MW01039587

The Navigation of Feeling

In *The Navigation of Feeling: A Framework for the History of Emotions*, William M. Reddy offers a new theory of emotions which both critiques and expands upon recent research in the fields of anthropology and psychology. Exploring the links between emotion and cognition, between culture and emotional expression, Reddy applies this theory of emotions to the processes of history. He demonstrates how emotions change over time, how emotions have an important impact on the course of events, and how different social orders either facilitate or constrain emotional life. In an investigation of Revolutionary France, where sentimentalism in literature and philosophy had promised a new and unprecedented kind of emotional liberty, Reddy's theory of emotions and historical change is successfully put to the test.

William M. Reddy is William T. Laprade Professor of History and Professor of Cultural Anthropology at Duke University. His previous books include *The Invisible Code: Honor and Sentiment in Postrevolutionary France, 1815–1848* (Berkeley: University of California Press, 1997), and *Money and Liberty in Modern Europe: A Critique of Historical Understanding* (New York: Cambridge University Press, 1987). He has been a Guggenheim Fellow, a Fulbright Fellow, and a Fellow of the National Humanities Center.

THE NAVIGATION OF FEELING

A FRAMEWORK FOR THE HISTORY OF EMOTIONS

William M. Reddy
Duke University

CAMBRIDGE
UNIVERSITY PRESS

PUBLISHED BY THE PRESS SYNDICATE OF THE UNIVERSITY OF CAMBRIDGE
The Pitt Building, Trumpington Street, Cambridge, United Kingdom

CAMBRIDGE UNIVERSITY PRESS
The Edinburgh Building, Cambridge CB2 2RU, UK
40 West 20th Street, New York, NY 10011-4211, USA
10 Stamford Road, Oakleigh, VIC 3166, Australia
Ruiz de Alarcón 13, 28014 Madrid, Spain
Dock House, The Waterfront, Cape Town 8001, South Africa

http://www.cambridge.org

First published 2001

Printed in the United States of America

Typeface Palatino 10/13 pt.   *System* QuarkXPress [BTS]

A catalog record for this book is available from the British Library.

Library of Congress Cataloging in Publication Data
Reddy, William M.
The navigation of feeling : a framework for the history of emotions /
William M. Reddy.
    p. cm.
Includes bibliographical references and index.
ISBN 0-521-80303-9 – ISBN 0-521-00472-1 (pbk.)
1. Emotions.   2. Sentimentalism – France – History – 18th century.   I. Title.
BF531 .R44   2001
152.4 – dc21

                                                                    00–066712

ISBN   0 521 80303 9   hardback
ISBN   0 521 00472 1   paperback

For Isabel

Contents

Preface

"In the past twenty years," psychologists Kurt W. Fischer and June Price Tangney remarked in 1995, "there has been a revolution in the study of emotion" (p. 3). As I quickly found after beginning this project, theirs was no understatement. In experimental psychology alone, hundreds of studies of emotion have been published and new paradigms proposed since the mid-1970s. Other disciplines have developed new interest in emotions, for their own reasons. But, despite the many positive findings this new research has generated, the revolution has done little to clear up the vexed question of what, exactly, emotions are. Disagreements persist, uncertainties abound. Some researchers (such as Panksepp 1992; or Drevets & Raichle 1998) are convinced they have identified the biological and neural substrates of emotional arousal. But others insist that hormones, skin conductance levels, and cerebral blood flows are not "emotions." "No psychologist knows what anger, fear, or shame are independent of folk knowledge," said one group of psychologists recently (Shaver, Morgan, & Wu 1996:83).

Perhaps, then, emotions are nothing more than constructs of "folk knowledge"? "Emotion is culture," says ethnographer Benedicte Grima (1992:6). Anthropologist Niko Besnier – like most of his colleagues, slightly more circumspect than Grima – comes close to saying the same thing: "I do not wish to claim that all emotions are socially constructed, and that emotions are socially constructed in all contexts of social life"; nonetheless "many emotions are collectively constructed and crucially dependent on interaction with others for their development" (1995a:236).

But are these our only choices? Must emotions be either cultural or biological? We need new approaches to emotion, says literary critic Adela Pinch, "approaches that could think, for example, about what

Wordsworth meant when he declared that the mind attaches itself to words, 'not only as symbols of . . . passion, but as *things*, active and efficient, which are of themselves part of the passion'" (1995:109, emphasis in original).

The fact is that there is not one revolution in the study of emotions going on right now, but three, proceeding almost independently of each other. Psychologists have found ways of applying laboratory techniques devised for the study of cognition to questions involving emotion, sparking one revolution. Ethnographers have developed new field techniques and a new theoretical apparatus for understanding the cultural dimension of emotions, sparking a second. Finally, historians and literary critics have discovered that emotions have a kind of history (but what kind is not entirely clear). Scholars working on the eighteenth and nineteenth centuries, in particular, have begun to trace out the rise and fall of an emotional revolution of the past, called "sentimentalism," or the "cult of sensibility" – a loosely organized set of impulses that played a role in cultural currents as diverse as Methodism, antislavery agitation, the rise of the novel, the French Revolution (including the Terror), and the birth of Romanticism.

The first two revolutions mentioned above, in psychology and anthropology, have at least some contact with each other. In addition, the trend in these two fields favors a convergence of views, at least on the level of findings if not on the level of theory or method. This convergence is toward a conception of emotions as largely (but not entirely) the products of learning. But historians and literary critics, with few exceptions (e.g., Stearns 1994), have shown little awareness of this development. They tend to regard ideas about emotions from the past as interesting, even fascinating, configurations to be understood as part of their own time. They have not asked themselves what relation such past ideas have to the "reality" of emotions.

For many anthropologists, literary critics, and historians, to ask any question about the reality of the self or experience these days is almost impossible. This is a problem that any attempt to develop a new theory of emotions must confront. It goes without saying, for many in these fields, that there is no one human reality, that human nature is plastic, a function of cultural and historical context. For this reason, many anthropologists consider research by cognitive psychologists (who *do* think they are examining what is really there) irrelevant to their own work. While I agree that psychologists often presume to know too much about human nature, I do not think this robs their work of all interest. Furthermore, contemporary critiques of empirical social science have their own problems. To presume that human nature is entirely variable (and therefore cannot be studied in a lab), entirely reshaped by every culture humans devise for themselves, is to open oneself to some glaring difficulties. Appreciation of these difficulties is an important preliminary step in the process of building the new theory of emotions presented here. This theory represents an attempt to get beyond these difficulties, without inadvertently sinking back into an ethnocentric, and aggressive, universalism.

One glaring difficulty with the presumption that human nature is entirely variable is that it implicitly abrogates any understanding of historical change. Why should a given historical context change, in any meaningful way, if it has the power to mold human nature and human experience, inside and out, to its own specifications? Suppose, however, that the context does change. The new cultural context is equally powerful; the life of the individual equally determined and confined by its structures. Why should such change matter to anyone? If we feel such change matters, perhaps it is just because of the peculiar cultural context that has shaped *us*. Another difficulty with this presumption is that it undermines any positive statements about rights and liberties. If human experience (including emotions) is perfectly malleable, if what we feel is purely a product of our cultural context, then why concern ourselves with the suffering of others or the liberty and dignity of the individual? Suffering, in distant times and places, becomes just another byproduct of a cultural context. Liberty becomes a purely modern Western preoccupation, of local significance only. No one is happy with these difficult implications of cultural relativism; but it is quite another thing to say, positively and convincingly, how to avoid them. Who would dare assert, today, without fear of falling into a conspicuous ethnocentrism, what human nature is or how human experience works?

By examining closely developments in all three of the ongoing revolutions, this study aims at elaborating a formal theory that establishes emotions as largely (but not entirely) learned. "Largely": the theory leaves plenty of room for cultural variation. "But not entirely": the theory establishes a core concept of emotions, universally applicable, that allows one to say what suffering is, and why we all deserve to live in freedom. With reference to this concept of emotions, historical change again becomes meaningful; history becomes a record of human efforts to conceptualize our emotional makeup, and to realize social and political orders attuned to its nature.

I am under no illusions as to the originality or likely salience of my efforts. Hundreds of scholars are working on all aspects of our thinking about the self, including the issues I am raising. Some will be discussed in these pages; others will not. To make the project manageable, I decided to keep the focus on work that deals explicitly and directly with emotions.

Others, already, have come very close to proposing a theory of emotions like the one offered here (e.g., De Sousa's [1987] notion of "bootstrapping" or Crapanzano's [1992] comparison of emotional expression with performatives). Numerous psychologists have noted in passing the issue that will prove to be central to this study. In 1989, Margaret Clark observed, "There is . . . some clear evidence that choosing to express an emotion or to cognitively rehearse it may intensify or even create the actual experience of that emotion while choosing to suppress it or not think about it may have the opposite effect" (p. 266). Phoebe Ellsworth has made a similar point: "The [emotional] process almost always begins before the name and almost always continues after it. The realization of the name [of the emotion] undoubtedly changes the feeling, simplifying and clarifying" (1994:192–193). But, until now, none of these insights has been put to use at the core of a new theory of emotion, designed to provide a framework for research within all three of the revolutions that are under way. This is not the first time in history such suggestions about emotional expression have been made. Wordsworth, in the passage cited above by Adela Pinch, was trying, it seems, to get at the same point. His contemporary, Germaine de Staël, made a very similar observation in a book published in 1800 (Staël 1800), where she argued that reading novels allowed people to have new, more nuanced, feelings. In this study, I accept that Clark, Ellsworth, Wordsworth, and Staël have it right. Emotion and emotional expression interact in a dynamic way. I provide evidence to suggest that this one aspect of emotional expression *is* universal, and I develop a framework for thinking about it. I try to show how this small concession to universalism is sufficient to ground both historical explanation and a defense of human liberty.

The study proceeds as follows. Part I provides a critical review of research and a new theoretical framework for dealing with emotions. In Chapters 1 and 2, I compare research in cognitive psychology and anthropology, to gauge the extent of convergence that is going on in these two fields, as well as the extent of conceptual blockage that has developed as new research findings have come up. In Chapter 3, I lay out a theory of emotions that accounts for the convergence of research results in these two fields, a theory that takes into account both (1) the reservations of poststructuralists about the implicit assumptions of a field of empirical research such as experimental psychology, and (2) the many critiques of the poststructuralist alternative to empiricism. In Chapter 4, I spell out how the theory presented in Chapter 3 offers a new way of understanding what I call "emotional regimes" and their relation to emotional experience and liberty. Part II offers a case study of historical change, using the proposed theory. I argue that emotions, as here conceived, had a direct impact on the course of change in that most important of transitions to modernity, the French Revolution. In Chapter 5, I examine the findings of new research into eighteenth-century sentimentalism and show how the theory of emotions presented here can explain the peculiar intensity of emotional expression in that period. In Chapters 6 and 7, I trace the changes in prevalent attitudes toward emotion that accompanied the transition from Old Regime, to Republic, to Napoleonic dictatorship, to a more stable constitutional monarchy. I show how emotions shaped this evolution, as well as how they were transformed by it. In Chapter 8, I provide an in-depth study of case material from the early nineteenth century, to show how the theory presented here can be applied to detailed research as well as to explore the kinds of emotional performance and suffering that characterized the aftermath of the Revolution. The Conclusion attempts to pull all the threads together and discuss, briefly, the implications of the study for our understanding of the present.

I have received a great deal of help during the preparation of this study. The National Humanities Center supported initial work on the project in 1995–1996. Papers derived from the research were presented to the Triangle French Studies Group, the Triangle Intellectual History Seminar, the European History Seminar at UCLA, and the Departments of History at Washington University in St. Louis, Johns Hopkins, Rochester, and the University of North Carolina. To the many participants in these seminars I owe thanks for their careful readings, helpful remarks, and encouragement. Aspects of the study were explored in articles that appeared in *Current Anthropology*, *Cultural Anthropology*, and the *Journal of Modern History*; I am grateful to the editors and their readers for their patient reviews of successive revisions of these progress reports, as well as to Frank Smith and the readers who helped with a near-final version of the manuscript at Cambridge. Constant and enthusiastic support, both material and emotional, has come from my spouse, Isabel Routh Reddy.

In the course of this project, I picked up the threads of many conversations I had in 1975–1976 with Michelle Z. Rosaldo, who was then at the Institute for Advanced Study working on her important ethnography of Ilongot emotions, and in 1976–1977 with Jerome Kagan, when, with a Research Training Fellowship from the Social Science Research Council, I had a year for postdoctoral work in developmental psychology. The questions those conversations posed for me stuck with me, and this book is, in a way, a belated acknowledgment of their importance to me and an attempt to continue them.

A note on translations: All translations from the French are by the author, except where otherwise indicated.

PART I

WHAT ARE EMOTIONS?

CHAPTER 1

Answers from Cognitive Psychology

What are emotions? To most of us, the question hardly needs asking; emotions are the most immediate, the most self-evident, and the most relevant of our orientations toward life. But from the moment the question is taken seriously, troubling difficulties of definition arise.

Emotions have been compared to colors.[1] Both emotions and colors have a strong subjective or experiential character; that is, it makes sense to individuals to describe the qualities and features of the perceived color or the experienced emotion, sometimes at length. In both cases, there is no way for an independent observer to check these "self-reports." However, these reported experiential qualities display great constancy from one person to another. Most agree, for example, that pink is a warm color, while blue is cool; most agree that fear brings excitement, rapid thinking, a readiness for action, whereas sorrow is inactive and renders one incommunicative. There is a long-standing common sense that says that both color perception and emotional experience are biologically based and therefore everywhere the same. The experiential qualities individuals report are, by this common sense, universal, "hardwired"; just as sugar always tastes sweet, so pink always looks warm and loneliness always feels cold. But while scientific evidence on color perception supports this commonsense view, research into emotions has failed to substantiate it. This contrast is instructive, a good starting point for appreciating the difficulties into which the concept of "emotion" plunges us.

In a study published in 1969, Brent Berlin and Paul Kay argued that color perception provided an instance of a universal, extralinguistic

---

[1] For comparison of emotions to colors, see, e.g., D'Andrade & Egan (1974); Lutz & White (1986:415); Church, Katigbak, & Jensen (1998:64).

category scheme. Linguists and anthropologists had been extolling for decades the power of language to shape perception and experience. But Berlin and Kay insisted that, in the case of color at least, our visual apparatus and the way it interacted with light shaped natural languages, not the other way around. The human retina contains cone cells with pigments that are most sensitive to three specific wavelengths of light (which English speakers associate with the color terms red, blue, and green). The visual cortex is able, by parsing this input, to identify what in English is called yellow. (Experts on color perception are in the habit of designating these specific wavelengths as "focal" red, "focal" blue, "focal" green, and "focal" yellow.) Berlin and Kay conducted interviews of native speakers of twenty languages, and added to this what they could find out about the color lexicons of seventy-eight more languages. On the basis of the evidence they gathered they concluded, among other things, that:

1. All languages contain color terms for white and black.
2. If a language contains three color terms, then it contains a term for red.
3. If a language contains four color terms, then it contains a term for either green or yellow (but not both).
4. If a language contains five color terms, then it contains terms for both green and yellow.
5. If a language contains six color terms, then it contains a term for blue.
6. If a language contains seven color terms, then it contains a term for brown.
7. If a language contains eight or more color terms, then it contains a term for purple, pink, orange, grey, or some combination of these (1969:2–3).

Berlin and Kay viewed these results as stunning evidence of the impact of biology on language. In a later study Paul Kay and Chad McDaniel (1978) nicely applied fuzzy set theory and more recent neurological research to the earlier linguistic data to argue that all informants, no matter how many or how few the color terms in their native languages, pick focal colors as the best examples of certain of their language's color terms. Speakers of languages with fewer than eight terms categorize unnamed colors as more or less poor examples of named colors. (Purple, for instance, might be categorized as a poor example of "red" in a language with no term meaning purple.) If the language in question has more than six color terms (including terms for black and white), then the excess terms' best examples will be derived, first, from the set referred to in English by the terms *brown, pink, purple, orange,* and *grey.* Berlin and Kay dubbed as "basic color categories" the colors referred to by these eleven English words: *black, white, red, green, yellow, blue, brown, pink, purple, orange,* and *grey.* By "basic" they meant that the designated wavelengths have a perceptual salience based on the structure of the human visual apparatus, and that human languages universally recognize this salience. That is, they were "basic" both in the sense of "hardwired" and in the sense of conceptually prototypical.

Berlin and Kay's work has not gone without challenge. Controversy has centered, for example, on whether neurological evidence of nervous-system color processing can be taken as a sure guide to the structure of cognition. Rather than speaking of "focal" colors, some researchers have argued, we need to analyze the color space. Color lexicons are structured in terms not of focal wavelengths but, given the number of color terms available, in terms of maximum contrast. (See Smallman & Boynton 1990; Jameson & D'Andrade 1994.) These disagreements have not raised doubts, however, about the finding that, whatever its exact character, color perception has nonlinguistic, universal conceptual features. (For more recent discussion, see Hardin & Maffi 1997.)

Efforts to uncover the hidden order among emotion words in various languages have yielded very different results. It is difficult, in the first place, to know just how to distinguish one emotion term from another in a given language. Where color terms can usually be associated with a specific segment of the electromagnetic spectrum, there is no such yardstick for emotion terms. Karl Heider published in 1991 the most thorough attempt to date to make sense of the inner logic of emotion lexicons. He asked speakers of three Indonesian dialects to give numerical ratings for the similarity or dissimilarity of emotion terms in their own language. Using such ratings, he developed semantic maps of related terms, diagrams in which the length of a line linking two words was inversely proportional to the speakers' sense of their likeness. The more similar they were in meaning, the closer they were on the map. Compare his diagram displaying the elusive relationships among Indonesian words for *happy* with Berlin and Kay's table schematizing their findings (Figures 1 and 2). In Berlin and Kay's table, the whole structure of a language's color lexicon can be designated with a few pluses and minuses. Heider, in contrast, must push the resources

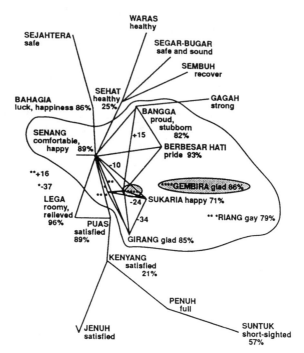

Figure 1. "Happy" cluster BI(M). From Karl G. Heider (1991), *Landscapes of Emotion: Mapping Three Cultures of Emotion in Indonesia* (Cambridge: Cambridge University Press), fig. 2.2, p. 147. Reprinted by permission of Cambridge University Press.

of numerical measurement and two-dimensional display to the limit to comprehend the relations among a few emotion terms from one language. Heider notes that even this representational strategy was not always equal to the complexity of his data. "[I]t often happens that A is close to B, B is close to C, but C very far from A. . . . Cognition goes where plane geometry cannot follow" (1991:26–27).

Other researchers have tried to cut through this sort of complexity by situating emotion terms in a space defined by two or more axes representing general characteristics of emotions. J. A. Russell in 1983 argued that in most languages "emotion-related words fell in roughly a circular order in a space definable by two dimensions: pleasure–displeasure and arousal–sleep" (see Figure 3). Lutz in 1986 offered a diagram of Ifaluk emotion terms using, as one axis, the pleasure–displeasure dimension and, as the other axis, a measure of whether the person experiencing the emotion was, in Ifaluk terms, in a strong or a

Type	No. of basic color terms	Perceptual categories encoded in the basic color terms										
		white	black	red	green	yellow	blue	brown	pink	purple	orange	grey
1	2	+	+	−	−	−	−	−	−	−	−	−
2	3	+	+	+	−	−	−	−	−	−	−	−
3	4	+	+	+	+	−	−	−	−	−	−	−
4	4	+	+	+	−	+	−	−	−	−	−	−
5	5	+	+	+	+	+	−	−	−	−	−	−
6	6	+	+	+	+	+	+	−	−	−	−	−
7	7	+	+	+	+	+	+	+	−	−	−	−
8	8	+	+	+	+	+	+	+	+	−	−	−
9	8	+	+	+	+	+	+	+	−	+	−	−
10	8	+	+	+	+	+	+	+	−	−	+	−
11	8	+	+	+	+	+	+	+	−	−	−	+
12	9	+	+	+	+	+	+	+	+	+	−	−
13	9	+	+	+	+	+	+	+	+	−	+	−
14	9	+	+	+	+	+	+	+	+	−	−	+
15	9	+	+	+	+	+	+	+	−	+	+	−
16	9	+	+	+	+	+	+	+	−	+	−	+
17	9	+	+	+	+	+	+	+	−	−	+	+
18	10	+	+	+	+	+	+	+	+	+	+	−
19	10	+	+	+	+	+	+	+	+	+	−	+
20	10	+	+	+	+	+	+	+	+	−	+	+
21	10	+	+	+	+	+	+	+	−	+	+	+
22	11	+	+	+	+	+	+	+	+	+	+	+

Figure 2. The twenty-two actually occurring types of basic color lexicon. (Berlin and Kay note, "Only these twenty-two out of the logically possible 2,048 combinations of the eleven basic color categories are found.") From Brent Berlin and Paul Kay (1969), *Basic Color Terms: Their Universality and Evolution* (Berkeley: University of California Press), tab. 1, p. 3. Reprinted by permission of the authors.

weak position vis-à-vis other actors (Figure 4). Kitayama et al. in 1995 diagrammed Japanese and American emotion concepts using, again, pleasant–unpleasant as one axis, and "engaged" vs. "disengaged" as the other (Figures 5 and 6). Both Lutz and Kitayama et al. chose their second axis on the basis of local ways of categorizing emotions. On Ifaluk, a Pacific atoll, emotions are primarily of moral and political importance and thus have to do with social position and authority. In Japan, emotions are comprehended in terms of the degree of dependence vs. independence they entail – anger, for example, being an independent emotion, love being a dependent one. The Japanese, who

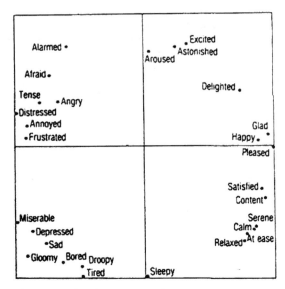

Figure 3. Two-dimensional scaling solution for 28 English emotion-related words. From James A. Russell (1983), "Pancultural Aspects of the Human Conceptual Organization of Emotions," *Journal of Personality and Social Psychology* 45, fig. 1, p. 1288. Copyright 1980 by the American Psychological Association. Reprinted by permission.

value dependence, they argue, regard pride as an unpleasant emotion, whereas Americans regard it as a pleasant one. Examples of this kind of variation are common; the Chinese regard love as a sad emotion, for example, as do the Ifaluk (Shaver et al. 1987:184; Lutz 1988). Does this mean that pleasantness–unpleasantness is a culturally variable feature of emotions? More fundamentally: Who is to say whether arousal is the more useful dimension to examine (in line with our belief about the biological basis of emotions) as opposed to authority or independence, as the Ifaluk and Japanese, respectively, would contend? There is no instrument, no spectrograph, that can solve these puzzles for us.

EMOTION AND COGNITION

Western specialists who study emotion cannot even agree on what the term *emotion* means. George Mandler, in 1984, remarked, "there is no commonly, even superficially, acceptable definition of what a psychol-

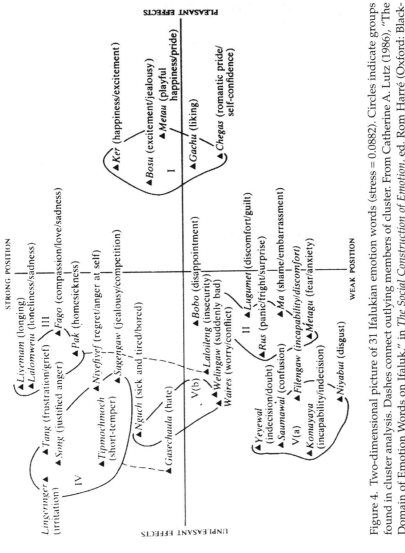

Figure 4. Two-dimensional picture of 31 Ifalukian emotion words (stress = 0.0882). Circles indicate groups found in cluster analysis. Dashes connect outlying members of cluster. From Catherine A. Lutz (1986), "The Domain of Emotion Words on Ifaluk," in *The Social Construction of Emotion*, ed. Rom Harré (Oxford: Blackwell), fig. 2. Copyright 1982 by the American Anthropological Association. Reprinted by permission.

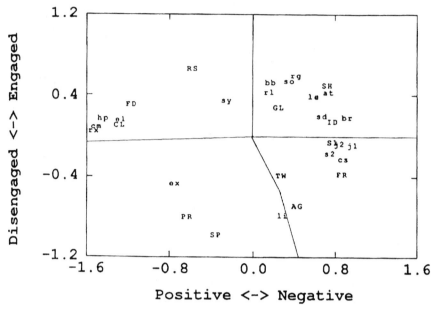

Figure 5. The structure of emotional experience: Japanese data. The following abbreviations are used:

Socially engaged positive emotions: CL, Feelings of closeness; FD, Friendly feelings; RS, Feelings of respect.

Socially disengaged positive emotions: PR, Pride; SP, Feelings of superiority; TW, Feeling like being at the top of the world.

Socially engaged negative emotions: GL, Guilt; ID, Feelings of indebtedness; SH, Shame.

Socially disengaged negative emotions: AG, Anger; FR, Frustration; S1, Sulky feelings (strong).

Others: at, Afraid of causing trouble for someone; bb, Feeling like being babied; br, Boredom; cm, Calm feelings; cs, Feelings of constraint; el, Elated feelings; ex, Excitement; hp, Happiness; j1, Jealousy (Higami); j2, Jealousy (Shitto); le, Feeling like leaning toward someone; li, "Licking" someone; rg, Resigned feelings; rl, Feeling like relying on someone; rx, Relaxed feelings; s2, Sulky feelings (weak); sd, Sadness; so, Feeling that one is superficially optimistic; sy, Sleepy feelings.

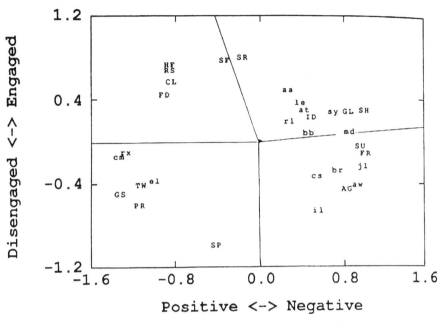

Positive <-> Negative

Figure 6. The structure of emotional experience: U.S. data. The following abbreviations are used:

Socially engaged positive emotions: CL, Feelings of closeness; FD, Friendly feelings; HF, Feeling happy for someone; RS, Feelings of respect.

Socially disengaged positive emotions: GS, Feeling good about oneself; PR, Pride; SP, Feelings of superiority; TW, Feeling like being at the top of the world.

Socially engaged negative emotions: GL, Guilt; ID, Feelings of indebtedness; SF, Feeling sad for someone; SH, Shame; SR, Feeling sorry for someone.

Socially disengaged negative emotions: AG, Anger; FR, Frustration; SU, Sulky feelings.

Others: aa, Afraid of angering someone; at, Afraid of causing trouble for someone; aw, Awkward feelings; bb, Feeling like being babied by someone; br, Boredom; cm, Calm feelings; cs, Feelings of constraint; el, Elated feelings; il, Ill feelings for someone; jl, Jealousy; le, Feeling like leaning on someone; md, Moody; rl, Feeling like relying on someone; rx, Relaxed feelings; sy, Sleepy feelings.

From Shinobu Kitayama, Hazel Rose Markus, and Hisaya Matsumoto (1995), "Culture, Self, and Emotion: A Cultural Perspective on 'Self-Conscious' Emotions," in *Self-Conscious Emotions: The Psychology of Shame, Guilt, Embarrassment, and Pride,* ed. June Price Tangney and Kurt W. Fischer (New York: Guilford Press), fig. 18.1B, p. 450. Copyright 1995 by the Guilford Press. Reprinted by permission.

ogy of emotion is about" (p. 16; quoted in Gergen 1995:17). In 1996 Shaver et al. noted that "No psychologist knows what anger, fear, or shame are independent of folk knowledge, and most studies of these emotions test hypotheses derived from intuition and everyday observations of self and others" (p. 83). In the 1970s Paul Ekman, Carroll Izard, and their associates tried to get beyond these difficulties of definition by linking emotions firmly with facial expressions. Like the color cards used by Berlin and Kay, photographs of faces showing carefully posed expressions of emotions could be shown to subjects around the world. It was a simple matter to ask subjects to link faces with emotion terms from their own language or with briefly described emotional situations, such as "This man is about to be attacked by a crocodile." The evidence thus collected seemed to prove that there was substantial worldwide agreement on the meaning of a simple set of basic facial expressions. From this agreement, Ekman (1972, 1980), in particular, concluded that there were only six biologically based emotions, each one associated with a specific, universally recognizable facial expression: happiness, sadness, fear, anger, surprise, and disgust. This new approach rapidly gained followers. It seemed possible, as well, to relate facial expressions with evidence about heart rates, tear-duct secretions, skin conductivity, hormone levels, and similar biological measures, so that a single schema of biologically preset emotion states could be identified. In the 1980s, however, this research began to run into serious difficulties. The data on autonomic and endocrine system states turned out to be more ambiguous than it at first seemed. Both fear and anger, for example, seemed to be associated with the same range of arousals of heart and skeletal muscles, and the same glandular secretions. In addition the approach faced two other nagging problems: (1) What happened to emotions when arousals subsided and the face returned to neutral? (2) How were emotions such as love, shame, or nostalgia to be fit into the scheme, when they had no obvious single facial expressions to go with them (Fischer & Tangney 1995)?

These problems were examined in detail in a stinging critique of the basic emotions theory by Ortony and Turner in 1990, who argued that all emotions were assemblages of components, and that such assemblages could vary almost infinitely. Compare fear of a bear that is about to attack with fear of cancer, Ortony and Turner suggested. "These two varieties of fear have . . . been assembled out of partially overlapping sets of elements, the nature of which depends on the details of how the situation is appraised by the person and how he or she attempts to cope with it" (p. 327). Fear of a bear will bring adrenaline into the blood-stream, for example, but not fear of cancer. In 1994, J. A. Russell published a sweeping review of research on the link between facial expressions and emotions, concluding that subjects' responses displayed much greater variation and uncertainty than had previously been realized. Most experiments based on Ekman's thesis had been carried out in the form of forced-choice tests. That is, subjects were not free to pick any emotion term to characterize the facial expression they viewed; they had to make a match with a limited, preselected list provided by the experimenters. In addition, many had been given initial training sessions to help them understand what was expected. While there was significant agreement, from many areas of the globe, on the meaning of happy faces, other types of facial expressions garnered far less agreement as to their meaning. College-educated subjects always did better than those without education. Uneducated persons from rural areas agreed least on the meaning of facial expressions, suggesting that exposure to movies or television (or other influences) may have pretrained the educated urban subjects to share experimenters' norms. In the absence of forced choice and pretest training, agreement on other than happy faces was weak. If photographs of spontaneous facial expressions were used (i.e., naturally occurring ones, rather than the carefully posed ones of the initial tests), agreement sagged further. Thus, the evidence for a few, universally recognized (and therefore biologically based) facial expressions of emotions was at best ambiguous – and this, after twenty years of work by many researchers.

Problems of definition plagued another area of active research that emerged in the 1980s, that of the relation between emotion and cognition. R. B. Zajonc launched a lively debate on the issue in a 1980 article in which he argued that emotional reactions occur entirely independently of cognition. R. S. Lazarus (1982) countered that a prior cognitive evaluation was an indispensable starting point of any emotional reaction. A heated series of exchanges followed. According to Parkinson and Manstead who reviewed the debate in 1992, the problem lay with the definition of the two terms. Zajonc defined emotion broadly and cognition narrowly; Lazarus the reverse. If cognition was defined so as to include all "recognition processes" (and not just "conscious rational, or purposive processes"), then cognition had to precede emotion by definition. As Bornstein put it (1992:252), "*Obviously*, a certain amount of cognitive processing is required to respond to *any* stimulus" (emphasis added). On the other hand, it was impossible to explain attitude or purpose in purely cognitive terms. As Nico Frijda put it,

I think that there is no disagreement whatever on the possibility of noncognitive elicitation of affect and mood. . . . With cognitive judgments, there is no reason, other than an affective one, to prefer any goal whatever over some other. Cognitive reasoning may argue that a particular event could lead to loss of money or health or life, but so what? What is wrong with death, other than that it is disliked? What I am trying to say is that tracing the affective effect of a stimulus to its cognitive conditions allows one, in the end, to find a stimulus that evokes affect *without cognitive mediation.* (1994:199, emphasis added. For a similar view, see Argyle 1991:167.)

In a series of experiments Bless, Clore, Schwarz, and their associates have tried to resolve this difficulty, in part, by developing an "affect-as-information" hypothesis. (See Schwarz & Clore 1983; Clore & Parrott 1991; Schwarz & Bless 1991; Bless et al. 1996.) They have found that it is easy to induce mood shifts in subjects by asking them to write about a happy or sad episode in their lives or by showing them carefully chosen video clips of happy or sad situations. Once a happy or sad mood has been induced, it influences subsequent cognitive processing styles in measurable ways. Happy individuals, they suspect, regard their environments as benign and are not motivated to expend cognitive effort to understand them; sad individuals sense that something needs to be corrected and are far more attentive to potential anomalies. Happy individuals therefore employ "top-down processing with considerable reliance on preexisting general knowledge structures," whereas sad individuals use "bottom-up processing" with much greater attention to detail (Bless et al. 1996:665). Keith Oatley (1992) has proposed a similar approach to emotions, regarding them as "non-semantic" control signals that intervene in cognitive or attentional processes in order to direct them to urgent or goal-relevant issues. But none of these researchers have offered an explanation of how a "non-semantic" emotion or mood can influence a cognition without itself, in some sense, being a cognition. If a happy mood conveys the information that the environment is benign, then why not conclude that a happy mood simply *is the cognition* that the environment is benign? If a sudden sense of fear redirects attention to a dark corner of the room, why not conclude that this sense of fear *is the cognition* of the potential danger of that corner? No experimental or test procedure has been offered so far that would allow one to rule out this possibility; it is resisted solely on the grounds that it counters the commonsense belief that emotion is something separate from thought, something opposed to "reason." This often unstated assumption is one that philosophers have recently begun to frown upon (Solomon 1984, 1992; De Sousa 1987; Greenspan 1988; Meyer 1991). Many psychologists have also begun to see the futility of maintaining the distinction. O'Rorke and Ortony (1994:283) flatly remarked that "emotions and cogniton are inextricably intertwined." Barnett and Ratner, in a recent review of research into emotional development, saw this issue as so important that they proposed a new word for what we do when we think-feel: "cogmotion," a term better able than words currently in use to represent "the interactive and inseparable nature of cognition and emotion" (1997:303).

By the folk wisdom of the West, emotions are involuntary; they come over us irresistibly, or steal upon us when we least expect it. The will, aided by reason, must master them or be mastered by them. Psychologists have therefore looked for effects of emotion on "automatic," "subliminal," and "unconscious" cognitive processes. It must be stated at once, however, that the meaning of these terms is as much in debate as the meaning of the term "emotion" itself. It is hardly in dispute that attention is limited and that the range of things that can be attended to at any given moment is only a tiny fraction of what is available through ongoing sensory input or from the vast store of procedural and declarative memory. What has proved difficult is drawing a bright line between what lies in attention and what does not, what counts as voluntary or controlled, and what counts as involuntary or automatic. As attempts to clarify this distinction proceed, the place of emotion in the larger life of the self is necessarily being constantly reformulated by psychologists. There is currently no end in sight to this process of rethinking. However, some important trends are evident, and their implications for research in other fields – such as anthropology or history – are far from negligible.

In an anthology of 1989 called *Unintended Thought: Limits of Awareness, Intention and Control*, edited by J. S. Uleman and John A. Bargh, researchers acknowledged the defeat of initial hopes to identify and understand "automatic" cognitive processing. Uleman described automatic processing (following Shiffrin & Dumais 1981:121 and Schneider, Dumais, & Shiffrin 1984:1) as a "fast [<300 milliseconds], parallel, fairly effortless process that is not limited by short-term memory (STM) capacity, is not under direct subject control" that is not itself intended, and that is difficult to inhibit because it tends "to run to completion" (Uleman 1989:430). Few cognitive processes could be shown to fit this stringent definition, however. Candidates for such "automatic" processing often turned out to take up processing capacity, to be susceptible to conscious manipulation, or to be affected by short-term memory content.

Alice Isen and Gregory Diamond, in the same anthology, reviewing research on the relation between emotions and automatic processing concluded that "the influence of automatic processes increasingly can be viewed as subject to modification and intervention rather than as inevitable and irresistible. Moreover, the occurrence of seemingly automatic processes may sometimes be the result of earlier decisions to deploy attention elsewhere" (1989:147). The research showed, they concluded, that emotions were not always automatic. "[B]ecause we find that affect can have an automatic impact, this does not mean that affect *must* always have automatic effects, or that it is in the *nature* of affect to be automatic. Not only may affects differ in this regard, but also the requirements of situations may influence whether stimuli are processed automatically, or whether automatic processes have effects or not" (p. 144). Insofar as emotions were automatic, according to Isen and Diamond, they resembled overlearned cognitive habits. Their review of the research led them to the following general remarks, worth quoting in full:

[T]o the extent that affect can have an influence automatically – without attention or intention and seemingly irresistibly – it can be understood as a deeply ingrained, overlearned habit, or as a process of chunking and organizing the situation. Thus, . . . seemingly irresistible feelings might be addressed in much the same way that other overlearned processes are understood, or in the way that other broad constructs or conceptualizations are refined (differentiated or "unpacked").

We are reminded of the way in which little boys have often been taught to keep from crying by substituting anger for sadness: "When something bad happens don't get sad, get mad." Thus, people may be able to regulate their feelings, through their focus and through changing what they learn in given situations. Similarly, they may be able to change the impact of certain kinds of feelings, again by directing thoughts along certain lines. In this way, problem emotions, even though they feel automatic and uncontrollable, may be alterable. This does not mean that unwanted affective reactions will be easy to change (old habits die hard), but it does suggest that change may be possible and that the very sense of inevitability may be misleading. (p. 144)

In this conclusion, one notes, as so often in this research, the likening of emotion to a form of cognition, and the dependence of both on the impact of conscious, intentional action – at least over the long run of an individual's life.

Research since 1989 has continued to confirm the complexity of the interrelation between automatic and intentional processes and has offered further support to Isen and Diamond's likening of emotion to overlearned cognitive habit. A variety of recent studies of automatic, subliminal, or unconscious cognition (e.g., Ste-Marie & Jacoby 1993; Strayer & Kramer 1994; Greenwald, Klinger, & Schuh 1995; Logan, Taylor, & Etherton 1996; Besner, Stoltz, & Boutilier 1997; Cohen & Schooler 1997) suggests that "most tasks involve a mixture of automatic and strategic processes" (McNally 1995:751). Test results repeatedly indicate that "attention" follows strategies, both during learning and during performance, deciding "what is taken out of memory at retrieval time as well as what gets into memory at encoding" (Logan et al. 1996:620). Carr and Dagenbach (1990) hypothesized a "center-surround" attention mechanism that can "enhance activation of sought-for codes and . . . inhibit related codes stored nearby in the semantic network" (p. 341).[2] As Ste-Marie and Jacoby put it: "Recognition may never be spontaneous in the sense of being fully divorced from intention or from the activity in which a person is engaged" (1993:787). Or, in Strayer and Kramer's words, "Automatic processing was characterized by an enhanced build up of evidence and a strategic setting of response criteria that capitalizes on the enhanced drift rate" (1994:339). Yet again, according to Balota and Paul, subjects "have considerable control over the influence of a given processing pathway, depending on the constraints of a given task" (1996:843). Greenwald et al. (1995:22), like Erdelyi (1992:786), comment on the malaise that underlies psychologists' lexical indecision, when, in their research reports, they pit against each other, with slightly varying definitions, words such as *unconscious, implicit, automatic, unattended*, on the one hand, and words such as *attentional, strategic, intended, aware, controlled*, on the other.[3]

---

[2] Greenwald et al. (1995:39) note how this finding coheres with their research.
[3] See also, on the question of choice of terms, Isen & Diamond (1989:147); Uleman (1989).

Greenwald et al. (1995; see also Greenwald & Drain 1997) argue forcefully that they have discovered "the statistically most secure evidence now available" for genuinely unconscious cognition. Unconscious cognition, as they stringently define it, means cognition that is fully dissociated from conscious cognition and influences performance outside the subject's awareness. But in order to find traces of such cognition, they admit, they had to examine linear regression of variance in accuracy of responses on Stroop-type subliminal interference tests of over two thousand subjects. When subjects were asked to evaluate the position of a word on a field (either left or right of center), the accuracy of their response was slightly influenced in cases where the word itself (visible for 200 milliseconds [ms], but dichoptically masked) was either of the words *right* or *left*. Under these conditions, according to Greenwald et al., the words were impossible to recognize at a conscious level. But some subjects, when the word *left* was flashed on the right, responded that the word had been flashed on the left side of the visual field and vice versa. In other tests by the same authors, subjects were asked to evaluate semantically whether a word flashed for 200 ms (but masked) was pleasant or unpleasant, pushing a key to the right for pleasant and to the left for unpleasant; in these tests, the subliminal flashing of the words *right* or *left* had no effect whatsoever on which button was pushed.

Admitting that the effects of unconscious cognition they found were "small" (p. 40) and that others might well hesitate to attempt to replicate them, in view of the fact that at least 900 subjects would have to be tested to find them, Greenwald et al. do not suggest that they have found a door into an entirely separate, unconscious sphere of cognition. They do, however, suggest that their findings add to the growing weight of evidence against the once-prevalent linear model of cognitive processing, by which "perceptual analysis proceeds in a single path through successive stages that are often identified as sensory registration, preattentive processing, attention, and response selection." Instead, they support alternative models, such as the "parallel distributed network form" proposed by Rumelhart, McClelland, et al. (1986), according to which "any stimulus input can readily develop independent pathways to different responses and multiple pathways to the same response" (Greenwald et al. 1995:38).

Similar ambiguous results continue to be reported by researchers attempting to measure the relation between affect and cognition. Sinclair, Hoffman, and Mark (1994) had subjects do a sentence completion task involving choices from a list of either highly emotionally negative or highly emotionally positive phrases (e.g., *cheerful I ran laughing*, or *knife slashed the stabbed*). Each subject received either all-positive or all-negative items. Half the subjects were then asked to exercise vigorously for two minutes, then asked to wait until they felt they had returned to a fully rested state. The other half were asked to wait three minutes (no exercise) after completing the sentence tasks. Both were then given a twenty-item questionnaire about their emotional state. All subjects' reports of their emotional states showed the influence of the sentence-completion task; those who worked on negative words were in a more negative state and vice versa. However, those who had exercised misinterpreted their residual arousal from the exercise as an emotional arousal, and consistently reported stronger affect than those who did not exercise. Sinclair et al. do not conclude that this misattribution was the result of "unconcious" or physiological influences, however. Instead, they believed the subjects' reports of heightened affect reflected their conscious evaluation strategies. "Because people do not exhaustively search memory when making judgments, but rely on readily accessible information . . . it appears that subjects searched for readily accessible explanations for their current arousal state and thus interpreted the arousal in terms of the primed concepts [i.e., the positive or negative words used in the sentence completion tasks]" (p. 18).

Likewise Mogg, Bradely, and Williams (1993), searching for differences in perception among nonclinical, anxious, and depressed subjects, administered a modified Stroop color-naming task to three groups. Their aim was to test two hypotheses, suggested by earlier studies: (1) that anxious individuals screen incoming perceptual data at a preattentive level for threatening cues, and are therefore more sensitive to threatening perceptions than are normal individuals, and (2) that depressed individuals seem to introduce bias at "later, controlled stages of processing, such as elaboration, that occur after the information has entered conscious awareness." Their findings were consistent with these two hypotheses. Subjects were presented with five types of words, either supraliminally or subliminally (1 ms exposure), while being exposed to a 1 ms flash of color. The five types of words used were (1) words related to anxiety (such as *embarrassment*, *cancer*), (2) words related to depression (such as *misery*, *discouraged*), (3) positive words (such as *adorable*, *bliss*), and two types of neutral words. When shown words related to anxiety or depression (that is, any emotionally negative word), at subliminal speeds, subjects who scored as anxious on post-test interviews took roughly 20 ms longer to correctly identify the color they had been exposed to than did either depressed or normal subjects. All subjects who identified the color correctly took a bit more than half a second to respond. Anxious persons therefore took about 3 percent longer to correctly identify the color that was flashed simultaneously with a 1 ms flash of an emotionally negative word. Subjects were independently tested to confirm that they could not consciously detect the presence of words exposed for 1 ms. Thus, the 20 ms delay of anxious subjects' responses appeared to be the result of a genuine subliminal interference. In conclusion, the authors reason, it may be that individuals suffering from general anxiety disorders, in contrast to depressed individuals, experience cognition biases "that are inaccessible to the patient and that cannot be assessed by self-report methods" and cannot, either, be treated by therapies that deal only with conscious thoughts or images. However, Mogg et al. concede that the effects they discovered were small. "Proof of subliminality is a difficult and controversial issue," they note (p. 310). In other tests, anxious individuals have responded more selectively and more strongly to words related to their specific anxieties, rather than to emotionally negative words in general. Mogg et al. speculate that these other tests allowed "increased opportunity for more elaborate processing of the semantic content of the word stimuli" (p. 309) than did their own 1 ms exposure times.

The boundary between what counts as conscious or controlled and what counts as unconscious or subliminal seems to shift with great sensitivity to the precise test procedures and contexts. There is increasing doubt about the existence of inflexibly separated structures or processes such as "registration" or "preattentive processing" and increasing credence given to the idea that there may be multiple pathways leading to any given response profile. No privileged entry point has been found where affect can exercise consistent "subliminal" influence over thinking, although the influence of affect on cognition is evidently widespread and complex. Evidence continues to mount in favor of the approach suggested by Isen and Diamond in 1989, that emotions operate very much like overlearned cognitive habits. No experimental procedure yet designed suggests that emotions are something entirely different from cognition, since the presence of emotions is always tested indirectly, through cognitive biases or through changes in skin conductance levels or heart rate. None of these things are "emotion" itself (Ortony & Turner 1990:319).

Depression, in particular, is increasingly seen as a cognitive disorder, and cognitive therapies have been developed and applied with success. (See, e.g., Moretti & Shaw 1989; Schwarz & Bless 1991; Baker & Channon 1995; Wenzlaff & Bates 1998.) Uncontrollable negative self-evaluative thoughts are a common feature of depression. Sufferers have no sense that these thoughts are biased and no way of checking their accuracy; these thoughts are associated with heightened emotional arousal and themselves enjoy a "chronic accessibility" to consciousness (Moretti & Shaw 1989:389). Cognitive therapies involve training sufferers to recognize such thoughts when they surface and to exert effort persistently to shift attention away from them. Grief and stress have also been shown to have a strong impact on cognition. The thinking of subjects who have suffered a recent trauma is less broad, less self-referential, and less emotional; these characteristics are regarded as resulting from strategies of avoidance and heightened mental control. (See, e.g., Pennebaker 1989; Hughes, Uhlmann, & Pennebaker 1994; Matthews & Harley 1996.)

EMOTIONS, GOALS, AND MENTAL CONTROL

Isen and Diamond's conclusion that emotions operate like overlearned cognitive habits and may be learned, altered, or unlearned by conscious decision must be tempered, however, by two types of consideration: (1) Most psychologists agree that emotions have a special relationship to goals. They have a "valence" or "hedonic tone" that renders them either inherently pleasant or inherently unpleasant; and they have an "intensity" that determines how easy or difficult it is for a person to override them. (2) New work on the nature of mental control shows that there are special constraints on the kind of learning or unlearning that involves emotions.

1. Valence, Intensity, and Goals

Most psychologists consider that emotions have both valence and intensity and that these characteristics distinguish emotions sharply from cognitions. Nico Frijda put it very simply. "With cognitive judgments, there is no reason, other than an affective one, to prefer any goal whatever over some other. Cognitive reasoning may argue that a particular event could lead to loss of money or health or life, but so what? What is wrong with death, other than that it is disliked?" (1994:199).

Emotional valence – the pleasantness or unpleasantness of emotional reactions to things, events, or situations – Frijda suggests, is the origin of all goals. Bower (1992:4) put it this way: "Emotion is evolution's way of giving meaning to our lives." A human organism, according to Bower, must be able to detect the urgency of various needs, prioritize, plan routines, and monitor internal and external states for unexpected developments. "A system with these components will exhibit 'emotions' as a byproduct of translating its concerns into goal-directed actions in . . . an unpredictable environment." That every emotion is either pleasant or unpleasant and that every emotion has a certain intensity is variously regarded as either shaping one's goals or reflecting one's goals. But, despite the widespread acceptance of these views, they present some important complexities that must be sorted out.

First, emotional intensity cannot be represented on a simple scale from low to high (Frijda et al. 1992). There are at least two different kinds of intensity, and each has several possible configurations. First, there is physiological arousal. Lang (1995) reviews neurological research that has identified two different types of physiological arousal, which he dubs "aversive" (i.e., negative or unpleasant) and "appetitive" (i.e., positive or pleasant); each of these can vary from low to high, and they are mutually exclusive, in Lang's view; that is, these two arousal states do not occur at the same time. But there is also widespread evidence that suppressing strong emotions results in still a third configuration of physiological arousal, in which some systems are aroused and not others (Gottman & Levenson 1988; Gross & Levenson 1993; Hughes et al. 1994). Arousal represents a complex terrain that psychologists have by no means completely mapped. Second, there is a type of intensity I would call "goal relevance"; it has been succinctly described by Clore (1994:391): "the more an event is seen to affect specific goals, the more intensely one may react in the sense that it may influence emotional feelings and preoccupation over time." Clore gives the following example:

Consider an intense emotional experience, such as grief over the death of a spouse. Assuming the marriage involved a close relationship of long standing, there might be few aspects of the grieving person's life that would not be changed or for which the mental representations would not be restructured. The experience might be intense to the extent that the person has to accommodate mentally to an endless number of violated assumptions about the other's presence. (pp. 391–392)

This kind of intensity, Clore concludes, "depends on the desirability of the event" which occasions the emotion; and this, in turn, depends on "the centrality of relevant goals, and hence *on the amount that a change in the goal dislocates the rest of one's network of goals*" (p. 392; emphasis added).

Second, valence is by no means a straightforward characteristic of emotions. Feldman Barrett, for example, in a recent study found that

First, the desirability of a mood and the hedonic quality [valence] of a mood are related, but not identical entities. Secondly, the desirability of a mood is also related to the level of arousal the mood denotes. Thirdly, desirability components are related to the self-report ratings of mood, but the ratings also reflect the hedonic tone and level of arousal describing the internal state of the respondents. (1996:47)

Another way of stating this finding might be as follows: Just as there is a goal-relevant type of emotional intensity, there would appear to be a goal-relevant type of emotional valence, what Feldman Barrett calls "desirability" as opposed to "hedonic tone." Fear, for example, may be inherently unpleasant in some sense, bringing about, in many cases, various intensities of "aversive" arousal (Lang 1995). But it is also apparent that, in some instances, fear is sought out and enjoyed. Bungee jumpers, spectators of a horror or suspense film, and roller coaster riders routinely experience pleasure in the fear induced by the chosen activity. Similar positive experience of fear may be associated with certain professions: pilot, police officer, emergency medical personnel, professional football player, golfer, tennis player, to name but a few. All these specific instances of enjoyed fear point to a more general sense in which none of us simply minimize fear in our lives. Full embrace of such a goal (of avoidance of all fear) would render life immediately unlivable. Other negative emotions may also be rendered positive by their goal relevance; under proper circumstances, nostalgia, melancholy, sorrow, anger, even grief can become sources of satisfaction or fulfillment, and occasions which produce them may be sought out (Stearns 1994:16–57).

Valence and intensity may therefore be misnamed, mispackaged concepts. On the one hand, one can indeed identify various configurations of physiological arousal; these may be categorizable into pleasant and unpleasant, in a hardwired sense, just as sweetness is pleasant to the tongue and a pinprick hurts the skin. Such valenced arousal patterns are not emotions, however. On the other hand, there are configurations of thought activation which vary in intensity and in their desirability/undesirability according to their total goal relevance.

Emotions are often viewed, by both expert and lay observers, as badges of deep goal relevance (Frank 1988; D'Andrade 1992; Oatley 1992:162). By "deep goal relevance" I mean the relevance of an action, event, or circumstance to goals which are pursued "for their own sake," not as intermediate steps on the road to some higher goal. Goals may be pursued for their own sake because they are integrated into a "network" of goals so deeply that it is impossible to regard them as a mere means to an end. For example, we generally pursue health for its own sake; but it is obvious that health is a means or condition for the pursuit of many, many other goals. As a result, pursuit of health as a means and pursuit of health as an end in its own right are likely to be indistinguishable (both to observers and to the person involved). Likewise, loss of health is widely regarded with fear or anxiety. Such fear or anxiety is a "badge" of the deep goal relevance of health. A person who avoids cheating even when he or she would not be caught may do so because being trustworthy has deep goal relevance for that person. Trustworthy behavior may be part of a code of honor which that person applies in many circumstances. He or she may avoid cheating out of a knowledge of the feeling of shame that would result. Shame is in this circumstance a badge of the deep goal relevance of trustworthiness for that person. If an observer witnesses the person's shame at a small infraction, the observer will know that the person in question is trustworthy (see Frank 1988).

Roy D'Andrade makes this same point: "The network of connections between goals and drives is extremely complex, involving 'many-to-many' mappings; these relations are so intricate that they can rarely be empirically determined" (1992:31). D'Andrade and his associates (e.g., Holland 1992; Quinn 1992; Strauss & Quinn 1997) have argued that humans simplify this complexity by identifying, learning, and implementing "schemas," many of which become invested with "motivational force" – that is, with great emotional significance. Schemas may represent sets of goals integrated by means of complex mutual means/ends relationships. For example, a person who embraces both a "marriage" schema and a "successful career" schema may view going to college as an important means to both ends. If so, he or she may also invest a "going to college" schema with great motivational force in its own right.[4] In Oatley's (1992) view, emotions which come up unexpectedly – for example, when viewing pictures at a museum, or while walking through a forest – reflect a monitoring process that makes up, in part, for the narrow focus of consciousness at any given moment. "By inserting issues into consciousness," Oatley argues, "and because they imply goals that may be inexplicit, emotions can point to aspects of our goal structures that we may have been unaware of" (p. 39). Not only are emotions badges of deeply relevant goals, but also we track the relevance of such goals to the current context in a manner that goes beyond the capacity of attention or consciousness, by monitoring our emotional reactions.

The goal-relevant "valence" of emotions and their goal-relevant "intensity" reflect the fact that deeply integrated goals are themselves sustained by overlearned cognitive habits which the individual has little or no capacity to evaluate or change, at least in the short run. The working through of intense (in the sense of duration, as in Clore 1994, quoted above) emotions such as grief, shame, chronic anxiety, *is* the process of changing such deeply integrated goals.

2. Mental Control

Because the goal-relevant valence and intensity of emotions indicates their close association with deeply pursued goals, emotions are also constantly implicated in efforts of "mental control," a set of processes that has been the subject of much new research. Central to the functioning of mental control, according to Daniel Wegner (1994), a leader in this area, is the so-called reflexivity constraint. Wegner expresses it as follows: "Any processes of control that are represented in consciousness during the exertion of control must be compatible with the state of mind that is the goal of the control mechanism" (p. 42). Positively formulated mental control tasks – such as attempting to think only pleasant thoughts – are less likely to violate this reflexivity constraint, because it is easy to check one's success without defeating one's purpose. Negatively formulated control tasks are quite different, however, and result in what Wegner calls "ironic processes." Asked not to think of pink elephants, a human being confronts an initial problem:

---

[4] Ortner (1989) and others have developed a parallel concept of schema in their application of practice theory to ethnographic analysis; for further discussion, see Strauss & Quinn (1997).

how intentionally to avoid thinking about something. One must think about it in order to identify that which one wishes to avoid. Once this difficulty is surmounted, there is another: how to be sure one is succeeding without recalling the forbidden thought, and thereby failing, at least temporarily. Because of the "reflexivity constraint" mental control is at best a sometime thing. "[O]ur attention jiggles and shimmers," Wegner remarks, "no matter how much we wish it to converge to a hard point. Ironic processes provide a way to explain this Achilles' heel of concentration" (p. 42).

These ironic processes look very much the same in laboratory tests, whether the goals of mental control are cognitive or emotional. Whether one sets out to avoid thinking about the number five or a lost love, the difficulties one faces are identical, although avoiding "chronically accessible" thoughts associated with strong emotions presents special challenges. Wegner hypothesizes that a decision to engage in mental control initiates two processes, an "operating process" and a "monitoring process." "The operating process creates the desired change by filling the mind with thoughts and sensations that are relevant to the desired state. The monitoring process searches surreptitiously for mental contents that indicate when control is needed, and so regulates whether or not the operating process will be initiated at any given time" (p. 34). The search carried out by the monitoring process is "not conscious, requires relatively little cognitive effort, and continues until the attempted mental control is terminated by a conscious choice." Of course, the unconscious character of such monitoring is essential to any effort of mental control. It is by definition impossible for any gatekeeper operation aimed at excluding certain contents from consciousness to be conscious. That there must be such gatekeeper operations seems also unavoidable; consciousness, by its very essence, is limited, "focused" or selective. Wegner reads the research as showing that, if the operating process fades or is set aside because of other cognitive demands that soak up available mental capacity, then the monitoring process "can be our undoing." In one test, Wegner and Erber (1992) gave subjects the task of avoiding thoughts of a target word. They were then prompted with words and asked to give associated words, under time pressure. The time pressure creates a cognitive "load," because the effort it calls for weakens the operating process that is censoring the target word. Under these conditions, subjects "responded frequently with the target word to target-relevant prompts, blurting out the very word they had been trying not to think about." "More important," Wegner continues, "suppression with time pressure boosted responses of the target word to target-relevant prompts over even the level of subjects under time pressure who were actively trying to think about the target" (Wegner 1994:42). Suppression efforts result in a "heightened accessibility" of the suppressed thought due to the monitoring process. When vigilance fades, suppressed thoughts "rebound" (Wegner & Gold 1995:783). Wegner cites research showing that such ironic rebound effects are common in efforts to quit smoking (trying not to think about smoking results in more frequent desire for a cigarette), in efforts to cure insomnia, in efforts to believe a given proposition, and in self-presentation tests when subjects were instructed to lie, or to present a favorable image of themselves.

Researchers examining the ironic effects of emotional control have come forward with similar findings. Wegner and Gold (1995) divided subjects into two groups. The first was composed of persons who had a former lover for whom they still felt a strong desire or a strong sense of loss; for them, their old flame was still a "hot flame." The second group had former lovers for whom they no longer felt desire or a sense of loss; their old flame was now a "cold flame." Both groups were given three 8-minute tasks: (1) to "think aloud 'of the person whose initials you gave earlier'" (i.e., the former lover); (2) to "try not to think of the person whose initials you gave earlier, but mention it if you do"; and (3) again to "think aloud 'of the person whose initials you gave earlier.'" For each group, control groups were told, for task no. 2, to "try not to think of the Statue of Liberty, but mention it if you do." Results showed the the "cold flame" group, whose former lovers were no longer objects of desire or loss, and who were told not to think of that person during task 2, experienced a rebound of thoughts about that person, speaking more of him or her during task 3 than those who tried not to think of the Statue of Liberty. The "hot flame" group who suppressed thoughts of the old lover did not experience a rebound, however. Nonetheless, their skin conductance levels did increase during task 3. Skin conductance levels commonly increase during efforts of emotional suppression. (See studies cited in Wegner & Gold; see also Gross & Levenson 1993; Hughes et al. 1994.) Wegner and Gold therefore concluded that the "hot flame" group were resisting instructions to talk about a painful subject and experienced heightened control efforts to combat the rebound effect.

Wenzlaff and Bates (1998) examined links between ironic effects of mental control and vulnerability to depression. They identified three

groups of subjects: nondepressive, at-risk, and depressive. Each group
was given three sets of twenty scrambled sentences and was instructed
to unscramble them, under time pressure. They were told to unscramble the first set "to form whatever statement comes to mind first"; the
second set they were to unscramble "to form a negative statement"; the
third set was to be unscrambled "to form a positive statement." Half
the participants were asked to hold a six-digit number in memory
during the tests; this was intended to supply a cognitive "load" that
would weaken or disable suppression efforts and to thus render ironic
effects more likely. Members of the nondepressive group formed positive statements consistently when instructed to do so, failing in only 2
percent of cases, whether or not they were under load. Members of the
depressive group failed to form positive statements in 14 percent of
cases under no load, and in 19 percent of cases when under load.
Members of the at-risk group scored nearly as high as nondepressives
in the no-load condition, but failed to form positive statements 17
percent of the time – nearly as high as depressives – when under load.
The researchers concluded that persons at risk of depression may be
avoiding depression by means of high levels of conscious thought suppression. If so, their vulnerability to depression may rebound when
they are under stress or high cognitive load. Because of the danger of
such rebound effects, "Full recovery may be more likely if individuals
do not routinely rely on thought suppression to avoid depressive
thoughts" (p. 1569).

Generalizing on this kind of research, Wegner and Smart (1997)
argue that there are three quite distinct states of thought activation.
"Surface activation" is the state of thoughts currently in consciousness
which are not likely to be retained in memory or to be accessible once
they leave consciousness. Examples are the color of cars passing by on
the road or thoughts of little interest which individuals focus on as dis-
tractors, such as the content of a television news broadcast or of a mag-
azine read in the doctor's office. "Full activation" entails both presence
in consciousness and ready accessibility to consciousness. Examples
would be conscious thoughts of significant others – family members,
friends – or of often repeated habits – a golf swing or a favorite recipe.
A third type of activation, which Wegner and Smart term "deep activation," consists specifically of those thoughts that have been the
targets of suppression efforts and have therefore been ironically activated by the unconscious monitoring process that accompanies mental
control efforts. Finally, thoughts may be in a fourth state of no activa-

tion; such thoughts and memories remain outside of consciousness without expenditure of cognitive effort. In addition, according to Wegner and Smart, activation of thoughts generally has three types of sources. First, perceptual input can generate any of the three types of activation – including "deep activation." In Wegner and Smart's view, tests of subliminal cognition like those carried out by Greenwald et al. (1995) show that perceptual input can activate thoughts without bringing them into consciousness. Second, many thoughts are in a state of "chronic or habitual activation." This is a highly significant status, according to Wegner and Smart.

Each person seems to have a chronic array of active thoughts, ones that are accessible all the time. Depending on the person's motivation to allow these thoughts into consciousness or to try to control them, chronically accessible thoughts may or may not appear in consciousness as well. It is probably safe to say that for many thoughts that are chronically accessible, their occurrence in consciousness sets off no special alarms. A person may have certain interests or preferences, for example, that often move directly from unconscious accessibility to conscious thought, and these are therefore often fully activated. It would be especially difficult to live a life in which chronically accessible thoughts are not desired in consciousness, thus yielding chronic deep activation – but this is probably the state of many individuals who suffer from certain psychopathologies. (1997:986–987)

Finally, they posit a third source of thought activation, "intentional activation" which they consider to be identical to "the operation of mental control." "[W]ith the proper resources, mental control often does work quite effectively, at least in the sense that it can produce intervals in which the desired conscious state of mind is achieved." But mental control always involves a cost, because it "introduces an ironic monitoring process that increases the accessibility of the very thoughts that are least desired in consciousness." They speculate that the ironic occurrence of deep activation can help to explain the great difficulty individuals encounter in trying to diet, break drug habits, overcome phobias, avoid morbid thoughts, or fall asleep. Mental loads break down control efforts; in daily life, such loads may include "not just stresses or distractions, but also alcohol or other drugs that influence attention, and any dispositional tendencies toward poor attention" (p. 987). When ironic effects are induced experimentally "they appear to cause experiences like those had by individuals suffering certain varieties of psychopathology" (p. 988). They cite evidence, as well, that intentional suppression of "emotional thoughts" can lead to a "disinhibition of the emotion in the period following – a disinhibition so upsetting that participants elected to continue trying to erase the thought from consciousness" (p. 989).

"Quite simply," they conclude,

> here we have a state of mind [deep activation] that is demonstrably set to change. A thought is poised to enter consciousness, and yet for some motivated or situational reason, is not allowed to be there. When this happens, it makes sense that associative pathways could be activated beneath consciousness, ones that lead to the expression of the accessible thought in other ways. These indirect eruptions of deep activation into thought or behavior would seem to be particularly likely to occur in areas that are not so obviously related to the thought that they generate conscious monitoring. Deep activation may produce effects that are just far enough away from the thought to allow the state of deep activation to continue unperturbed. (p. 991)

These kinds of effects may easily resemble classic symptoms and mechanisms of neurosis in Freudian theory: phobias, obsessions, projections, sublimations. In addition, deep activation, despite its unstable nature, often finds ways of perpetuating itself in a kind of unstable equilibrium, Wegner and Smart speculate.

How is deep cognitive activation maintained despite its unstable nature? In many cases, it is not maintained. When happy thoughts are deeply activated, for example, there is usually little tendency to perpetuate the state. A creative insight, for example, or a memory that one hopes to retrieve, is not prone to yield intrusions or emotions that will prompt the person to reinstate suppression or avoidance. The thought is welcomed to consciousness and full activation is produced. It is probably the case that deep cognitive activation is maintained primarily when the person achieves conscious glimpses of some thought that is too painful or unfathomable to allow in consciousness. That is, there may well need to be at least one undesired intrusion every once in a while to motivate continued mental control and so promote the maintenance of deep cognitive activation. (p. 991)

Wegner and Smart are not alone in insisting that "activation" of thought material can no longer be considered a simple "on/off" condition. Carr and Dagenbach's "center-surround" hypothesis, mentioned above, bears some remarkable similarities to Wegner's conception of paired (conscious) operating and (unconscious) monitoring processes. Balota and Paul (1996) posit a kind of "forward-spreading" activation; like Besner et al. (1997), they are attempting to chart the differences between "lexical-" and "semantic-level" activation – that is, recognition of mere letters and words, versus recognition of meanings and their relationships – types of activation that are proving to have quite different characteristics. Work by Drevets and Raichle (1998) and others attempts to track different forms of activation using cerebral-blood-flow imaging.

CONCLUSION

In sum, psychologists have moved away from linear models of cognition toward models involving multiple pathways, multiple levels of activation and types of activation, involving complex combinations of suppression and enhancement. Departure from linear models has forced psychologists to drop, as well, neat dividing lines between conscious and unconscious, supraliminal and subliminal, controlled and involuntary processes. These shifts have brought in their train a sweeping reconceptualization of the nature of emotion – a "revolution in the study of emotions," as Fischer and Tangney have noted (1995:3). Traditionally, emotion was associated both with nonlinear (free-associational, poetic, or symbolic) thinking and with physiological arousal (blushing, adrenaline flow, changes in heart rate, and so on). These two types of phenomena were linked in that they both departed from a vision of conscious, rational, voluntary action that was believed to be the hallmark of human intelligence. Symbolic thinking is not strictly rational; physiological arousal is not strictly under voluntary control. But as notions of "voluntary" and "conscious" have broken down, and as thinking has increasingly been regarded as reflecting multiple levels of activation, attention, and coherence, it has become difficult to sustain the distinction between thought and affect. As we have seen, many researchers uphold the distinction as a matter of faith and use it as a heuristic tool for organizing their thinking about laboratory results; but no one has found a way to probe or measure an emotion directly. Blushing may be a good indicator of embarrassment, but embarrassment often occurs in the absence of blushing. Sexual arousal may be an indicator of (romantic) love; but the two are quite independent of each other in many circumstances. Clenched fists and a furrowed brow may be good indicators of anger, but anger often subsists for long periods without yielding any physiological, facial, or behavioral signals.

Recent research has continued to confirm the analysis of Isen and Diamond in 1989 that emotions can be regarded as overlearned cognitive habits; they are involuntary (automatic) in the short run in the same sense that such cognitive habits are, but may similarly be learned and unlearned over a longer time frame. However, the learning of what we conventionally call emotions must often involve both deep goal relevance and mental control. For example, much training in childhood entails attempts to instill feelings of shame over failures of impulse control. Children throwing food on the floor at dinner, wiping their noses on their sleeves, openly showing anger in front of guests are repeatedly reprimanded and reminded to control such impulses. The end point of such training is a quite spontaneous and involuntary sense of shame and embarrassment at lapses of decorum or etiquette. However, such learning involves mental control. The individual must set out to search for impulses to blow his or her nose or to shout out in anger so that they can be suppressed. Such searching and suppressing is always carried out under the difficult conditions imposed by the "reflexivity constraint." Different strategies of avoidance will yield different degrees of success. Consciousness itself has its own unconscious gatekeepers, as it must. A great deal of "activated" thought may lie outside of consciousness, as with Wegner and Smart's notion of "deep activation"; or outside of consciousness part of the time, as with Wegner's "monitoring process," or Carr and Dagenbach's "center-surround" activation pattern. Other thoughts may be activated in certain circumstances, by sensory input or by a monitoring process, without ever entering consciousness, as with anxiety-prone individuals' responses to negative words in Stroop color-naming tests.

An individual cannot, therefore, fashion or refashion just any emotion or any set of emotions he or she wishes. Limitations derive not only from the mutual means-ends relationships of deeply relevant goals, but also from the "architecture" of mental control, as Wegner and others have outlined it. Thus, certain strategies of emotional training – such as those which rely too much on thought suppression – may fail, or may yield a stable pattern of repeated failure.

Cognitive psychologists have reached a stage where old assumptions have been brought into doubt and the building of sweeping new models has come into vogue; increasingly, emotions are being included in these models as something "inextricably intertwined" with cognition (O'Rorke & Ortony 1994:283). Over the same period, anthropologists working on emotions have confronted difficulties very similar to those confronted by psychologists. But they have dealt with them in the context of a more generalized crisis that continues to refashion their discipline. In the next chapter I will examine anthropologists' efforts to make sense of emotions, and show how this effort has been implicated in the discipline's larger political and epistemological questioning. I will also try to show, in a preliminary way, how the findings of cognitive psychology might be employed to point a way forward, out of the current crisis.

CHAPTER 2

Answers from Anthropology

If emotions are not biologically based or genetically programmed, then they must be cultural, or at least deeply influenced by culture. If emotions operate like overlearned cognitive habits, as many psychologists would now agree, then they must be shaped, to a significant degree, by the environment in which the individual lives. What is culture, for the individual, if not a set of overlearned cognitive habits?

As psychology has experienced a "revolution" in the study of emotions, anthropologists, aware of developments in the other discipline (see, e.g., Lutz & White 1986:405), have been quick to fashion new definitions of emotion and new research methods suitable to exploring emotions in the special kind of evidence they use. Over the last quarter century, as a result, the anthropology of emotions – virtually unknown in 1970 (Levy 1984:214) – has become one of the discipline's most vital new subfields. Anthropologists' fieldwork has uncovered a fascinating array of different conceptions of emotion, different emotion lexicons, and varying emotional practices from around the globe. But the anthropology of emotions has not been free of controversy. Just as psychologists have disagreed over the relation between emotion and cognition, anthropologists have disagreed over precisely how, and to what extent, emotions are influenced, shaped, or "constructed" by culture.

However, these disagreements have gained complexity from their resonance with larger currents of debate in the field of anthropology. Anthropology has been in a period of prolonged crisis. This crisis reflects a larger "debate about the production of knowledge" (Marcus 1992:viii) related to the rise of poststructuralist approaches in a number of humanities and social science disciplines. But in anthropology, the debate has been more acute because, as George Marcus put it,

34

First, . . . unlike most other disciplines affected, the debate in anthropology has occupied a central focus of attention in which the identity of the discipline itself is at stake for its practitioners. And second, the critique of knowledge in anthropology was produced by a working alliance of scholars inside and outside of anthropology, that is, of historians and critics, focusing upon the discipline, and of practitioners within it. This alliance across the boundaries of the discipline made the critique both more provocative and more difficult to dismiss or marginalize among anthropologists. (p. viii)

The existence of culture has itself been brought into question, because anthropologists' prior idea of culture was linked to a particular idea of the "production of knowledge" that no longer seemed tenable. The discipline's identity was, up to that point, so closely linked to this idea of culture that many wondered if it could survive the loss of its most cherished model. The rebuilding effort has concentrated on several axes. The political implications of fieldwork and the cultural status of gender and ethnic identity have become subjects of heated discussion. Anthropologists have become acutely sensitive to individual variation, resistance, and historical change. The anthropology of emotions has, as a result, matured in an atmosphere of self-searching and uncertainty, responding to some of the pulls and tugs of the larger debates, but not to others. The very nature of the self, in relation to its social context, has come into question, opening up an extraordinary opportunity to rethink the mission of the social sciences.

THE CONSTRUCTIONIST APPROACH

One of the pioneers of the anthropology of emotions, Michelle Z. Rosaldo, set out to demonstrate that, while emotions may have some physiological facets, nonetheless, "what individuals can think *and feel* is *overwhelmingly* a product of socially organized modes of action and of talk" (M. Rosaldo 1984:147; emphasis added). Although little of the new psychological research on emotions was available at the time she carried out her fieldwork in the mid-1970s, Rosaldo drew support for her approach from the earlier research of S. Schachter and J. Singer (1962). In their classic study, Schachter and Singer found that subjects injected with epinephrine reported experiencing a variety of emotions from elation to anxiety, depending on what effects the experimenters told them to expect from the injection. (For discussion, see Laird 1987;

Lakoff 1987:406–408; Sinclair, Hoffman, & Mark 1994; Gergen 1995.) The evidence established, in Rosaldo's view, that emotions included a biological component (arousal), that was rather ambiguous and unimportant in itself, coupled with an all-important interpretive component that was learned and therefore cultural.[1]

Rosaldo's work on the Ilongot people (hunters and swidden farmers of a mountainous, forested region of the Philippines) demonstrated that their most intimate emotional experiences were shaped by their language's emotional lexicon and by the practices that flowed from this lexicon (M. Rosaldo 1980). Most important in the Ilongot lexicon was the concept of *liget*, a term that encompasses a number of English notions, including anger, energy, envy, heat. Possession of liget was positively valued and highly admired. Liget provided the motivation to garden and to hunt, as well as to protect one's clan from attack and to avenge injuries. Liget could be heightened by grief at death, whether or not the dead person was a victim of violence. Central to the possession of liget was the male activity of headhunting. Traditionally, a young man was expected to take a head before achieving adult status. Adolescent males would become full of liget, to the point of obsession and confusion – a danger to themselves and their families – until elders agreed to take them on headhunting raids. Following the return of a successful raiding party, a community would break into blissful celebration, performing dances and songs that gave expression to the joy brought by liget's fulfillment.

The centrality of liget to the Ilongots' lived experience of self was brought home to Rosaldo on her second field trip to the region. In the intervening period, headhunting had come to an end due to a crackdown by Philippine authorities. When Rosaldo played a tape recording of an earlier headhunting celebration – at her hosts' urgings – the Ilongots present quickly demanded that she turn the machine off. The sound of their earlier joy was too painful for them, now that such celebrating had ceased; to their own surprise, what they had so ardently wished to hear turned out to be unbearable. She found that many Ilongots were converting to Christianity in the belief that the new religion would take away the pain of liget unrealized and replace it with a milder, more placid emotional character. She observed one group of Ilongot Christians playing volleyball at a child's funeral, because, they

[1] Based on a number of in-depth discussions between M. Rosaldo and the author in 1976 and 1977.

said, they no longer had any reason to feel grief. These new developments of the second field trip showed that the activities motivated by
liget were not just empty performances of cultural scripts, the application of fixed symbolic structures. They reflected a profound emotional
engagement, but an emotional engagement that was itself a product of
culture operating at a deeper level than previous anthropologists had
recognized.

By Rosaldo's approach, the human self was almost infinitely malleable; when Western psychologists thought they were studying universal characteristics of the human psyche, they were, more often than
not, only charting the local characteristics of Western emotional culture.
In other times and places, the self and its feelings were quite differently
constituted, by culture.

Not all anthropologists were prepared to go so far. Robert Levy (1973,
1984), another pioneer of the anthropology of emotions, held that underlying emotions were similar from one culture to another; what differed
was the extent to which a culture emphasized or valued an emotion.
Each of a common human set of emotions was either "hypercognized"
(emphasized and consciously rehearsed, expressed, and discussed)
or "hypocognized" (not named, denied, concealed). In Tahiti, where
Levy did fieldwork, the language lacked words for sadness or grief.
What we consider sadness and grief Tahitians seem to regard as mere
physiological disturbances, of no interpersonal significance.

People would name their condition, where I supposed that [the body signs
and] the context called for "sadness" or "depression," as "feeling troubled"
(*pe'ape'a*, the generic term for disturbances, either internal or external); as
"not feeling a sense of inner push" (*'ana'anatae*); as "feeling heavy" (*toiaha*);
as "feeling fatigued" (*hauman*); and a variety of other terms all referring to
a generally troubled or subdued bodily state. These are all nonspecific
terms, which had no implications of any external [social] relational cause
about them, in the sense that being "angry" implies an offense or a
frustration. (1984:219)

Yet Levy observed that Tahitians who suffered loss displayed symptoms of grief even if they identified those symptoms as emanations of
illness or fatigue.

From the very beginning to this day, the anthropology of emotions
has been caught on the horns of this dilemma: how much influence to
attribute to culture, how much to attribute to underlying universal
psychic factors. Does death bring grief everywhere, or just in those

cultures where the individual is highly valued? Is romantic love a universal human experience, celebrated in some cultures, suppressed in others – or is it just the creation of Western individualism? Is depression a neurological illness that can strike down anyone, anywhere, or is it a cultural artifact of modern, clinical treatment and modern social isolation? The debate has paralleled the controversies among psychologists over the existence of "basic" emotions, over the meaning and character of different arousal states, and over the relation between cognition and affect. In anthropology, however, this debate has had an extra dimension to it and has taken on an added, highly charged, political significance.

In psychology, the question of emotion takes the classic form of a nature/nurture controversy – like debates over intelligence, schizophrenia, drug addiction, and other conditions. But anthropologists of emotion cannot debate the influence of culture in this simple either/or form, because in recent years the culture concept itself has come under serious challenge. In anthropology, one has the strange prospect that certain followers of Rosaldo – those prepared to attribute the greatest role to "socially organized modes of action and talk" in the shaping of emotions – are also paradoxically the most vocal in their denunciation of the culture concept. For them, the idea that emotions are cultural in origin has become just as distasteful as the idea that they are biological in origin. This highly illuminating standpoint bears careful examination.

In 1986, Lila Abu-Lughod published a study of the Awlad ʿAli, a Bedouin group of the Egyptian desert, showing that, here as with the Ilongots, the individual's most intimate, most private feelings were deeply shaped by social practices and norms. Abu-Lughod examined how women used snatches of *ghinnāwa* poetry to express sentiments of resistance to elders' wishes, or sentiments of profound grief over the effects of their commands. But she argued that such expressions, prompted by commitment to the deeply held Bedouin value of personal independence, only served to underscore the personal cost of obedience (another deeply held value), thus increasing the honor of the one who suffered. The ghinnāwa is a traditional form, requiring mastery of a literary language not used in everyday life and memorization of numerous examples. The apparent spontaneity of ghinnāwa usage in certain circumstances is itself a carefully cultivated effect. For example, Abu-Lughod examined an unusually difficult marriage involving Rashīd, a man in his early forties, and Fāyga, his second wife, who was twenty years his junior. Rashīd showed undue preference for Fāyga by spending almost all nights with her, shunning his first wife, who deserved at least equal treatment. The issue was widely commented on in the village. When Fāyga ran away, Rashīd did everything he could to get her back, angering many relatives who felt her departure was an insult. He ought to give her a divorce, and not even ask for the return of his bridewealth, they felt, as a way of insulting Fāyga's relatives in return. Among Bedouin communities divorce is relatively common early in a marriage, and sometimes offers men and women a way out of situations imposed on them by elder kin. But honor is always supposed to take precedence over attraction or affection. Many couples who felt affection, Abu-Lughod reports, kept it a strict secret and would have been quite embarrassed if it were known, even among close family members. Rashīd completely disregarded this injunction against the display of affection.

Fāyga felt a strong aversion for her new husband, longed to return to her family, and dreamed of being married to another, younger man she had only heard about, but never seen. She recited snatches of ghinnāwas, from which some of her female in-laws gleaned knowledge of her true feelings (as they understood them). Abu-Lughod carefully recorded a number of these bits of poetry.

> You want, oh dear one, to be disappointed
> and to fight about something not fated to be . . .
>
> On my breast I placed
> a tombstone, though I was not dead, oh loved one . . .
>
> If a new love match is not granted
> the ache in my mind will continue, oh beloved . . .
> (1986:217–219)

Because of their artfully arranged structure, these bits of poetry could not be construed, in some simple way, as spontaneously revealing what was otherwise hidden, but true, sentiment. Abu-Lughod did not find, either, that such use of ghinnāwas reflected resistance to the political status quo, norms, or customs of the community. Those who used them remained as committed as ever to their own, and their lineage's, honor, and as ready as before to obey elders. What ghinnāwas did make possible, Abu-Lughod concluded, was the depiction of the self as able to creatively master strong divergent feelings – an ability that played a central role in the ideal of honorable independence so many Awlad 'Ali strove to achieve. Thus Fāyga demonstrated, through her poetry, that her resistance to Rashīd was not a shameful failure to obey her elders, but an expression of commitment to independence, to an independence so deeply valued that even her limited obedience had a high cost. Abu-Lughod found no split between cultural and subjective "selves"; instead, like Rosaldo, she discovered people whose deepest feelings were already in conformity with, constructed by, their community's outlook and values.

Abu-Lughod's work was unprecedented in the context of Bedouin ethnography. As a woman of Arab parentage, Abu-Lughod had been barred from doing the traditional kind of "public" fieldwork anthropologists had long taken as normal and adequate. Her Bedouin hosts treated her like a relative; she was subject to the same constraints on movement and socializing and the same expectations about work and obedience as any other woman of the community. Rather than succumb to discouragement about her inability to work along established ethnographic lines, she set about examining what was available to her. Only after she had gained acceptance and become fully integrated into the household was she able to witness the poetic performances that became the focus of her work. For her, the discovery that the intense emotions expressed in ghinnāwas were "not outside of culture" (p. 256) simultaneously legitimated her unorthodox methods, raised questions about the established procedures of (largely male) anthropologists, and undermined a traditional Western ideology about gender difference. Prior ethnographers' indifference both to emotions and to the female sphere of the Bedouin household reflected their unquestioning acceptance of the Western idea that emotions were more biological than cultural and that women were more emotional (less specifically cultural) than men. Prior accounts of Bedouin culture were therefore distorted by a Western, male-dominated lens that determined both the kinds of questions ethnographers asked and the methods they adopted to answer them. The resulting picture was too neat by half, based as it was on an unrecognized complicity between the ethnographers' male-centered assumptions and the Bedouins' own (different, but still) male-centered assumptions about gender and emotion.

Two years later, Catherine Lutz published an important ethnography of emotions on the Pacific atoll of Ifaluk (Lutz 1988). Not only was her approach "constructionist," like Rosaldo's and Abu-Lughod's (in finding that emotions are local, social "constructions"), but she reinforced this stance with a stinging critique of Western belief about emotions, reviewing its historical development from the seventeenth century down to the present. In Lutz's view, the notion that emotions are biologically based is not simply erroneous, it is part of a larger, insidious, gender-biased Western view of the self that privileges alleged male rationality over the supposedly natural emotionalism of women. Expert and lay assumptions coincided, Lutz charged, in regarding emotions as internal, involuntary, irrational, potentially dangerous or sublime, and female. Men were rational and therefore better suited to action in the public sphere. Ethnographic research showed, however, that emotions were a product of social interactions and showed, as well, that outside the West, emotions were generally not distinguished from thinking in the peculiarly sharp way Westerners distinguished them, and were generally regarded as an outcome of social interaction, rather than as rising up, ineffably, from within.

On Ifaluk, Lutz found, there was no denigration of women or of emotion. Thought and emotion were not distinguished there; political authority was associated with the expression of an emotion called *song*, which Lutz translated as "righteous anger." Women were invested with such authority as frequently as men. Recognition of and submission to such authority was associated with another emotion, *metagu* ("fear/ anxiety"); and both emotions were highly valued.

Both of these anthropologists needed an analytical tool more refined than the concept of culture in order to make their arguments clear. They could not use the concept of culture as it was in fact used by Rosaldo. Rosaldo drew her notion of culture from the influential writings of Clifford Geertz (1973), who defined culture as a symbolic system, as a "model of" social life that was routinely used as a "model for" the carrying out of social performances. But, if culture in this sense determines both our thinking and our emotions – indeed, everything about us, motivations, dreams, desires – then there are no possible political grounds on which a culture can be criticized. If everything we want is merely an outgrowth or an artifact of our culture, then it is impossible for us to want to be free of that culture, or to want to change it. This implication has, in fact, been one of the grounds on which the Geertzian culture concept has been most severely and consistently criticized. Yet it was on these very grounds that Rosaldo built her claim that emotion was a properly anthropological concern. Emotion was, for her, the last bastion of subjectivity, the final fortress of individuality, the most intimately individual domain. That culture reigned here implied that there was nothing left over.[2] Yet if there was nothing left over, on what grounds could the West's peculiar view of emotions be criticized?

---

[2] Both Spiro (1992) and Chodorow (1999) have noted that Rosaldo carefully qualified her position, granting that a residuum of the self might belong to psychology rather than to culture. However, both argue that her qualifications were halfhearted and inconsistent.

Even if the Western view was "wrong" because it "constructed" the domain of emotion as a "natural" one, and women as especially emotional, this could not change the fact that, for Westerners, it thereby *became* a natural domain. If it made no sense for Rosaldo to criticize her Ilongot informants for feeling grief over the end of headhunting, then it made no sense for Lutz or Abu-Lughod to criticize Western social science for being male-centered and for seeing emotions as natural and peculiarly female.

For this reason, like many anthropologists in the 1980s, Abu-Lughod and Lutz distanced themselves from the culture concept, preferring to speak of "discourses" rather than using Geertz's concept of culture. "Discourse," in Foucault's thought, is recognized as a locus for the exercise of political power. Discourses, for Foucault, by the very categories they employ, give rise to disciplinary activities and license institutional structures of domination. Discourses differ from culture as Geertz understood it in that they are potentially multiple (more than one may be available at a given time), in that they change over time (although how they come to change is not explained in Foucault's writings), and in that they may be resisted (although how resistance can be organized without generating yet another dangerous "discourse" is not explained).[3] While Foucault had next to nothing to say about emotion in his work, Abu-Lughod and Lutz extended the concept of discourse to explain the social construction of emotion. "In enabling people to express experiences," Abu-Lughod concluded, *"these discourses may enable them to feel these experiences"* (Abu-Lughod 1986:258; emphasis added). "Like Foucault," Lutz stated, "I am interested in how the emotions – like other aspects of a culturally postulated psyche – are 'the place in which the most minute and local social practices are linked up with the large scale organization of power'" (Lutz 1988:7, citing Dreyfus & Rabinow 1983:xxvi).

In 1990, Lutz and Abu-Lughod jointly authored a more programmatic statement of their approach that drew heavily on Foucault's notion of discourse. Like other "discourses" Foucault had identified (such as those of the clinic or of the prison), discourse about emotions, they argued, creates the object it purports to be about; and, in doing

---

[3] These difficulties in Foucault's work have been widely remarked; for further discussion see Chapter 3; see also Reddy (1992, 1997a). Geertz, of course, was prepared to recognize that cultures were not unified and that they changed; however, both his theoretical principles and his ethnographic practice focused on timeless, tightly coherent cultural configurations.

so, such discourse establishes a structure of domination. They urged anthropologists to reject the idea that talk about emotions is expressive of something inside the self; "we argue that emotion talk must be interpreted as *in* and *about* social life rather than as veridically referential to some internal state" (Lutz & Abu-Lughod 1990b:11; emphasis in original). Acceptance of this standpoint will allow anthropologists to treat "all those productions in a community that could be considered cultural or ideological," including emotions, as "social practices, tied to relations of power as well as to sociability" (p. 10). Abu-Lughod, writing in the same anthology, was particularly critical of Western emotional practices. She took as an example a New York radio talk show she had heard, in which callers sought emotional advice from a professional psychologist.

What struck me most about what I heard was that the psychologist kept asking over and over, "How did you feel?" – How do you feel when this happens, what did you feel when he said that, what did you feel when he did that? She took for granted this mode of getting at the truth, this focus on emotions as touchstones of personal reality. And I suspect that the poor caller, had she later gone into therapy, would have learned to populate her narratives about herself and her relationships with a legion of emotions too. She would have learned to practice on herself and on others, to adapt a notion from Foucault (1985:5), a hermeneutics of feeling. (Abu-Lughod 1990:24)

She noted that the Bedouin women she worked with would have regarded such a question as nonsensical, and she agreed.

It is nonsensical, first, because it implies that there is a satisfying explanation to be had by resorting to the inspection of emotions and, second, because it presumes that the sentiments one would talk about in this publicly broadcast confessional would be the same as those in other social contexts and in other forms or media. In short this question assumes that emotions could be detached in meaning and consequence from the flow of social life. (pp. 24–25)

But there is a difficulty here. Why should a New York talk show host and her callers be regarded as engaging in a nonsensical practice while Bedouin women reciting ghinnāwas before carefully selected intimates are regarded as engaging in a sensible emotional practice? If Western practices make no sense, then surely Bedouin practices are equally arbitrary. Yet Abu-Lughod is careful to avoid critical remarks about Bedouin discourse or practice. Up to a point, such restraint reflects a laudable professional caution; she is not herself Bedouin; she cannot presume to have plumbed the depths of the Bedouin self or of the fates of Bedouin women. Certainly it is for them to decide, and not a Western-educated expert, whether and when they wish to demand change. Certainly Abu-Lughod is right not to read some form of protofeminist resistance into their poetic performances. However, the conceptual problem involved cannot be dispensed with that simply. Abu-Lughod has no grounds, on the basis of the concept of discourse, for criticizing any emotional practice. She cannot show that there is a free or right discourse; she cannot show that there is a kind of emotion or emotional state or practice "beyond" discourse, that can serve as a polestar by which we can navigate out of the grip of discursive domination of one kind or another.

Many anthropologists working on emotions, cautious about such difficulties, equally uncomfortable with the culture concept, have backed away from a total embrace of the "constructionist" standpoint. One finds frequent expressions of a circumspect stance, from which the anthropologist asserts that he or she is concerned with emotions only insofar as emotions are shaped by culture or by practice. Fred Myers, in his study of the Pintupi of Australia, said he wished to speak of a "cultural subject," in a way that "leaves open . . . the relation between cultural models and psychological organization" (Myers 1986:104–105). Watson-Gegeo and Gegeo (1990:164) likewise drew a sharp line between "social meanings and relationships, together with their implications for handling conflict," on the one hand, and "subjective or personal meanings" on the other. Niko Besnier, in 1995, echoed the views of many anthropologists in the field when he issued the following disclaimer: "I do not wish to claim that all emotions are socially constructed, and that emotions are socially constructed in all contexts of social life"; nonetheless "many emotions are collectively constructed and crucially dependent on interaction with others for their development" (Besnier 1995a:236). Having enunciated such caveats, however, Besnier, like Myers, Watson-Gegeo and Gegeo, and others, has followed a form of ethnographic interpretation hardly different, in practice, from Rosaldo's, Abu-Lughod's, or Lutz's. In terms of the practice of fieldwork and interpretation, constructionist method, if not constructionist doctrine, is probably the most common stance among anthropologists of emotion.

For example, the year 1990, in which Lutz and Abu-Lughod offered their programmatic statement about the power of emotional discourses, also saw the publication of an anthology of studies on emotions in India (Lynch 1990) that was insistently constructionist in orientation, and another anthology on conflict resolution practices in the Pacific (Watson-Gegeo & White 1990) that showed how emotional expression was shaped by political authority and rank in a wide variety of island cultures. More recently work by Besnier (1995b), Fajans (1997), Collier (1997), and others shows how a constructionist approach to emotions is gradually being integrated into ethnographic practice, following strategies first laid out by Rosaldo.

Virtually all of this work lacks historical depth and political coherence. Ethnographers who practice constructionism (whatever their theoretical allegiance may be) continue to write in the ethnographic present about communities presumed to be culturally uniform, even when they show great sensitivity to issues of political authority, gender, and conflict. Where historical change is discussed it is generally seen as coming from the outside, from the impinging forces of the modern world (e.g., Lutz 1988; Abu-Lughod 1990; Besnier 1995; Collier 1997). Where diversity is acknowledged, it is treated as secondary or ancillary (Grima 1992).

The problem of history has been with the anthropology of emotions from the very beginning. It is striking that Michelle Rosaldo's pioneering work on Ilongot emotions (M. Rosaldo 1980) appeared simultaneously with an historically oriented ethnography of the Ilongots written by her spouse, Renato Rosaldo (R. Rosaldo 1980). These two gifted anthropologists had carried out their fieldwork side by side, read each other's rough drafts as work on the manuscripts proceeded, and appreciated each other's efforts to make a decisive new contribution to cultural anthropology. Yet, just as Michelle Rosaldo's work has nothing to say about historical change, Renato Rosaldo's ethnographic history makes no attempt to consider whether Ilongot emotions changed over time. The difficulty did not arise from a lack of sources. The Rosaldos' informants represented a wide range of generations and changing generational experiences. The problem arose because it is impossible to account for emotional change unless one can draw on some conception of the universal features of emotional life. If emotional change is to be something other than random drift, it must result from interaction between our emotional capacities and the unfolding of historical circumstances.

Fifteen years later, Niko Besnier, author of a series of brilliant ethnographic works on emotions, continues to be plagued by the same conceptual problem. In his book-length monograph on emotions and literacy among the roughly three hundred inhabitants of the island of Nukulaelae (Besnier 1995b), he carefully examines the historical background that has shaped present-day social life on the island. He documents the islanders' apparent enthusiasm for conversion to Christianity and for the acquisition of literacy in the late nineteenth century – both of which were brought to the island by the London Missionary Society's "native teachers" after 1865. From that time to the present, social, political, and religious authority on the island have been closely linked. But when he turns to emotions, he speaks exclusively in the ethnographic present. In addition, while he is an acute observer of the relation between emotional performance and political authority, he offers no political judgments about the nature of this authority or its legitimacy.

In a close examination of letter writing, Besnier shows that private letters to relatives off-island are occasions for intense expression of longing and sorrow. Because those off-island are generally earning money, islanders plead with them to show *alofa* (love, empathy, compassion) by sending gifts of money or commodities; they enjoin moral principles of solidarity and personal discipline, and provide news and gossip – establishing a genre of communication starkly different from oral speech, resembling oratory, with the obvious political purpose of reinforcing a sense of membership on those who have departed.

Besnier has also looked closely at gossip and the delivery of sermons – both also highly emotional and politically charged forms of communication. In oral gossip, Besnier finds "Nukulaelae speakers communicate affect in prosody, deictic adverbs, and the rhetorical style of the quote, while maintaining every appearance, at more overt and transparent levels, of presenting an exact rendition of the quoted voice" (1993:176–177). These strategies allow a speaker to censure a third party implicitly by reenacting the third party's own inappropriate affect and behavior. In a small face-to-face community, where overt anger and overt criticism are regarded with extreme distaste, this kind of gossip allows strict social control efforts to proceed without ruffling the smooth, nonjudgmental surface of social interaction. Sermons, Besnier finds, delivered at Sunday services by select members of the congregation, "play an important role in establishing authority and entitlement, and in defining a privileged relationship between the oral delivery and the truth" (1995b:139). Thus, while Besnier is acutely aware of the political implications of emotional expression, he speaks consistently in the ethnographic present, englobing all Nukulaelae islanders routinely in his descriptions. He fails to offer a sense of the dynamic inherent in political authority, emotional management, and the negotiation of status. He fails, likewise, to provide a conception of the process of submission and possibilities of resistance, or the trajectory of change. Doubtless, direct evidence on such issues is difficult to come by. But there is also a conceptual failure here; Besnier has no theoretical grounds for a critique of Nukulaelae emotional behavior and its political implications, although the picture he paints is of a highly regimented community. Besnier is hardly alone in this regard.

These weaknesses are no accident. Because we associate emotions so closely with goals, motivations, and intentions, insofar as one treats emotions as culturally constructed, one becomes unable to attribute to individuals any goals, motivations, or intentions that come from outside culture. Thus the individual cannot want anything unless the culture has taught him or her to want it. Conflict cannot be important, unless the culture teaches individuals how to engage in conflict. Political power and political oppression in a culture other than our own, as a result, lack significance for us because it is only in terms of the emotional makeup of members of that culture that suffering, oppression, or desire for liberty can be defined for them. In such a constructed emotional world, history leads to no meaningful change because, even when a culture changes, individuals continue to suffer or to be happy in just the ways their culture prescribes. There is no way in which we can say that such change leaves them better off or worse off.

How can we conceive of individuals whose emotions are culturally constructed and who nonetheless remain capable of taking meaningful action, making meaningful change, or engaging in meaningful conflict? The greater the power we suppose culture or discourse to have over emotions, the more we are likely to disregard individual desire and choice as epiphenomenal. How are we to respond to Ilongots crying out in grief over the end of headhunting? With empathy? With revulsion? With clinical ethnographic detachment? What are the stakes for us in their suffering? Lutz, Abu-Lughod, and a few others among constructionists stand out in that they have positive answers to these questions. But their answers only underscore the political incoherence of constructionism and its related inability to grasp historical change. If many recognize these weaknesses, no one to date has offered a way of correcting them.

PSYCHOCULTURAL APPROACHES

A significant number of anthropologists who work on emotions continue to reject constructionism vigorously. An important alternative has been provided by what Hollan and Wellenkamp (1994:2) call "psychocultural anthropology." Taking their orientation, like Levy, from Western personality psychology, the psychocultural school has sought to eschew that discipline's normative, diagnostic stance, while retaining its psychodynamic understanding of affect. In the field Hollan and Wellenkamp conduct what they call "loosely structured life history interviews" (Hollan 1992:48) – seeking to find, like other practitioners in this subfield, a kind of midpoint between ethnographic and clinical methods. They pose carefully translated questions for respondents about life satisfaction, joys, anxieties, grief, and allow them a free hand in responding. That respondents understand such questions and find them interesting enough to answer at length shows that individual emotional life and emotional suffering are culturally salient. (However, such salience is surely not universal; Fajans [1997] has recently documented a carefully cultivated indifference to life histories among the Baining of Papua New Guinea, for example.) Obeyesekere's (1985, 1990) caution against the danger of intrusive clinical judgments in this kind of work has been widely recognized. His work in Sri Lanka has shown that "the work of culture" can transform emotional states – states that appear (to Westerners) to require clinical intervention – into the starting points of meaningful spiritual or social growth. Good and Good (1988) have offered a penetrating analysis of the impact of the Iranian revolution on the experience of grief in that country; once an emblem of resistance, grief is now an emotion mandated by the state.

No one has gone further than Arthur Kleinman and Joan Kleinman in exploring and making political sense of the relation between individual feeling and state power. (See Kleinman & Kleinman 1991, 1997; A. Kleinman 1995, 1996.) They have done so by redefining, in what they hope is a culturally neutral fashion, the key Western concepts of *suffering* and *experience*. These carefully amended concepts, especially the first, allow Kleinman and Kleinman to isolate the individual and to attribute states of "suffering" to that individual that are politically deplorable. They thus seek to mobilize our political judgment in explicit ways. Arthur Kleinman and Joan Kleinman's field work in China confronted them with the personal aftereffects of massive political terror and repression. In this context, they have linked individual cases of dizziness, headaches, and depression (which can be shown to fit Chinese ethnopsychological models) to what they call "a society-wide delegitimation crisis" (Kleinman & Kleinman 1991:283). Following Kleinman and Kleinman, Jenkins (1991) has proposed that the "political ethos" of repressive regimes that use violence and torture to maintain themselves in power has emotional consequences that might be termed "psychosocial trauma." Jenkins found depression to be common among refugees from El Salvador, and also discovered somatic symptoms among sufferers that were culturally specific (as Kleinman & Kleinman had in China), and which therefore easily lead to misdiagnosis in U.S. clinics.

The work of this school, as with anthropologists who lean toward constructionism, has produced extraordinarily rich research. Each stance is based on a bald assertion, however, not on evidence. Practitioners of the psychocultural approach simply claim that there is a broad underlying commonality in human emotions, just as the practitioners of the constructionist approach either claim that there can be no such commonality or at least that anthropological research cannot address it. Particularly noteworthy are the political implications of each stance. Good and Good, Kleinman and Kleinman, Jenkins, and others are concerned with the emotional implications of political oppression and authoritarianism *within the states* that are the sites of their research. Lutz, Abu-Lughod, and their followers focus, in contrast, on (1) the politics of *the local household and family*, where gender and related distinctions legitimate concentrations of authority, and (2) the political implications of emotion ideologies *in the public sphere to which they address their work*. Constructionism allows one the fullest opportunity to raise doubts about mainstream Western culture's oppressive political implications, whereas a psychocultural approach allows greater clarity in identifying sufferings inflicted by local regimes that do not respect Western ideals of freedom and equality. (This is not to say that the latter group are complacent about the politics of Western culture, far from it.) Neither emotional constructionists nor psychocultural anthropologists attempt to deal with historical change. Even when looking at the aftereffects of revolution or dictatorship, the latter group makes no effort to see how culturally specific emotional factors may have lain at the origin of historical change or may have served to heighten the likelihood of crisis or repression. Emotions are affected by history, but are not part of history.

Constructionism seems to offer greater safeguards against the insidious effects of unnoticed ethnocentrism, but at the cost of a relative
inability to conceptualize oppression and emotional suffering within
the communities that are the objects of research. But the psychocultural
approach, basing its work on sometimes vague notions about human
commonality, cannot offer guarantees against the kind of Eurocentric
condescension Abu-Lughod has condemned with particular eloquence
(1991). What the anthropology of emotion most sorely lacks, at present,
is a unified conception of emotions as part of the historical unfolding
of politically significant institutions and practices.

OTHER APPROACHES

Some anthropologists, rather than trying to resolve these thorny issues,
have simply sought to go around them, by establishing entirely new
approaches to emotion. While distancing themselves from clinical
models, they have registered strong dissatisfaction with constructionist approaches. Renato Rosaldo (1989), for example, insists that emotions have a "force" independent of culture; and he encourages
ethnographers to be attentive to linkages – such as that between grief
and anger. Such linkages may exist universally, unaffected by the cultural context. Unni Wikan (1990, 1992) has argued for the existence of
a nonverbal "resonance" that allows for empathetic communication
across wide cultural gaps. Such resonance is utilized by almost all
ethnographers, she contends, but seldom acknowledged by them,
because of the discipline's historic focus on explicit symbolic material.
Margot Lyon has argued that emotions derive not directly from culture,
but from the way in which bodies are associatively linked in a social
structure. We are urged to pursue this link through a kind of ceteris
paribus calculus, which is alluded to without much elaboration: "[A]ll
other things being equal, it could be said, for example, that any action
by one person or group of persons that is *interfered with* by another
group or person can give rise to anger" (Lyon 1995; emphasis added).
How *interference* is to be defined without cultural interpretation is not
explained, however. John Leavitt (1996) asserts that what he calls
"feeling" is about the body in the same sense that "meaning" is about
the mind. Leavitt believes that ethnographers routinely depend on
empathy without acknowledging it, and that it is time they did so.
Attention to the realm of feeling, he predicts, will allow anthropology

to find a way out of the constructionist dead end. I have also in the past used this term "feeling" as if it referred to a special entity, wholly independent of thought, without defining it further (Reddy 1997a). Obviously, current research on emotions by psychologists raises difficulties for such a view, with its increasing inability to distinguish emotion from cognitive habit.

"Force," "resonance," "interference," "feeling," and similar terms, as with Kleinman and Kleinman's notions of suffering and experience, seem to offer an extracultural dimension of existence that we share with persons of all cultural contexts. This extracultural dimension allows us direct emotional access to them and, in certain cases (especially for Kleinman & Kleinman, Jenkins, Wikan, and Lyon), provides a basis for political judgments. But all of these concepts lack the elaboration necessary to ensure us against the danger of ethnocentrism.

A number of studies have attempted detailed examinations of the nonverbal dimension of affective communication, drawing on linguistics, musicology, and literary criticism (e.g., Feld 1982, 1995; Urban 1988; Irvine 1990, 1995; McNeill 1992). Such studies offer the promise, eventually, of providing a concrete bridge of findings about emotional signaling that might get us over the conceptual roadblock that divides constructionist and psychocultural approaches. Greg Urban, for example, identifies certain "icons of crying" in the ritual wailing of three Brazilian Amerindian groups. These "icons" make their wailing easily identifiable to Americans as expressions of sadness or grief. They include: "(1) the 'cry break,' (2) the voiced inhalation, (3) the creaky voice, and (4) the falsetto vowel" (1988:389). He shows how such elements are artfully inserted into sung recitations of texts of greeting or mourning. Following Urban, Steven Feld has found similar elements in ritualized wailing among the Kaluli, an ethnic group of Papua New Guinea. There, too, Feld concludes, the cry-break, "sonically realized as a diaphragm pulse accompanied by friction" is "the most transparent index of a crying voice" (1995:96). This kind of comparative work promises conceptual tools that may allow us to say, with much greater precision, why certain performances appear to be transparent to emotional interpretation for outsiders and insiders alike. In conjunction with work such as that by Hatfield et al. (1994), the promise is a full understanding of all the ways nonverbal signs and "body language" are used in different locations, with a good sense of commonalities and the range of variation. But such technically brilliant analyses, to date, still leave us far from a standpoint where political judgment might be possible.

These same drawbacks characterize the work of cognitive anthropologists who have sought to shed light on the cultural workings of "cognition" or the "mind." D'Andrade's (1992) insightful discussion of "goals," as noted in the previous chapter, struggles creatively with the problem of the roots of motivation; Strauss and Quinn (1997) have rightly insisted on the mutual relevance of research into culture and cognition; and their version of "connectionism" points to the usefulness, for cultural interpretation, of psychological notions such as "activation" or "automatic" processing. However, the political implications of these proposals have been left unexplored so far.

Kleinman and Kleinman, Veena Das, Talal Asad, Margaret Lock, and others recently contributed to an important anthology that explores "social suffering" (Kleinman, Das, & Lock 1997). Their concept of "social suffering" is aimed at reminding us, as Kleinman and Kleinman insist in their contribution, that simply to report, merely to speak of an event such as a famine, in the context of a given public discussion – whether journalistic, academic, or clinical – is to appropriate it for new uses. Suffering is already socially situated before we hear of it; even our own suffering is already interpreted before we can express it. In her contribution to this anthology and several other recent essays, Veena Das explores the political implications of this dilemma in a way that says a great deal about the current state of play in the anthropology of emotions. On the one hand, she insists on the constructive power of language. Those who have mastered a language, she argues, have not learned how to speak about feelings such as hope and grief which they already experienced. Instead, the "grammar" of that language "tells us what kinds of objects hope and grief are" (Das 1998:188). Das examines, in the "social suffering" anthology, the plight of women abducted and raped during the Indian Partition violence of 1946–1948 (Das 1997). Hindu and Muslim tradition in the Indian subcontinent agree on treating violated women as worse than dead. In the Hindu epic, the *Rāmāyana*, even the possibility of violation is sufficient to warrant Rāma's rejection of his perfect wife Sītā (Dimock et al. 1974:56–71). During the Partition of India and Pakistan, as many as one hundred thousand Muslim and Hindu women were taken from their homes, raped, kidnapped, sometimes marched naked in the streets with political slogans written on their skin (Das 1998:180–181). Some stayed with their abductors, others were eventually returned to their families. When asking women about those days, Das found "a zone of silence around the event."

It was common to describe the violence of the Partition in such terms as rivers of blood flowing and the earth covered with white shrouds right unto the horizon. Sometimes a woman would remember images of fleeing, but as one woman warned me, it was dangerous to remember . . .

This code of silence protected women who had been brought back to their families through the efforts of the military evacuation authorities after they were recovered from the homes of their abductors, or who had been married by stretching norms of kinship and affinity since the violation of their bodies was never made public. Rather than bearing witness to the disorder that they had been subjected to, the metaphor that they used was of a woman drinking the poison and keeping it within her. (Das 1997:84–85)

For such women, Das notes, the heroic task of breaking the silence, of "using our capacity to 'unearth' hidden facts" to denounce past wrongs can easily turn into a "weapon" against the victims themselves (Das 1997:88). How, then, can we speak of such matters at all? For Das, the answer is to bear witness to such suffering in a manner sensitive to the grammar in which it occurs.

[T]o find my way [with another's pain] is similar to letting the pain of the other happen to me. My own fantasy of anthropology as a body of writing is that which is able to receive this pain. Thus while I may never claim the pain of the other, nor appropriate it for some other purpose (nation building, revolution, scientific experiment), that I can lend my body (of writing) to this pain is what a grammatical investigation reveals. (Das 1998:192)

This response is at once inspiring and troubling. It is inspiring because of the faith expressed that ethnography can somehow penetrate the unsayable distances that separate one language from another. It is troubling because, at the same time, Das seems to foreclose the possibility of making any political use whatever of what she thereby renders intelligible.

But it may be possible to go further than this, and the research we have already examined suggests some important ways forward. The common dilemmas, and parallel achievements of cognitive and anthropological research into emotions, I believe, give good reason for hope that a universal language for talking about emotions may be possible.

THE UNIVERSAL FEATURES OF EMOTIONAL LIFE

To summarize the argument so far: Emotions have been the object of a new wave of research in both cognitive psychology and cultural anthropology since the 1970s. Research in both fields has tended to undercut the received Western common sense about emotions.

Among psychologists, the idea that emotions are biologically pre-programmed responses has been replaced by a consensus that they operate like overlearned cognitive habits. As psychologists have probed the boundary between attention on the one hand and unconscious, automatic, or subliminal processes on the other, they have found this boundary to be a broad gray zone pierced by many pathways. Emotional habits and expectations have come to be seen as having subtle and far-reaching influence on the processing of perception and on strategies of task completion. The idea that emotions vary along two simple axes, from mild to intense and from unpleasant to pleasant, has been set aside in favor of a deeper understanding of the complex dimensions of arousal and the importance of goal relevance to emotional response. Most recently the constraints of mental control have been shown to shape the ways in which we learn, manage, and suppress emotions as well as thoughts.

Among anthropologists, a prevalent tendency to regard emotions as culturally constructed has led to a wide range of new and persuasive ethnographic accounts of worldwide emotional variation. At the same time, this approach to emotions has run up against both theoretical and political difficulties. The idea that emotions are culturally constructed provides grounds for a political critique of the Western common sense that identifies emotions as biological and feminine. At the same time, this idea robs anthropologists of any grounds for a political critique of the local emotional practices they study. Ultimately, indeed, a thoroughgoing constructionism cannot even critique Western views and practices – which are simply another construction, no better and no worse than any other. Alternative conceptions of emotion that have been proposed recently allow a way out of this difficulty, but some suffer from vagueness and they may not be as culturally neutral as their defenders wish to believe.

Can research in cognitive psychology be enlisted to help resolve the conceptual obstacles that have emerged in anthropology? Many would say no, on purely theoretical grounds. But the possibilities are so obvious and so intriguing that one wonders if the theoretical objection might not be set aside somehow. In this section I will briefly examine these possibilities. In the following chapter, I will turn to the theoretical difficulties posed by using laboratory evidence in conjunction with ethnographic reports. I will elaborate a new theoretical approach to emotions that can encompass both kinds of research results and that can open the way to a politically engaged, and historically grounded, anthropology of emotions.

Psychological research supports the constructionist approach to emotions common among anthropologists only in part. Insofar as psychologists' findings continue to confirm Isen and Diamond's (1989) view of emotions as overlearned cognitive habits, emotions can be regarded as no different from any other cognitive content. All cognition is deeply influenced by social interaction. Like cognitive habits, emotions are as malleable as any other dimension of community life that involves symbols and propositions, such as religion, cosmology, kinship, moral principle, or political ideology. But insofar as emotional learning involves mental control, it is subject to the hazards and variability of any strategy aimed at "not thinking about x." And, insofar as psychologists continue to regard emotions as possessing goal-relevant valence and intensity, emotions must constitute a domain where mental control is of the utmost importance for the individual. If emotions are closely associated with the dense networks of goals that give coherence (however limited) to the self, and if they aid the individual in managing the conflicting tugs and contradictions that the pursuit of multiple goals must give rise to, then exercising mental control over emotions may be a high-priority task, whose accomplishment is always partial at best.

One would therefore expect communities to give emotions a high priority. If there is to be any unity of purpose or ethos in social life (which is, patently, not always the case, but often the case), then emotions must play a central role in its maintenance. To this extent, there is a strict limit to the range of possible emotional "cultures" – or perhaps one should say emotional "regimes" – that can be successfully elaborated. We would expect to find two features universally: (1) that communities construe emotions as an important *domain of effort*, and (2) that they provide individuals with prescriptions and counsel concerning both *the best strategies* for pursuing emotional learning and *the proper end point or ideal* of emotional equilibrium. Emotional regimes would be essential elements of all stable political regimes.

There is widespread evidence in anthropological research on emotions that confirms both of these expectations. No matter what the theoretical allegiance of the researcher, the ethnographic data routinely contain traces of collective shaping of emotional effort and collective elaboration of emotional ideals. Particularly striking is evidence from the constructionist ethnographies of M. Rosaldo (1980), Abu-Lughod (1986), and Lutz (1988). All three of these pathbreaking studies contain indications that the two features mentioned above were central to local emotional practice. The Ilongot, the Awlad 'Ali, and the inhabitants of Ifaluk all have an important local term for characterizing successful emotional control. Among the Ilongot, the concept of *beya* (which Rosaldo translates as "knowledge") is as important as that of liget ("anger" or "energy"). It is the beya of elders that successfully contains and channels the rising liget of adolescents. Beya allows the elders to hold back the impetuous violence of young men until proper targets are identified; beya allows elders to plan carefully for a raiding expedition, to remain hidden in the forest during the long march, to strike only when it is safe, and to resist the confusion that often accompanies attacks, so that a successful escape can be made. Beya ensures that the liget of women is tempered by experience, so that their gardening and care of the young are efficacious. Among the Awlad 'Ali, as in many Arabic-speaking communities, emotional control is included in the meaning of the term *'agl*, which Abu-Lughod translates as "reason." In the incident described above, for example, in which the middle-aged Rashīd openly displayed undue affection for his new, adolescent wife, Rashīd's conduct was regarded as demonstrating a deficiency of 'agl. "By relinquishing control over his feelings, he allowed himself to be controlled by another person. . . . Through this episode Rashīd lost the status appropriate to his age, that of the man of honor who is master of himself and others – a status that he had until then held" (1986:97). The use of ghinnāwas, by contrast, was fully in accord with the dictates of 'agl, according to Abu-Lughod. These snatches of poetry, when recited in front of strategically chosen intimates, by their artful and expressive character, showed not a failure of control, but "the profundity of that which had been overcome." Poetry gained its efficacy, Abu-Lughod notes, because it was "a sign of *powerful feeling creatively managed*" (p. 246; emphasis added). On Ifaluk, children are said to attain *repiy* (which Lutz translates as "social intelligence") by the age of six. This faculty enables them to learn the principal social emotions, *fago* ("love/compassion/sorrow"), which binds people together, and *song* ("righteous anger"), the emotion of moral judgment and political authority.

In each of these contexts, individual reputation rests on both a record of past action and an appreciation of the individual's mastery of emotion and conformity to emotional norms. That emotion is understood as a domain of effort in this way does not prevent these communities from being very different in other respects. Shame and guilt are not important emotions among the Ilongots; failure to control violence may bring unfortunate consequences, but it does not bring humiliation or judgment (M. Rosaldo 1984). Honor is central among the Awlad ʿAli, by contrast; pursuit of honor is their only publicly admissible motive; emotions are, in general, regarded as dangerous. Among the Ifaluk, emotion is itself the site of moral judgment; good action derives from good emotions. Despite these stark differences, all three ethnographies reveal that emotion is regarded as a domain of effort of the greatest importance; and emotional mastery, recognized to be difficult and changeable, is highly valued in oneself and admired in others.

Anthropologists working on the role of emotions in the Hindu tradition have found a conception of emotions that seems ideally suited to a constructionist interpretation. But a closer look shows that this tradition, too, is all about the difficulties and uncertainties of emotional control, and its importance in relation to community goals and standards of behavior. Central to that tradition is the concept of *rasa*, a Sanskrit term meaning "juice," "sap," or "flavor." Here is A. K. Ramanujan's widely cited definition of rasa: "The feelings of an individual are based on personal, accidental, incommunicable experience. Only when they are ordered, depersonalized and rendered communicable by prescriptions do they participate in *rasa*. . . . *Rasa* is a depersonalized condition of the self, an imaginary system of relations" (Dimock et al. 1974:128). In artistic contexts, rasa constitutes an esthetic ideal, in religious ones, a spiritual ideal. In traditional Sanskrit drama, for example, the performance is intended to lift the spectator out of his or her ordinary, particular feelings (called *bhāva*) and into the realm of rasa. By identifying with the characters, and feeling emotions inspired by their actions and the twists of the plot, spectators come to feel a dominant rasa – that is, a specific depersonalized emotion or mood, sanctified by its universality. Traditional Hindu musical patterns called *raga* are also understood as expressions each of its own type of rasa (see, e.g., Goswami 1995; Widdess 1995). Legend likewise states that

Vālmīki invented the *śloka* meter of epic Hindu poetry when expressing spontaneous grief at the death of a heron. The two-line poem he
uttered transformed his particular and personal bhāva into rasa by rendering it communicable, by giving it a compelling, universal form
(Dimock et al. 1974:54–56).

Modern-day Krishna sects of the Mount Ghovardan region, as
described by Toomey (1990), carry out complex rituals aimed at accomplishing this same end, the transformation of bhāva into rasa. Each sect
concentrates on a particular relationship with Krishna. The Vallabhite
sect focuses on the maternal love of Yashoda, Krishna's foster mother.
They perform elaborate food offerings, consisting of bland and sweet
dishes suitable to infants, which are set before an icon of baby Krishna.
The food offerings are intended to stand for the maternal love which
the devotees bear for the god. By accepting these offerings, Krishna
transforms their mundane love (bhāva) into rasa. The Chaitanyaite sect
focuses on the illicit sexual love that the cowherd Radha feels for
Krishna. This sect regards *viraha* (love-in-separation) as the purest form
of love. In their meditations they concentrate on this kind of forlorn
longing, and by accepting their food offerings Krishna transforms their
longing into rasa. Devadasi dancers at Jagannatha temple, as described
by Marglin (1990), similarly attempt to arouse in the spectator a generalized, depersonalized erotic desire which is sanctified through food
offerings. The dancers are said to be courtesans of the god. They may
have temporary sexual liaisons with men, but they may not marry or
have children – such enduring, particular attachments being inimical
to their mission of feeling and conveying a universalized eroticism.
Trawick's (1990) examination of joint family life in the Tamil-speaking
region shows that the concept of rasa has moral implications. Displaying open love or affection for one's own spouse or children is considered dangerous and dishonorable; nieces, nephews, or cousins,
however, may be safely coddled and pampered. When relations are
more distant, display of affection partakes of rasa because it is less particular, closer to the universal. (Significant here are the myths in which
Krishna is cared for by his *foster mother*, Yashoda.) Breaking purity rules
is a common method of displaying affection, as when cousins eat from
each other's hands, or a woman shares food with her low-caste maidservant. This is because love in its sanctified form, so close to depersonalized universality, easily becomes confused about persons. The
rasa concept can also shape relationships of deference and authority, as
Appadurai (1990) has shown. When underlings display their submis-

sion to a superior, according to Appadurai, "What matters are the emotional effects of praise, which, when properly 'performed' creates a
generalized mood of adoration or admiration or wonder that unites the
one who praises, the object of this praise, and the audience if there is
one" (p. 109).

As all these, and other, anthropologists have noted, the Hindu transformation of bhāva into rasa requires collective performances, whether
of a drama, a ritual, or a custom. There is a palpable sense in which the
emotions that count in the Hindu tradition truly are social constructions. However, there are plentiful traces of recognition in Hindu
performances that arriving at a certain feeling is unpredictable and
involves planning and effort. The traditional staging and elaborate
gestural language of Sanskrit drama, as well as the characterization
and plots of the great plays, and the high skill required of actors and
audience alike, all point toward an understanding of the rasa state as
an outcome of effort. The individual must work in order to get out of
his or her particular feelings, and into the generalized mood of the
play; success is by no means certain. The high erudition required to
perform and appreciate such plays points toward an implicit element
of competition, as well. Sectarian ritual, too, is just one step in the
prescribed path by which the faithful search for spiritual fulfillment;
long meditation on myths and the feelings that go with them is essential. Speaking of Sinhalese healing rites, Kapferer (1979) concluded that
participants in rituals *often actually feel* what they express" (p. 153;
emphasis added). "Rather than view the structured and regulated
display of emotion in ritual as representative of the normative and customary I regard it as problematic, problematic for participants as well
as for the anthropologist. . . . Performance both expresses and creates
what it represents" (pp. 153–54).

If ritual is regarded, not as a simple cultural text to be correctly interpreted, but as the blueprint for a collective effort to mold feeling, then
the Hindu tradition as a whole offers strong confirmation of the relevance to anthropology of recent psychological research on the goal-
relevance of emotions and the difficulties of mental control. Brenneis
(1995), working on the Fiji Indian village of Bhatgaon, remarks that he
became "increasingly bothered by the question: 'how did rhetoric *work*
for those who hear it?'" (p. 242; emphasis in original). He notes that
the villagers themselves speak of collective emotions as being "made"
or "built" (p. 245) and concludes, "As in Bhatgaon, we perform
emotion as well as talk about it. As interlocutors, listeners and

coproducers, we and those whom we study are engaged in active and broad-gauged interpretation not only of terminology but of those complex interactions which emotion words might implicate" (p. 249). Such a process necessarily entails both effort and the management of uncertainty. Effort, uncertainty, goal-relevance: these are not constructed, they are givens which the tradition must come to grips with.

The element of effort and the importance of control are quite apparent in studies whose authors embrace a constructionist approach to emotions, and therefore have no theoretical reason to pay attention to effort or control. But effort and control become all the more salient if the anthropologist is paying attention to them. Wikan's (1989, 1990) work on Bali demonstrates what a difference such attention can make. Prior anthropologists from Mead and Bateson to Geertz had all agreed that the Balinese were nearly emotion-free. A calm cheerfulness prevailed in social life with almost complete uniformity. Bali was listed as the single place (in a survey of seventy-three cultures) where death was not followed by mourning. Wikan, however, engaged in fieldwork similar to Abu-Lughod's – establishing intimate relationships with a few women – and was able to see beyond the displays meant for public consumption. She witnessed the drama of one young woman who, at the sudden death of her fiancé, managed to appear only mildly inconvenienced by the news in most circumstances, but occasionally broke down in secret tears. Wikan saw how others tried to encourage her cheerful performances by joking about the death or by teasing the young woman if she seemed on the verge of a lapse. The ostensible reason for such ferocious efforts at concealment and mastery was not hard to locate. Wikan estimated that the Balinese she worked with attributed roughly 50 percent of deaths to the effects of black magic. What made one vulnerable to black magic, above all, were sadness and anger; inappropriately expressed anger, or impoliteness, were, moreover, the behaviors most likely to cause another to retaliate through black magic. The maintenance of cheerful moods at all cost was, therefore, as she put it, a matter of "public health" for the Balinese (Wikan 1989:303). They possessed, as well, a "double-anchored" concept of the self (Wikan 1990:104–105), in which the "face" and the "heart" mutually influence each other. To put on a "bright face" (*mue cedang*) when feeling grief stricken, for the Balinese, is not dissembling, because the face can help the heart to change. The bright face is quite explicitly embraced as both a means and an end, a safe haven – which not even grief over a death can be allowed to perturb – which is also an instrument. The effort of maintaining it leads the heart away from the sadness or anger that, literally, threaten one's life.

That negative emotions are frequently associated with illness and with magic underscores their importance as objects of effort. Such associations are reported for the Chewong (Howell 1981), the people of Toraja (Hollan & Wellenkamp 1994), Calabria (Pandolfi 1991), the Cheyennes (Strauss 1977), the Kwara'ae (Watson-Gegeo & Gegeo 1990), Guadeloupe (Bougerol 1997), and the inhabitants of Santa Isabel (White 1990a, 1990b, 1991) – to mention but a few. In each case, fear of physical or magical consequences provides an added incentive to bring one's emotions (not merely one's emotional expressions) into line with social norms. Gossip also frequently comes into play as a disincentive to poor emotional equilibrium. On Nukulaelae, according to Besnier, as noted above, criticism of third parties often takes the form of an imitation of their speech patterns, using high and variable pitch to suggest the target's emotional immaturity and irrationality (Besnier 1990a, 1993, 1995b). Besnier comments, "gossip is often primordially *about* emotions, in that emotions often are the explicit focus of gossip interactions. . . . Most straightforwardly, conversationalists can *name* emotions and attribute them to the victims of their gossip" (Besnier 1995a:224). Brenneis (1990a) remarks that fear of embarrassment or shame is intense in Batghaon and, as a result, limitation of gossip is one of the principal purposes of the *pancayat*, a village council that simply explores different versions of events in dispute, without rendering judgment. Lutz (1988:162) reports that gossip is the principal sanction imposed on persons who become the object of *song* (justifiable anger). (See also, on gossip, White 1990a, Bougerol 1997.) Gossip, illness, black magic – such widely reported instruments for disciplining emotion or punishing emotional lapses offer further confirmation that high goal relevance and uncertain mental control are universal features of emotion and universally a focus of local theories of the person and of local norms, customs, religious beliefs, and political institutions.

This brief review suggests that emotional "regimes" may vary across a vast range of possibilities, but that this range is subject to two constraints: (1) Because emotions are closely associated with the dense networks of goals that give coherence to the self, the unity of a community – such as it may be – depends in part on its ability to provide a coherent set of prescriptions about emotions. (2) Because intentional shaping of emotions (insofar as they are cognitive habits) is possible, subject to the constraints of mental control, a community's emotional order must take the form of ideals to strive toward and strategies to guide individual effort. These two constraints, should they prove to be universal, would be of the greatest political relevance. Because of these constraints and their consequences, it might be possible to conceptualize an ideal of emotional freedom and to evaluate individual emotional regimes on the basis of this ideal.

However, many anthropologists would object that there is a philosophical and epistemological gap between experimental psychology and ethnographic interpretation. On this ground, they would regard the evidence presented in this section as unimportant or as reflecting patterns that were less general than I imagine. Any consequences drawn from this analysis would be infected by the limited philosophical perspective of Western experimental science, and highly ethnocentric. Dealing with this objection will be the first task of the next chapter.

CHAPTER 3

Emotional Expression as a Type of Speech Act

The conceptual difficulties that have emerged in the anthropology of emotions represent an opportunity. Because they stem in part from anthropology's openness to interdisciplinary influences, and the discipline's related political engagements, these difficulties can only be removed by a new theory of emotions of broad interdisciplinary significance. In this chapter, I will examine the philosophical difficulties that such a theory of emotions must overcome, and then lay out a theory that answers these difficulties.

FROM PROCESS TO TRANSLATION

Many would object that, in the last section of the preceding chapter, I made a fundamental error, and that, therefore, my pursuit of evidence of universal features of emotional regimes was entirely misguided. By finding evidence in ethnographic studies that supports the conclusions of laboratory tests, the argument would go, I have compared apples with oranges. Psychologists are engaged in an empirical science of the mind, of consciousness, or of experience (Cohen & Schooler 1997). To undertake such scientific inquiry, they must make certain assumptions, assumptions which are not necessary to ethnography and which may, themselves, be tainted by an inadmissible Western ethnocentrism (Lutz 1988; Lutz & Abu-Lughod 1990b; Gergen 1995). Doubtless ethnographic evidence about emotional ideals, rituals, gossip, and black magic is intriguing. But it cannot be used as a basis for a claim about universal features of emotional life, unless one has already established solid theoretical grounds for believing that certain aspects of human culture or experience might be universal. Therefore ethnographic evidence alone cannot be used to resolve the conceptual difficulties that stand in the way of progress in the ethnography of emotions. There is considerable force to this argument.

However, I believe I can show that the findings of psychologists' laboratory experiments can retain significance even when stripped of the assumptions of empirical epistemology. I will propose that cognitive "processing" be regarded as a type of "translation." When an individual correctly identifies an outline drawing as representing a bird, for example, I simply propose that this feat of cognitive "processing" be regarded as an act of translation from the code of the outline drawing to the code of everyday English categories. As developed by philosophers such as Quine, Davidson, and Alcoff, the concept of translation allows one to speak of the relation between language and the world in a way that is neither Cartesian (distinguishing sharply between subjective and objective conditions, as most psychologists continue to do) nor poststructuralist. It allows one to say, meaningfully, that there are kinds of thought that lie "outside" of language, yet are intimately involved in the formulation of utterances. Emotions, I will argue, are among the most important of such kinds of thought; and, when we speak of our emotions, they come into a peculiar, dynamic relationship with what we say about them. I will formulate a theoretical framework for comprehending this peculiar dynamism of emotional expression, modeled on J. L. Austin's speech act theory. This framework will provide the grounds needed for regarding both psychologists' laboratory findings and ethnographers' discoveries in the field as evidence for universal features of emotional life. The following chapter, building on this theory of emotional speech acts, will offer a definition of emotional liberty, and examine how that definition can be used to ground political judgments about Western and non-Western societies alike as well as to account for historical change in emotions.

Cartesian Dualism in Psychology

Experimental psychologists routinely assume that there is an experiential or "subjective" side to the phenomena they examine, such as arousal states, performance on reading tests, or reported thoughts and affect. In 1984, Izard, Kagan, and Zajonc – three very eminent practitioners – stated that most psychologists regarded emotions as consisting of three elements: "neurophysiological-biochemical, motor or behavioral-expressive, and subjective-experiential" (p. 3). This approach has not changed in the intervening years. Experimentalists continue, routinely, to explain their findings by assuming that the three elements named by Izard et al. in 1984 are closely, but by no means perfectly, coordinated. Anomalies, delays, mistakes are assumed to give evidence of the complex ways in which this imperfect coordination works itself out. Suppose, for example, that a face has been flashed at high speed, and subjects apparently cannot identify it or remember it, yet respond more positively to it on second presentation than to faces they have not seen before. Such results are said to indicate that the high-speed exposure of the face had no "subjective" effects, only "neurophysiological-biochemical," or "motor or behavioral-expressive" effects (cf. Niedenthal & Showers 1991). "Subjective-experiential" effects are usually accessed by asking subjects direct questions; their "self-reports" are deemed to have privileged status as evidence of subjective experience, because subjective experience is assumed to be the special province of "consciousness" and language use is assumed to be its special instrument.[1]

Reporting on research into emotional suppression in 1993, for example, Gross and Levenson stated that "some researchers . . . assert that *expressive behavior* is so important to an emotional response that the other aspects of an emotion (*subjective experience and physiological response*) are greatly diminished if its behavioral expression is stifled. . . . Other researchers . . . disagree, arguing that the inhibition of expressive behavior leads to increases in the other aspects of an emotional response" (p. 970; emphasis added). Feldman Barrett in 1998 argued that individuals vary according to whether they focus on the valence of an emotion or its level of arousal. She summarized her findings as follows:

Valence focus is defined as the extent to which an individual incorporates pleasantness or unpleasantness into their *conscious affective experience*, and may be associated with a tendency to attend to the *pleasant or unpleasant aspects of a stimulus*. Arousal focus is defined as the extent to which an individual incorporates *subjective experiences of arousal* into a conscious affective experience, and may be associated with a tendency to attend to the *internal sensations* associated with an affective experience. (p. 580; emphasis added)[2]

---

[1] It is noteworthy, however, that this special status of self-reporting has been challenged; see Kagan (1984:55); Erdelyi (1992:785); Ste-Marie & Jacoby (1993); Schooler & Fiore (1997).

[2] For other remarks on this issue, see Ortony and Turner (1990); Frijda et al. (1992); Greenwald et al. (1995:23–24); Gergen (1995).

Experimental psychology's approach seems to reflect continued allegiance to a Cartesian dualism, that is, a sharp distinction between mind
and body, of a kind that has been widely criticized by philosophers
going back as far as Hegel, and including twentieth-century giants as
diverse as Heidegger, Dewey, Wittgenstein, and Quine, to name but a
few. This dualism comes into play both in the method of experimental
psychology and in its assumptions about its subjects. The method pre-
supposes that the experimenters are themselves trapped in the realm
of subjective experience, which is uncertain, changeable, insubstantial.
Replicable experiments with appropriate controls are therefore necessary to circumvent the shortcomings of subjective perception. The
experiments, in turn, focus on the shortcomings of the subjects' own
experiences and cognitions, as well as the subjects' own imperfect
"control" of their bodies (Plutchik 1994:171–184). The aim is to explain
both types of shortcomings in terms of their grounding in neurophys-
iological and biochemical mechanisms.

Cartesian dualism of this type is the most widespread Western
model of the "subject" – that is, of the subjective self that is a locus of
unique experiences. It is just this notion of the self that has sustained
the Western common sense about emotions, according to which
they are viewed as a naturally occurring composite of involuntary
physiological arousal states and subjective "feelings."[3] The anthropological evidence clearly shows that this view of emotions is just
one local cultural construct. How, then, can a critique of anthropologists' constructionism, such as the one I offered in Chapter 2, avoid
begging the question of what emotions are, when its claims are derived
from experimental psychology, a discipline built on Western dualist
assumptions?

The most influential critique of the Western notion of the subject in
recent years has been elaborated by poststructuralism, a philosophical
movement which many anthropologists – including anthropologists of
emotion, as we have seen – have explicitly made use of in developing

---

[3] Descartes himself worked out a basic-emotions theory to explain the relation between
the body and reflective consciousness, a theory with a number of remarkable similarities to those that have been proposed in the last thirty years (Meyer 1991:216–223).
Descartes's list included admiration (similar to Ekman's concept of "surprise"), joy,
sadness, love, hate, and desire. Like psychologists of the present day, Descartes found
it difficult to account for the cognitive component of emotion. Meyer (1991), in fact,
argues that this problem has plagued philosophical understanding of the passions
throughout Western history.

their own method, and which has also had a profound impact on the study of history, literary criticism, historical sociology, philosophy, and feminist theory. Can the poststructuralist critique of psychology be turned aside? Or can something useful be salvaged, once the strengths of this critique have been taken into account? In what follows I will attempt to present the salient tenets of poststructuralism in a clear fashion, and to show how they raise questions about psychological research. I will in addition offer a discussion of the weaknesses of post-structuralism and reexamine the import of psychological research in light of these weaknesses.

The Poststructuralist Critique of Social Science

According to poststructuralists, what comes before us as knowledge is fundamentally semiotic or linguistic in character. We have access to signifiers; each signifier represents a signified; the two together constitute a sign. But signs are always multiple and therefore must have a systematic character. Signifiers come in groups (such as the lexicon of a language); within such a group each signifier must be distinguishable from the others in order for it to have a relation to what it signifies. For example, in English, the word *mile* signifies a measure of distance. *Mile* is the singular form, *miles* is the plural form. The presence or absence of an *s* (called a phoneme in linguistics) is easily distinguishable. This clear and simple "distinctive feature" is a prerequisite of signification. Before the word *miles* can have a relation of reference to lengths over 5,280 feet, it must have a relation of distinctness to the word *mile*. Likewise the word *mile* itself must be readily distinguishable from other units of the lexicon before it can be given a definition. Without this systemic character, signs cannot signify anything. Because this systematic distinctness is a prerequisite of using signifiers clearly, their relation to what they signify is purely arbitrary. The sound and the associated markings that constitute the signifier *mile* could be used to signify anything. Only convention determines its use to represent a measure of distance. The syntax of language may be regarded as a method for combining signs (derived from the lexicon, already constituted in such a way that words are distinguishable from each other) into more complex signifiers (utterances) that may stand for very complex signifieds. In the manipulation of systems of signs, one never has direct access to the raw signified – the shadowy second half of the sign that always stands behind its front end, the signifier (Derrida 1973:140). To name what a signifier stands for is simply to substitute another signifier for it; even to point at something is to make of one's finger a kind of signifier. Thus, "everything becomes discourse" (Derrida 1967b:411).[4]

This characterization of the sign and of language derives from early twentieth-century structural linguistics. Structuralism and poststructuralism grew out of an effort to apply these ideas from linguistics to thought itself. The basic categories that we use to classify things, it was claimed, must have the same systematic mutual distinctness that the words of a language have. In this sense they constitute a "discourse," just as the words of a language constitute a lexicon. As part of a discourse, the category *subjective*, for example, must be distinct from the category *objective* before it can serve any representational function. Just as words must be distinct before they can be given a definition, so the definitions of these categorical words must be distinct before they can be used to talk about the world. But this implies that the definition of such categorical words cannot be checked against the world, because we cannot talk about the world unless we have some fundamental categories already in place. The important thing is that the definition of *subjective* be clearly demarcated and distinct from the definition of *objective*, just as *mile*, the singular form, is clearly distinct from *miles*, the plural. Only then can these terms be properly and clearly used in a discourse. But it follows that this definition's relation to the world is just as arbitrary as the relation of the sound *mile* is to the length 5,280 feet. Categorical words, the elements of discourse, cannot be tested, at least not if one is using them. If one is using them, one can only make statements that they allow. For example, these categories do not allow one to assert that phenomenon x is neither subjective nor objective. In a world where everything must be one or the other, there is no space left for such a phenomenon. Extrasensory perception is an example of a phenomenon that seems to defy the barrier between subjective and objective; and its status as uncanny and therefore suspect is a direct result. If one is using some other set of categories (or discourse) to talk about the world – suppose, for example, one divides it up first into sacred and profane instead of subjective and objective – then, of course, the distinction between subjective and objective will appear secondary, irrelevant, even absurd. But this is, by itself, no test, no adequate

---

[4] But Derrida immediately qualifies this remark as follows: "on condition that we agree on the meaning of this word – that is, a system in which the original, transcendent signified is never absolutely present outside of a system of differences."

critique of the categories subjective and objective, because other category schemes, or discourses, labor under the same drawback as the subjective-objective one. They cannot be tested either. Each of them, too, appears secondary, irrelevant, even absurd from the vantage point of any of the others.

This idea that the definitions of words must have the same mutual systematic distinctness as do the bare words and phonemes of languages is fundamental to both structuralism and poststructuralism. It implies that our first step toward knowledge, the creation of a set of mutually distinguishable concepts, is always arbitrary, and that this arbitrariness infects all the thoughts and propositions that can be formulated in a discourse – all human thought.

This pessimistic view was first popularized by Claude Lévi-Strauss and other practitioners of "structural anthropology" who used this approach largely in attempting to understand non-Western societies. Poststructuralism proper derived from the attempt simultaneously to go further down this road of semiotic analysis and to apply it to the critique of Western knowledge.

Jacques Derrida's (1973) notion of *différance*, for example, invites one to reflect on the question, How does a concept, or category, become distinct from another in the first place? How is the first step made that leads one to fall into, or embrace, a categorical – that is, a discursive – structure? Derrida finds that this first step is an effect of time. To distinguish, to note a difference, in the flow of signifiers – to abstract a system of signs from a stream of talk or text – is to "defer" (in French *différer*) one's understanding of any given sign until one grasps the whole system of signs. *Différance* is "the movement by which language, or any code, any system of reference in general, becomes 'historically' constituted as a fabric of differences" (p. 141). Derrida, in addition, criticized the idea that speakers have intentions that they express through their utterances. One should regard a set of utterances just as one regards a set of phonemes or words. They cannot have meaning except by being mutually distinct. It is arbitrary to assume that all the utterances coming from a single person or found in texts by a single author should derive their meaning from "representing" what that speaker or author meant or intended to communicate. They actually gain their meaning by the way they are distinct from the whole corpus of texts and utterances of the language. One can, if one chooses, rearrange bits of text into other sets and find quite different meanings in the new sets of mutually distinct text fragments. This is the game of "deconstruction."

Derrida also argued, as a direct result, that the apparently quite real presence of another person was itself only the byproduct of an arbitrary assumption about a certain unity to be found in the flow of signifiers (Derrida 1967a). All signifying was like writing, because it was all, in the first place, depersonalized, in the sense of giving access to signifiers alone. Persons only come into view *within* one or more arbitrarily embraced discursive structures. One can only find persons after one has embraced a certain discursive structure that assumes their existence as the source of signification. Cartesian dualism is an example of such a discursive structure, one that allows us to find persons as the "subjective" source of all signifiers. But for Derrida this is actually a definition, not a discovery, and, as such, is thoroughly arbitrary and untestable. The subjective/objective structure, once accepted, allows one to identify texts and utterances with their authors. But there can be no justification for accepting this structure, however neat it looks after the fact.

Michel Foucault moved in a different direction. He argued that one could differentiate periods of history according to the views of language that prevailed in each. The modern period was dominated by the semiotic approach, precisely Saussure's and Lévi-Strauss's structuralism, the idea of the mutual systematic distinctness of words and their definitions. But earlier periods had other ideas. The Renaissance had regarded words as in a relation of part-to-whole with the things they meant. The eighteenth century had seen words as capable of independent representation of things; it was the job of the mind to bring these independent representations together into systematic tableaux, as Linnaeus did for plants, or into correctly formed grammatical sentences. When history shifted from one of these views to another, the past became virtually incomprehensible to the present. In fact, these notions about language were not really "views"; no one held them, since they constituted the conditions under which people initiated the formulation and debate of "views" (Foucault 1966). Thus, their history – the only important history – had to be recovered by a difficult process Foucault likened to archaeology (Foucault 1969). By examining fragments of text from the past, one attempted to discern what relation between word and thing was presumed in them. One had to be prepared to discover apparent absurdities, because any discourse different from the one we use now will appear absurd, just as the one we use now will appear self-evident because it cannot be tested.

For poststructuralists, the Cartesian dualism so easily discernible in the prose of cognitive psychologists constitutes a discourse with an arbitrary semiotic structure. The division of phenomena into subjective and objective, with its implication that objective knowledge and reason can be achieved by the application of certain privileged methods, is a constant, implicit target of poststructuralist critique. Even our experience of ourselves as subjects in modern society – as individual persons who have subjective experiences and feelings and who pursue sets of deeply valued goals, making choices, and carrying out plans – is utterly without foundation. It is, of course, no better and no worse than any other discourse in this respect.

For Foucault, however, the unfounded, arbitrary character of this modern discourse about the subject provided grounds for an open attack. Linda Alcoff recently offered an illuminating account of Foucault's view of the social sciences. Despite the fact that they were, as she puts it, "only tenuously grounded by commonly accepted scientific standards," these sciences exercised

an inordinate authority in criminal and judicial matters, legal determinations of competency for a range of behaviors, and the promulgation of "universal human norms" imposed as measures of judgment on us all. They are used to justify everything from forced institutionalizations to removing children from their parents. Foucault's question thus becomes, how might one account for this disparity between their social authority and their scientific status? (1996:120)

Foucault argued that this disparity arose because of a certain coherence between the kind of arbitrary knowledge Cartesian dualism allowed one to produce and the political legitimacy of modern institutions. Modern institutions – such as factories, department stores, mental hospitals, prisons, armies – all reflected in their structure the presumption that individuals are subjects with intentions, desires, needs, who depended on these institutions to mediate between their needy subjectivity and a harsh objective world, to impose discipline on their behavior so as to produce a world safe for subjectivity.

For those who follow Foucault, including some important feminist anthropologists of emotion, as we have seen, modern psychology is simply one more cog in this machinery of domination.

Experimental psychologists believe they are measuring cognitive, memory, autonomic, attentional, or automatic "systems" within their subjects, objective systems which surround and serve a subjective kernel of consciousness or attention. But poststructuralists would insist that, since these objects of measurement are constituted discursively – that is, fabricated as illusory signifieds of a system of signifiers – the "findings" of this "science" are a foregone conclusion. For example, since "subjective" and "objective" are opposed signs of a fundamental character in this discourse, it follows that it will be impossible to find any signified that belongs to both categories at the same time. Such a signified cannot be represented in the discourse without wiping out the opposition that maintains these two signifiers as distinct. Indeed, it turns out that psychologists have had a great deal of difficulty identifying "bridge" phenomena. What counts as subjective (intentional, conscious, experiential) in one experimental approach often turns out to count as objective ("neurophysiological-biochemical, motor or behavioral-expressive") in others. As Erdelyi (1992) succinctly put it, with regard to research into subliminal perception, "when laboratory psychologists try to discover the true divide between the subliminal and the supraliminal, their efforts inevitably bog down in a tangle of methodological problems that in fact are covers for conceptual problems" (p. 785). As the review in the last chapter suggested, psychologists have been unable to distinguish, in the laboratory, between emotion, conceived as a "non-semantic," or "neurophysiological-biochemical" phenomenon, and cognition conceived as intentionally directed process. Yet this has not prevented them from continuing to speak with confidence about the two as if they were separate phenomena. As Barnett and Ratner (1997) note, psychologists continue to employ categories derived from Aristotle, drawing "artificial boundaries" around cognition and emotion in particular, leading to futile debates over which comes first, "as if they could be divided into 'pure' forms" (pp. 305–306). That psychologists continue, in spite of these difficulties, to pursue evidence for subliminal (that is, objective, not subjective) thought processes, and continue to distinguish emotion from cognition suggests a determination based more on conceptual, than on empirical, grounds.

Foucault was harsh in his criticism of this kind of social science. "Man and his doubles," he insisted, were chasing each other's tails (Foucault 1966). "Man," being the modern subject, a consciousness tenuously attached to the world through the senses of a body, had to study that world using scientific method in order to gain "objective" knowledge of it. But, inevitably, looking through his weak eyes into this alien world, he discovers others like himself, who, in their turn, become the objects of scientific inquiry. Science then "discovers" that they are a composite of subjective and objective features, and pursues ever more exact knowledge of this spurious composite.

Many anthropologists have taken this line of criticism with the greatest seriousness and have striven, in the last twenty years, to rid their discipline of the kind of dualist presuppositions that poststructuralists have denounced (e.g., Clifford & Marcus 1986; Clifford 1988; R. Rosaldo 1989; Behar & Gordon 1995). They no longer pose as scientists of culture, scouring the globe for interesting phenomena to be used in the building of a single, objective theory of human cultural capacities. They have refounded their discipline as an interpretive (not scientific) one, aimed at understanding discourses, meanings, the "poetics" of practices and customs. It could reasonably be argued, in fact, that a poststructuralist anthropology is possible, whereas a poststructuralist experimental psychology is not. Many anthropologists have therefore, as we have seen, disputed the relevance of psychological research to their own work.

Critiques of Poststructuralism

However, poststructuralism has itself been widely criticized. I will mention two of its most frequently examined weaknesses in passing and then concentrate on a third. Once these criticisms are taken into account, it becomes possible to read experimental psychology in a very different light.

First, poststructuralists have been criticized for "performative contradiction," that is, acting in a way that is not consistent with their doctrines (e.g., Habermas 1987; Matusik 1989). If there are no modern Western subjects, except as artifacts of a discursive order, why publish books, give lectures, comment at conferences with the aim of persuading such subjects that they have no authentic existence? This is a criticism which many poststructuralists have themselves carefully considered, however. Their writing and their interventions have borne the imprint of this consideration. Poststructuralists' works are notoriously difficult, for example. Their penchant for obscure jargon and overly complex extended metaphors; their tendency to speak of abstractions as if they were persons or forces; their disregard for the conventions of scholarly exposition; their apparent perversity vis-à-vis their audiences and their readers – all reflect a search for a very different, new practice that would adequately embody a dissatisfaction with practices of writing and reading appropriate to the Western subject. Whether they have found such a practice is uncertain; it is quite clear, however, that they have explored the irony of arguing, and attempting to persuade others of, their views. The use of irony in this way can certainly serve important ends in intellectual endeavors.

Second, poststructuralists, especially Foucault and his followers, have been criticized for their inability to positively specify political conditions that would constitute liberation from the arbitrary rule of discourses. It is meaningless to denounce certain discourses as oppressive, if one cannot say what would count as a just or free kind of discourse. This point I have already discussed in relation to the work of Lutz and Abu-Lughod in Chapter 2. As Carolyn Dean (1994) has remarked, succinctly but pertinently, "In the process of recovering and exposing exclusions, many theorists often sacrifice meaning and agency in favor of sweeping references to 'discourse,' 'culture,' 'power,' 'disciplinary formations,' and 'undecidability'" (p. 274). As a result, "Most theorists are currently struggling with this question about how Foucault's work effaces experience in one way or another" (p. 275; see also Ferry & Renault 1985; Fraser 1992; Reddy 1997a, 1999).

Without a subject, there is no public to read critiques of the subject. There is also no clear idea of what it is that has rights and liberties and therefore is capable of being oppressed or exploited. We have already explored the implications of this weakness in examining the drawbacks of the constructionist approach to emotions. If I feel a deep culturally constructed loyalty to Louis XIV, can we say I am oppressed by this feeling? If so, then there must be some free feeling (unconstructed, natural) I would feel if I could. But if there is no such true, free feeling, then there is no oppression in obeying an absolute monarch.

Alcoff, in her recent work on epistemology (Alcoff 1996), has defended Foucault against such charges. Alcoff claims that Foucault has a strategic sense of theory as a domain at once of power and truth; by siding with the "subjugated knowledges," he opposes not only the political domination of a disciplinary discourse but also its (false) claims to universality. Foucault thus has, not just political, but also "epistemic reasons to reject hegemonic discourses." Subjugated knowledges, Alcoff continues, involve less "violence, distortion, and omission" than global knowledges require, "and their recalcitrance to total subsumption helps to block a hegemony that would claim dominion over each and every infinitesimal social and discursive event. Thus they have a *different* relationship to power, and given power's role in the 'constitution of a field of knowledge,' this different relationship will constitute a different field" (p. 155; emphasis in original). Foucault was aware, Alcoff insists, of the danger that his own epistemology might entail claims to hegemony of the very type he denounced. "Foucault considers this charge in the same lecture in which he defines genealogy. He says that the genealogical project he has developed has not yet achieved dominance, and thus 'the moment at which we risk colonization has not yet arrived.' Therefore his project does not yet incur the dangers and problems of global theory" (p. 157, quoting from Foucault 1980:86).

This position is similar to the view defended by Judith Butler (1992) that the theoretical positions that ground a given politics of liberation ought to be held only contingently. Butler (1997) has noted, in addition, that an absence of specification about the precise aspects of human nature that justify freedom can be regarded as itself a kind of political strength. Refraining from saying who or what should be liberated, we rule out no claims before they have had a hearing. The expression of such restraint in the form of positive law or policy remains an issue fraught with ambiguities, however.

Poststructuralism, Translation, and New Realisms

The third weakness of poststructuralism, which I will concentrate on here, lies in the idea that one can "never" gain access to a signified that is not already a signifier in its own right, not already part of an insidious discursive structure with its own limiting presuppositions. This is the idea that "everything becomes discourse." What access could we possibly have to something that is not already incorporated in a discursive structure? the poststructuralist asks. Merely by naming it, we betray ourselves, for the name we use is inevitably an element in a system of signs. To this seemingly incontrovertible argument, one can easily object as follows: Any statement of the form "one can never know or never gain direct access to *x*" can be dismissed as trivial and meaningless. This is obvious when someone insists that there are little blue gremlins in every coffee cup, but they can "never" be seen. It is less obvious, but still the case, when someone insists that, even if you mutely point at something, you are not designating a raw signified, you are actually creating a sign that consists of you in conjunction with the thing pointed at. It appears to follow that this sign is subject to the constraints of semiotics just like all the others. But, if we are to accept that we *never* have access to raw signifieds (signifieds that are not just other signifiers in their turn), that we never have access to the "original" signified (Derrida 1967b:411), then the concept of "raw" or "original" signified gives us access to nothing. Only if the concept "raw signified" were the one exception to the general rule "we never have access to raw signifieds" could the rule itself be different from a claim of the kind "we never have access to the invisible blue gremlins in every coffee cup." But there are no grounds on which such an exception can be justified. If "raw signified" gives us access to nothing, then the claim of poststructuralists that "everything is a text" is equivalent to the claim that "we never have access to nothing."

One must choose: either (1) the distinction between signifier and signified renders talk of discourse just another type of metaphysics like Cartesian dualism; or (2) there is some special way in which "raw signified" can be given meaning that differs from the way in which "objective fact" can be given meaning, when an empiricist asserts that we never have direct access to objective facts. Cartesian dualism treats all objective facts as independent of the (shaky and questionable) subjective efforts of humans to know them, and therefore what we "know" to be fact is never securely objective at all, so that all knowledge, all being we have access to, becomes tainted with subjectivity. Likewise, one could easily charge, poststructuralism is similarly metaphysical in character, when it treats the "raw signified" as an unreachable, pure example of the category "signified," revealing that all knowable signifieds are just a subset of signifiers, and therefore the concept "signifier" becomes equivalent to everything there is. The concept of signifier thus becomes equivalent to the concept of being, a notoriously slippery concept that distinguishes nothing from anything else.

While many influenced by poststructuralism fail to confront this difficulty, the classic statements of the approach by Derrida, Foucault, and others show they are perfectly aware of it, and that their position is the second one mentioned in the previous paragraph, that there is something special about the sign concept that exempts it from the pitfalls of metaphysics. Indeed their claim is not that they have escaped this problem, but instead that certain notions of text, language, discourse, or semiotics – all of which involve borrowing doctrines from Saussurian linguistics – offer a privileged way of expressing, and enhancing our awareness of, a certain insoluble puzzle about thinking that metaphysicians (such as Descartes, Rousseau, Kant, Hegel, or Husserl) claimed, spuriously, to be able to solve. I have elsewhere noted that all these metaphysicians made similar distinctions between themselves and their predecessors, and that the history of the making of such distinctions in philosophy deserves closer study than it has heretofore attracted (Reddy 1992). Here I wish only to point out that the privilege claimed for notions of discourse, text, or language (as opposed to Descartes's clear and distinct idea, Kant's categories, Hegel's Absolute, Husserl's phenomenology of consciousness) trades on a certain potential for confusion that is necessarily deleterious to the poststructuralist cause itself.

To claim that notions of text, language, or discourse offer a privileged way of thinking about the quandary of the concept of being is to imply that Kant's notion of the space-time manifold or Hegel's notion of the dialectic are somehow inferior. It is to claim that the quandary of metaphysics is a kind of side effect of our ability to speak, read, and write. There is a residual, and all-too-comforting empiricism implicit in this idea. Only the most vigilant poststructuralist can resist its reassuring implications. The comforting error, committed by all too many scholars influenced by the work of Derrida and Foucault, is to imagine that we find utterances and texts in the world of nature, that we do so as secular scientists or interpreters of human society. Only then, within utterances and texts, do we discover the problem of being in the form of the distinction between signifier and signified. We then presume that we can discuss this problem and its effects on social existence, as professional social scientists writing our monographs and preparing our research reports.

But poststructuralism preaches that social inquiry is spurious in the first place, because there is no such thing as humanity or society (which are just more signifiers without raw signifieds) and no reason to engage in research into humanity's behaviors or conditions of existence, no grounds for any kind of social science or social interpretation. The only grounds for engaging in "social" interpretation, indeed, would be to examine the absurd effects which spurious categories such as the "social" have on our ways of thinking and acting with each other. The only proper social interpretation available to a poststructuralist is to denounce the "social" as nonexistent, as a signified never encountered. Ironically, the tendency has been quite the opposite, to enshrine a certain vision of the social as mysteriously all-powerful, because the social is insinuated into consideration as the context that gives rise to language and to discourse. To guard against the kind of misreading which I am suggesting poststructuralism easily gives rise to, it would have been better to recast the argument entirely in a new set of terms. But if the social were not available as a shadowy and comfortable way of thinking about the context in which discourses arise and texts are produced, poststructuralism would not have been useful in so many contexts of present-day scholarly endeavor, where one must justify one's professional standing by investigating something social, whether it be literature, history, culture, or "social" relationships.

However, my aim here is not to repair potential misreadings of poststructuralism, although I hope I have effectively suggested that its special pretensions are nothing new, and that its arguments require the same kind of indulgent reading that every metaphysical argument requires – indulgent in the sense of recognizing that the text is developing approaches to, not solutions for, insoluble problems. My aim, instead, is to propose a concept of "translation" as a replacement for the poststructuralist concept of "sign." By using the concept of translation, I will argue, one can avoid the problem of the raw signified. One can, if one chooses, think of the signified as just another signifier within its own semiotic system. Or, one can think of it as something other than a sign. Either way, I propose, one can fruitfully think of the signified as being "translated" when one attempts to apprehend it, when it is "found" as the shadowy complement of a signifier. I use the concept of translation because of the way translation has been discussed in English-speaking philosophical circles in the last thirty years; I depend particularly on Alcoff's (1996) recent examination of this discussion and her brilliant exploration of its similarity to poststructuralist preoccupations. When the work of cognitive psychologists is examined as an effort to understand the activity of translation, its relevance to the current problems of anthropologists and historians is immediate and obvious.

To demonstrate the advantages of this borrowed approach, I begin with a simple example. There is a difference between a picture, on the one hand, and a set of propositions (a text), on the other, that allows one to specify the picture uniquely and completely, and, if necessary, to replicate the picture exactly.

Item 1. A picture:

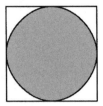

Item 2. A textual specification of the picture:

> *A square, one inch on a side, contains a circle with a diameter of one inch; the center of the circle is one-half inch from the top of the square and one-half inch from the left side of the square. The square is white; the circle is gray.*

If we regard Item 2 as signifier and Item 1 as its signified, the poststructuralist doctrine that we never have direct access to raw signifieds invites us to recognize that Item 1 may be regarded as just another signifier in its turn. The interpretation of geometric figures, one might argue, is just as arbitrary and conventional as the interpretation of language. It is only convention, for example, that dictates our interpretation of Item 3 below (a fragment of Item 1) as the meeting and then separation again, of two independent lines, one curved, one straight.

Item 3. A fragment of Item 1:

A different convention might encourage us to see this figure as two pointed objects touching at their points. Even if everything available to us is already in the form of signifiers, however, there are still two quite distinct sets of signifiers in play in Items 1 and 2. Two distinct languages or codes are in use. Item 4 below, for example, fails as a representation of the figure specified in Item 2 because it mixes these two distinct languages or codes.

Item 4. A figure with mixed codes:

In this example, not only are the textual and geometric codes mixed, but the textual specification "gray" is attributed to the letters of a piece of text, rather than to a "circle" item within the code of geometric figures.

As a way out of the poststructuralist conundrum, I would propose that we regard the relationship between Item 1 and Item 2, not as the relationship of signifier to signified, but as a relationship of translation.

Regarding this relationship as one of translation allows one, as noted above, to make two moves. First, one can incorporate into the discussion a debate about the nature of translation that has occupied a number of philosophers in the analytic tradition. Second, I will argue that translation is something that goes on, not just between languages and between individuals, but among sensory modalities, procedural habits, and linguistic structures. This idea points, not toward a reconstitution of a Cartesian type of subjectivity, but toward a conception of the individual as a site where messages arrive in many different languages or codes, and where some of the messages are successfully translated into other codes, while others are not. By this approach, the work of cognitive psychologists gives us access to better understanding of how the activity of translation is carried out in varying circumstances and in pursuit of varying aims. Cognitive research also helps to understand the limitations, incompleteness, and imprecision of translation work. It is significant, for instance, that psychologists have repeatedly found that certain "cross-modality transfers" require attention. The term "cross-modality transfers" refers to the connection of input from various senses or "modalities," for example, the identification of a spoken word with a written word. Apparently, it is quite difficult to make such transfers (a specific type of what I would call translation) automatically (Ste-Marie & Jacoby 1993:786; Brooks & Stein 1994:10; Jacoby, Yonelinas, & Jennings 1997:28; Drevets & Raichle 1998:357). Attention is, above all, I would argue, a translator. This way of thinking about cognition points toward a novel understanding of the relation between feeling and utterances, since the latter must always constitute translations into speech of the former.

In a number of works, W. V. O. Quine (see, for example, Quine 1969) argued that all translation was indeterminate. He offered the example of a linguist attempting to learn a new language from informants who spoke only that language. Suppose the linguist pointed at a rabbit and uttered the English word "rabbit," after which one of his or her informants pointed also, and uttered a word. Quine noted that it would be impossible for the linguist to tell if the foreign word meant "rabbit," "undetached rabbit part," "rabbit stage," or even "rabbithood." The linguist's tendency to assume that his or her informants also meant "rabbit" was based on a theory about the world he or she held unreflectively. All the translations which the linguist would painstakingly develop would therefore be only contingently accurate. Their correctness would depend on the linguist and his or her informants' sharing the same theory about the world. But there would be no way for the linguist to check whether they shared this theory, because he or she already translated whatever the informants said on the basis of the assumption that they did share it. Quine viewed all communication as similar to this kind of "radical translation," of the field linguist (Quine 1969:46; Davidson 1984:125–139; Alcoff 1996:87). Successful interpretation of another's utterances, Quine argued, was always contingent on the sharing of a theory, which sharing could not be checked.

The problem Quine was bringing forward was similar to that which preoccupied the poststructuralists who were writing at about the same time in France. They, too, saw that the relation between an individual word and the thing it supposedly represented was tenuous to say the least.

Donald Davidson subsequently developed a critique of Quine's position. First he noted that, although translation may be indeterminate, nonetheless, a difference that could never be checked was no difference at all (Davidson 1984:139; Alcoff 1996:108). Second, he posed a "Principle of Charity," by which we must assume that successful communication does occur (Davidson 1984:136–137). The linguist is justified in applying his or her theory about the informants' pointing activities on the grounds of the Principle of Charity. The Principle of Charity also implies something new about the relation between words and the world. On the basis of this principle, it is reasonable to hold that, if there is an important defect in the theory that backs up one's translations, then it will probably turn up sooner or later.

Building on Davidson's critique of Quine, Hilary Putnam has developed what he calls "internal realism." By this view conceptual schemes that are internally coherent (such as Cartesian dualism) are very powerful, but not all-powerful. There are ways, ways we cannot specify, that both the world and the mind are implicated in such schemes and thus their weaknesses will lead them to be supplanted in due time.[5] Alcoff has offered to improve on Putnam with her notion of "immanent realism." In Alcoff's view, not just the conceptual scheme or theory, but also its "historical, spatio-temporal, and social location" – that is, its "context" – should be considered (Alcoff 1996:218). This allows one to capture not just the categorical scheme or "discourse" in play but also the institutions and the political relationships that the scheme underwrites. "On an immanent realist view," Alcoff concludes,

---

[5] Here I am following Alcoff's discussion of Putnam in Alcoff (1996:161–200).

truth is an emergent property of all the elements involved in the context, including but not limited to theory. Immanent realism can therefore acknowledge more readily the formative effects that language, discourse, and power/knowledges have on the production of truths, rather than privileging the knowing subject as the necessary center of the knowing process. Here, then, might lie the route to a nonauthoritarian epistemology, one that incorporates an ineliminable partiality and a context-based account of knowing which is, in effect, a more plausible description of real knowing. (pp. 219–220)

One does not have to follow every turn of Alcoff's conclusion to recognize that her discussion accords with my proposal to equate "translation," as Quine understood it, and the "sign" in structuralist and poststructuralist thought. Just as signifiers must always have a systematic mutual distinctness before they acquire any power to signify, so translation must be based on a theory about the world. Just as signifiers, in the end, can only refer to other signifiers, not to any real thing, so translation is always indeterminate. The various realisms that have been proposed as critiques of Quine are just as powerful as challenges to poststructuralism.[6]

The advantage of the notion of translation over that of the sign, for the present analysis, is that translation implies the existence of two mutually distinct languages or codes, what Quine calls "theories," *within* what poststructuralists would call the sign, dividing the signifier from the signified. By applying the notion of translation to Items 1 and 2 above (the figure and its textual specification), I am proposing that we regard vision as a skill analogous to, but quite separate from, the mastery of a language, and that we regard the ability to point at something in the visual field, such as a rabbit, as a third skill, a skill in translating. It might be argued that the ability to point at a rabbit is inherent in knowing the English language, or at least in knowing what the word *rabbit* means; but this is obviously not the case. I often read novels that mention different varieties of plants and animals without being able to say what they look like. I frequently ask my spouse to identify things in the woods, even very familiar things, such as a holly bush, a beech tree, or a woodpecker, even though I have heard and understood all these words since childhood. I remember being distinctly intrigued to discover the faint, but definite, resemblance

[6] As this statement implies, I regard Alcoff's immanent realism as quite a step beyond Foucault, even if it builds on his work.

between the appearance of a woodpecker in the woods and the appearance of the cartoon figure, Woody Woodpecker, familiar to me from television. Identification is a separate skill, and I am proposing that it be treated as a translation skill in its own right. My spouse is quite dependent on me when we go to France, because she knows little French. My translating for her in France and her helping me in the woods are very similar activities, and we have frequently remarked the parallel.

The translation task inherent in pointing and naming ("ostension") is indeterminate in just the ways Quine claims. Only repetition and induction reduce the indeterminacy to workable levels; no one disputes Quine's contention that a certain residuum of indeterminacy always remains.

Such translation skills are frequently the focus of psychological testing. Psychologists, in fact, frequently use words and fragments of text in their tests; word recognition and reading are the subjects of a flourishing subfield, as well. The Stroop color-naming test offers a good example to consider. Variations of this test have been used in over five hundred studies (Besner et al. 1997). The original study, carried out by J. R. Stroop in 1935, consisted of presenting subjects with words printed in various colors and asking them to identify the color the word was printed in. Stroop found that, if the color of the word was, say, blue, and the word itself was the name of a different color – say, the word was *green* – then subjects' recognition of the color was delayed. They hesitated for a moment before naming the color the word was printed in. Examples of the interesting variations that have been made on this test were mentioned in Chapter 2: Mogg et al. (1993) found that, in subjects judged to be anxious, words related to anxiety or depression could delay recognition of the color the word was printed in. Greenwald et al. (1995) found increased errors in placement recognition of a word (difficulty recognizing whether it was to the right or left of center of a screen) if the word *right* was found on the left of the screen, or the word *left* was found on the right. Such tests tend to indicate that aspects of the recognition task are "automatic," that is, recognition goes on and influences response even if it is irrelevant to the assigned task. In the original Stroop test, the subject cannot help but notice the meaning of the word, despite instructions to concentrate on the color, and is delayed by this meaning in identifying the color of its letters; this is called "semantic" interference.

Recently, Besner et al. (1997) challenged standard interpretations of Stroop-type tests. They do not believe that the delays or errors in recognition represent irresistible, "automatic" processing. Instead, delays reflect reasonable expectations of subjects who intentionally choose certain recognition strategies, causing "activation" to spread or be blocked at various levels. In their laboratory, they changed the color of only one letter of the word. They asked subjects to identify the color of the colored letter. The colored letters were inserted in words, some of which were color words for different colors. They reasoned that the Stroop effect, the delay in recognition, if automatic, should not be changed by this alteration. Yet it was; in one test, the delay disappeared entirely. Besner and his associates surmise that, because subjects concentrated their efforts on searching for a *letter* of a different color, their attention was diverted from the word-recognition, or lexical level, of processing, and, as a result, semantic-level processing was blocked.

But the precise interpretation of these results is irrelevant here. One does not have to explain recognition delays or errors as some combination of automatic ("objective") processing and intentional ("subjective") strategies or goals. One may still accept that there is a difference between a green patch of color and the word *green*. One may grant, if someone wishes it, that the patch of color is not "raw sense data," nor a "raw signified," but just another signifier within some kind of discursive structure. One can still assert that the color green and the word *green* are not from the same set of signifiers, are not in the same code or language. Others may wish to insist that the color green is not a signifier, but an objective fact, or an extralinguistic nervous system state resulting from stimulation of certain phosphors in the retina. However one characterizes it, this "not-same-ness" of the color green and the word *green* requires translation to make the bridge between the two. Translation involves an element of indeterminacy, which may be of no significance; but if it is of significance it will have an impact, it will make a difference, sooner rather than later. Translation sometimes requires effort, sometimes, by force of habit, it seems to "run to completion" on its own; each kind of translation is a task that must be learned and can occur only if we are able, and inclined by circumstances, to carry it out. In the Stroop test and its variations, subjects hesitate because they are translating both image and word based on rapid, well-developed habits. But they are also obliged to translate the instructions given by the experimenters into proper performance; they do not have habits for this and must rehearse the details of the instructions, which rule out consideration of the meaning of the word and require attention only to the color of the letters. Most cognitive research, including laboratory research on affect, may be regarded as an effort to understand how and when translation tasks of various kinds occur. There is no need to force the results into a Cartesian mold in order for them to offer illuminating glimpses into translation and its limitations and side effects. (On this issue, see Kosslyn 1994.)

Mere coordination of the five senses already involves a remarkable work of translation. Infants routinely stare fixedly at their hands and feet as they move them through complex patterns or in attempts to manipulate objects. An apple that is beginning to rot has a particular appearance, a particular feel, smell, and taste. If it is thumped it will sound different from a fresh apple. Coordination of these inputs to gain a coherent impression of a rotten apple involves establishing their mutual equivalence. The complexity of such a translation task can be simulated within language, using separate phrases to characterize each sensory modality, as follows:

input a = round, red object with stem, and with several oval brown spots. Within the brown spots, puckers and wrinkles in the surface are evident.

input b = hard, curving, smooth surface, with areas that are softer, bumpy, and damp.

input c = sweet tangy odor with an overlay of pungent acidity.

input d = partly hard, crisp resistance to teeth, partly soft, mealy, yielding; mixed textures on the tongue, sweet, sour flavor.

input e = complex noise when struck or bitten, a stiff, deep echo accompanied by softer, looser reverberations.

We do not need to decide whether any of this sensory input is happening inside or outside of "language" or a "discourse." To gain an impression of a rotten apple requires that the messages in these different codes be coordinated, that is, mutually translated. A person who has been blind from birth, suddenly cured, will not at first recognize a rotten apple by sight alone. The *Odyssey* in the original Greek and the same work in an English translation are also both, in the same way, the same and indeterminately different. Likewise, the textual proposition "This apple is rotten" can be arrived at by a further translation of the sensory inputs. It, too, is both the same and not the same as what it translates. If one were a guest in another's house, one might prefer to say, "This apple appears to have gone bad." The word *appears* suggests doubt; *gone bad* is less abrupt than rotten. The aim would be to avoid insult or the suggestion of ingratitude. Here, considerations of personal relationships, of honor, of reciprocity, of political authority, must also be translated into appropriate wording. This new proposition could also be viewed, profitably, as a translation of "This apple is rotten" – a translation into a code determined by a context of personal relationships. Every utterance, every expressive act, can be viewed as the outcome of convergent translation tasks. Sensory, linguistic, relational, and status codes are all in play in the articulation of the expression.

Translation in this sense is one of the principal tasks that human beings carry out when they are awake; it is a kind of task imposed by pursuit of the most rudimentary goals such as eating a piece of food or walking. The very formulation of longer-term, life-organizing goals involves translation through transposition of short-term goals into higher-level frames of reference with their own codes. The step from "I like food" to "I like farming," or, alternatively, to "I like money" involves translation of one target into appropriate equivalents in two different codes. This step requires what Quine called a "theory" and entails a degree of indeterminacy. Within the theory that anything is available for money, for example, money is equivalent to, and can be exchanged for, food, clothing, shelter, love, admiration, esteem. But applying such a theory to life entails constant translations from other codes, codes in which the theory cannot even be stated. Such translations may constitute real tests of the theory, in the sense that an actor may find them troubling or satisfying, adequate or faulty.

Goals themselves must be "translated" into action; stating them as explicit propositions involves still another, quite different, task of translation. Bourdieu developed his notion of habitus to take this last difference into account (Bourdieu 1977; see also Strauss & Quinn 1997). All such translations have an element of indeterminacy. The term *blue* does not have the capacity to capture everything that visual interpretation offers about blue-ness. A dancer cannot draw a picture of, or write out in words, what a dance allows him or her to express. He or she may try; the attempt may be interesting, illuminating; but it is not exhaustive of what dance does. Even within the frame of linguistic utterances, we can easily, sometimes inadvertently, shift among theories and hold interpretations only as "drafts" while awaiting further developments (Dennett 1991). One of the important things that an "art" or a "medium" such as dance offers to us is an occasion for interesting translation work.

Psychologists categorize the kinds of things that stand in need of what I am designating as "translation" (using a linguistic metaphor where they would use the mechanical metaphor of "processing") roughly as follows: (1) sensory inputs, including proprioceptive and internal bodily sensations as well as pleasure and pain; (2) "procedural" memory, including cognitive and practical skills such as the capacity to use language, to read and write, or to hammer a nail; (3) "declarative" memory, that is, memory stored as preformulated narrative fragments and propositional strings. (See, for example, Erdelyi 1990, 1992; Wegner & Smart 1997; Schneider & Pimm-Smith 1997.) This categorization scheme must be regarded with considerable caution; "goals," for example, could be found represented in all three types of things, in sensory input (as when thirst guides one's perceptions of a cooler full of soft drinks), in procedural memory (as when a desire to win is virtually pre-encoded in a tennis player's back swing), as well as declarative memory (where we would expect to find some goals explicitly formulated). In addition, it is hard to imagine a person being awake without having a certain number of ongoing translation tasks up and running in the background. A certain range of things are, in this sense, always already translated before a "person" – an agent embodying goals and intentions – has access to them. Nevertheless, what this category scheme brings out forcefully is the fact of the vastness and diversity of the stuff translation must work on – which I will call here, for lack of a better term, *thought material*. It also brings out the extraordinary gap at any given time between what is available for possible translation work and what is now undergoing translation.

This gap is analogous to the gap in structural linguistics, taken over by poststructuralism, between *langue* and *parole* – that is, between language as a semiotic system (*langue*), and the specific utterances it makes possible (*parole*). The principal difference is that thought material exists in many codes, linguistic and extralinguistic. The tendency in both structural linguistics and poststructuralism was to emphasize the limitations which the structure of the system imposed on what could be uttered or "thought" by utilizing it. In the poststructuralist view, these limitations are so great as to rob utterances and texts of any independent significance whatever. The structure of concepts that underlies a "discourse" determines everything that can be "said" or "written" within it so completely that the individual "using" this structure to say something is robbed of all real choice, robbed of agency, reduced to epiphenomenal status. What Saussure called the "associative relation-ships" of signifiers (Wells 1947:9), I claim, are relationships of transla-tion. When one admits this correction, and along with it, the idea of extralinguistic, or nonverbal, thought material (or, if one prefers, thought material in visual, aural, gestural, etc., codes), and when one accepts, in addition, that utterances and texts (parole) are more or less indeterminate attempts at translation of such material, the relationship between langue and parole changes. It changes because we must rec-ognize the possibility that an utterance may be regarded as a failure, as a bad translation. One's visual language may not be constrained by Cartesian dualism, for example. Thus, one may see things one does not know how to translate into the terms of that "theory" (to use Quine's terminology) or "discourse" (to use Foucault's). Utterances can, in this case, by repeated failures, lead to the questioning or restructuring of the lexicon or discourse itself. This introduces the possibility of human agency, of trial and error, as well as of a historical dynamic that has been sadly lacking in poststructuralist theory (White 1978). Cognitive psychology itself, for example, may be on the verge of recognizing the inadequacy of the subjective/objective distinction for comprehending its laboratory results. Our ability to check, and reject, translations is no more mysterious than our ability to translate in the first place. Or, rather, both are mysterious because both entail a capacity to work with indeterminacy as a permanent irritant, which is also a condition of the possibility of having new thoughts.

Translation, Activation, and Attention

When psychologists working in the laboratory look at this gap – between the vast array of available thought material and the minus-cule part of it that is actually undergoing translation – they move in an entirely different direction from poststructuralists. What attracts their notice is the ephemeral activity that occurs between the two. They look at very short time horizons, measured in thousandths of a second, and discover that different facets of what I am calling translation tasks occur with different time intervals that can be predictably manipulated. To explain these differences, as noted in Chapter 1, they have recourse to many concepts that are often ill-defined and problematic: "subliminal," "unconscious," "automatic," "controlled," "strategic," and so on. I will argue here that two commonly used concepts are free of dualist impli-cations and can be retained as tools for talking about how translation tasks are coordinated, namely, "activation" and "attention."

Especially important is the notion of "activation." Used very widely, although represented by means of a variety of models sculpted to fit various experimental findings, the concept of "activation" identifies a state or a set of similar states that "inputs," "thoughts," or "memories" (what I am calling, collectively, "thought material") can occupy and that render them more or less available to be "processed," that is, translated. Equally important is the concept of "attention" (preferred by many to "consciousness"). Attention is not the only place where translating occurs, but it is a location of the greatest intensity of translation work and where novel translation efforts (learning) must be carried out. Wegner and Smart (1997), as noted in Chapter 1, attempt to explain the ironic effects of mental control by regarding activation as either "surface," "full," or "deep." Surface activation is within attention, but transitory, as when one temporarily remembers a telephone number one is dialing. Full activation renders thoughts readily available to attention over a much longer term and ensures that they frequently enter attention. Deep activation results from active attempts at suppression, rendering thoughts "unconscious" – that is, not currently available for attentive translation into declarative sentences or intentional action – but also strongly activated, and therefore likely to intrude when vigilance is relaxed or weakened by cognitive "load." This scheme applies equally well whether the objects or the goals of mental control involve emotions, moods, or cognitions. Wegner and Smart further consider that both full and deep activated thoughts can be in a state of "chronic" activation that makes them highly likely to leap forward into ongoing translation tasks. The concept of chronic activation is, in fact, frequently used to explain a variety of experimental results, especially those involving the influence of anxiety or depression on cognition (e.g., Moretti & Shaw 1989; Hughes et al. 1994; Rudman & Borgida 1995; Joseph et al. 1996).

Psychologists' interest in these ephemeral intermediate states is of the greatest importance in any theoretical consideration of emotion because the term *emotion*, in English usage, is frequently employed to refer to that which is activated but not yet in attention, to material that is available to, even calls for, attention but has not got it. This kind of activation often occurs because of the multiple pathways (Greenwald et al. 1995) that translation tasks must follow. Emotions frequently involve activated thought that is not yet in attention because emotions are associated with what I called in Chapter 1 "deep goal-relevance"; goal networks with complex "many-to-many" mappings that constitute "schemas" of action may all be activated at once by a particular circumstance (D'Andrade 1992; Quinn 1992; Strauss & Quinn 1997). Some of these goals may be formulated within the same framing "theory" or code, others may require mutual translation. Here are two examples:

Suppose a sister steals her eight-year-old brother's favorite toy. The brother's activated thoughts may, within the first instant of discovery, include the following features (none of which are articulated):

1. She may steal something else.
2. Mom and dad may not punish her.
3. If I tell, mom or dad may punish her.
4. If I hit her she might stop stealing things.
5. She is sneering at me as if I were to blame for something.
6. If I steal something from her, she might stop.
7. She really does not like to be pinched.
8. She hurt me really badly last week.
9. If you steal in school, you can get expelled.
10. We could have had fun playing together with that toy.
11. She has her favorite watch on.
12. Her eyebrows are ugly.
13. If I throw something instead of hitting her, I might not get punished.

Activated thoughts 1 through 4 and 13 above may be said to share the code or frame of reference or "theory" of familial interaction. Thoughts 5 through 8, 11, and 12 may be said to be embedded in the code or theory of immediate interaction. Thoughts 9 and 10 may be said to derive from a high-level moral or normative code. My formulation of this list was somewhat arbitrary; it could easily be extended. Each of these quasi-propositions derives from a code or theory, and there is no ready method of determining in what way these different theories gel or conflict, to what extent or with what indeterminacy each theory's statements can be translated into statements in the other theories. There is no easy way of telling how such quasi-propositions, as they occur, get involved in the activation of a dense network of goals. In effect, there is no way, in language, to convey the richness of even the simplest such reactions to routine situations. This failure of language is similar to language's inability to capture all the meanings of a dance (or dance's, to capture those of a text). A number of possible scenarios of interaction (from "procedural" memory) are applied to the situation, and a number of drafts of utterances are surveyed (Dennett 1991). All of this can be regarded as translation work. As the boy works through this material, his autonomic nervous system may prepare for action; the face or voice may betray the violent actions that are occurring to him, even though he is deciding to say something in a placating tone. Within a short time, a great deal has been accomplished and a plan is "translated" into action. Even so, many aspects of the thought complex activated by his sister's theft escape the preliminary work of attention that constituted a search for an adequate response. The eight-year-old boy in the example experiences what in English-speaking regions would be considered an "emotion," specifically, one kind of "anger"; if asked, "How do you feel?" at this moment, an American boy might say, "I'm really angry." Or he might convey the same sense in conventionally threatening, linguistic extremes associated with anger, such as shouting "I *hate* her!" or "I'm going to kill her!" (On anger, see, e.g., Lakoff 1987; Gottman & Levenson 1988; Gross & Levenson 1993; Hughes et al. 1994; Hess, Philippot, & Blairy, 1998.)

A common Western conception of romantic love, if articulated in propositions, would include three desires or action tendencies (see, e.g., Averill 1985; Grimal 1988; DeJean 1991; Hatfield & Rapson 1993; Spurlock & Magistro 1994; Daumas 1996; Shaver et al. 1996):

1. a desire to promote the welfare, well-being, and happiness of the loved one;
2. a desire to be in frequent proximity to the loved one, sharing residence, meals, leisure;
3. a desire for frequent physical affection and sexual intercourse with the loved one.

For the purposes of discussion, I propose we accept for the moment that Westerners often do desire these three things with reference to another individual and that these "desires" often become high-level life goals in the social contexts created by Western institutions.[7] A great deal of learning and personal effort is involved in being capable of love as understood in the West. Once these goals are embraced with reference to someone, obviously, they raise a vast array of issues for

---

[7] The term "often" here takes into account Holland's (1992) interesting work on dating practices. I do not address, for the moment, the controversial question whether Western "love" is universal or ethnically distinct; for a review, see Shaver et al. (1996).

the individual. A stunning amount of both procedural and declarative knowledge, of monitored inputs and adjustments, and of life goals, intentions, and purposes are directly implicated in this list and will be altered both by the pursuit of these desires and by their fulfillment. Mental control goals of various kinds will suggest themselves. This is far more than can be handled by attention over a short time horizon.

Should the loved person come into one's presence, this complex of desires must be translated into immediate action; but there are many alternatives to be resolved, and often, a gnawing indeterminacy about the meaning of one's own and the loved one's actions. Later, one may become meditative attempting to retrace the multidimensional thoughts activated in the other's presence – surprise at one's own reactions ("Why was I so afraid?"), or appreciation of the loved one's appearance and sexual attractiveness, may vie with curiosity about that person's mood (out of both concern for the other's welfare and desire for closeness); with vivid imagining of goal-related scenarios (such as eating together, making love, buying a house, helping with the laundry); with admiration of the loved one's personality, pronunciation of words, choice of clothing, face, past woes and accomplishments. As these diverse associational trails try to lead thought off in many directions at once, one may be either "distracted" or "anxious" – or alternate between the two. In the loved one's presence, negative thoughts or disapproving thoughts may be avoided, or denied if activated, in order not to be unpleasant to the loved one.

The possible contradictions among the various desires one has may lead to obsessive rehearsal of certain issues. For example, if the loved one's well-being is in contradiction with one's desire to be close (as when the loved one must travel for work or schooling), one may attempt to think and rethink possible solutions. Another common contradiction: If the loved one does not appear to reciprocate one's desires, unpleasant implications must be explored. Is this disinterest linked to the positive features one discerns in the loved one? (One may end up asking, "Do attractive, good people in general tend to dislike me?") Movements and interactions in a present situation, long-term life goals, ethical or moral constraints – these and other considerations that impinge on action are couched in different codes, and a constant work of translation is necessary to ensure each has a satisfactory influence on action.

Many Westerners, if their attention is drawn to their involvement in such a complex of thoughts, which is beyond intentional manipulation in the short run because it is so vast, will realize "I must be in love." Translating love into action, in turn, requires coordinating many simultaneous translation tasks – involving linguistic, visual, bodily, and social codes – in a single stream of strategic expression and behavior.

Grief at the death of a loved one, like love, for many Westerners, will also draw attention into a labyrinth of related thoughts on many dimensions quite beyond the capacity of attention to encompass either at once or in a short time. Grief, like love, therefore has a certain life span. Much procedural knowledge – making breakfast or washing clothes – when remembered, will recall the loss anew (just as, when in love, admiration is excited anew as one imagines scenarios of interaction). (See discussion by Clore 1994 mentioned above; see also Lofland 1985; Abu-Lughod 1986:203; Tait & Silver 1989; Stearns 1994:83; Drevets & Raichle 1998:370.)

These examples could easily be extended. Even a starkly simple situation, such as the need to escape a charging bear, will have multiple ramifications. As she struggles in panic to climb a tree, a middle-class American might find herself thinking of her ten-year-old child ("What will she do when I am dead?") or the new house she had hoped to buy. Emotions involve complex, multipathway activations linking dense networks of goals, which lie in closely related strata of varying codes or theories.

In sum, this discussion has established that the findings of psychological research can be described and reflected upon without recourse to the Cartesian dualism that psychologists themselves so frequently employ to parse their data. Viewed in this way, such findings reveal the importance of translation tasks and the complexity of the bridging of "activation" that renders thoughts, memories, or perceptions ready or available for attention.

The importance of attention's translation tasks comes into view when one examines two weaknesses of poststructuralism. First, it is meaningless to assert that there is nothing outside of discourse, language, or text. Even accepting such an assertion, it remains legitimate and important to distinguish between signifieds that are more "inside" language and those that are less "inside" – such as the word *blue* and the color blue. This distinction uncovers the multiplicity of types of "input" that must be mutually translated – raw percepts, procedural memories, narratives of past events. Second, the distance between langue and parole is vast. It is necessary to conceptualize intermediate phenomena. The notion of activation, as developed and variously applied by psychologists, represents a useful way of thinking about why some translation tasks and not others are accomplished. The notion of attention as a limited area of heightened translation capacities helps to explain why parole must be linear and obey syntax. Within what is activated, although it is a small fraction of the whole range of available thought material, there are, nevertheless, still many options to explore, much indeterminacy and potential contradiction in the coded messages awaiting attention's translation, and many doors that remain unopened. Within what is activated, it is possible to recover a sense of agency and of history. This is the terrain of "emotions." It is certainly legitimate, therefore, to bring psychologists' findings directly to bear on reports of ethnographic research; evidence that emotions are widely regarded as goal-relevant and as objects of mental control is highly suggestive, as noted in Chapter 2, that the current lines of research that psychologists are pursuing may be meaningful well outside their Cartesian homeland.

A new, working definition of *emotion* is now both necessary and possible. It is necessary to redefine this term at this juncture because, as the many critiques of Western ideas about emotions have shown, this term is fraught with implications we need to avoid. Thinking through the research findings and the epistemological puzzles associated with emotions has forced us to conclude that emotions are not a bridge between body and mind, are not a set of hard-wired arousal systems, are not something radically distinct from reason or thought. What, then, can we say the term *emotion* as commonly used is about? I propose the following as a preliminary response: An emotion is a range of loosely connected thought material, formulated in varying codes, that has goal-relevant valence and intensity (as defined in Chapter 1), that may constitute a "schema" (or a set of loosely connected schemas or fragments of schemas); this range of thoughts tends to be activated together (as in the examples mentioned above, of "angry at sister" or "in love") but, when activated, exceeds attention's capacity to translate it into action or into talk in a short time horizon. Its loose and often variegated character is a reflection of the complexity of translation tasks (including the formulation and application of goals). Episodes of particular complexity give rise to the emotionally configured thought material in the first place; renewed episodes reactivate such configurations.

Are all such loosely aggregated thought activations to be considered "emotions"? My preliminary answer is yes. Any time activations of a wide variety challenge attention's capacity for translation, native speakers of English are likely to say that they are aware of an emotion or feeling. Even if the activations relate to the problem of proving a theorem in topography, or designing the dashboard of a new automobile, English speakers are likely to agree that they are reacting "emotionally," or having a feeling about the matter. They are likely to find certain terms from the English emotion lexicon appropriate to describing the challenge such activations pose for attention: for example, *wonder, anxiety, satisfaction, depression, elation, tranquility.*

This definition of emotion makes possible a new conceptualization of the self. While drawing on psychologists' research we have set aside Cartesian dualism in favor of a conception of attention as a translator beset by an extraordinary array of translation tasks. Such tasks, with all their indeterminacy, must be carried out before a person can achieve the coordinated pursuit of a goal, however simple. Because the translation tasks are always incomplete, and the translations always indeterminate, the kind of self that is possible, by this approach, is a "disaggregated" self. It is disaggregated because memory traces, perception skills, goal hierarchies lie about in various stages of activation, with various patterns of mutual coordination established by habit, and with innumerable latent conflicts and contradictions capable of coming to the fore depending on the context. This disaggregated self is different from both the Cartesian subject and the poststructuralists' vision of an illusory self generated as a byproduct of a discursive structure. Like the poststructuralist self, the disaggregated self has no inherent unity. However, its disunity derives directly from the fact that it has constantly before it flows of signifiers in many different codes or languages, both verbal and nonverbal, in constant need of translation. In addition, its translation work takes the form of drafts provisionally held, based as they are on theories that can be, somewhat mysteriously, retained or reformulated.

Obviously such a self is a collective construct in the sense that the integration which a self achieves, always provisional, builds on social interaction and learning.[8] However, it is not just any collective construct; some way of thinking about the difficulty and contingency of translation efforts must be included. There must be, among other

---

[8] This approach to the self joins many other recent efforts to get beyond Cartesianism, psychodynamics, and poststructuralism, especially among anthropologists. See, for example, Ewing (1990, 1997); Battaglia (1995); Strauss & Quinn (1997); Dennett (1991).

things, a way of talking about emotions as just defined. It is now necessary to turn to these ways of talking and the constraints they impose on every community.

EMOTIVES: SPEECH ACTS IN THE CONTEXT
OF TRANSLATION

The emotional lexicon of English and most other European languages may be regarded as a code for talking about the kinds of thought activations that characterize the disaggregated self. The Western concept of emotion represents a well-developed method for talking about the complex multipathway activations that are an omnipresent aspect of waking life. Such activations spread well beyond the capacity of attention. Some of the material activated at any given moment may organize itself, on inspection, as recognizable chains of Boolean logic or causal inference. Other material may represent tentative coordination of multisensory inputs or other multidimensional arrays. Other material may establish metaphorical or synecdochal links, arithmetic relationships, scenarios of action. (I am employing these technical expressions, somewhat at random, to evoke the extraordinary variety of codes that may be involved in what is activated at any given time.) Some minimum of cohesive translation of the contents of these various fragments is necessary for the smooth apprehension of an environment of action. The most rigorous mathematician simply chooses certain of these chains of activation to the exclusion of others, according to strict rules. Even as he or she does so, he or she has "feelings" about it; that is, great arrays of new thought material beyond the capacity of attention are constantly activated, and from them derives the sense that sticking to the rules of mathematical reasoning requires "effort" – the effort of refusing to follow any of the alternate paths that activation opens up – and that sticking to the rules likewise brings the "joy," "wonder," "awe," "boredom," or "frustration" of mathematics.

But suppose this mathematician were manipulating formulas in which the variables represented the states of activated thought that these very manipulations produced (or were a part of). How could formulas or propositions retain any rigor or rule-governed order if they were about the activated (but not fully attended) thoughts that accompanied or were triggered by their elaboration and their contemplation by their author? This is the dilemma that has convinced many scientists and mathematicians to scoff at the idea of rigor when speaking of or contemplating the self. But perhaps there is a minimal rigor, greater rigor than has been achieved in the past, available if we attempt to characterize with greater accuracy the peculiar structure of this dilemma. To accomplish this I wish to build, by analogy, on Austin's notion of *performatives*.

J. L. Austin established a subfield of philosophy, called "speech act theory" with ideas expounded in his 1962 work, *How to Do Things with Words*. Austin's core insight was the recognition that not all statements are descriptive. The previous history of philosophy had been taken up exclusively with considering the truth conditions and truth value of descriptive, or what Austin called "constative," statements or utterances. But these were just one class of utterance, in Austin's view. Another class of utterances existed which do not describe at all, he insisted. He called them "performatives," because these were utterances that people used to perform or accomplish something, rather than to describe something. Examples are the "I do" of a wedding ceremony, by which bride becomes wife, groom becomes husband, or "I order you to close the door," where the verb *order* is used in such a way as to make the utterance into an order. Such utterances are neither true nor false, Austin noted. However, they do not perform what they appear intended to perform unless certain conditions are met. To say "I do" as an actor on a stage, in a play about a marriage, does not make one into a spouse. Only in the context of a properly performed marriage ceremony does such an utterance perform. If a private says to a sergeant, "I order you to close the door," the utterance is not an order in the military sense. Austin distinguished performatives as either "happy" or "unhappy" depending on whether they occurred in a context that rendered them effective, or in a context that rendered them ineffective.

Austin's ideas were quickly taken up, not only by philosophers, but also by anthropologists and literary critics who found the notion of performatives both intriguing and powerful.

Early on, the question was raised whether all utterances did not, in fact, have a performative dimension. Even the most purely descriptive of utterances, such as "The grass is green," could be taken as having an implicit performative element that situated the utterance vis-à-vis the speaker, such as "(I assert that) The grass is green," or "(I think that) The grass is green." But to some, this idea seemed to open a Pandora's box of possibilities, allowing observers to attribute all sorts of performative intentions to speakers with no evidence the speakers were aware of them. Austin did distinguish between the "illocutionary force" of every utterance and its "perlocutionary force," where illocutionary force meant its status as a performative and its perlocutionary force its status as a descriptive or constative utterance. For example, "I order you to close the door," has perlocutionary force in that it implies that there is an open door in the immediate vicinity and illocutionary force in that it refers to itself as an order. Searle, one of Austin's most prominent disciples, has tried to clear away some of the confusion by arguing that, for example, the utterance "Close the door" is a *performance*, but that, without an initial phrase "I order you to" or "I request that you," it is not a *performative* (Searle 1989).

But, even as philosophers worked to hone the necessary definitions and distinctions allowing us to see performatives for what they were, anthropologists, students of religion, and literary critics recognized the analytical power the concept of performatives offered them for understanding ritual, law, fiction, and other literary production – all of which consist of texts, utterances, or performances produced in specific institutional contexts that gave them a certain illocutionary force. But the context of any utterance, practice, or text which endowed it with a certain illocutionary force merely consisted of other utterances, texts, or practices. Therefore performatives existed in, and derived their meaning from, a whole field of illocutionary forces. In a traditional Christian wedding, for example, the happiness of the "I do" is dependent on the minister's or priest's subsequent utterance of the performative: "I now pronounce you man and wife." The happiness of that performative is, in turn, dependent on the fact that the laws of the state and the regulations of the minister's church endow that minister with the power to perform marriages. And this condition depends on some ceremony in which a church official pronounced "I now ordain you minister," or some such performative formula, and on procedures by which legislatures and courts passed and upheld laws ("I urge you to support . . ." "We do hereby enact . . ." "Objection sustained . . ."). The interlinking of such chains of happy performatives stretches out to the horizon and curves back upon itself.

Marshall Sahlins, in one influential discussion that follows the lines just sketched out (Sahlins 1985), has proposed that culture be considered nothing more than a series of recipes for the happy carrying out of performatives that transform the social status of actors vis-à-vis each other and the cosmos. Sahlins's purpose in making this suggestion was to historicize a concept of culture that was too rigid and synchronic. Viewed as recipes for performatives, culture becomes a series of guides that actors can strive to follow. When historical circumstance prevents the carrying out of the recipes – as occurred, according to Sahlins, in Hawaii when the first British ship arrived in 1778 – then actors are forced to innovate, to improvise, to contend for authority; historical change is the result. Because circumstances always vary, however slightly, history is introduced consistently into accounts of culture in this manner. Literary critic Sandy Petrey made a parallel proposal in a discussion of the French Revolution (Petrey 1988), when he noted that the resolution by which the Estates General turned itself into a "National Assembly" in June 1789, thereby implicitly claiming sovereignty, represented a performative with no predetermined institutional context. The question whether this performative was "happy" or "unhappy," in other words, could be determined only by the conflict that culminated in the fall of the Bastille and the capitulation of the king the following month. (And the legitimacy of even this event was rejected by some, who would, even today, insist that the revolutionary resolution was never "happily" performed.)

By now, the concept of performatives has wide currency in the humanities and social sciences, so that Sarah Maza, in a recent review of historical methodology, can state, "[A]s recent developments in cultural history suggest, cultural products and practices are performative as well as reflective (a novel or ritual does not just reflect social experience, it also constructs it)" (1996:1494). Performance theory has been elaborated by anthropologists and feminist theorists to make sense of ritual, sexuality, ethnic identity, and modernity (see, e.g., Butler 1990; and for a review, Schein 1999).

But statements about the speaker's *emotions* (as that term is used among speakers of English) are prominent examples of a type of utterance that is neither constative (descriptive) nor performative, neither "doing things with words" nor offering an account or representation of something beyond the reach of words. Emotional utterances of the type "I feel afraid," or "I am angry" – which I will call *first-person, present tense emotion claims* – are treated by Austin as being "merely reports" (Austin 1962:78–79) similar to statements such as "I am sweating." But Austin, and his followers, were concerned strictly with the character and properties of utterances. They recognized that the "happiness" of a performative depended on its social and institutional context, but, like poststructuralists, they did not concern themselves with the kind of intermediate extralinguistic phenomena that psychologists have studied – including the key issues of translation, activation, and attention, discussed in the previous section. When viewed in that context, first-person, present tense emotion claims have (1) a descriptive appearance; (2) a relational intent; and (3) a self-exploring or self-altering effect. (Other types of emotional utterances, that concern, for example, the past or other persons, have derivative effects that are discussed below.)

(1) DESCRIPTIVE APPEARANCE. First-person, present tense emotion claims have a descriptive appearance in the sense that emotion words are used in predicates that apply to personal states. "I am sad" or "I have a heavy heart," "I feel elated," or "I am in a giddy mood, although the giddiness is tinged with anxiety" – these types of utterances present themselves at first glance as semantically the same as "I have red hair," "I am clean," "I feel ill" – which are genuinely descriptive or constative. In addition, statements attributing emotions to third parties, as in "He feels angry" or "The general felt no fear," *are* genuinely descriptive (just as "She orders him to close the door" is a constative, not a performative).[9] As descriptive statements, however, emotion claims do not admit of independent verification. The only way to determine the "accuracy" of an emotion claim such as "I am angry" is to notice the coherence of such a statement with other emotionally expressive utterances, gestures, acts, all of which make reference to something no one can see, hear, or sense. Instruments which monitor autonomic nervous system (ANS) states and endocrine system (i.e., glandular and hormonal) states offer a slightly wider spectrum of expressive cues, but still do not allow direct observation of "emotion" (see Ortony & Turner 1990:319).

(2) RELATIONAL INTENT. A large number of observers have noted that statements about emotions in social life occur most frequently as part of (or appear to designate) specific scenarios, relationships, or action orientations.[10] Some have gone so far as to argue that emotions are nothing but such scenarios. To speak about how one feels is, very

---

[9] The case of second-person emotion statements ("You are feeling upset") will be dealt with below.

[10] Here is a sample of specific citations: Averill (1994); De Sousa (1987:45); Lakoff (1987:397–399); Lazarus (1994:307); Lutz (1988:211); Quinn (1992); M. Rosaldo (1984:143); Sarbin (1986); Schieffelin (1985:169); Wierzbicka (1994:437).

often, to make an implicit offer or gift, to negotiate, to refuse, to initiate a plan or terminate it, to establish a tie or alter it. To say "I am afraid of you" may be a way of refusing to cooperate with someone or a request for a change in the relationship. To say, "I feel like going to a movie" may be to propose an outing; to say "I am in love with you" may propose or confirm a long-term sexual liaison. Hochschild (1983) noted that, in the United States, many professions (such as airline flight attendant, waiter, or teacher) require that one express a special range of feelings while on the job; continued expression of such feelings is, in effect, a contractual requirement of employment and to cease expressing them would quickly lead to termination. Familial relationships (in the United States) may offer a greater range of possible emotional expressions, but still impose, in that country as in many others, a set of normative expectations as to emotional expression. In many cultures, smiles have special uses, to signal embarrassment (Barrett 1993:154), to indicate a polite openness to contact (Ekman 1980:136; Fridlund 1992), even to respond to death or loss (Wikan 1989) – in addition to serving commonly as a signal of joy or contentment. Public grieving has also been widely studied in connection with funerary rites in many parts of the world, and it takes on a variety of highly standardized patterns, performed both by those close to the dead and by more distant kin, friends, clients, or strangers. (See, e.g., Feld 1982, 1995; Urban 1988; Good & Good 1988; R. Rosaldo 1989; Grima 1992.) Such performances have raised many methodological difficulties; experts disagree about how to approach them. Is ritualized emotional expression insincere? Or do rituals aim at creating emotion? These questions have remained difficult to answer because researchers have too often neglected the third feature of first-person emotion claims.

(3) SELF-EXPLORING OR SELF-ALTERING EFFECT. However emotions are defined, psychologists tend to agree, as noted in the previous section, that they involve widespread activations of thought materials – variously called "appraisals," "cognitions," or "judgments" – some of which may only be automatic, habitual, semiconscious, or imperfectly glimpsed, and some of which may spill over into facial signals, laughter, blushing, ANS or endocrine-system arousal, tone of voice, gesture, posture, and so on.[11] As studies of automaticity show, the range

---

[11] For use of these terms, see: Averill (1994); Ortony & Turner (1990); Solomon (1984); Greenspan (1988); Frijda (1994); Bornstein (1992).

and complexity of thought material activated at any given time can be so great, and can so completely exceed the translating capacity of attention, that attempts to summarize or characterize the overall tenor of such material always fail. Such failure is, in the first place, a consequence of the indeterminacy of translation. To say "I am happy" about buying a new car and "I am happy" about a trip to see my mother is like pointing at a holly bush in the woods and saying "holly" and pointing to a plastic holly wreath used as a Christmas decoration and saying "holly." In both instances it is necessary to share a theory with the interlocutor to ensure appropriate interpretation of such utterances. But translating emotions into words is even more difficult than translating the sight of a holly bush into words. As Wierzbicka (1994:448) has argued, emotions are not "natural kinds" (see also Griffiths 1997); as a complex, specific thought activation, each emotion is sui generis. Theories that liken emotions to natural kinds (basic emotion theories), as noted in Chapter 1, have not held up. Simple emotion labels are oversimplifications.

An attempt to characterize an emotion in a brief phrase or two is, finally, an endeavor in which the activated thought material itself plays a role and in which very important relationships, goals, intentions, practices of the individual may be at stake. As a result, the attempt inevitably has *effects on the activated thought material* and may have the effect of activating or altering still other thought material within the vast terrain of currently inactive sensory input and procedural and declarative memory. Therefore, even if it were in principle possible to sum up the over-all character of activated thought material in a few words, the attempt to do so is already initiating changes in this material before it is fully formulated. The translation into an emotional code carried out by attention as it formulates and utters an emotional statement can be very far reaching in its consequences for the multivocal thought patterns that are excited or dampened down as attention works. A person whose current state includes an element of confusion may say "I love you" in order to find out if it is true; and the "truth" or "falsehood" of the statement depends on its effects on the speaker. D. C. Dennett (1991:246) cites the following passage from a biography of Bertrand Russell by R. W. Clark (1975:176):

It was late before the two guests left and Russell was alone with Lady Ottoline. They sat talking over the fire until four in the morning. Russell, recording the event a few days later, wrote, "I did not know I loved you till I heard myself telling you so – for one instant I thought 'Good God, what have I said?' and then I knew it was the truth."

A great range of outcomes are possible following an emotional claim. We could categorize them, in an oversimplified way, as confirming, disconfirming, intensifying, or attenuating the emotion claimed. Insofar as an emotion claim is *self-exploratory*, its effects on the self may tend to confirm or disconfirm the claim; insofar as an emotion claim is *self-altering*, its effects on the self may intensify or attenuate the state claimed. In the Russell example above, a combination of confirmation and intensification appears to have followed his avowal. This would appear to be a very common outcome (implicit in findings of Hochschild 1983 or Wikan 1990). The work of Wegner and his associates (Wegner 1994; Wegner & Smart 1997) on the ironic effects of mental control may help explain why intensification of an emotion is a common result of its expression. Emotion claims of the form "I am not afraid" suffer from the same defect as the command "Try not to think of your former lover" (Wegner & Gold 1995; see Chapter 1 for a discussion of this study). Positive emotion claims, on the other hand, especially ones that the individual has reason to espouse, set up a search that activates confirming material.

Such effects may be common, but there is no reason for them to triumph in every case. Over a longer period (of days or weeks) negative claims that are repeated and sustained may have greater chance of success. Erdelyi (1992, 1994) has found that subjects can be instructed to forget or remember an episode or event and, over a period of days, reduce or enhance the accessibility of that event or episode to attention in accord with the instructions. But such efforts are never perfect nor entirely predictable.

In addition, although the consequences of emotion claims can be categorized in these four ways (confirming, disconfirming, intensifying, or attenuating) for analytical convenience, the effects of emotion claims remain as complex and diverse as the multivocal activations they purport to "describe" and which they inevitably alter, sometimes very significantly. In effect, the flight attendant who feels grumpy may just have to try out cheerful behavior anyway, to see if it works, if it takes, and a better mood gels, even if only for a while. Practice makes a difference.

A number of researchers have remarked on the powerful effects which emotional utterances can have on emotions. As Margaret Clark has put it, "There is . . . some clear evidence that choosing to express an emotion or to cognitively rehearse it may intensify or even create the actual experience of that emotion while choosing to suppress it or not think about it may have the opposite effect" (1989:266). Jerome Kagan, in a frequently cited essay on emotional development, made a similar point in 1984: "The presence or absence of detection of internal changes is of extreme importance for the subsequent emotional state. I do not suggest that the undetected biological changes are unimportant, only that the evaluation that follows detection often changes the affect experienced" (p. 41). Phoebe Ellsworth recently reiterated the point: "The realization of the name [of an emotion one is experiencing] undoubtedly changes the feeling, simplifying and clarifying" (1994:193). In addition, philosopher Ronald De Sousa's (1987) concept of "bootstrapping" differs from the approach presented here only in that De Sousa regards the emotional effects of emotion claims as self-deceptive, or at any rate as diverging from a "true" state of affairs (Whisner 1989).[12] Wikan (1989:302) reports the Balinese presuppose that "emotional expression shapes and modulates feeling." Anthropologist Bruce Kapferer's remarks about ritual, discussed in Chapter 2, could also be cited here. No one, not even the most enthusiastic postmodernist, has argued that the wavelengths of light get broader or narrower according to how we name them. Emotion words, however, do have a direct impact on what they are supposed to refer to; this fact separates the question of emotion decisively from the question of perception. What is original to the present discussion is an attempt to theorize this impact as the most important facet of emotional expression, rather than simply noting its existence in passing.

The startling features of emotional utterances that take the form of first-person, present tense emotion claims warrant designating such utterances as constituting a form of speech act that is neither descriptive nor performative. I propose that we call such utterances "emotives." Performative utterances, by the way in which they refer to themselves, actually do things to the world. In the statement "I accept your nomination," the verb *accept*, used in this way, refers to or names the statement in which it appears, making the statement an acceptance. The acceptance, as an act of the speaker, changes the world, in a way

---

[12] Yet this is an important distinction, since De Sousa attempts to get by with existing conceptions of descriptive utterances, which I regard as inadequate for understanding emotional expression.

that a descriptive statement cannot, because it makes the speaker into a nominee. An emotive utterance, unlike a performative, is not self-referential. When someone says, "I am angry," the word *angry* is not the anger, not in the way that, in "I accept," *accept* is the acceptance. As a result, an emotive is not a distinct type of speech act in the original sense of the term, because the original theoretical domain of speech act theory was restricted to utterances, without reference to how they came to be formulated. An emotive statement seems at first glance to have a real exterior referent, to be descriptive, or "constative," in Austin's terms. On closer inspection, however, one recognizes that the "exterior referent" that an emotive appears to point at is not passive in the formulation of the emotive, and it emerges from the act of uttering in a changed state. Emotives are translations into words about, into "descriptions" of, the ongoing translation tasks that currently occupy attention as well as of the other such tasks that remain in the queue, overflowing its current capacities. Emotives are influenced directly by, and alter, what they "refer" to. Thus, emotives are similar to performatives (and differ from constatives) in that emotives do things to the world. Emotives are themselves instruments for directly changing, building, hiding, intensifying emotions, instruments that may be more or less successful. Within the disaggregated self, emotives are a dynamic tool that can be seized by attention in the service of various high-level goals. But emotives are a two-edged sword in that they may have repercussions on the very goals they are intended to serve. It is here, rather than in some putative set of genetically programmed "basic" emotions, that a universal conception of the person can be founded, one with political relevance.

Forms of Expression Related to Emotives

There are several types of utterances and forms of expression that share in the special features of the first-person, present tense emotion claim:

(1) FIRST-PERSON, PAST TENSE EMOTION CLAIMS. Statements such as "I was angry at you," or "I used to despise you" are interpretations of past states of the person. As such, they imply claims about the present state of the person (such as, that the emotion mentioned has now ceased) and, by means of that implication, acquire the full, present transformative force of first-person, present tense emotion claims. They are therefore also "emotives" in the full sense of the word as defined above.

(2) FIRST-PERSON, LONG-TERM EMOTION CLAIMS. Statements such as "I have always loved you," or "I will always be proud of you" are also emotives. When referring to a past time extending into the present, they represent an interpretation of past states combined with an explicit claim about the present state of the person; when referring to the future, they constitute explicit promises as well as claims about the present. As a result, these forms too have the full effect of emotives.

(3) EMOTIONALLY EXPRESSIVE GESTURES, FACIAL EXPRESSIONS, WORD CHOICES, INTONATIONS. With reference to nonverbal emotional signals, it is necessary to distinguish in principle (even if doing so in practice is difficult) between those signals that derive directly from the present action of attention and those that are inadvertent, deriving from effects of activated thought that "short circuit" attention (see, e.g., Argyle 1991:167; Niedenthal & Showers 1991:128–129; Hatfield et al. 1994). The former have the same self-transforming capacity as emotive utterances. The latter, because operating outside of attention, do not – which is not to say that their transforming capacity is zero. Emotion cues that are inadvertent cannot have the same transformative effect, unless they are drawn into attention after they occur. One may "discover" one's sadness on feeling tears begin to fall down the cheek; the tears may bring into attention a range of thought material that had been pushed out by mental control, or had slumbered in neglect. (See Besnier 1990b for a useful discussion of nonverbal emotional expression; see also McNeill 1992.)

(4) OTHER CLAIMS ABOUT STATES OF THE SPEAKER. Emotion states are not the only kind of state of the person that have descriptive appearance, relational intent, and self-exploratory or self-altering effects. Claims such as "I am thinking it over" or "I haven't the slightest idea," because they are also claims about states of the person that cannot be observed, can share in these three startling features of emotives. The same is true for claims about interlocutors' emotions, such as "I thought you loved me" – which is an interpretation of the present state of the speaker that has just as much power to influence that state or redirect it as do emotives. Therefore emotives, which are the focus of attention of this essay, are only a prominent subtype of a larger class of utterances that do not fit Austin's scheme. It is not advisable to insist too much on this distinction between emotives as subtype

and the larger class, because these other utterances, although they do not contain explicit emotion claims, are almost always accompanied by intentional cues as to the speaker's emotional state. One can easily imagine that "I thought you loved me," when uttered with a sad, downcast demeanor, becomes, by its combination with intentional emotional cues, an emotive. The question, what counts as an "emotional" expression, as opposed to expression of thoughts, judgments, or attitudes, is to a significant degree arbitrary, since it is based on customary English-language distinctions that are hardly universal.

(5) SECOND- AND THIRD-PERSON EMOTION CLAIMS. Second- and third-person emotion claims such as "You appear angry," or "He is afraid" are not emotives for the person who utters them, but they can elicit rehearsal of the claim by the person spoken to or spoken about, in the first-person present tense. Such a rehearsal is an emotive. When someone tells me what I feel or appear to feel, I immediately rehearse the claim for myself and, at that time, the claim has emotive impact. Because the claim does not derive directly from my own previous state or from an effort to put that state into words, it may enjoy a less significant self-exploratory or self-altering effect. On the other hand, the relation of the speaker to the person spoken to may be such as to enhance the impact of the emotion claim. A child, when told by its mother, "Don't be afraid," may accept at once that he or she is afraid. Or, in the case of a dispute between peers, the person spoken to might respond with a highly self-altering denial, such as "I am not afraid." I will call the emotive impact of second- and third-person emotion claims on the person who is the subject of the claim "presence effects." Claims about third persons who are not present are not emotives, of course; as noted above, they are descriptive or constative in form. But such third-person claims can have emotive impact if the third person gains knowledge of the claim. In any case, their truth value suffers from the same limitations as emotives, because such claims can only be considered true if the equivalent emotive were an efficacious one for the person characterized. Therefore, their use is very often colored by the management strategies and goals that govern the use of emotives. Both presence effects and the limited truth value of all emotion claims have important political implications that are discussed further in Chapter 4.

Sincerity and Self-Deception

Just as Austin noted that performatives are not true or false but either efficacious or ineffective ("happy" or "unhappy" in his terminology), so emotives are neither true nor false; as descriptions they always fail, because of the complexity of the personal states they describe in the first instance, and because of the effects they have on these states as they are formulated and uttered. But they may also be efficacious or ineffective, depending on whether their effects confirm or disconfirm their claims. One can easily imagine, for example, a person stating "I'm very angry with you" and then finding that, just by saying this, he or she had caused the anger to dissipate. It may be that a more common result is confirmation and intensification (angry thoughts are activated and quickly thereafter activate a range of strong, confirming links to related thought material). But there is no necessary relation of this kind between claims and results. More complicated outcomes can readily be envisioned: in which, for example, the anger remains strong, but other feelings about the person come to the fore as well, resulting in ambivalence or uncertainty.

Because of the powerful and unpredictable effects of emotional utterances on the speaker, sincerity should not be considered the natural, best, or most obvious state toward which individuals strive. On the contrary, probably the most obvious orientation toward the power of emotives is a kind of fugitive instrumentalism. One attempts to use this important tool to achieve ends that may be only tangentially related to the content of the claim. For example, one wants to sell a car, and so one says to a prospective buyer, "I am happy to meet you." Or one prays for good health, with words such as: "Dear God, I love you and submit entirely to your will." In both instances, there is no necessary insincerity; one intends that saying it will help make it so, and one discovers in the aftermath whether this aim is achieved. As in these examples, the relational intent and self-altering effects of emotives often go hand in hand; emotion claims which are implicit promises or refusals often do successfully call up feelings appropriate to the carrying out of the promise or to persistence in refusal. But sometimes the two diverge.

I use the term "fugitive" here in reference to such instrumental self-manipulation because it is always carried out in the service of one or more high-priority goals that are, at present, not implicated in the activated thought material whose alteration is aimed at. When the thought activations associated with an emotion disrupt or alter the balance of current goal orientations, it is impossible to sustain an instrumental attitude toward the "emotion." For example, if a flight attendant, after being attacked by a passenger, felt strongly that he ought to change to another career, he might suddenly find it much more difficult to sustain appropriate cheerfulness. I follow Wikan (1989, 1990) and Hochschild (1983) in calling such fugitive instrumentalism "management" of emotions. But, because instrumentalism often breaks down, because activated thought can easily, if unexpectedly, undermine the goals that currently direct management efforts, I introduce the idea of "navigation" to refer to the whole tenor of emotional life. (This issue is taken up again in Chapter 4.)

A person who becomes adept at tolerating divergences between the self-altering and the self-exploratory effects of emotives (the proverbial used car salesman or gigolo) may be said to lie about his or her feelings, although such a lie is not the same as a constative lie or the performative lie of, say, a bigamist. It is worth noting that routine acceptance of, and management of, divergences between relational intent and self-altering effect can result in one's giving up on the self-exploratory effects of emotives. One ceases to use them to find out what one feels because one is habituated to expect the worst: to being confronted with feelings that do not match the implicit promises one is making. This style may be called "self-deception" or "denial" – but only if one recognizes that no claims about the self have a straightforward truth value. Use of terms such as "self-deception" and "denial" will have its own potential emotive effects, as well as normative political implications. These terms are as prone to instrumental deployment as any other characterizations of "emotions."

Because of emotives' powerful effects and the likelihood that individuals will develop a set of "skills" in exploiting these effects, sincerity must be considered a specialized skill in its own right, that develops only in certain historical and political settings. Insincerity, or outright deception, likewise, cannot be considered the only alternative to sincerity; instead, it is at the opposite pole of a broad field of styles of use of emotives. Even though we must hold others responsible for their actions in certain respects, it is also true that no one can be faulted for not knowing everything that is going on with herself, given the inherent indeterminacy of the multiple translation tasks always under way. Social life entails operating with a generous margin for error, and constant correction, in emotion claims. This is one of the reasons (but not the only reason) that one always finds a divergence between social principle (the formal patterns of "culture" as publicly explicated) and social practice (the strategies and miscues of relation building), the divergence which Pierre Bourdieu enshrined in his well-known notion of "habitus." This divergence is sometimes protected by codes of "honor" that allow or prescribe concealment of breaches of norms – whether in terms of feeling or action. Social life must allow for self-exploration and self-alteration by means of claims about personal states. We are simply too complex, and it is too difficult for attention to cover all the terrain of thought that may be activated by varying circumstances, for us simply to fulfill the roles assigned to us like automata.

CONCLUSION

This chapter has offered two concepts aimed at bridging the gap between anthropology and psychology, concepts that resolve the difficulties faced by anthropologists engaged in ethnographic interpretation of emotions – first that of "translation," second that of "emotives."

In philosophy, the problem of translation has attracted a great deal of attention in recent decades, but generally it has been regarded as a problem affecting communication, an issue that comes up *between* persons (Quine, Davidson, Alcoff). It has not been widely recognized that translation must necessarily come up within the individual as well. The Stroop color-naming task and its analogues show, however, that the path from a perceived patch of color to the correct name for that color – even for the native speaker – is a long and circuitous one. By careful manipulation, experimenters can increase or decrease the length and the sinuosity of that path. Regarding "cognition," even "consciousness," as largely a matter of translation tasks allows a critique of the poststructuralist concept of language and points the way to an interpretive method that can utilize psychological test results without fear of slipping into Cartesian dualism.

In the context of cognition as translation, it becomes necessary to find new intermediary phenomena lying between langue and parole. Utterances are not based on one language alone; they are translations into that language of a small part of the flow of coded messages that an awake body generates. The intermediaries proposed here are "activated thought material" and "attention"; the former consists of a range of current matters in various codes, the latter is the locus of the most intense translation activity. Emotion can thus be defined as an array of loosely linked thought material that tends to be activated simultaneously (which may take the form of a schema), and that is too large to be translated into action or utterance over a brief time horizon. The examples of "angry at sister" and "in love" were offered to help visualize this definition.

Emotional expressions can thus be considered as utterances aimed at briefly characterizing the current state of activated thought material that exceeds the current capacity of attention. Such expression, by analogy with speech acts, can be said to have (1) descriptive appearance, (2) relational intent, and (3) self-exploring and self-altering effects. Because of this third property, emotional expressions, which I call emotives, are like performatives in that they do something to the world. As a first suggestion of the significance of the concept of emotives, it was noted that sincerity and self-deception must be redefined and rethought.

With this theoretical scaffolding now in place, we have already restored agency and historical significance to the disaggregated self. It now remains to construct a notion of emotional liberty as a political ideal that can be used to make judgments about emotional regimes both Western and non-Western, removing the conceptual roadblock that has developed in the anthropology of emotions. This will be the task of the next chapter.

CHAPTER 4

Emotional Liberty

The concept of emotives elaborated in Chapter 3, developed in response to a range of problems encountered by researchers on emotions, has broad implications for the understanding of social life and politics. The present chapter offers a preliminary exploration of these implications. They will be spelled out in greater detail in Part II, which examines a specific period of political and social change.

Researchers on emotions in fields other than anthropology have frequently neglected the political implications of their work. Psychologists have had very little to say on this issue. Philosophers and historians who have written on emotions in recent years have often expressed only tangential interest in the political dimension of their ideas (e.g., Solomon 1984, 1992; De Sousa 1987). Speech act theorists have, for the most part, treated their subfield as a highly technical one, concerning language and intention, requiring no exploration of political issues. A number of philosophers, historians, and literary critics concerned with gender have recognized the political implications of the West's gendered conception of emotions (e.g., Greenspan 1988; Jaggar 1989; DeJean 1991; Schiesari 1992; Burack 1994; Roper 1994; Pinch 1996 – in addition to the anthropologists mentioned in Chapter 2). But these observers have focused their attention too much on redressing this imbalance and too little on the larger implications of the whole mental ontology their work has put into question.

Anthropologists represent an important exception to the general aversion to politics displayed by researchers on emotions. But their work has been hampered by fear of ethnocentrism and the ongoing critique of the culture concept; and, as a result, those working on emotions tend to split according to whether they wish to offer political critiques of the West or political critiques of the social orders they study. Anthropologists working on emotions, in addition, have lagged far behind others in their discipline in conceptualizing historical change. In this chapter I will show how the concept of emotives can provide a foundation for a politically useful reconception of the relation between individual and collectivity, that is, a reconception of liberty. This idea of liberty will make possible, in turn, political analysis of cultural variation and explanation of historical change, and it will point toward a form of political engagement that is not reductionist, condescending, or ethnocentric.

LIBERTY AND HISTORY IN THE ANTHROPOLOGY OF EMOTIONS

As we saw in Chapter 2, anthropologists working on emotions have confronted a severe difficulty in attempting to make political judgments of emotional regimes. Some have chosen to formulate a harsh political critique of Western ideas about emotions, based on their findings in the field. In non-Western contexts, they have found, emotions are rarely regarded as private, quasi-biological responses that endanger our reason; much more often they are valued as collective performances. In addition, they have insisted that the wide range of variation in emotional practices undercuts the Western biological view. Other anthropologists have emphasized the emotional impact of political repression and exile in states such as Iran, China, or El Salvador, where the local governments have engaged in policies of systematic violence and disciplinary coercion that no Westerner would attempt to excuse. But no anthropologist of emotions has offered a conceptual basis for making political judgments about both Western and non-Western practices at the same time, including communities undergoing political crisis and communities whose way of life is not currently subject to severe pressure from outside.

This difficulty has been compounded by an inability on the part of anthropologists of emotion to talk about historical change in emotions or the performances associated with emotions. While most practitioners in the discipline have been won over to a strong awareness of historical change, anthropologists of emotions have continued to use the "ethnographic present" in describing their findings. There is a direct relation between this presentism and the roadblock to political judgment. Both stem from a problem in conceptualizing the emotional individual.

The problem with the politics of emotions is understanding in what way the individual submits and why it matters. Anthropologists of emotions have proven themselves highly sensitive to the workings of political institutions, deference, authority, and gender; but they have not been able to show what is at stake for the individual in submitting to such institutions, in accepting and feeling the emotions prescribed by specific family organizations, in embracing emotional styles that render them humble, obedient, deferential – or aggressive, independent, arrogant. Can a person who feels an emotion that is a learned response, a product of social construction, be oppressed – in the political sense of the term – by this feeling? The concept of emotions as used in the West is closely associated with the individual's most deeply espoused goals; to feel love for one's spouse or fear of one's opponent, presumably, is to be moved by those things one most authentically wants. It is hard to see how a person can be oppressed by his or her most authentic, most deeply embraced, goals. To make such a claim – that a certain person, group, or community is politically oppressed without knowing it – would require that one be prepared to assert something about the nature of the individual. Such an assertion, by definition, would have to apply to the individual as universally constituted, outside the parameters of any given "culture." Who would have the temerity, today, to make positive claims about this politically charged issue? The ethnocentric dangers of such essentialist discourse have been so thoroughly rehearsed that many have chosen to fall silent, despite the conceptual vacuum that results. Yet only on this evacuated terrain can one hope to formulate a critical political judgment about emotional culture. That power is exercised is of no consequence unless there is something at stake. What is it the individual loses by submitting to, embracing unreflectively, a collectively constructed emotional common sense? If nothing, then we have no grounds upon which to critique Western emotional common sense, and much of the feminist, poststructuralist, and cultural critiques of the Western individual offered in recent decades has no meaning or purpose. If there is something that can be lost, then it can be lost everywhere, by anyone.

There are two practitioners of the ethnography of emotion who come significantly closer than others in the field to providing a politically grounded historical depiction of emotions, Geoffrey White and Unni Wikan. Their work deserves a brief examination here, because both force us to appreciate the interlinked character of political judgment and historical explanation.

Wikan, despite the ill-defined character of her notion of resonance, offers a clear-cut, full, and original analysis of the political dimension of emotional expression, in her study *Managing Turbulent Hearts: A Balinese Formula for Living* (Wikan 1990). As noted in Chapter 2, where previous ethnographers had described the Balinese as almost devoid of feeling, Wikan insists that Balinese individuals are actually engaged in a constant struggle to match their emotional expression to the strict norms of the community.

To show how emotional management and political power interact, Wikan tells the story of a school teacher who was fired by the village council for encouraging too much independence among his pupils. Among those involved in firing him was his closest friend, a powerful local figure, who gave nothing away of the planned dismissal until the last moment. The fired teacher was openly disconsolate and embittered; he repeatedly berated his wife – who attempted to keep up a smiling face in the proper way, despite the humiliating and terrifying impropriety of her husband's reactions. He denounced his powerful friend to anyone who would listen. But his outbursts only ensured his increasing marginalization. As with his teaching, so with his personal response to dismissal, he was out of touch with the normative tone of village collective self-control. Years later he discovered that his good friend, far from being an instigator of the dismissal, had gone along with the plan only out of fear of losing his own influence. Just as this powerful villager revealed nothing of the plan to his friend, so he said nothing of his own efforts to counter it, leaving the former teacher to find out in his own way. In the end they were reconciled. Through this story, Wikan allows us to see that in Bali heroic, virtuoso self-management in conformity with collective norms brings status and power.

Close examination of a case of deviance is rare in the anthropology of emotions, precisely because most practitioners lack a conceptual framework for situating it. Wikan's capacity to examine the political implications of emotional expression is directly linked to her theory of the "double-anchored self" which is presented as an alternative, and a direct challenge, to the prevailing constructionism in the ethnography of emotions. A double-anchored self maintains an equilibrium by effortful pursuit of expression to modify feeling and pursuit of feeling to modify behavior – effortful pursuit aptly dubbed "management," so long as one remains aware that it is not easy to draw a line between what manages and what is managed within this self. A self that is double-anchored is a self that cannot be encompassed within a discourse or defined by a practice; it is a self that can be molded by discourse, altered by practice to a significant degree, but never entirely or predictably, never to the same degree from one person to the next. The double-anchored self, as Wikan conceives it, is quite close to the notion of the disaggregated self presented in Chapter 3, in which the broad range of activated thought material contrasts with the small scope of the material that attention can deal with actively at any given time. The Balinese concepts of face and heart capture this contrast and help them think about the management efforts this contrast readily gives rise to. But Wikan's study is oriented entirely toward the present and offers no account of historical change.

Geoffrey White does not propose to write a history of emotions in his important study of the island of Santa Isabel (Solomon Islands), *Identity Through History* (White 1991). But he has examined the performance of emotion on Santa Isabel in other studies (White 1990a, 1990b) and is alive to the process by which emotions are enacted and given collective force as norms. As a result his historical research allows us to glimpse, as perhaps no other historical ethnography has done, how a politically meaningful history of emotions might be framed.

White's painstaking collection and comparison of written and oral accounts of the conversion and subsequent colonial takeover of the island allow him to piece together a gripping picture of its recent social history. Prior to the first successes of Anglican missionaries beginning around 1890, the population of Santa Isabel had been greatly reduced by a period of endemic raiding. The operations of slave traders in the region encouraged seafaring groups from other islands in the Solomons, and from Santa Isabel itself, to make frequent expeditions in pursuit of captives. Captives were sold to slave traders in return for modern firearms and other supplies; captives were also used locally in rituals of human sacrifice and cannibalism. Groups less adept at such seaborne raiding moved into the highlands, concealing themselves in the forests and building sturdy wooden forts. Coastal villages, once the norm, all but disappeared. Both seafarers and hill groups embraced raiding, warfare, headhunting, and human sacrifice as methods of ensuring their own power and security. The political focal point of these raiding groups were "chiefs" whose status was partly hereditary, partly based on proven prowess; chiefly lineage shrines sporting lines of enemies' skulls along their walls, and the bones of predecessors inside, sites of frequent ceremonies, shored up chiefs' reputations as masterful possessors of secret knowledge and magical power.

Today, islanders emphasize the contrast between this violent, impoverished heathen past and the peaceful Christian present. White rightly refuses to accept this contrast at face value. At the same time, one is struck by the repetition of certain themes in the conversion narratives White analyzes, themes of missionary bravery and missionary magical power, as well as of chiefly recognition that a peace policy might enhance their rule. For reasons difficult to penetrate, many chiefs saw in Christianity a new form of secret knowledge that might serve as a potent source of legitimacy.

Central to Christian conversion was the new salience of an emotion called *nahma*, a complex term which denotes soothing, gift giving, compromise, settlement. The term is translated locally using the English term "love"; nahma is considered to be the essential orientation of the Christian person. In local practice, the new centrality of nahma was associated with the willingness of chiefs to unite under the leadership of great regional chiefs (already Christianized) who sent missionaries to reside in their villages and teach the new ways.

White notes that older inhabitants of Santa Isabel remarked "a perceived shift in ethos during their lives such that the constant vigilance which was once maintained against sorcery and tabu violation may now be somewhat relaxed" (1991:246). But the lives of the previous generation, the generation of conversion, must have seen an even deeper shift in ethos; open violence disappeared; sorcery and tabu – because pagan – went underground; then, in the 1930s, colonial officials named headmen of their own choosing, threatening the power of chiefly lineages. Nahma and skill at talking and negotiating replaced warrior prowess as instruments of influence; and because Christian conversion came prior to colony status, Christianity could serve as a badge of indigenous identity and indigenous competence for self-rule. The limits of this transformation are difficult to gauge; White notes that stories of the pre-Christian past still convey "a sense of vitality and accomplishment" and that fear of magic still shapes much daily behavior (p. 40). The practice of rule on Santa Isabel, within the newly independent state of the Solomon Islands, is a peculiar mix of traditional oligarchic elements, church influence, and Western-style parliamentarism that concentrates power in a few hands. Recent troubles on the island of Guadalcanal underscore the ongoing fragility of this newly established polity, which is certain to undergo further substantial

transformations. Still, it is hard not to empathize with those who celebrate the end of the raiding heyday of 1860–1900. Why should we not
celebrate the missionary heroes, both British and Melanesian, who
risked their lives to bring about this aim?

White notes that the feelings of *natahni* (sorrow) and *kokhoni* (sympathy) of the *thautaru* song, sung on the occasion of sons' inheriting the
houses and gardens of their fathers, also characterize the local sentiments toward the conversion period and its (chiefly and missionary)
heroes. They, like nurturant fathers, are invoked with sorrowful gratitude in special thautaru chants; their brave actions are retold in theatrical reenactments. We cannot complacently imagine that justice now
reigns on Santa Isabel. But a profound historical turn that has enhanced
the place of nahma, natahni, and kokhoni on that island, replacing violence, slave trading, and malevolent magic as the foundation of political legitimacy, ought to engage our respect and our gratitude.

How can we build a firm foundation for this kind of political judgment, so that it is not vacuously Eurocentric and "humanist" (Abu-
Lughod 1991)? From the foregoing review of the anthropological
literature emerges a list of requirements: We need a conceptual frame
that acknowledges the importance of management (as opposed to construction) of emotion, that allows political distinctions among different
management styles on the basis of a concept of emotional liberty, and
that permits the narration of significant historical shifts in such management styles. In the section that follows, I will build such a frame on
the foundation of the concept of emotives elaborated in the last chapter.

COORDINATION OF GOALS AND
EMOTIONAL NAVIGATION

In the following discussion, I employ the concept of "goal" in deference to its widespread current usage among psychologists. As Oatley
(1992) and Wegner (1994) note, any control mechanism must include
two functions: (1) the capacity to initiate and terminate an operation,
(2) a means of checking the status of the operation. These two functions correspond to the two parts of "if . . . then" commands in soft-
ware programs or to the two elements of a smoke detector: the
chemically sensitive switch and the alarm which it turns on and off.
The nervous system of any animal obviously accomplishes thousands
of similar control functions. Within cognition, thoughts that are capable

of both triggering and terminating subordinate thoughts or actions are referred to as goals. Baars et al. (1997), for example, refer to the goal a person is currently pursuing as a "goal image," because this coherent thought must supply sufficient details to allow many unconscious automatisms to initiate and terminate component tasks. Uttering a sentence requires coordination of more or less automatic application of rules of syntax, more or less automatic search of a lexicon, command of facial and oral muscles, and other capacities. It requires, in addition, that the performance be monitored, so that slips or false starts can be corrected. We are all aware of how halting and hesitant speech often is, as monitoring is accomplished and interruptions or restarts are initiated to keep the performance on track. Some hesitation may also reflect shifts in the precise character of the goal of the utterance itself.

While psychologists have not explored the implications of goal coordination very much, all recognize that goals overlap and mutually implicate each other and that they must be organized into hierarchies. Bower (1992), Oatley (1992), Clore (1994), and anthropologist D'Andrade (1992), as noted in Chapter 1, have all pointed out the close relationship that must exist between coordination of goals and emotion. Strong emotions such as joy or grief indicate the relevance of high-priority goals to a present condition; sudden emotions such as the rapid onset of fear or anger indicate that a goal not currently being pursued must be given higher priority in response to a surprise or disappointment in the environment. In Chapter 1, I argued that it is the goal-relevant intensity and valence of emotions that renders them inherently enjoyable or inherently uncomfortable. It is precisely here that emotions become politically relevant, because they are capable of guiding action long after explicit threats or explicit rules have been forgotten.

It is obvious by now that an adequate theory of emotions must be built on an entirely new terrain, with newly defined terms as free as we can possibly make them of suspect ethnocentric implications. We must take nothing for granted and provide an account for every issue that may turn out to be important when we begin examining particular cases.

Goal coordination is, quite simply, an issue of bewildering complexity, for those who do it, for those who attempt to understand it. The environment is challenging; life will not continue unless a certain number of goals are accorded high priority and their coordination is assured. Coordination of behavior with others is also extraordinarily rewarding. Where there are continuing communities of successfully surviving individuals, we may presume that most members are constantly engaged in the pursuit of a dense network of interrelated goals, and that the community has deeply influenced the construction of most individuals' networks. Consider the example of a person who says, "I am looking forward to getting married next week, but I just don't want to breathe any more." Or, "The only reason I wear clothes is because my mother told me to." Such statements would be regarded as deviant in many cultural contexts, not just in the West. Westerners would regard them as evidence of emotional disturbance. The English word *emotion* is often used to refer to thought material activated by coordination and priority problems; and these utterances would represent evidence of a startling breakdown of normal coordination of goals. As discussed with the examples of "angry at sister" and "in love" in the last chapter, emotions often entail sweeping orientations of goal networks, built up over time, as a consequence of hundreds of actions, and cannot be evaluated or rebuilt on short notice. Such orientations, when they come before attention activated by a sudden development in the environment, do often seem to be involuntary. At the same time, without them, it would be absurd to talk of doing anything "voluntarily"; emotions are a kind of precondition of volition and motivation; they convey the weight of hundreds of past volitions and motivations into the present. Specific activities almost always represent combinations and compromises among many goals.

The preparation of a meal, for example, may involve consideration of goals with reference to relationships, nutrition, time usage, "esthetic" or taste expectations, religious observances or prohibitions, monetary expenditure, usage of available perishables or seasonal foods. The particular can only be apprehended as an intersection of innumerable properties that can be variously categorized, each of which may call up its own goal or set of goals. Here is where strict logic leaves one most at sea, either in deciding what to do or in understanding how others have combined such factors in a decision. This is the original domain of personality psychology or of cultural interpretation, when these are conceived as the study of "nonscientific" or "nonrational" dimensions of behavior. Scientific experiment represents an attempt to eliminate multiple determinations, so that "causes" may be isolated. For this very reason, scientific method has run up against a brick wall when it has attempted to explore this dimension of human behavior. No one chooses recipes for dinner, or accords their political allegiance, on the basis of a single "cause." There is no unidimensional way to decide what to make for dinner, or what to wear, or what to say next. Human behavior is, in this sense, "overdetermined."

The constant activation of thought material associated with the complex tasks of goal coordination – emotion as defined here – comes up, inevitably, as an issue in its own right, about which special goals must be formulated. In the simplest case, activated thought material signals the existence of a goal conflict that cannot be resolved except by rejection outright of one of the goals. A soldier, about to kill his first opponent on the field of battle, feels a sudden, cold fear as a wave of guilt and revulsion threatens to paralyze him. The goal of nonviolence and the goal of soldiering are in conflict, conflict of a kind that can be resolved only by setting one aside. If nonviolence is set aside, mental control will be marshaled to eliminate it from attention, so that the complex activities of soldiering may continue without interference. Mental control of this kind derives from a sense of self. The self must become an object of "cognition," and must also be viewed as a terrain of action in which there is something at stake. The vast range of activated thought material which calls for attention to provide guidance for goal coordination suddenly comes before attention as a source of danger. These activations must somehow be trimmed and reordered.

Emotives are one instrument for attempting such trimming and reordering. But, because they have exploratory as well as self-altering effects, they do not always represent compliant tools of mental control. They may as easily, inadvertently, activate material that is capable of subverting the mental-control goals they are formulated to serve, and they may also heighten what Wegner and Smart (1997) call "deep activation." To maintain equilibrium by use of such utterances requires experience; their effects are idiosyncratic and difficult to predict, and also vital to the social identity of the speaker. Even to know what kind of "equilibrium" one might wish to maintain may take some searching, some choosing among available models or norms. Hence the sense, quite widespread in the world's communities as reported in ethnographic work on emotions, that emotional control requires constant effort and that those who do it well are relatively rare, deserving of admiration and authority. A normative style of emotional management is a fundamental element of every political regime, of every cultural hegemony. Leaders must display mastery of this style; those who fail to conform may be marginalized or severely sanctioned. In other cases, there may be a hierarchy of contrasting styles, failure to conform to one or another renders one's identity unclear, subject to exclusion.

But the political implications of such normative styles cannot be appreciated unless it is recognized that "management" is an inadequate metaphor for encompassing everything that emotives do. This term has been used by both Hochschild (1983) and Wikan (1989, 1990) to name the use of emotional expression as a tool for altering emotions, in a way that brings both researchers very close to the concept of emotives being proposed here. But to "manage" is to organize means to a certain known end or goal. Emotional management styles are organized around normative goals. However, emotives are both self-exploring and self-altering. It is never certain what effect they will have. Unexpected effects are sometimes costly. (Edmund Muskie, for example, was forced to drop out of a U.S. presidential primary race in 1972 because, trying to express anger, late one night, he began crying on television.) The complex thought activations that are emotions often tend toward changes in goals or ideals, often expose tension or conflict among them. As a result, management can easily break down; or a given set of management strategies can be put to new uses. The self that is managing, and its intention to manage, are always subject to revision. "Navigation" might be a better metaphor than "management," for what emotives accomplish, because navigation includes the possibility of radically changing course, as well as that of making constant corrections in order to stay on a chosen course. But even "navigation" implies purposive action, whereas changes of goals are only purposive if they are carried out in the name of higher-priority goals. Goal changes at the highest level of priority cannot be "intentionally" carried out; they have no goal. Such changes reflect complex reorderings of the many-to-many mappings of goal networks. They are the result, often, of unexpected self-altering effects of emotive utterances or of emotional activations. "Navigation" is used here to refer to a broad array of emotional changes, including high-level goal shifts. "Navigation" thus encompasses "management," which is the use of emotives' self-altering effects, in the name of a fixed set of goals.

EMOTIONS AND POLITICAL REGIMES

Emotional Liberty, Emotional Suffering, Emotional Effort

The idea of navigation as a universal, central characteristic of emotional life makes possible a preliminary definition of "emotional liberty" as the freedom to change goals in response to bewildering, ambivalent thought activations that exceed the capacity of attention and challenge the reign of high-level goals currently guiding emotional management. This is freedom, not to make rational choices, but to undergo conversion experiences and life-course changes involving numerous contrasting, often incommensurable factors.

The idea that emotives make possible navigation – in which the self both undergoes changes of goals and seeks to maintain consistency around the pursuit of certain goals – allows for a politically relevant definition of "suffering." It is one thing to suffer from pneumonia or cancer. It is quite another to suffer while concealing information under torture.[1] The suffering of such torture is precisely the suffering that results when high-priority goals come into conflict. Torture to extract information or confession presumes that preservation of one's health, wholeness, and freedom from pain is a high-priority goal. In situations of political conflict, opponents may artificially bring this goal of health and wholeness into conflict with another goal or set of goals that the individual previously held as quite compatible with health and wholeness, such as the honor of one's family, clan, or party, or the moral integrity of one's commitments, or the health and wholeness of comrades. Whether the individual resists the torturers or gives in, he or she will experience emotional suffering either way.

Suffering that results from goal conflicts is seen also in love relationships when, for example, the desire to be with the loved one or to engage in sexual acts with the loved one comes into conflict with the desire to further the loved one's own goals. This happens most obviously when the loved one makes clear a desire to avoid the lover or be free of the relationship. Suffering results not only from the thought that one is unworthy of the loved one, but also, and especially, from the conflict of goals. When and in what ways ought one to seek out the loved one in order to bring about a change of heart? When and in what ways ought one to accept the loved one's expressed aversion for oneself? Emotional suffering occurs when high-priority goals are in conflict in this way, and when all available choices seem to counter one or more high-priority goals. Seeking out a loved one may realize a high-priority desire to be with that person, but it may also expose one to open rejection – and thus to the knowledge one has not embraced the loved one's own goals – as well as to puzzles involved in valuing highly someone who does not reciprocate. Revealing a truth to a torturer may end the physical pain but require the sacrifice of a moral or political ideal. Resisting the torturer seems to implicate one in

---

[1] Torture to gain information is a specific kind of torture; see Asad (1997); Caron (1999).

self-harm. Torture victims thus continue to suffer emotionally long after the physical pains have ended.

Spousal abuse, a matter of international concern in recent years, is one of many violent relationships where the victim is often, to some extent, willing. The victim holds the abusive goals of the partner higher than his or her own goal of personal health and wholeness. But resolving the goal conflict this way, by the effort of holding the abusive spouse's goals above health and wholeness – it is widely believed – involves acute suffering, in the sense that I am using the term: Either the victim believes the violence is justified, holding the self in contempt, or else he or she constantly undergoes conflict between the goals of embracing a loved one's goal and pursuing one's own health and wholeness. Holding the self in contempt is an automatic source of goal conflict and therefore suffering, just because the more highly the self prizes a goal, the more that goal comes in danger of taint from the contempt aimed at the self who prizes.

Defining emotional suffering as an acute form of goal conflict makes it possible to elaborate on the concept of emotional effort proposed in Chapter 3, in the section entitled "Translation, activation, and attention." Physical effort is the maintaining of an action or exertion in spite of rising pain or loss of strength in skeletal musculature. The metaphor of "emotional effort," as it will be used here, refers to the maintaining of a goal or action plan in spite of rising suffering due to goal conflict. Athletic effort almost always involves a combination of physical and emotional effort. The emotional effort consists of maintaining the goal of skillful performance against conflicting desires for physical comfort and enjoyment or freedom to pursue other activities.

Emotional suffering and emotional freedom, when so defined, are not opposites; a state of emotional freedom would not be one devoid of suffering, nor require no effort to sustain. Emotional suffering, as elaborated here, is likely to accompany any important shifts in life goals, both in a preliminary stage, before the shift is embraced, and in a "working-through" stage, where the suffering may be supplanted by grief or may take the form of guilt or shame.

Induced Goal Conflict

Central to the life of individuals, open to deep social influence, emotions are of the highest political significance. Any enduring political regime must establish as an essential element a normative order for emotions, an "emotional regime." Such emotional regimes can be placed, in a preliminary way, on a spectrum. At one extreme are strict regimes which require individuals to express normative emotions and to avoid deviant emotions. In these regimes, a limited number of emotives are modeled through ceremony or official art forms. Individuals are required to utter these emotives in appropriate circumstances, in the expectation that normative emotions will be enhanced and habituated. Those who refuse to make the normative utterances (whether of respect for a father, love for a god or a king, or loyalty to an army) are faced with the prospect of severe penalties. Those who make the required utterances and gestures, but for whom the appropriate emotions are not enhanced or habituated, may seek to conceal their lack of zeal. If they are unsuccessful, they, too, face penalties. The penalties may come in the form of torture, aimed at extracting a change through induced goal conflict, or in the form of simple violence, confinement, deprivation, exile. Either way, the prospect of such penalties induces goal conflict not just in their present victims but in all those who do not react within the normative range to the emotive utterances required by the regime. Such goal conflict, for many, significantly increases the likelihood that required emotives will have the appropriate effect. The prospect of severe penalties, because of the goal conflict it induces whenever deviant emotions occur, renders the emotional enhancement effects of normative emotives soothing, even pleasurable. Many will find that the strict emotional discipline of their regime works well for them, shoring up a personal emotional management style that serves as the core of a coherent, rewarding way of life.

At the other end of the spectrum are regimes that use such strict emotional discipline only in certain institutions (armies, schools, priesthoods) or only at certain times of the year or certain stages of the life cycle. These regimes set few limits on emotional navigation outside these restricted domains. In them, many individuals, operating without the management tools of induced goal conflicts, encounter difficulties coordinating their goals or holding to a single course over time. Rather than promoting a core of conformists and a marginalized minority, such a regime may serve as an umbrella for a variety of emotional styles. Some individual life paths will stray across two or more of these varieties; others will cling faithfully to the one most familiar from birth. Subgroups may form (cults, mafias) on the basis of shared preferences for certain stronger penalties (verbal abuse, torture, death) that shore up their emotional management more firmly than those offered by the prevailing regime. These must be combated, however, because they threaten to reshape the existing regime in their own image.

Thus, very roughly, one might generalize that strict regimes offer strong emotional management tools at the expense of allowing greater scope for self-exploration and navigation. Loose regimes allow for navigation and allow diverse sets of management tools to be fashioned locally, individually, or through robust subgroup formation. Why should we favor one type of regime over another? Against the strict regimes, two points may be made: (1) They achieve their stability by inducing goal conflict and inflicting intense emotional suffering on those who do not respond well to the normative emotives. (2) When such regimes pronounce anathemas on all deviation, they set themselves against an important human possibility – or vulnerability, the vulnerability to shifting purposes or goals, to conversion experiences, crisis, doubt. Possibility, vulnerability – the pairing of these terms is significant. The higher the level at which goal shifting occurs, the less the element of intention or choice enters into the change, because the notions of intention or choice imply a preexisting goal or aim – a notion of self, a long-term plan – in terms of which the shift is chosen. The highest level determination of goals must occur, by definition, "for no reason." It is here, at the highest level, that multivocal thought activations may impinge upon the arrangement of those goals that steer attention. When change comes here – where certain goals may have long resided without ever coming before attention as objects of reflection – the individual has no sense of anticipating or "choosing." Strict regimes exploit the power of emotives to shape emotions, to serve as management tools, but ignore or denounce the power of emotional activations to "impose" unanticipated or "unwanted" change on the individual. They thus offer, in the end, an incomplete and contradictory vision of human nature and human possibilities. In the short run, as institutions cope with war, epidemic, famine, scarcity, or the harsh labor requirements of certain technologies and certain environments, the induced suffering a regime depends on and the incompleteness of its notion of humanity may have little importance. In the very long run, they are of the greatest importance. They become particularly salient in situations of conquest, colonization, or expansion, when the normative management strategy must be imposed on new populations. Emotional suffering becomes epidemic.

When it comes time to say what we stand for and what we oppose, the incompleteness and contradictory character of the strict regime's notion of humanity represents a political failure that can only be rejected. This incompleteness coincides with a higher incidence of emotional suffering than would prevail under a loose regime. It is the conjunction of an incomplete or contradictory vision of humanity and of induced suffering aimed at sustaining allegiance to such incompleteness that renders certain regimes unjust.

But what forms of induced emotional suffering are allowable under a regime of emotional freedom? This is a familiar problem in all definitions of political liberty – spelling out what limits on liberty are acceptable in the interest of liberty – but an answer must be offered, in any case. One answer is to pronounce as allowable and necessary the inducing of emotional suffering, through penalties, in all those who espouse induced emotional suffering as a means to any end other than the maintenance of emotional freedom. This is an answer compatible with the liberal tradition and with the notion of the rule of law. Another answer is to assert that one cannot force people to be free; one cannot, by means of induced emotional suffering, bring people to forswear induced emotional suffering as a tool, as an instrument of rule or of community. In the short run it is not necessary to decide between them. Both answers are compatible with a political stance in favor of reducing induced suffering to a minimum – a stance that would motivate critical judgments of all existing polities.

The ideal of reducing emotional suffering to the necessary minimum has implications for political action as well as for political judgment. Political action against undue use of induced emotional suffering cannot be effective if such action itself makes undue use of induced emotional suffering in order to win compliance with its aims. Fighting fire with fire may only perpetuate the ills one seeks to end. (This point is illustrated vividly in the case of the French Revolution, discussed in Part II.)

Of course, this schematism encounters problems as soon as it is applied to a real social order. Capitalist democracies, for example, appear to offer great scope for navigation, but, in practice, capacities and options are limited by contractual relationships (that is, by access to money and property). Those who depend on a single contractual relationship for their income and social identity (married women under certain legal regimes, salaried employees) are, in practice, severely limited in the types of emotional management strategies they may adopt – even though these strategies vary widely from one enterprise or household to another. Within families, beyond the reach of legal action, still other types of strategies may be common. (See, on these issues, Reddy 1987, 1997a). Such societies thus belong more to the middle of the spectrum and produce all sorts of configurations: conforming majorities, marginalized minorities, varying management strategies within the majority, organized cults and mafias. A large industrial society offers the prospect of many different social relationships and emotional management styles, the rich and well educated uniting around one, the laboring poor being subjected to a variety of others. Gender-based and ethnic variation are usually also marked and exploited to sustain a complex and inequitable division of labor. Vital, large-scale exchange of money and goods, rather than serving as a unifying factor, can harden and consolidate stark differences. Adult male coal miners, women garment workers in a sweatshop, or flight attendants have very different social relationships and live in very different emotional atmospheres, whereas the executives who command them have much more in common.

In practice, such complex social orders can also offer individuals the opportunity to create relationships or localized organizations that provide them with emotional refuge. In these contexts norms are relaxed or even reversed; mental control efforts may be temporarily set aside. Affective connections, otherwise illicit, may be established, even celebrated. Such emotional refuges may take a great variety of forms, from private understandings, to informal sociability, to Carnival-type ritual, to international secret brotherhoods. They probably play a role in most emotional regimes. Their significance is polyvalent. They may make the current order more livable for some people, some of the time. For others, or in other times, they may provide a place from which contestation, conflict, and transformation are launched.

The theory being elaborated here has, by this time, given rise to a series of special definitions of terms that it would be convenient to list.

> *emotions.* Goal-relevant activations of thought material that exceed the translating capacity of attention within a short time horizon.
>
> *emotives.* A type of speech act different from both performative and constative utterances, which both describes (like constative utterances) and changes (like performatives) the world, because emotional expression has an exploratory and a self-altering effect on the activated thought material of emotion.

emotional management. Instrumental use of the self-altering effects of emotives in the service of a goal. May be subverted by the exploratory effects of emotives.

emotional navigation. The fundamental character of emotional life. Emotions are a sphere of "fugitive instrumentalism," in which the exploratory and self-altering effects of emotives sometimes work in tandem, cooperatively, under the guidance of certain high-priority goals and, in other instances, part ways, such that the individual may either sink into "self-deception" or undergo a "conversion experience."

emotional liberty. The freedom to change goals in response to bewildering, ambivalent thought activations that exceed the capacity of attention and challenge the reign of high-level goals currently guiding emotional management. This is freedom, not to make rational choices, but to undergo or derail conversion experiences and life-course changes involving numerous contrasting incommensurable factors.

emotional suffering. An acute form of goal conflict, especially that brought on by emotional thought activations. Political torture and unrequited love (both in the Western context) are examples of emotional suffering.

emotional effort. Maintaining a goal or action plan in spite of rising suffering due to goal conflict.

emotional regime. The set of normative emotions and the official rituals, practices, and emotives that express and inculcate them; a necessary underpinning of any stable political regime.

induced goal conflict. The effects at a distance (that is, the deterrent or exemplary effects) of policies of punishment, torture, exclusion, or imprisonment which sanction deviance from an emotional regime.

emotional refuge. A relationship, ritual, or organization (whether informal or formal) that provides safe release from prevailing emotional norms and allows relaxation of emotional effort, with or without an ideological justification, which may shore up or threaten the existing emotional regime.

This set of interlinked concepts is sufficient to allow historical analysis that is at once ethnographically rich, sensitive to deviance and diversity, and politically engaged. The idea is not to apply these terms mechanically to a given body of evidence, but to hold them ready in the background. They can provide points of reference that guide our interpretive endeavor beyond relativism, toward a defensible commitment to liberty.

POLITICAL EVALUATION OF CASE MATERIAL

This array of concepts frees one of the necessity of theorizing culture, power, or identity characteristics, such as race, class, gender, or ethnicity, which have preoccupied scholars so much of late. The only questions that need to be asked are, Who suffers? Is the suffering an unavoidable consequence of emotional navigation or does this suffering help to shore up a restrictive emotional regime? That is, is this suffering a tragedy or an injustice? In developing specific answers to these questions, identities, the cultural field, and political institutions come back into play as historical phenomena, but not as independent theoretical entities. We seek conceptualizations of these things that will best allow us to grasp emotional suffering. In Part II of this study, I will examine historical material on France for the period 1700 to 1850. An appreciation of one episode of emotional history will breathe life into the theoretical language we have just explored. By way of conclusion for this chapter's analysis, however, I wish to show briefly how the above schema can be immediately put to use evaluating individual instances of conflict and deviance. To do so I turn to two cases of arranged marriage, one from nineteenth-century France, one that of Rashīd and Fāyga, derived from Abu-Lughod's (1986) study of the Awlad ʿAli, already discussed in Chapter 2.

In 1840, in the village of Meudon, about two miles southwest of Paris, a marriage was arranged between Palmyre Désirée Picard and Nicolas Marie Gogue.[2] The bride's mother owned a small vineyard and sold wine out of her home, both for resale and for immediate consumption. The groom's family also owned vineyards in the neighboring village of Clamart. The day after the wedding, the husband began complaining loudly to whoever would listen that his new wife was two months' pregnant by another man. "I thought I was entering a

---

[2] The material on the Gogue case is derived from the Tribunal civil de Versailles, in the Archives de l'ancien département de Seine-et-Oise, in two different series: (1) 3U Registre d'audiences et de jugements civils, 1ᵉ chambre, 1839, 1840, judgments of 15 November 1839, 31 March 1840, 19 May 1840, 25 November 1840; (2) 3U 0246[48], *Enquête* of 26 June 1840, *Contr'enquête* of 1 July 1840.

garden full of flowers," he repeated to at least two of his new in-laws, "but I was entering a desert." The husband's father thought that the trouble began when Gogue saw how his new wife behaved toward a certain Guillaume during the wedding party. This Guillaume had worked for Mme Picard and was also a frequent customer in her wineshop. But, whatever cause Gogue may have had, his statements constituted public insult, a matter recognized in law as one of the few legitimate grounds (including cruelty and violence) for marital separation. (Divorce was not possible at that time.) Soon there was word of violence occurring in the new household. The whole village knew within days that the couple were "not getting on together" ("ne fait pas bon ménage ensemble"). Palmyre began sleeping separately from her husband. About three months after the marriage Gogue attacked his wife more severely than usual, dragging her from her bed by her hair, beating her, then attempting to strangle her. Her cries brought several neighbors into their bedroom; soon the village police officer (*commissaire de police*) arrived. Witnesses reported marks on her leg and on her neck. Palmyre moved back to her mother's the next day and sued for a separation. The evidence of strangulation, seen by several villagers, coupled with the public insults made the wife's case quite strong; a separation was granted later in the year.

In his deposition, the police agent noted that the husband's violence was aggravated by the fact that the woman was visibly pregnant. Although none of the other thirteen witnesses – including the mother of the wife and the father of the husband – had mentioned the pregnancy, this comment suggests Gogue was right, that his new wife was pregnant at the wedding. According to the wife's brother, their fights had begun on their wedding night, hardly leaving time for an interlude of intimacy. Right or wrong in his charges against his wife, Gogue had been severely scolded three days after the marriage by his father, who told him to "hold his tongue" and beg pardon from his wife and mother-in-law. Gogue went to his wife and fell to his knees, in tears, asking to be forgiven. His wife accepted the apology. But within a few days, Gogue could not contain himself and began denouncing her again. The father reproached Mme Picard for continuing to receive Guillaume in her wineshop after the wedding, which only exasperated his son further. "He was no longer in possession of all his faculties," Gogue's father maintained; "if only his mother-in-law and his wife had taken a few precautions, they could have brought him to reason."

None of the fourteen witnesses in the case suggested the young wife had done anything wrong – to have done so under oath would have constituted public insult in itself – but the protestations about her virtue were few and vague. The unspoken assumption of all, including Gogue's father and uncle, appeared to be that the truth of the matter was irrelevant. Gogue must protect his wife's reputation, even if undeserved, thereby protecting his own. He must make the best of the situation. Gogue's father and uncle were nonetheless angry that his wife had persisted in her suit for separation; she, too, ought to devote herself to damage control and give her husband another chance. They blamed her mother for convincing her otherwise.

Central to the case, then, was Gogue's tendency to work himself into a state of heightened jealousy, grief, and rage with emotives so striking witnesses repeated them: "I thought I was entering a garden full of flowers, but I was entering a desert." "If you were not pregnant," he said to his wife on one occasion, "I would kill you." This strategy went against the norms of the community. Even his own family acknowledged he was in the wrong.

An historicist, or constructionist, approach to this episode would emphasize the distinct character and strength of the code of honor that ruled in this society, a code that allowed for a great deal of deviant behavior, so long as it was accomplished discreetly, a code that dictated the strongest family solidarity around matters of reputation. Since we do not live by such a code, the constructionist would insist, we are not in a position to make moral or political judgments about the choices made by these people.

The concept of emotives allows one, in contrast, to appreciate that this honor code dictated behaviors, and silences, that could have a strong shaping impact on one's emotions. Far from being a mere cultural construct or discourse, this code was an essential part of an emotional regime and favored a certain style of emotion management. From this perspective the actions of Gogue's elders take on a fascinating new significance. They urged him to express satisfaction with, and affection for, his pregnant wife and commitment to her child. They prescribed emotives for him. They believed that if he worked at such expressions he could master his jealousy and disappointment, save the marriage, and enjoy many possibilities that were closed off by a legal separation. He could have established a tolerant closeness with his wife, or at least a de facto estrangement, that would have minimized gossip and family dishonor and allowed for the possibility of legitimate offspring. Gogue's father believed that Mme Picard could have helped Gogue regain emotional equilibrium if she had closed her door to Guillaume, whose continuing visits to her house he believed only stimulated Gogue's suspicions. These were strategies of emotional management, and no interpretation of this episode can be complete that does not recognize their centrality.

In some respects the emotional regime Gogue was told to submit to was very rigid, in others, quite loose. (This regime will be considered in greater detail in Chapters 7 and 8.) As far as certain public behaviors and nonverbal cues were concerned, strict self-control was required. A duel might result from an eyebrow raised at the wrong moment (Nye 1993; Reddy 1997b). Those who gained mastery of themselves, and of the game of appearances demanded by honor, however, could entertain many choices about how one actually led one's life. The family members who scolded Gogue knew that there were many ways, besides marriage, to find one's "garden full of flowers," and many ways to find it even in marriage, so long as one's ideas about it were not too fixed. At the same time, the very silences enforced by the honor code could encourage false expectations, especially among the young, among those who tended to mistake appearances for realities or who, for whatever reason, could not tolerate compromise.

Where the honor code dictated silence, it was impossible to enunciate explicit public norms. Young Gogue may have been entirely unprepared for the ideas that his father, his uncle, and his new mother-in-law tried to communicate to him urgently in the days after his marriage. If he had heard of men whose wives were unfaithful, it was in the form of gossip, or in newspapers, novels, or plays – that is, in contexts that encouraged judgment and distancing.[3] The extent to which a man ought to tolerate in silence a wife's infractions was, in any case, a highly personal matter. Precisely because norms could not be enunciated openly, each person had to find his or her own way. Gogue was apparently thrown into prolonged turmoil by the discovery of his wife's pregnancy. It appears that he tried to reconcile with her after an initial outburst, but subsequently found he was unable to contain his shame and anger. To be happily married was a high-priority goal for him. But

---

[3] For further discussion of public norms and the circulation and influence of newspapers, novels, and plays, see the discussion in Chapter 7; see also Lyons (1987); Reddy (1993); Nye (1993); Cornut-Gentille (1996); Houbre (1997).

in a society where divorce was ruled out, one false step might put Gogue's goal out of reach. At first he sought to repair the situation in line with his father's advice. But the emotives his father wisely counselled him to utter (apologizing to wife and mother-in-law) did not have the desired effect. His management effort failed, and he chose, in the end, a different path. Violence against his wife was not apparently aimed at compelling her to take a given course of action. Instead it was simply a way to impose on her emotional suffering that matched the suffering he believed she had knowingly imposed on him. If scandal followed, scandal was what she deserved.

An honor code of this type combines flexibility and rigidity. Severe penalties await those who openly break its injunctions. Public opprobrium, gossip, disgrace of deviants such as Gogue and his wife (for both diverged from the norm) induce powerful goal conflict in a broader audience. But, so long as one remains adept at keeping up appearances, one can navigate one's way to many personal compromises. Court records of the period reveal many peculiar arrangements: husbands and wives who lived apart for years, still others who spent a few days a month together, others who married for reasons that had little to do with sexuality. The vast majority of such arrangements were kept silent, however, were known only to a few, and left no trace in the records. In the cases that found their way into the courts, something went wrong; one of the parties violated implicit understandings or had an unexpected change of heart (Reddy 1993, 1997b). In all cases the man's preferences were crucial; he could legally force his wife to live with him; her infidelities were illegal and punishable by imprisonment if he chose to lodge a formal complaint. His infidelities, so long as accomplished outside the home, were not illegal and even enjoyed a certain tolerance.

In her important study of emotion among the Awlad ʿAli, already mentioned, Abu-Lughod (1986) examines an unusually difficult marriage involving Rashīd, a man in his early forties, and Fāyga, his second wife, who was twenty years his junior. As was noted in Chapter 2, Rashīd showed undue preference for Fāyga. But Fāyga felt only aversion for her new, middle-aged husband; when she ran away, Rashīd did everything he could to get her back, angering many relatives who felt her departure was an insult.

The ghinnāwas Fāyga recited to give expression to her (otherwise) concealed feelings actually take the form of emotives. (This is true of most of the ghinnāwas reported in Abu-Lughod's study.)

> You want, oh dear one, to be disappointed
> and to fight about something not fated to be . . .
>
> On my breast I placed
> a tombstone, though I was not dead, oh loved one . . .
>
> If a new love match is not granted
> the ache in my mind will continue, oh beloved . . .
>   (1986:217–219)

In Abu-Lughod's view ghinnāwas make possible the depiction of the self as able to creatively master strong divergent feelings – an ability that played a central role in the ideal of honorable independence so many Awlad ʿAli strove to achieve. The concept of emotives, however, allows one to regard ghinnāwas as powerful tools for shaping and disciplining emotional material that stands in tension with the emotional regime's prevailing norm of tough, honorable independence. They may not always work as planned, however. Where many women used them to express feelings they wished to master, Fāyga, in the end, acted on her deviant feelings by running away and later by openly showing her aversion to spending nights with her new husband – very immature behavior. The concept of emotives allows us (1) to accept as an important insight Abu-Lughod's insistence that ghinnāwas do not express "real" or "genuine" feelings, and (2) to recognize that, nonetheless, they are more than mere forms of self-fashioning, because they play a role in the navigation of difficult seas. They may serve to assure or to demonstrate mastery, but their exploratory effects may as easily intensify nonconformist sentiment.

The concept of emotives and the notion of navigation outlined above suggest that any successful emotion regime must allow for wide personal variation. But also, the story of the Gogue marriage indicates the high price exacted by regimes that accommodate variation by treating it as a deviation that must be concealed, and that impose stricter expectations on women than on men. The difficulties of navigation ought to be openly recognized and allowed for, with equal treatment of all. The articulate elaboration of alternatives and consequences – the freedom to be open to shifts of high-priority goals – mitigates goal conflict and its emotional suffering and aids navigation. The ease of navigation of one's close collaborators (whatever their gender) is as important as one's own to the reduction of emotional suffering.

Where honor codes allow for deviance from norms through concealment, individuals often establish what we might call informal emotional refuges. At a minimum, emotional refuge is a relationship in which one may display one's deviant feelings openly, and sometimes realize deviant desires as well. Arrangements of this sort were common in relations between men and women in early nineteenth-century France, as they were between siblings and certain close friends (see Vincent-Buffault 1995; Houbre 1997; for further discussion, see Chapters 7 and 8). Gogue's father, for example, may be read as encouraging his son to tolerate his bride's extramarital connection so long as she took care to conceal it. Marriage based on love was by this time a widely accepted, but by no means universal, norm in France. Gogue signaled his acceptance of this norm by his references to entering a garden. The norm of arranged marriage was still very much alive, however; and, within this latter standard, ready acceptance of extramarital relations (as in aristocratic marriages of the eighteenth century) remained a possibility. Had Gogue been able to accept such a line of conduct, his marriage might have become an emotional refuge in the sense that both partners accepted the absence of love between them. Each would be then able to pursue additional refuge in extramarital relationships. As I have noted, nothing about these choices was easy, straightforward, or standard. Every arrangement was idiosyncratic.

In the case of the Awlad ʿAli, Abu-Lughod notes the occurrence of a very different kind of emotional refuge, namely, the development of affectionate, even romantic, feelings between spouses who were expected to remain distant, emotionally independent, mutually respectful, devoted to their separate roles. Here, too, such arrangements were idiosyncratic and depended on the agreement of both parties. Rashīd's difficulties may be seen as deriving from his failure to secure such an agreement from his young bride, as much as from his failure to remain discreet about his intentions. In another case discussed by Abu-Lughod, a divorced woman openly displayed her longing for her ex-husband in front of dismayed friends; later, when he returned to her, she displayed with equal indiscretion her considerable joy. The breach here was twofold: If she could not resist such feelings, she should at least conceal them.

Where honor codes reign, concealment allows for all kinds of compromise, a rich field for improvisation and for navigation to many interesting shores and safe harbors. (This is, in effect, what is meant by the term *honor* in English and its equivalent in French.) At the same time, the individual is left very much to her own devices.

In the marriages of Gogue and Picard and of Rashīd and Fāyga, young women with hardly any experience of the world were thrust by parental authority into long-term sexual submission to men they knew nothing of. In both cases the norm for marriage was that of loyal cooperation, hard work, production of offspring, and wifely submission to the husband's authority. In the French case, due to Christian teaching, to the circulation of sentimental novels, and the popularity of innumerable melodramas and songs, marriage also included an ideal of romantic love that stood in strong tension with the norm of arranged marriage. In the Awlad 'Ali case, romantic love played a less salient role, as an outlawed alternative to marriage, but was still well known through the plots of traditional poetry. In both cases, the result was a very difficult mix, in which the newly married were likely to face significant goal conflicts and emotional suffering. To be confronted with such stark choices, to be presented with the tools of self-management represented by the searing shame of public breach of the honor code, or the all-or-nothing acceptance of a male partner of unknown character – this is political oppression.

I am not arguing for a simple progressive view of history, in which the passing of the centuries leads gradually but inevitably toward a kinder, gentler social organization. Nor do I wish to condemn certain non-Western ways, thereby potentially adding yet another burden of shame, another insult, to lives already too weighted with insult and fear of insult. I plead only for recognition of two things: (1) that the people involved in these episodes, even though they did not formulate explicit political grievances, were struggling to find a better way, or to improvise a personal variation on prevailing norms; (2) that this struggle, this navigation, is our own.

Armed with these two recognitions, it would be possible to write a history of emotions that takes into account their full political significance. In such a history, the modern West would not play the role of latest and best approximation of perfection, but that of a promising, although variegated, failure of world-historical proportions, a failure whose promise lies in its vast scope. A civilization, better than some alternatives, the fruit of collective striving, but off-course, awaits a change of navigation.

PART II

EMOTIONS IN HISTORY:
FRANCE, 1700–1850

CHAPTER 5

The Flowering of Sentimentalism (1700–1789)

In 1692, Louis XIV demanded that his nephew, the duc de Chartres, marry one of his illegitimate daughters, Mlle de Blois – a severe blow to the young man and his parents. On the day the engagement was to be announced, the duc de Chartres's mother was seen in the corridor outside the king's apartment sobbing with rage. But that evening, during supper, the duc de Chartres and his mother gathered their wits and behaved with marginally acceptable decorum.

The king appeared completely normal. M. de Chartres was next to his mother, who looked neither at him nor at her husband, Monsieur. Her eyes were full of tears, which fell from time to time, and which she wiped away, looking at everyone as if she wished to see what kind of facial expression each was making. Her son also had reddened eyes . . . I noticed that the king offered Madame almost all the dishes that were before him, which she refused with a brusque manner that, to the very end, failed to put off the king or temper his polite attention.

Everyone noticed that, at the end of dinner, as all were standing in a circle in the king's chamber, the king made a very low bow to her, but she turned to leave so quickly that, on lifting his head, he saw nothing but her back, as she advanced toward the door (Saint-Simon 1947–1961:I, 35). Far from disquieting the king, her behavior appeared to suit him perfectly. He did not seek mastery over her emotions. Submission of the will, displayed through a minimal compliance with etiquette, was quite sufficient. The literature of the period often shows a similar lack of interest in inner complexities. Molière's *Dom Juan* (1665), for example, says little about the charms which the infamous aristocrat used to seduce women; their attraction to him is a given, their emotions about him are depicted as intense, but left unexplored. The plot

141

turns solely on the struggles to which this attraction gives rise. Even in Lafayette's pathbreaking *La princesse de Clèves* (1678), the main characters fall in love at once, with little explanation or understanding.

A hundred years later, both literature and high politics had undergone a sea change. Choderlos de Laclos's *Liaisons dangereuses* (1782) devotes hundreds of pages to minute narration of the means of seduction, means that are emotional in character. The hypocritical Valmont arranges for his prey, the beautiful and devout Mme de Tourvel, to witness his benevolent gestures toward the poor; he seeks to convince her of his *sensibilité* – that is, his emotional sensitivity, his capacity to love, his capacity to be reformed by her.

In the summer of 1789, as the Estates General prepared to alter forever the constitution of the kingdom, Germaine de Staël rejoiced in the lack of artifice the French displayed. "*A sincere and disinterested enthusiasm* inspired at that time all the French; public spirit was everywhere, and, in the upper classes, the best were those who *desired most ardently* that the nation's will count for something in the direction of its affairs" (Staël 1818:114–115; emphasis added).[1] But her mother, Mme Necker, expressed a profound disquiet about the constant, insincere talk of feelings: "Love of country, humanity, vague terms empty of meaning which men invented to hide their insensitivity under the very veil of sentiment" (Diesbach 1983:90). This divergence between mother and daughter rested on a deeper agreement, a shared belief that sincere emotions were of great political importance.

After the fall of Robespierre, however, the role of emotions in politics was brought into question. Within a few years, reigning ideas about emotions were radically altered; even their role in prior decades was covered over and denied. This erasure has remained in effect until the last few years. From 1794 to the present, the history of the Enlightenment has been presented largely as a matter of science, rationality, social contract, and natural right. The Revolution has come to be seen as an attempt to apply these new ideas, an attempt that somehow went astray. Both the Revolution's outbreak and its radical phase, the so-called "Reign of Terror" under the Jacobin Republic in 1793–1794, have been explained in sociological terms. This radical republic, it was

---

[1] "Un enthousiasme sincère et désintéressé animoit alors tous les François; il y avoit de l'esprit public; et, dans les hautes classes, les meilleurs étoient ceux qui désiroient le plus vivement que la volonté de la nation fût de quelque chose dans la direction de ses propres intérêts."

believed, represented a doomed effort on the part of the laboring poor to impose participatory democracy by coercion and to level the social hierarchy by violence and expropriation. Yet the Jacobins, in reality, were never interested in the poor as such; for them what mattered were certain natural moral sentiments, which the poor happened to feel more readily than others. Even the atmosphere of the period has been misrepresented by the selective eye of the film industry; only its spoofs and cautionary tales have been considered worthy of revival: *Tom Jones,* *Les liaisons dangereuses, Sense and Sensibility* – but not *Pamela,* not *La vie de Marianne,* not *Paul et Virginie,* not *Delphine.*

When examined through the lens of recent research, the era of the French Revolution presents itself as an extraordinary moment in Western history. For a few decades, emotions were deemed to be as important as reason in the foundation of states and the conduct of politics. After 1794, not only was this idea rejected, even its memory was extinguished. The French Revolution, as a result, offers a case especially well suited to testing the utility of the theory of emotives, both because of its inherent importance and because of its vexing new appearance. Puzzling out the startling new appearance of the Revolution requires a theory of emotions suited to historical explanation. It is not enough to offer close readings of the texts, or to trace, decade by decade, without seeking to understand, the gradual and thorough alteration in emotional common sense that occurred between 1650 and 1789, and which was so radically and swiftly altered again after 1794. Joan DeJean, one of the pioneers of research into this transformation, has put her finger on the difficulty we face.

This modern crisis in subjectivity forces us to return to the eternally vexed question central to the relation between words and things: can phenomena exist before the words to describe them? In this case, we must ask if the French *felt* differently once they had access to *émotion, sentiment,* and *sensibilité* [key words in the new emotional lexicon]. Evidence from domains as disparate as medicine, literature, and theology indicates that either this was the case, or at the very least that individuals became able, as we would now say, to access previously unrecorded affective possibilities. (DeJean 1997:93; emphasis in original)

Having raised this question, DeJean immediately drops it. In the context of this study, however, it is possible to approach this kind of question from an entirely new angle. The concept of emotives suggests that when words change their meaning, their emotive effects change as well. It allows us to say this without requiring us to say exactly what any given person did feel. In addition, as we have seen, it allows us to examine the political implications of such change and to make judgments for or against the politics associated with new conceptualizations of emotion.

Two centuries ago, Germaine de Staël anticipated and fully understood DeJean's question; for her, the answer came easily: words and ideas enriched and educated feelings. Her *De la littérature dans ses rapports avec les institutions sociales* (1800) was a veritable history of emotions in Europe. As she conceived this grand narrative, first Christianity, then the spirit of northern peoples had reformed the misguided stoicism of the ancients. Finally, the modern novel had begun to inculcate "man's highest sentiment," which was "friendship in love" between a man and a woman (Staël 1800:100, 176). In passages like the following one on the introduction of Christianity, Staël made clear she saw an intimate interaction between word and sentiment:

Man's happiness grew with all the independence which the object of his tenderness had obtained; he could believe himself loved; a free being had chosen him; a free being obeyed his desires. *The perceptions of the mind, the nuances felt by the heart multiplied with the ideas and impressions of these new souls*, who were trying out a moral existence, after, for so long, having languished in life. (Staël 1800:171; emphasis added)[2]

"New souls" grew from new ideas, but not just any ideas, only ideas that opened one to the nuances of freely chosen and freely expressed love. Staël's conception was the fruit of a century and a half of reflection and exertion, especially by female writers from Scudéry, to Lafayette, to Riccoboni, to Wollstonecraft. *De la littérature* was also one of the last expressions of this school. As she wrote from exile in Switzerland, its memory was already being expunged in Paris. Without embracing Staël's teleological thesis, one may recognize that her agenda is both ambitious and worthy of emulation. It challenges us to understand the history and the political implications of how people feel.

---

[2] "La félicité de l'homme s'accrut de toute l'indépendance qu'obtint l'objet de sa tendresse; il put se croire aimé; un être libre le choisit; un être libre obéit à ses désirs. Les aperçus de l'esprit, les nuances senties par le cœur se multiplièrent avec les idées et les impressions de ces âmes nouvelles, qui s'essayaient à l'existence morale, après avoir longtemps langui dans la vie."

Four features of the period 1660 to 1789 marked its emotional history. First, under Louis XIV, an aristocratic honor code was consolidated and elaborated via new standards of etiquette and personal comportment imposed in Louis's glittering court at Versailles. The tendency of all honor codes to tolerate concealed deviance was in this period pushed to new extremes, at least for certain types of behavior, even as the formal rules governing publicly visible behavior achieved unprecedented elaboration. The prevailing honor code, an essential part of noble identity for centuries, was transformed into an instrument of monarchical rule. Louis ruled the aristocracy by strategic whim, favoring some, exiling others – inducing emotional suffering that enhanced his power dramatically. His growing bureaucracy's rule over the rest of the country was buttressed by the carefully wielded threat of arbitrary force. For the first time in history, France knew law and order, but a law and order based on that sharp emotional suffering brought by the threat of capricious coercion.

Second, in this forcibly pacified realm, new forms of sociability developed offering emotional refuge from the increasingly elaborate honor code. These forms appealed to those who found no satisfaction in the mere concealment of deviance (the approved form of emotional refuge under an honor code). Many of those involved had felt the pain of Louis's disfavor. In the salons of the *précieuses*, small, intimate groups suspended the strict hierarchical rules of interaction that prevailed elsewhere. In the salon, friendly groups pursued at first esthetic, later intellectual pleasures; noble and commoner, wealthy patrons and penniless writers mixed on a basis of companionate equality. In some instances, sexual liaisons based on "inclination" were celebrated. By the early eighteenth century, Masonic lodges also began to spread, offering an all-male model of warm companionship that bridged rigid social boundaries. Both salons and lodges were linked by correspondence; letters took on a new, warm, intimate tone.

Third, a new optimism about human nature spread widely, an optimism based in part on new confidence in the power of human reason, in part on the belief that certain natural sentiments, sentiments that everyone was capable of feeling, were the foundation of virtue and could serve as the basis for political reform. The optimists who spread these beliefs often worked through salons and Masonic lodges as well as print media, the academies, and the arts. These new intimate gatherings were regarded as living proof of the strength of positive natural sentiment, and as models for a future, happier social order.

Fourth, attractive new models of emotional refuge came to be disseminated in hundreds of novels, plays, paintings, and operas. These
models took a number of important new forms: the marriage based on
affection, the household of the benevolent father or father figure, the
natural communities that were imagined to exist on tropical islands or
in New World wildernesses. This literature also depicted the fragility
of emotional refuges as well as the horrific consequences of abandon-
ing convention if one failed to find such a refuge.

This period, as noted above, has often been thought of as an "age
of reason" in which a new science of nature was popularized and new
political and economic doctrines, such as the idea of the social contract,
or the laws of supply and demand, acquired great prestige. More
recently, historians have focused on the rise of new public institutions,
such as art exhibits, libraries, cafés, and a new reading public served
by a vigorous publishing industry. Salons, Masonic lodges, and lively
private networks of correspondence have been seen, following Habermas, as integral parts, along with these other institutions, of a new
"public sphere." The Revolution has come to be seen not as a concerted
attempt to apply new political ideas, but rather as an outgrowth of the
new political practices (of a new "political culture") this public sphere
gave rise to.

But here I wish to insist on the special emotional character of some
(but not all) of these new practices, on the novel view of emotions as
a force for good in human affairs, and on the enthusiasm for emotional
expression and intimacy – for emotional refuge from a prevailing code
of honor – expressed by many actors central to events leading up to
and following the outbreak of the Revolution. I propose to call these
linked features of the age collectively "sentimentalism," and I propose
to sketch their history briefly here. By viewing these developments
through the lens of the theory of emotives and the related vocabulary
worked out in the last chapter, I also propose to show how that theory
can point toward new, more powerful accounts of at least some features of the age that have defied understanding. If the theory of emotives is right, then sentimentalism's view of human nature was wrong
in interesting ways. (And in saying it was "wrong" I am purposefully
breaking with a relativist stance vis-à-vis the subject matter of my
research.) The theory allows one to see, further, how sentimentalism,
wrong as it was, inspired such widespread, fervent support, making
its erroneous implications about emotional management all the more
explosive in their impact. Although few historians have remarked the

fact, the Revolution, as we shall see in Chapter 6, began as an effort to transform all of France, by means of benevolent gestures of reform, into a kind of emotional refuge. But the eighteenth century's misunderstanding of emotions, coupled with the paradoxical effort to enlist the coercive power of the state in the service of benevolence and generosity, transformed the emotional refuge aimed at in 1789, in four short years, into the acute emotional suffering of the Terror.

In a final section of Chapter 6, I will briefly suggest how the eighteenth century's positive view of emotions and the utopian political hopes it attached to them were both firmly rejected after the end of the Terror in 1794. A new pessimism about the role of emotions in human life was inaugurated; its development is the subject of Chapter 7. Not only were emotions rejected, their very historical role was overlooked and denied. Gradually, sentimentalism as an intellectual and political program was rejected, then forgotten; it was erased from the history books, until recent research (much of it inspired by new interest in gender) began to rediscover it.

HONOR AND EMOTIONAL REFUGE IN THE ABSOLUTE MONARCHY

In the eighteenth century, people lived out their lives in a society where a certain governmental, religious, and familial system of authority was shored up by a newly elaborated set of norms of emotional expression known as "civility." By the end of Louis XIV's reign (1715), France was a "policed society," in Muchembled's (1998) words; and by this he means policed both by effective, bureaucratically controlled officers of the crown and by an effective type of personal training. In this context, the emotional expression recommended by sentimentalist ideas presented itself at first as something strictly forbidden.

For two centuries, from 1450 to 1650, the crown had struggled intermittently to bring its over-mighty subjects to heel. Great aristocrats, who controlled vast resources of wealth and patronage, had repeatedly plunged the country into disastrous civil wars, the final such episode being the so-called Fronde of 1648–1652, a rebellion against a regency government during Louis XIV's minority. Fearful of a recurrence of such rebellion, Louis, during his vigorous adulthood, forced the high nobility to reside permanently under his watchful eye at the grandiose palace of Versailles. There he imposed on them an elaborate round of ceremonial activities and an equally elaborate code of etiquette. His successful centralization of authority, and his tendency to give out favors or penalties somewhat capriciously at court, made this code of etiquette into an essential tool of advancement. For those not privy to court practices, its rules were laid out in popular etiquette manuals, and practices in other milieux rapidly came, more or less, into conformity with Versailles. This new style of civility was built of disparate ingredients, drawn ultimately from humanist writings as much as from the outlook of the noble warrior elite (Elias 1978; Revel 1986; Gordon 1994; Muchembled 1998). But its unifying preoccupation was the avoidance of insult. Avoidance of insult involved two concerns: (1) recognition of one's interlocutor as a person of honor by means of marks of esteem; (2) appreciation of refined distinctions of rank. The first concern was aimed at soothing the testiness and aggressiveness of the independent warrior nobleman (Neuschel 1989). The second concern reflected the limits of the unity imposed by the monarch. This unity was only achieved by giving to each his due; the great submitted to royal authority because they generally emerged as winners (Beik 1985). One of the ways in which they won was in the flow of new offices, pensions, and authority the king sent their way; another way in which they won was reflected in the subtle but unmistakable marks of deference in the manners of those around them. The new etiquette organized the whole country into a single series of cascades of disdain. If Louis XIV brought domestic peace to France, it was in the form of a prolonged aristocratic truce. Etiquette reaffirmed one's temporary commitment to this truce. The failure of efforts to suppress dueling among the nobility was a nagging reminder of its limits (Billacois 1986).

Both king and society exerted what we today can only regard as extraordinary authority over the individual. Marriages were arranged by parents in both town and country, at all levels of society. To protect the honor of families, and the power of fathers over their offspring, Louis XIV developed the so-called *lettre de cachet*, a royal order of imprisonment that circumvented normal judicial procedures. This powerful tool for the protection of family honor was another of the side benefits of submission to his rule. A father, whose disobedient son had eloped with a chambermaid, could have both son and wife imprisoned indefinitely with such an order – perhaps while pursuing an annulment in an ecclesiastical court (Daumas 1988, 1996). A child or spouse's criminality or insanity could also be hushed up and contained by such an order. Members of the high nobility sought such help directly at court; but royal officers were also allowed to issue *lettres de cachet* for the more humble. Thousands were issued in the eighteenth century (Farge & Foucault 1982). Many aspects of status were fixed in this society and enforced by law. Apprentices and journeymen, for example, were treated as parties to contracts in some respects, but in others they were treated as minors subject to the paternal authority of their masters (Sonenscher 1989). An apprentice walking the streets during work hours was subject to arrest. Journeymen were required to have certificates of good conduct when looking for work; their brotherhoods were illegal. The vows taken by priests and nuns changed their civil status and were enforceable in civil courts.

It is only against this backdrop that the salon, the literary correspondence, the Masonic lodge, friendship, and affectionate marriage can be understood as forms of emotional refuge. These freely chosen connections between persons were based not on family, office, or rank, but on merit or personal inclination. The rigidity of etiquette was ostentatiously set aside in favor of a more open, more egalitarian manner, which, as the eighteenth century wore on, became increasingly sentimental (Revel 1986; Vincent-Buffault 1986).

The new practices in some instances predated the new ideas that explained and popularized them. In the aftermath of the Fronde, certain aristocratic women, banned from Versailles due to their association with the rebellion, established the first salons, regular meetings of friends and literary collaborators for mutual entertainment. Typical products of such collaboration were the writings of Madeleine de Scudéry which, after 1652, increasingly emphasized a certain natural tenderness of the noble soul and praised liaisons of "inclination" between men and women (DeJean 1991, 1997).

Intellectual discussion was particularly difficult to arrange in the social world of absolutism. As Goodman (1994) has pointed out, the schools of the period instructed students in an art of disputation that was confrontational and personal. One put one's own honor on the line when defending a position, and defended it by every means possible; the implicit model was that of legal pleading. In most situations of mixed company, involving men and women of differing ranks, it was considered essential to avoid discussion of any matter of importance. In more public venues, such as cafés or the walkways of the Palais Royal, intellectual discussions became, in Melchior Grimm's words, "combats to the death" in which "the loudest was the most respected and men of letters and refined minds acquired the tone and habits of porters" (Craveri 1982:411).

The famous literary salons of the eighteenth century – those of the marquise de Lambert, Mme de Tencin, Mme Geoffrin, Mme du Deffand, Julie de Lespinasse, and Suzanne Necker are the best known – provided a way around this impasse. Differences of rank were set aside on entry. Differences of opinion could be expressed openly, without insult, because the hostess encouraged their expression and sought to ensure that discussion was entertaining, and that everyone had a chance to express his views (most guests were male). The hostess herself derived the immense advantage from her salon that it was an engaging, even a consuming activity, providing her with a quasi-public role, yet without drawing her away from the domestic realm to which honor confined her (Goodman 1994).

Each salon had its own character. Deffand, one of her biographers reports, was discouraged by the skillful hypocrisy required by the manners of her time and "tormented by suspicions that, with the passage of years, took on an ever more pathological character." A frequent guest remarked that she displayed a "stark frankness [*une franchise outrée*] about everything that came before her judgment, whether people, or their works." She valued in d'Alembert his "sometimes brutal sincerity," and, with his collaboration, encouraged a kind of honesty greatly appreciated by the young intellectuals she attracted (Craveri 1982:88). She battled recurrent "ennui" as well as the grief brought on by an encroaching blindness; correspondence and dry wit were her principal weapons.

While guests came to Deffand's salon to listen and admire, as much as to speak, they appreciated in Geoffrin her ability to facilitate conversation. "She had the intelligence to speak only about things she knew very well," said Marmontel of her, "and to yield the floor on everything else to men of learning, always politely attentive, without even appearing bored when she was not listening; she was even more adept at presiding, overseeing, and holding in check" the guests of her twice-weekly gatherings.[3] In his eulogy of her, the poet Antoine-Léonard Thomas remarked

---

[3] "[E]lle avait le bon esprit de ne parler jamais que de ce qu'elle savait très bien, et de céder sur tout le reste la parole à des gens instruits, toujours poliment attentive, sans même paraître ennuyée de ce qu'elle n'entendait pas; mais plus adroite encore à présider, à surveiller, à tenir sous sa main ces deux sociétés naturellement libres" (Jean-François Marmontel, in his memoirs, cited by Craveri [1982:416]).

These sorts of societies that, in order to survive, cannot be too constrained, but that, with the liberty of democracies, are sometimes beset with agitation and movement, require a certain power to temper them. It seems that this power is no better held than in the hands of a woman. She has a natural right that no one disputes and that, in order to be felt, has only to be shown. Madame Geoffrin used this advantage. [In her salon], the reunion of all ranks, like that of all types of minds, prevented any one tone from dominating. (Quoted in Goodman 1994:100–101; Goodman's translation)

But it was Deffand's young protégée, Julie de Lespinasse, who most perfectly embodied the spirit of the *salonnière* as self-effacing facilitator. The comte de Guibert said of her

I have tried to understand the principle of that charm which no one possessed as she did, and here is what it seems to me to consist in: she was always devoid of ego [*personalité*], and always natural. . . . She knew that the great secret of how to please lay in forgetting oneself in order to become occupied with others, and she thus forgot herself constantly. She was the soul of conversation, and she thus never made herself its object. Her great art was to show to advantage the minds of others, and she enjoyed doing that more than revealing her own. (Quoted in Goodman 1994:103; Goodman's translation)

Jean-François de La Harpe spoke of Lespinasse in similar, admiring terms: "I can say that I have never known a woman who had more natural intelligence, less desire to display it, or more talent for bringing out the intelligence of others. No one knew better, either, how to welcome guests into her house. She put all her friends in their place, yet left everyone content" (quoted in Craveri 1982:150). After she established her own salon in 1764, Lespinasse came to preside over a group, including d'Alembert, Condorcet and Mme Condorcet, Suard and Mme Suard, that espoused deep friendship and expressed intense affection toward each other.

After 1720, freemasonry spread rapidly in France, as well as in Britain. By 1789 there were from thirty to fifty thousand members of these all-male secret societies in France alone (Halévi 1984:16). Agulhon (1968:198) concluded that, by 1789, almost all local elite males in Provence had abandoned religious confraternities in favor of Masonic lodges as their preferred form of sociability. The life of the lodges was built out of non-Christian symbol and ceremonial, drawn from ancient Greek mythology and other sources. A candidate for admission was required to believe in God, to have high moral standards, and "to be his own master" (Agulhon 1968:181). Nobles and commoners mixed freely in the lodges; most commoners were well-to-do, but a minority, perhaps 15 percent, were master craftsmen of the better trades (watchmaker, wigmaker). In the lodges, such craftsmen met on a plane of equality with powerful local aristocrats and well-heeled merchants and barristers. In the meetings, ceremonies, and banquets, gaiety, mutual affection, and mutual solidarity were to reign as the very raison d'être of the association. Attendance at a fellow Mason's funeral was obligatory. When traveling, Masons were welcomed with open arms into local lodges along the way. Toward the rest of mankind, Masons were expected to display their profound feelings of benevolence by carrying out good works; lodges constantly taxed their members for specific charitable causes. The Masons worked to counter public criticism suggesting they were no more than drinking societies; and they attempted to suppress factions or exclude lodges that favored drinking to excess. Gaiety must never "exceed the bounds of decency" (Agulhon 1968:181).

Like the salon, Masonic lodges of the eighteenth century have been the object of important new scholarship in recent years (e.g., Halévi 1984; Jacob 1991a, 1991b). Both have been examined principally as institutions that foreshadowed the deliberative practices and egalitarianism of Revolutionary assemblies, and of the nineteenth-century public sphere more generally. But in the context of Old Regime society, these were also places in which a special emotional tone reigned, of a kind that later deliberative institutions entirely lacked. At the opening ceremony of a new lodge in Mézin in 1785, the abbé de Laroche Bouscat told its members,

We will found the reign of a gentle harmony and of a perfect equality over all human desires, envies, and passions; and that self-interest that corrupts all will not sully our loving hearts. . . . We will thus see reborn that primitive force of nature that unites all men instead of creating those insulting distinctions which have only generated arrogance on one side and hatred on the other. (Quoted in Halévi 1984:34)[4]

---

[4] "Nous fonderons le règne d'une douce harmonie et d'une parfaite égalité sur les désirs de l'envie et les autres passions humaines; et l'intérêt qui corrompt tout ne souillera pas no coeurs aimables. . . . Alors nous verrons revivre cette force primitive de la nature qui unit tous les hommes au lieu de créer des distinctions injurieuses qui n'ont jamais enfanté que l'orgueil d'un côté et la haine de l'autre."

For eighteenth-century Masons, equality went hand in hand with a kind of natural, gentle harmony. Ranks proliferated within the movement, it is true, and protocol was often elaborate. But after 1773, all offices became elective; merit was explicitly linked to a quality "peculiar to this fraternity" that could not be put in writing (Halévi 1984:26–27).

This special emotional tone stood in stark contrast to the requirements of self-control expected in other venues, where power, influence, and rank were expressed. The royal academies of Paris and their provincial imitators, the annual art exhibitions at the Louvre, the new cafés and reading rooms of the larger towns – these are also frequently cited as foreshadowing later practices. However, none of these latter institutions seem to have provided that sense of refuge, of a letting down of vigilance, so characteristic of the salon and the lodge.

The affectionate marriage and a new kind of intense friendship should also be placed on the list of forms of emotional refuge that spread in the eighteenth century. The ideal of love hardly changed from the sixteenth through the eighteenth centuries, as Daumas (1996) notes. From the Renaissance through the end of the eighteenth century, this ideal was characterized by five features: (1) the loved one is placed above the self; (2) fidelity; (3) equality between the partners; (4) reciprocity of giving and receiving; and (5) exclusivity. What changed, in Daumas's view, is the relation between this ideal and its context. In the earlier period, lovers spelled out the relation of their love to religion, either invoking God's protection or deploring their own weaknesses (see also, on this, Febvre 1944). By 1700, however, love fashions its own morality and may be invoked to set aside conventional moral norms. In the earlier period, love, especially passionate love, is seen as incompatible with marriage, an institution shaped by economic, political, and lineage calculations. By 1700, however, love within marriage takes on the status of an ideal, in which friendship and sexuality are linked, and familial affection becomes a natural model of love. In the earlier period, women penning love letters agree that their sex lacks constancy, but insist that they are exceptions to the rule. By 1700, men and women focus on feminine tenderness as the ideal form of love, and men love womanhood itself through their women. These changes are perfectly in line with sentimentalist thought. However, Daumas's evidence is anecdotal, based on a few precious caches of love letters as well as a few well-publicized cases of elopement. Vincent-Buffault's (1995) examination of friendship is equally limited in its scope, drawing evidence only from the writings of a thin, well-known elite. But so far, this limited research confirms that many in the eighteenth century were beginning to seek emotional refuge in these relationships (see also Darnton 1985:215–256).

The claim here is not that emotional refuge was something new; on the contrary, one would expect that any society which imposes strict emotional discipline will generate various practices, relationships, and venues that provide temporary, local suspension of the mental control efforts prescribed by the emotional regime in place. It is probably the case that many practices and institutions begin their histories as forms of emotional refuge. The Christian ascetic impulse in fourth- and early fifth-century Rome and its reemergence in eleventh-century western Europe, the Beguine communities of the thirteenth century, at least some of the illicit relationships of the courtly love tradition, the underground conventicles and holy cities – Zurich, Strasbourg, Geneva – of the Reformation era: any and all of these phenomena may have provided emotional refuge for a significant number of those who made them.

What was distinctive about Masonic lodges, salons, and new forms of affectionate marriage and friendship after 1700 was that these practices gradually came to draw legitimacy from a developing conception of sentiment – a secular, naturalistic, and political bundle of ideas close to our own notion of emotion. This conception of sentiment gradually came, in turn, to possess a powerful ideological thrust.

SENTIMENTALISM IN RECENT RESEARCH

In recent work the term *sentimentalism*, originally the label for a literary genre, has gradually been extended. David Denby, for example, concludes that "sentimental narratives occupy a central place in the project of the French Enlightenment," because "reason and sentiment can no longer be posited as contradictory polarities in eighteenth-century cultural formations." The eighteenth century assumed that "rationality can be accessed experientially and affectively, just as the constitution of reason as a historical category uses textual procedures entirely consonant with sentimental narratives" (1994:240). In addition, in Denby's view, the Revolution followed the Enlightenment's lead, taking shape as "the ultimate sentimental event" (p. 96). In simpler terms, emotion was, for a time, considered equal to reason in the formulation of political doctrines and policies. This marks the Revolutionary period as extraordinarily unusual in the whole history of political ideas and practices. Never in ancient or modern times had emotions been considered a worthy source of political insight or direction.[5] Lynn Hunt's well-known work (Hunt 1992) shows the Revolution was infused with new ideas about family and patriarchal authority produced by the sentimentalist wave. This wave, as she indicates, was carried by a great number of novels, plays, paintings, political pamphlets, and pornographic libels in the decades before the Revolution. Sarah Maza (1993) has demonstrated that in certain show trials of the 1770s and 1780s ambitious barristers fashioned their pleadings into melodramas, with their clients playing the role of innocent commoner victims (and sentimental family members) while their opponents appeared as scheming, arrogant, hypocritical aristocrats. James Johnson (1995) has tracked the transformation of music and opera in Paris from around 1770 into a vehicle for eliciting tearful empathy and pity from a new public of avid listeners. Nicole Fermon has urged a reevaluation of Rousseau's politics recognizing that he regarded "emotions as both the basis of human associations and antecedent to conceptions of interest" (1997:180).[6]

The impact of sentimentalism was just as great in England as it was in France; but there it was more readily accepted (see, e.g., Langford 1989). According to work by G. J. Barker-Benfield (1992), Richard Teichgraeber (1986), Frank Baasner (1988), as well as Denby (1994), sentimentalism in England gained early impetus from the Earl of Shaftesbury's attack on Locke in his 1711 book, *Characteristics of Men, Mannners, Opinions, Times*. Shaftesbury felt that Locke's vision of human nature was impoverished and could not account for a great deal of human behavior, especially the bonds that united families. He claimed that in addition to the senses enumerated by Locke, men were equipped with an "inward eye" that enabled them to perceive the morally good. Moral perceptions became available to the mind via inborn sentiments. Feelings of benevolence, pity, love, and

---

[5] A notable exception is that, in rhetoric, appeals to the passions were viewed, from the Greeks on, as an important tool in persuading *others*; they were never considered as a useful guide for one's *own* deliberations. See Conley (1990).

[6] See also Blum (1986), who argues that Jacobin violence was prefigured in certain tendencies of Rousseau's thought; his desire to meld with others in empathic union and a certain disgust, even rage, against those who resisted virtue were reverse and obverse of the same coin. See also Revel (1986).

gratitude gave shape to moral judgment and rendered moral action pleasurable.

Here are some pertinent reflections on virtue in Shaftesbury's own words. First on the positive side, comparing animals and men:

It is impossible to suppose a mere sensible creature originally so ill-constituted and unnatural as that, from the moment he comes to be tried by sensible objects, he should have no one good passion towards his kind, no foundation either of pity, love, kindness or social affection. It is full as impossible to conceive that a rational creature, coming first to be tried by rational objects and receiving into his mind the images or representations of justice, generosity, gratitude or other virtue, should have no liking of these or dislike of their contraries, but be found absolutely indifferent towards whatsoever is presented to him of this sort. . . . [The soul] must needs find a beauty and a deformity as well in actions, minds and tempers as in figures, sounds or colors. If there be no real amiableness or deformity in moral acts, there is at least an imaginary one of full force. Though perhaps the thing itself should not be allowed in nature, the imagination or fancy of it must be allowed to be from nature alone. Nor can anything besides art and strong endeavor, with long practice and meditation, overcome such a natural prevention or prepossession of the mind in favor of this moral distinction.

Sense of right and wrong therefore being as natural to us as natural affection itself, and being a first principle in our constitution and make, there is no speculative opinion, persuasion or belief which is capable immediately or directly to exclude or destroy it. (Shaftesbury 1711:178–179; emphasis in original)

Second, on the negative side:

And thus if there be anything which teaches men either treachery, ingratitude or cruelty, by divine warrant or under color and presence of any present or future good to mankind, if there be anything which teaches men to persecute their friends through love or to torment captives of war in sport or to offer human sacrifice or to torment, macerate or mangle themselves in a religious zeal before their god or to commit any sort of barbarity or brutality as amiable or becoming, be it custom which gives applause or religion which gives a sanction, this is not nor ever can be virtue of any kind or in any sense but must remain still horrid depravity, notwithstanding any fashion, law, custom or religion which may be ill and vicious itself but can never alter *the eternal measures and immutable independent nature of worth and virtue.* (Shaftesbury 1711:175; emphasis in original)

Teichgraeber examines the powerful impact of Shaftesbury's ideas on the Scottish philosopher Francis Hutcheson and, through Hutcheson, on the thinking of both David Hume and Adam Smith. "The gist of the moral sense argument in Hutcheson," Teichgraeber says, "was that moral judgments are products of a human faculty distinct from reason and analogous to the ordinary five senses" (1986:36). "Practical dispositions to virtue" were, according to Hutcheson, implanted in human nature, creating "a universal determination to benevolence in mankind" (p. 42). But Hutcheson cautioned that there were also dangerous passions at work in human nature and that governments were best founded not on an expectation that benevolent action will win out naturally, but on an effort to channel rational self-interested action toward beneficial goals. Hume considered that natural benevolence normally extended only to the limits of the family; in his view, it explained the existence of families, an issue which Locke had entirely skirted. Beyond the family, however, Hume did not think benevolence could be counted on; the idea of justice was not natural, he argued, but a historical product of competition among men, who gradually learned the value of limiting and policing their competition. Smith, like Hutcheson and Hume, did not believe that a state could be built on natural benevolence alone; but he did see such benevolence as operative in the origins of property. Only a natural ability to sympathize with others (not reason) could confirm a person's claim to a right over the fruits of his or her own labor. Still, the state was better off if it confined itself to specifying primarily men's "negative duties" rather than counting on their natural benevolence (Teichgraeber 1986:139). His devotion to freedom of trade, therefore, derived from a belief that acquisitiveness was a good balance point between benevolent sentiments and selfish passions.

Barker-Benfield (1992) shows how Shaftesbury's ideas were transmitted to Samuel Richardson, whose *Pamela*, best-selling English novel of the century, created a sensation when it appeared in 1740. Richardson, a printer by trade, was already familiar with a new kind of novel, written by and for women, that had grown in popularity early in the century. In *Pamela*, he integrated its conventions with the new ideas about the origins of morality in natural sentiment. The protagonist, a young, simple, and innocent chambermaid, fends off the advances of her imperious master. She is literate and loves to read; she writes detailed accounts of the attempts on her virtue to her mother and her father (a bankrupt schoolteacher). Her master, for a time, kidnaps her, but repeatedly, on the point of violating her, relents. Her devotion to virtue, one of her principal charms, both sharpens his desire and inspires his respect, driving him into an ambivalence of increasing intensity until, having seized her letters, he is disarmed by their honesty and depth of feeling. Her voluminous letters, displaying a modest education, are proof of her innocence; she has nothing to hide from her parents and, like a child, tells them all. She is sincere and open even about the first stirrings of love for her master, which dismay her. Finally, he undergoes a conversion and, setting aside his pride, offers to marry her.

Pamela presented a number of the essential doctrines of sentimentalism cast into a compelling and readable form: (1) that superior virtue is linked to simplicity, openness, and lowly rank, because virtue is an outgrowth of natural sentiments we all share; (2) that women are more likely to develop such virtue; (3) that men are more likely to be enslaved to their stronger passions; (4) that true beauty lies in virtuous innocence and sincerity; (5) that reading (especially novels) and writing are important instruments for the cultivation of sensitivity and virtue; (6) that romantic attachment is the proper foundation of marriage; and (7) that a marriage so founded is both a refuge and a school of virtue. These ideas were in stark contrast to an age-old common sense about virtue. Virtue, in the opinion of the centuries, was built on a rejection of passion in favor of reason; that men were more readily able to achieve it; that superior social rank and superior virtue more or less coincide; and that marriage ought to be arranged to preserve the coincidence of rank, rationality, and virtue. Richardson depicted the gentry as, by and large, dissolute and corrupt; he refrained from spelling out the political implications, but others would not. Richardson's ideas became conventions and were developed and explored in the novels of Fielding, MacKenzie, Burney, Wollstonecraft, and many others. Often, the virtuous woman instructed, and helped to convert to virtue, a male driven by sexual attraction. In other cases, female virtue in distress was saved by a "man of feeling" (Barker-Benfield 1992:247–253; Maza 1993:303). In still other cases, sensitive hearts were simply overwhelmed by the unfeeling ways of society, notably in Richardson's second novel, *Clarissa* (1747–1748).[7]

---

[7] For discussion of this more somber treatment of sensitivity, see Baasner (1988:89–94, 169); Denby (1994:22–30).

In France, Joan DeJean (1991, 1997) has found, new ideas about sentiment developed by women novelists had been linked with new medical theories about the heart and the circulation of the blood as early as the 1680s. By 1705, with the publication of Gamaches's *Système du coeur*, an "exceptionally powerful complicity between medicine and fiction" had been established, within which certain sentiments could be viewed as both natural and good (DeJean 1997:88–91). Montesquieu explored the question of moral sentiments in *Lettres persanes* (1721). In the parable of the Troglodytes, he depicted a society incapable of organizing itself until two Troglodytes, who had "humanity," and who felt only pity for their compatriots, retired to live apart. They loved their wives and were "tenderly cherished" in return. They allowed their children to choose their own mates. They were prosperous and multiplied. In their communal festivals, they prayed for "healthy fathers, united brothers, tender mothers, loving and obedient children" (Montesquieu 1721:41).[8] But their decline from virtue seemed certain when they decided to choose a king – an outcome signaling a certain ambivalence on Montesquieu's part. This is hardly the only trace of reflections on moral sentiments in the work, however. Roxanne, Usbek's favorite wife, for example, won his favor in a manner that anticipated Pamela's conquest of Mr. B., by stiff resistance to his advances.[9] Jean Ehrard has argued that *L'esprit des lois* (1748) bears the imprint of a continued commitment to natural moral sentiment. Montesquieu's opposition to slavery, for example, went further than prior natural-right theorists because, Ehrard notes, for Montesquieu, "slavery must revolt sensitive souls" while, from another perspective, reason easily demonstrates its violation of natural law (Ehrard 1970:287–295, quote from p. 289). Voltaire also accepted that moral sentiments were natural; even a savage, he noted, would feel pity and fear, on seeing a baby about to be devoured by an animal (Baasner 1988:103). Germaine de Staël expressed deep admiration of Voltaire's early tragedy *Tancrède* precisely because it depicted with such force the "friendship in love" of a man and a woman. Tancrède's death at the end of the play brought the audience to tears because, she noted, it entailed the loss of that incomparable good just at the moment Tancrède discovered he possessed it (Staël 1800:280). Baasner has noted that Voltaire saw himself as a "man

---

[8] "la santé des pères, union des frères, tendresse des mères, l'amour, l'obéissance des enfants."
[9] For further discussion, see Schaub (1995).

of feeling" and that his attacks on religious intolerance were carried
out in the name of natural benevolence. His denunciation of religious
persecution in the Calas affair, for example, was built upon a depiction
of the Calas family as united by profound, natural sentiments of mutual
love (Baasner 1988:135–136, 143–145; Maza 1993:31–33; see also Gordon
1994:187).

As Voltaire's journalistic writings illustrate, French social thinkers
displayed a much greater tendency to enlist sentimentalist ideas in
their political polemics than did their British counterparts. But in
France, as in Britain, even moderate voices paid homage to sentimentalist doctrine. D'Alembert, in his introduction to the *Encyclopédie*,
insisted there was a kind of "evidence of the heart" that was as irresistible as the "evidence which the mind attaches to speculative truths"
(Baasner 1988:161). Condorcet referred to "those habitual movements
of an active, enlightened benevolence, of a delicate sensibility, whose
seeds nature planted in every heart, and which wait only for the gentle
influence of understanding and of liberty to develop" (Baasner 1988:
150). Where thinkers differed was on the question of how powerful
such natural sensibility was on its own, to what extent it had to be
shaped, preserved, or educated. Rousseau, and those who followed
him, put much greater emphasis on the natural origins of virtue, and
tended to view the development of civilization in a negative light, as a
source of hypocrisy, falseness, and debauchery. But even his opponents
did not question the natural foundations of virtuous character.[10] Suard,
in his reception speech before the Académie Française, insisted on the
necessity of proper cultivation of natural feelings. "There are virtues
that are the sole fruit of knowledge. The very word *humanity* was
absolutely unknown in the era of ignorance. It is a virtue of educated
people, that can only be born in souls whose natural sensibility has
been purified by reflection" (Gordon 1994:149). Rousseau agreed that
natural sensitivity, unguided, did not produce virtue; but its proper formation required a training quite different from that suggested by
Suard. One model he offered of this training was republican in character, and found its exemplars in Geneva, Sparta, and Rome. One
model was familial, and found its exemplar in Julie's reluctant submission to parental authority in *La nouvelle Héloïse* (1762). Rousseau's
attempt to bridge the gap between ancient, republican civic virtue and
modern, natural moral sentiment was not, at first, widely followed. But

---

[10] On the controversies surrounding Rousseau, see Gordon (1994:149–190).

his originality can only be appreciated against the backdrop of broad acceptance of the importance of "sensibilité."[11]

The picture emerging from recent research is, then, one of a remarkable consensus among the educated elite about the centrality of natural sentiment to virtue, a consensus that, while encompassing some significant variations of emphasis, stretched from the highest intellectual protégés of the courts to the lowliest scribblers of melodrama, including painters, composers, and pamphleteers along the way.

THE EXCESSES OF SENTIMENT AND THE THEORY OF EMOTIVES

The 1770s and 1780s in France was the period of the cult of Rousseau and of the great show trials examined by Maza (1993). Rousseau was not, according to Baasner, an aberration in the Enlightenment context, not a foreshadowing of nineteenth-century Romanticism, as was once believed. However, Baasner does recognize what he calls a "trivialization" of sentimentalist ideas in the 1770s and 1780s (Baasner 1988:332–333). The escalation of emotional expression of these decades is a long-established puzzle for experts in the field. The new students of sentimentalism have shown themselves no more at ease with this issue than were an earlier generation of scholars. "Bourgeois crybabies" was Daniel Mornet's conclusion in 1929 about the adherents of sentimentalism's period of "trivialization" (cited by Denby 1994:6). Robert Darnton, in 1985, proclaimed Rousseau's *La nouvelle Héloïse* to be "unreadable"; best-selling French novel of the eighteenth century, it nonetheless leaves modern readers cold, Darnton said, because they are not used to "six volumes of sentiment unrelieved by any episodes of violence, explicit sex, or anything much in the way of plot" (p. 242). The current spate of analyses continues to echo these complaints. Sarah Maza, in a recent article, noted that the new "serious" dramas of the period are seldom produced today. "Modern spectators," Maza observes, "would find their hyperbolic sentimentalism – the weeping, collapsing, exclaiming, and pontificating – at best comic, and more likely, tedious and embarrassing" (1997:227). Lynn Hunt proposes a

---

[11] Rosenblatt (1997) has shown Rousseau drew on Genevan thinkers and theologians in attempting to link ancient civic and modern natural conceptions of virtue. See also Blum (1986); Fermon (1997); Baasner (1988:303–311).

Freudian approach to this kind of evidence, which is, she admits, "confounding and mysterious." The French, she surmises, were in the grip of a "collective political unconscious" that generated feelings, shaped choices of symbol and metaphor, and impelled them on courses of action which they barely understood (Hunt 1992:xiv, 13).[12]

Maza, Denby, and Vincent-Buffault all explore the stunning frequency of references to "breaking down in tears" in documents of the end of the Old Regime (Vincent-Buffault 1986; Maza 1993; Denby 1994). Vincent-Buffault speaks of the "unregulated sentimentality" that began to appear in private letters of the 1730s and of the "jubilant frenzy" evident in discussions of friendship (Vincent-Buffault 1995:28, 46). James Johnson, in his recent examination of the sentimentalist craze in opera sparked by Gluck's works of the 1770s, finds it hard to believe all the shedding of tears was genuine. "Even if the audience seemed to cry on cue," he remarks with obvious skepticism, "the very pretense of personal affect presented itself as a good deal more subjective in response than had the reactions of audiences thirty years earlier" (Johnson 1995:68). Maza is openly doubtful of the sincerity and accuracy of expressions of extreme feeling in the celebrated lawyers' briefs she analyzes. We can easily agree that the tears of an ambitious lawyer are hardly to be taken without question. But why did this same observation, quite rudimentary to us, not occur to the public of that day?

Denby argues that the period was preoccupied with the problem of bridging the gap between inside and outside, and sought in tears and in hyperbolic emotional outpourings – trembling, sighs, falling to one's knees, endlessly repeated claims of extreme feelings – the sure exterior signs of inner feeling (1994). But this still does not explain why, today, our first reaction is often the opposite: that all these effusive displays, so relentlessly pursued, must be false. Maza believes that sentiment was being offered as a new foundation for social bonds and social identities threatened by commercial expansion and consumerism (Maza 1997).

These arguments have considerable merit. But do they fully account for the extremes of expression that fill the documents of the period – not just novels and plays, but personal letters, autobiographies, newspapers, and acts of government? This new style seemed to divide people even as it gained new adherents. Some, like Julie de Lespinasse,

---

[12] Hunt would be the first to agree.

the young Germaine Necker, Marie-Jeanne Phlipon, and her fiancé Jean-Marie Roland, embraced effusions, expressing frustration at the inadequacies of language, especially written language, to convey feeling, peppering their prose with exclamation points, hanging sentences, references to tears (Vincent-Buffault 1995:195–206; Daumas 1996; Baasner 1998:194–198). Others, such as Riccoboni, Sénac de Meilhan, Baculard, and Genlis, began to fault, in Sénac's words, "the reign of beautiful sentiments delivered with fake warmth" (quoted in Basner 1988:335).[13] Grimm, in 1773, protested, "Today all our novelists pretend to have a somber, lachrymose, and sentimental philosophy. Have we become more philosophical or more sensitive? No, only weaker, more fainting, sadder" (quoted in Baasner 1988:345). It was partly a matter of generation, partly of inclination. When fifty-three-year-old Mme de Charrière met twenty-three-year-old Germaine de Staël in 1793, she sought to excuse the younger woman's sentimental outpourings: "It is with perfectly good faith that I pardon Mme de Staël for being a woman of her age . . . but I cannot go along with it, any more than I can make myself younger than I am. I detest that affectation" (quoted in Diesbach 1983:157). Thus a growing unease about insincerity was part and parcel of sentimentalism's triumph.

How can the theory of emotives and the connected concept of emotional liberty help to explain both sentimentalism's remarkable triumph and the signs of disquiet and suspicion discernible by the 1780s?

Most of the people who welcomed and used the characteristic forms of emotional refuge in the eighteenth century understood them in terms of sentimentalist notions. If they had no prior knowledge of sentimentalism, it was easy to pick up elements of it in these refuges themselves. The Masonic preference for non-Christian forms of symbolism reflected an effort to imagine mutual affection, gaiety, and benevolence as universal, natural feelings. There was an implicit rejection of the doctrine of original sin and the penitential style of Counter Reformation sociability. In salons frequented by or in correspondence with any of the major figures of the period – Montesquieu, Voltaire, Diderot, d'Alembert, Rousseau – as well as many lesser figures, from Marivaux to Suard – one could hardly have avoided hearing sentimentalist ideas discussed and witnessing friendships that were expressed and understood in sentimentalist terms.

---

[13] "le règne des beaux sentiments débités avec une chaleur factice."

Sentimentalism implicitly offered numerous recipes for the formulation of powerful emotives. According to its propagators, pity, benevolence, love, and gratitude were one and the same natural sentiment, the root of morality and the foundation of all social bonds. Stimulating these feelings, further, was the best protection against unruly passions and a necessary training for virtue. A person who embraced these ideas, and who said "I love," or "I feel pity," would regard any stirrings of feeling that confirmed these claims as deriving from an inborn sense, beyond consciousness or rational direction, needing stimulation, the source of all good and beauty. If such emotive claims were effective, then their success confirmed for the individual that he or she had indeed tapped a well of natural sentiment. Because nature was overtaking him or her, intensity and sincerity went together. As Diderot put it, speaking of theater, "To say that one must not move [the audience] beyond a certain point, is to suppose that they must not come away from a play too enamored of virtue, or too cool toward vice" (quoted in Fried 1980:80).[14] Here, the didactic character of art and the role of extremes of feeling in the learning of virtue are both spelled out.

The concept of emotives suggests that, with practice, great facility might be developed in eliciting from oneself intense feelings – not "sincere," not "natural" feelings as sentimentalism inclined one to believe, feelings that were learned and cultivated. But all feelings are learned and cultivated.

Because feelings were deemed natural, they united people rather than isolating them; they were shared by all, a public resource. Public expression of intense feeling, rather than causing embarrassment, was a badge of generous sincerity and of social connectedness. In this, too, facility could be developed with practice. Because feelings, whether inspired by fiction or by life, were the same – and were more important than the occasions that gave rise to them – the difference between art and life was attenuated. Recognition of emotions and expression of them would lead to right action, whether in the realm of art, politics, or private life. Hence the tendency toward didacticism in fiction, theater, and the arts. Beauty and moral instruction were the same thing; therefore to adorn one's novel or play with long sermonlike speeches, sociological or political reflections, or philosophical speculations was

---

[14] "[D]ire qu'il ne faut les émouvoir que jusqu'à un certain point, c'est prétendre qu'il ne faut pas qu'ils sortent d'un spectacle, trop épris de la vertu, trop éloignés du vice" (from the *Entretiens sur le fils naturel* [1757]).

to enhance its moral utility and its beauty at the same time. The natural beauty and innocence of a young protagonist, the beauty of the prose that expressed her feelings and perceptions, and the beauty of the moral ideas that guided her were all of a piece. Theater was singled out as an especially appropriate tool for eliciting and shaping sentiment, because, like no other art, it allowed the reality of the story to be directly sensed (Baasner 1988:188–200). Painting, according to Diderot, must strive for the same effects as drama; it must attract, arrest, and enthrall the observer, and then teach a great lesson (Fried 1980:90, 92). In the theater, character and action should be drawn, not from ancient or mythical stories, but from the present-day lives of the middling ranks, whose simplicity rendered them easy to identify with. Anticipating what psychologist Elaine Hatfield and her associates have dubbed "emotional contagion," Diderot recommended that the spectator be so convinced by the play that he or she become ready to jump up and join the action (Baasner 1988:190; Hatfield et al. 1994; Maza 1997:227).

The figure of Diderot has emerged with remarkable frequency in recent work as a contributor to, and propagator of, sentimentalism. His first published work was a translation of Shaftesbury's essay on moral sentiments; he later wrote an *Eloge de Richardson*, in which he praised the novelist in ecstatic terms, calling his novels a new kind of scripture, capable of gripping the attention of the reader and sparking emotional reactions as intense as real life (Chartier 1999). His editorial role in the *Encyclopédie* project ensured it contained many expositions of sentimentalist ideas. He is regarded as, at once, the most important art critic of the middle decades of the century, and the most influential theorist of the new *genre sérieux* in theater (Maza 1997:224–225). In effect, as Fried (1980:55) emphasizes, what we find most distasteful today in the art Diderot admired – its simple narratives pitting good agains evil, its cheap moralizing – is precisely what Diderot and other critics of the period found most praiseworthy.

Painters such as Greuze, Fragonard, and David strove to provide depictions of those simple, compelling episodes of daily life best suited to grab attention and inspire moral admiration: betrothals, newborn babies, oaths of loyalty – including, notably, young women reading sentimental novels. Playwrights of the end of the century carried forward these expectations and built on them. From the audience's natural, involuntary emotional reactions to characters and events, Beaumarchais theorized, a self-questioning would follow; some would recognize their need for reform, others, who found their own character to be good, would cherish the play that gave them this pleasurable confirmation (Baasner 1988:192–193). By the time Mercier began his career as a playwright in 1769, he found that audiences expected "to be touched and to cry at his play" (quoted by Baasner 1988:205). A complicity had been established among playwrights, actors, and audience, a complicity that required training feelings in ways now alien to us. When Gluck arrived on the scene in the 1770s, similar conventions were applied to opera, with enthusiastic response from Paris audiences (Johnson 1995). Under the Terror, Johnson reports, actors were sometimes arrested for playing monarchists on the stage. The trend had reached its logical end point; person blended with persona (Johnson 1995:121). As art became didactic, its effects were supposed to appeal not to knowledgeable observers who understood its esthetic rules and aims, but to the simplest, the least instructed, the humble Pamelas. Its impact was to be achieved via the observer's inner rehearsal of the feelings depicted. This was an art virtually designed to take advantage of the power of emotives to manage feelings. It was also an art that increasingly depicted the world with bright contrasts of good and evil.

Two love letters exchanged between Jeanne-Marie Phlipon and her future husband Jean-Marie Roland at the beginning of their courtship in 1777 illustrate further the blurring of boundaries between reality and fiction, between public and private, in self-expression of the late eighteenth century. According to the editor of their letters, "This unpublished correspondence reveals Marie Phlipon establishing with Roland and composing, almost like an expert author, a novel that led to their marriage" (Join-Lambert 1896:iii). Like the protagonists of their beloved Jean-Jacques's novels, the lovers constantly mixed general remarks and specific expressions of sentiment, explaining the intensity of their feelings by references to maxims and principles of sentimentalist ideology. The resulting style was at once expository and personal, emotional and abstract. Like so much of the writing of the period, in effect, these letters are packed with elegant, pointed emotives whose effects on those who wrote or spoke them is an issue historians must consider.

In the earliest surviving letter, of 17 September 1777, Roland explains to Phlipon why, after a long delay, he had decided to write to her. He had been on a long journey through Italy and southern France, doing research into manufacturing and trade. During this journey, certain losses had brought him an unusual dose of pain and grief. "I know only two remedies to grief," he wrote:

friendship and violent shocks; I have made much use of shocks [through traveling]; don't judge me ill if I turn, a little, towards you for the other remedy; you spread about you, anyway, so many of those kinds of charm that sharpen and support feeling, even as they please and reassure the mind, that, if I have the recipe right, I doubt not I am turning to the right source as well.[15] (Join-Lambert 1896:2)

He writes of having given up on life. "[M]y friends, my friends alone, have been able to place an obstacle to my consent to destructive feelings" (p. 3).[16] His knowledge of Phlipon's own suffering suggests to him that his complaints will be understood: "You have been ill, you have lost friends, you have looked into the dark: we have much in common. This reassures me a little about the melancholy tone which I fear has left its trace in my letter" (p. 3).[17] In this letter Roland asks if Phlipon would be willing to look at his voluminous research notes from the recent voyage. (She had already agreed to help him write up reports based on earlier notes.) Phlipon responded with urgent enthusiasm, in a letter of 2 October 1777, which begins:

I am struck, delighted, sorrowful; I pity you, I scold you, I . . . I wish I had several tongues and could use them all at the same time. Is it possible you value even a little the memory of me, and yet waited so long to try to recall it? Is that forgetfulness or confidence? The first of these would be desperate and, anyway, you prevent me from believing it; I would prefer to pardon you for your presumption in being so confident of me, if I could say it was presumptuous. You are very lucky to be so pitiful! If I valued you less, I would fear you; but I would not tell you. Your letter made me cry, yet I am happier since I received it. (p. 5)[18]

---

[15] "Je ne connais que deux remèdes aux chagrins: l'amitié et de violentes secousses; j'ai fait grand usage de celui-ci; ne trouvez pas mauvais que j'aie un peu recours à vous pour l'autre; vous y répandez d'ailleurs tant de ces sortes d'agréments qui aiguisent et soutiennent le sentiment, en même temps qu'ils délectent et corroborent l'esprit, que, si j'ai bien jugé de la recette, je ne juge pas moins biens de l'adresse" (Join-Lambert 1896:2).

[16] "[M]es amis, mes seuls amis ont pu mettre quelque obstacle au consentement d'un sentiment destructeur" (p. 3).

[17] "Vous avez été malade, vous avez perdu de vos amis, vous avez eu du noir: voilà bien des conformités. Tout cela me rassure un peu sur le ton mélancolique dont je crains que ma lettre n'ait quelque empreinte" (p. 3).

[18] "Je suis pénétrée, ravie, désolée: je vous plains, je vous gronde, je vous . . . je voudrais posséder plusieurs langues et pouvoir me servir de toutes à la fois. Est-il possible que vous mettiez quelque prix à mon souvenir et que vous soyez resté si longtemps pour chercher à vous y rappeler! Est-ce oubli ou confiance? Le premier serait désespérant et d'ailleurs, vous m'empêchez d'y croire; j'aimerais mieux vous pardonner la présomption de la seconde, si je pouvais dire avec vérité que cette confiance fût

This is an extraordinary paragraph, packed with intimations, revealing an impatience for contact, and amounting to an avowal of love. The avowal is, to some degree, unsurprising. It was highly improper in that day for unmarried men and women to exchange letters, even more improper that the woman should write first, as Phlipon had done (although her first letter is lost). Therefore, Roland's reference to "a little" friendship is disingenuous; Phlipon's initial letter was already an avowal simply in being sent. His response, although slow in coming, was all she could have hoped for.

Sentimentalism shapes every sentence of this exchange. Roland explains his letter as the application of a principle: that shocks and friendship remedy grief. He esteems Phlipon's friendship as especially useful in this regard because of her charms, which are both emotional and intellectual, and because she has also suffered. These are the special sentimental virtues which women are supposed to possess. In her response, Phlipon indicates the extremes of feeling that his letter caused. Because virtue grows out of feeling, extremes of feeling, especially those deriving from love or "friendship," as in this case, are virtuous. Phlipon explains that her high estimation of Roland allows her to be sincere toward him, to reveal to him the many emotions his letter caused. ("If I valued you less, I would fear you; but I would not tell you.") This is another sentimentalist principle: virtue is sincere, sincerity is virtuous. Knowing Roland is virtuous, Phlipon is sincere with him. The centrality of sincerity to virtue also explains why it is in line with sentimentalist principle that virtue must and can override conventional proprieties. The improper exchange of letters is itself a sentimentalist gesture, and an offer of emotional refuge.

That these letters are gracefully written in a high style as if for a large audience is further evidence of sincerity (not insincere self-consciousness, as we would tend to imagine today). So is the fact that they were carefully conserved. Our natural feelings are all the same, virtue lies in not hiding them, feeling them fully, and acting on them. Roland and Phlipon have nothing to hide; the example of their virtue may uplift others. That their language is attractive, expressive, public, is still another seal of their virtuous openness.

présomptueuse. Vous êtes heureux d'être à plaindre! Si je vous estimais moins, je vous craindrais beaucoup; mais je ne vous le dirais pas. Votre lettre m'a fait pleurer, et cependant je suis plus heureuse depuis que je l'ai reçue" (p. 5).

Were Phlipon and Roland sincere? Or should we, as historians, avoid this unanswerable question and satisfy ourselves with noticing how they gave voice to widespread presuppositions of the age? The concept of emotives offers a third alternative. It is to suppose that, more often than not, the emotives in their letters were effective, eliciting a confirming response and intensifying emotional inclinations that were already there. A good sentimentalist, moreover, would take such a confirming response – a very common response to emotives – as evidence that the emotion expressed was indeed a natural one. The more intense it was, the more likely it was to be natural and good. This conviction could make possible a kind of vicious circle, a kind of escalation of intensity, as individuals fine-tuned emotives in search of a natural elevation of sentiment.

Anthropological research offers many examples of practices that aim at enhancing approved emotions to high intensity. The Chaitanyaite sect of northern India concentrates on developing the feeling of *viraha* (love-in-separation) for Krishna through an arduous ascetic regime (Toomey 1990). The Paxtun women studied by Grima (1992) expend constant effort talking about and expressing *gham* (grief); moments of loss such as death or departure are seen as central, defining features of a life, and the feelings they bring are overwhelming at the time and constantly rehearsed afterward. The epistolary excesses of some late sentimentalists are much easier to understand in the context of such anthropological findings.

Germaine de Staël's extravagant style, for example, has frustrated more than one of her biographers, just as her personal manner frustrated her mother, Mme de Charrière, and others in her own day. Often her letters lack the grace of the Rolands' initial exchange. Take, for example, the following excerpt from a letter written by Germaine de Staël to her lover, comte Louis de Narbonne, in October 1792:

Do I deserve this atrocious death you have inflicted on me? You have allowed a mail delivery to pass without writing me. I have taken up a kind of passion for you that absorbs my whole being. I will owe you everything if you do not abandon me. If you took me to New Zealand, you would be my guardian and my God. And if you abandoned me on the throne of the universe, you would be my assassin. There is nothing exaggerated about this statement. (Diesbach 1983:129)

Four years later, a new lover, Adolphe Ribbing, was receiving equally unqualified assurances: "I love you, I would expose myself to anything

for you, I think only of your happiness" (p. 181). Narbonne, she assures
Ribbing, was never as important to her: "[T]hat which is called love,
that invincible attraction of the eyes as well as of the heart, I never felt
it for him" (p. 182). Staël's biographer, Diesbach, who cites these letters,
does not consider her to be "a character out of *Liaisons dangereuses*, as
some of her political adversaries accused her of being"; still, he
expresses surprise at her "bad faith" (pp. 102, 182). Balayé (1979), one
of the foremost authorities on Staël's life and work, explains that,
although Staël shifted constantly from one strong feeling to another,
with little interval, she was not, as some have charged, faking. As we
have seen, many contemporaries, including Mme de Charrière and
Mme Necker, felt the new style of emotional expression was artificial
and insincere. But terms such as "affectation" and "bad faith" may be
terms that miss the underlying consistency of Staël's self-perception.
She viewed emotional expression as merely an attempt to describe
something natural, powerful, morally pure, and urgent. For her, natural
feeling and truth were the same thing.[19] When she sought to drink at
the wellhead of this inner flow of natural truth, it seems likely that she
often formulated emotives that intensified her feelings, thus confirming her hope that she had "found" a true and genuine sentiment to
"describe." At other times, if the emotives were not efficacious, she
might rightly regard statements she had made as deficient and, therefore, as neither true nor binding on her. This is not to say that she was
unconcerned about sincerity. She simply regarded those feelings which
she believed she "found" within herself as sincere by definition, even
though she was actively managing them in accord with her sentimentalist convictions. The young Benjamin Constant proved himself to be
her match in this kind of vigorous management of "natural" feeling. In
1795, after months of fruitless courting of Staël, Constant woke up a
country house full of guests one night with his violent convulsions. He
was dying of love, he claimed, and demanded to see her, scandalizing

---

[19] Here are some representative citations: (1) from a 1798 manuscript: "Tous les sentiments naturels sont des idées justes" (cited in the introduction by Gérard Gengembre
and Jean Goldzink to Staël [1800:23]). (2)"[L]e talent exprime avec d'autant plus de
force et de chaleur les affections sensibles, que la réflexion et la philosophie ont élevé
plus haut la pensée" (Staël [1800:152]). (3) "Mais la parure de la vérité, dans un pays
libre, est d'accord avec la vérité même. L'expression et le sentiment doivent dériver
de la même source" (Staël [1800:310]). (4) The "foyer naturel" of eloquence is "la puissance des sentiments sur notre âme" (Staël [1800:403]). For similar ideas in Vauve-
nargues and Diderot, see Baasner (1988), pp. 155–156, 190.

some witnesses, impressing others with his effrontery. But Staël was convinced and began to soften toward him (Diesbach 1983:165–166).

Barker-Benfield (1992) notes both the origin of Wesley's ideas about emotion in sentimentalist doctrine and the resemblances between his sect's emphasis on emotion and sentimentalist practice. Whether sentimentalism was a "cult" or a "religion" is unimportant here; what is important is that it encouraged the systematic exploitation of the power of emotives to shape feeling in the name of a doctrine of natural feeling. The result was an emotional style which, like grieving among the Paxtun (and in many other locations), encouraged the pursuit of excess. Those for whom such emotives did not work, or for whom they worked some of the time and did not work other times, doubtless also often regarded their contemporaries with the same thinly veiled frustration that Paxtun men often express toward their women. But when they recognized the astonishing effects of emotives on others they formulated their recognition as a problem of "sincerity" because sentimentalism taught that feelings were either natural or hypocritical.

The plots of sentimentalist novels, plays, and operas were often Manichean in structure, that is, they pitted good against evil in an effort to arouse empathy and right moral judgment. Maza has shown how plot structures and intense emotionality could be easily exploited by lawyers to fashion compelling printed briefs for their clients, briefs that circulated in the tens of thousands in the years before the Revolution (Maza 1993). In these briefs, politics, society, sentiment, and morality were fused together into an attractive reformist vision. Some read like novels (again fiction and reality were blurred). To us, this seems odd. But at the time, the novel genre was praised by its defenders for its unparalleled realism, source of its didactic force (Chartier 1999); attorneys believed the conventions of the genre themselves were a kind of badge of sincerity. The briefs were printed to skirt the secrecy of Old Regime courts; public opinion was a higher tribunal, whose judgment of the case had greater weight than that of the established courts. Public opinion's judgment was of greater weight because the public was sensitive to natural feelings of benevolence and pity, and therefore capable of discerning the sincerity and the suffering of the injured party. The injured party was usually depicted as a commoner (like the public as a whole), his opponent as an aristocrat (concerned with appearances, artificiality, etiquette, luxury, debauchery). The court, its manners, and its fashions became the epitome of immorality and corruption. The injured party's willingness to tell all to the public was itself a proof of his innocence, because aristocratic honor required concealment; the guilty must lie, their lies are devoid of natural feeling and easily penetrated, therefore they try to keep silent. Putting sentimentalism to practical use in this way gave the Manichean plot structures of its literary genres a sinister new political import (Maza 1993:14). While offering implicit support to calls for popular political participation, more than any abstract theorizing could have done, such a strategy also necessarily heightened the concern about sincerity – both one's own sincerity and that of others. In the cases of the 1780s, both sides sought to deploy the same sentimentalist strategy. Which side was faking? Doubts about sincerity had to arise, when open emotionality no longer gave an unambiguous message. Lack of sincerity, in turn, came widely to be regarded as a certain sign of evil intent. As Maza has noted, the contours of thinking that would characterize the Terror were already visible in 1789.

THE COMING CRISIS

By the end of the 1780s, royal ministers were grappling with the most serious fiscal crisis to face the government in sixty years, and a general consensus was forming that the solution must lie in profound reform of the whole system of privilege. These were also the years in which the conventions of late sentimentalism – its Manicheism, its appeal to audiences who had learned through practice to find the wellsprings of pity within themselves on short notice – were coming to play an increasing role in political debate itself. The summer and fall of 1788 also saw the worst harvest failure of the century, ensuring that the following spring would bring high food prices, widespread beggary, even famine. This was the concatenation of circumstances that gave rise to the Revolution. In the next chapter, I will not try to provide a narrative of this extraordinary episode in European history, but I will try to highlight those features of the Revolution that seem to reflect the power of emotives, as focused by late sentimentalist presuppositions, to shape feelings. From this interaction, utopian hopes, at first, gained sway. Revolutionaries for a time were gripped with the idea that all of society could be transformed into an emotional refuge, like close friends meeting in a salon, like an audience in tears at a performance of Gluck's *Orphée et Eurydice*. But when these hopes proved ill founded, sentimentalism collapsed and disappeared with remarkable suddenness.

CHAPTER 6

Sentimentalism in the Making of the French Revolution (1789–1815)

In 1780 Jeanne-Marie Phlipon, the young daughter of an engraver, married Jean-Marie Roland, a well-off inspector of manufactures. We have already seen that they lived their own courtship and marriage as if they were characters in a kind of sentimentalist novel. When the Revolution broke out nine years later, Jeanne-Marie was much more engaged and more resourceful than her husband in taking part in the new world of politics that opened up. (On her life, see May 1970.) She wrote articles for Jacques-Pierre Brissot's successful new paper, *Le Patriote français*. She urged her husband into politics, taking a large role in shaping his views and determining his allies. On 15 January 1793, when Roland resigned as minister of interior, he read out before the Convention a forceful defense of his stewardship and a call for a full reorganization of the government. But the Convention, preoccupied with the trial of Louis XVI, ignored his recommendations. The manuscript of that speech, which has survived, was written in his wife's hand. The Rolands had by this time ranged themselves with the moderates, the so-called Girondins, who opposed the execution of the king. The king, however, was condemned to die shortly afterward, and mounted the scaffold on 21 January. In the subsequent months, disagreements between the Girondins and their chief rivals, the rising Jacobin faction, only worsened. Party rivalry spread to the provinces, breaking out in open violence in some cases. During these troubled months, the Rolands kept a low profile. Nonetheless, when the Commune of Paris and the National Guard finally rose up to expel the Girondins from the Convention on 31 May 1793, officials ordered the arrest of Roland for unspecified reasons. As her husband went into hiding, Jeanne-Marie Roland climbed into a hired carriage and rushed to the Convention to denounce this illegal act.

When she got to the Tuileries Palace, she found the Convention under guard, the doors closed. She struggled to get a message in to the presiding officer, so that it could be read from the rostrum, but to no avail. She found an usher she knew and persuaded him to ask an old associate, Pierre-Victurnien Vergniaud, to come out and speak with her. To Vergniaud she unfolded her desire to make a speech to the Convention. "If they will let me in," she told him, according to her own account of the day,

I will dare to say what even you cannot express without being accused; I fear nothing in the world, and if I do not save Roland, I will at least express with force truths that will not be without utility to the Republic. Warn your worthy colleagues, a surge of courage can have a great effect [*un élan de courage peut faire un grand effet*] and will be at least a great example. (Roland 1905:I, 13)

She believed that she could have made a great impact, perhaps even saving the day for the moderates.

I was, in effect, in that state of mind that makes one eloquent; full of indignation, beyond all fear, enflamed for my country whose ruin I foresaw, everything I love exposed to the greatest danger, feeling strongly, expressing myself with facility, too proud to speak other than with nobility. I had the greatest issues to discuss, a number of arguments ready to defend them, and I was uniquely situated to make those arguments with effect. (p. 13)[1]

But Vergniaud told Jeanne-Marie Roland that there was no way she could be admitted to address the Convention. It was already deeply involved in the debate over the Commune's call to expel the Girondins; at the very least, there would be an hour-and-a-half wait, while other speakers came to the rostrum.

Later that evening, Mme Roland returned to the Tuileries in another hired carriage, to try again. To her surprise, however, the session had already been adjourned. This could only be bad news, she thought. Why adjourn, unless the Convention had delivered itself into the hands of the Jacobins and their allies in the Commune and the National

---

[1] "J'étais effectivement dans cette disposition d'âme qui rend éloquent; pénétrée d'indignation, au-dessus de toute crainte, enflammé pour mon pays dont je voyais la ruine, tout ce que j'aime au monde exposé aux derniers dangers, sentant fortement, m'exprimant avec facilité, trop fière pour ne pas le faire avec noblesse, j'avais les plus grands intérêts à traiter, quelques moyens pour les défendre, et j'étais dans une situation unique pour le faire avec avantage."

Guard? As she turned to get back into her carriage, the driver noticed a stray dog and decided to bring it home for his son. They began rolling out of the Place du Carrousel, but the carriage suddenly stopped. The dog had jumped off. "Little one! Little one! Come back!" called the driver. For a moment, Roland did not understand. Then,

I remembered the dog. I thought it was sweet and friendly to have a driver at that time who was a good man, a father, sensitive [*un bon homme, père et sensible*]. "Try to catch him," I said, "you can put him inside the carriage and I will guard him." The good man, full of joy, got the dog, opened the door, and gave me a companion. That poor animal seemed to sense that it had found protection and asylum. I was well caressed. I remembered that story called *Saadi* about an old man who, tired of human company, put off by their passions, retires to a forest where he makes himself a hut. He passes his time by adopting a few animals who repay his kindness with signs of affection and gratitude, which satisfied him – since he could not find any with his own kind. (p. 17)

Mme Roland herself was arrested the following day. Released about three weeks later, she was arrested again in August and guillotined on 8 November 1793. When her husband, still in hiding in Rouen, heard of her death, he committed suicide.

To the very end, Jeanne-Marie Roland spoke a language of emotions that is strange to us today, and which we must struggle to understand. Of course, it is not odd that she wished to defend her husband. Nor is it odd that she should feel sympathy for a stray dog or affection for a man who wishes to care for it and give it a home. But we are not pre-pared to appreciate that Mme Roland, in effect, exulted in the extremes of feeling that overcame her as she thought of speaking to the Con-vention in a crisis. She regarded these feelings, not as impediments to effective public speaking as we might now, not as dangerous to her purpose and needing to be contained, but as the very wellspring of eloquence. Doubtless, in doing so, she thought along lines anyone in the Convention would have understood. Poised before them as a loyal wife, concerned at once about both her husband's and her fatherland's fate, tears running down her face as she begged the assembly to find its courage and resist the pressures being brought to bear upon it, she would have made a subject worthy of a David painting. She would have absorbed her audience's attention and won its empathy, in just the way Diderot prescribed for the playwright, for the painter.

We are also not prepared to appreciate that, while petting a stray dog in a hired carriage, Roland's mind turned almost at once, not to the pleasures and companionship dogs can offer to young children, not to pets she or her family or friends may have had, but to a story about an old man who has retired to a primeval forest. This man finds in the companionship of animals the affection men and women have denied him. It is a typical sentimentalist trope: civilization corrupts and dries up the flow of natural feeling; primitive nature restores it.

On 30 May 1793, the day before these events, a young Jacobin, Antoine-Louis Saint-Just, had been elected to the Convention's powerful Committee of Public Safety, the quasi-executive agency that would organize the Terror. It was he who would deliver a report to the Convention later in July condemning the Girondins and justifying their arrest. Ironically, Saint-Just felt about animals much the same way as Mme Roland. In an unfinished essay, called *De la nature*, found among his papers after his own death (on the guillotine, along with Robespierre, on 28 July 1794), Saint-Just praised the sociability of animals. Every species that breathes, he said, has laws governing its independence, its social relationships, its defense against other species.

These laws are their natural relationships, these relationships are their needs and their affections; according to the nature of their intelligence or their *sensibilité*, animals associate with each other to a greater or lesser degree.

Some gather in springtime. Others in many seasons; they meet without mistreating each other or fleeing from each other. (Saint-Just 1976:141)

Man alone has a problem, according to Saint-Just. Originally he, like animals, formed groups according to his ("social") affections, and defended his group against others according to his ("political") independence. The social realm was the realm of *sensibilité*, the political realm that of force. But, in history, gradually, force came to be used within groups, instead of only between them. The natural social affections that tied humans together were corrupted by the political reign of force within society.

People originally associated in order to protect themselves, it was said. But against whom? The original form of society "was not a prey to politics; it was ruled by natural law. Man became savage only when he confused the laws that ought to govern nations with those which ought to govern men" (pp. 143–144). Like Mme Roland, Saint-Just believed that the business of the Revolution was to restore this natural state. Just as her encounter with a stray dog became for her a kind of figure of her own homelessness in a polity gone astray, so Saint-Just regarded his struggle as one of natural man against corrupt political force. Both believed that force had to be met with force, in order for the Republic to be founded. This was unfortunate, but for Saint-Just the implications of natural law were crystal clear. He who used force was putting himself outside the group, into a state of war. Hence his famous dictum during the trial of Louis XVI, that "no one can reign innocently." "Louis," Saint-Just charged, "is a stranger in our midst" (quoted in Blum 1986: 175, Blum's translation). Likewise, the prevalence of force in Old Regime governance had resulted in such widespread corruption that only a reign of terror, a special kind of "revolutionary government," could rid society of those who conducted themselves like strangers within it, those who believed force to be legitimate.

For Saint-Just as for Mme Roland, politics was entirely emotional. "We must not," Saint-Just warned, "confuse the sentiments of the soul with the passions. The first are a gift of nature and the principle of social life. The others are the fruit of usurpation and the principles of savage life" (Saint-Just 1976:140). "Terror" was precisely the passion republicans wished to inflict on the corrupt, to make way for the soulful sentiments of natural society. In the dire circumstances of 1793, a true patriot combined "a cool spirit and the fire of a pure and ardent heart" (quoted in Higonnet 1998:89).[2]

In this chapter I wish to accomplish three things: (1) I will argue that sentimentalist doctrines, whose history up to 1789 was briefly examined in the preceding chapter, remained central to the unfolding of events, from the outbreak of the Revolution in May–June 1789 down to the end of the Terror in July 1794. (2) I will show that these same doctrines were quickly suppressed thereafter, so much so that it became difficult even to mention them. In the end, as we will see, it became hard to remember that they had ever possessed any influence whatever. (3) I will consider how the concept of emotives can help explain both the Revolution's rapid evolution to ever greater radicalism up until 1794, and its sudden shift, after the fall of Robespierre in July 1794, to a decidedly moderate republicanism.

SENTIMENTALISM: THE MISSING INGREDIENT

A great deal of research has been focused on explaining the extremism and violence of the Revolution in recent years. As the idea of class conflict has lost its explanatory power, and cultural and

---

[2] "la froideur de l'esprit, le feu d'un coeur ardent et pur."

poststructuralist methods have gained influence, the constant "escalation" of the Revolution toward radical democracy – accompanied by the breakdown of law and order, civil war, and widespread judicial murder – has become a puzzle.

François Furet (1981) emphasized that the Revolution began with the breakdown of royal government, leaving a vacuum of power, a vacuum that for a time could only be filled by individuals manipulating key abstractions such as "the people," "liberty," or "the nation." Carol Blum (1986) traced out the close affinity between certain peculiarities of Rousseau's thought and the concrete policies and assumptions of the leading Jacobins on the Committee of Public Safety. Rousseau believed that he discovered his innocence and his virtue when he looked within himself, that these characteristics united him with all others. A virtuous man, he could fuse with other virtuous persons. Death might be the appropriate penalty for those who refused such virtuous togetherness. The resemblance between these ideas and those of Saint-Just, Robespierre, and others on the Committee is, indeed, striking. Lynn Hunt (1992) has noted the uncanny similarity between the way the Jacobins talked about violence, especially about the death of the king, on the one hand, and, on the other, Freud's theory about the role of parricide in the founding of states in *Totem and Taboo*. Patrice Higonnet (1998) argues that Jacobin ideology was optimistic and humane to the bitter end. However, their ideals were at once communitarian and individualistic. When forced to choose between these two opposed values, Jacobin leaders all too often fell back on certain attitudes deriving from the Old Regime: the idea of "quasi-mystical loyalty" to the state, Catholic intolerance toward dissent, and a vivid sense of the "majestic public purpose" of the state (Higonnet 1998:70–73). Patrice Gueniffey agrees that the Revolutionaries were led by a "fatal spirit of imitation" and that Revolutionary crowds possessed a long-standing "culture of punishment" (Gueniffey 2000: 95, 99). Timothy Tackett has recently proposed that the widespread fear of conspiracy that plagued the Revolutionaries, based in large measure on the frequent occurrence of real, localized conspiracies, "exerted a profound effect on the origins of a Terror mentality among political elites in the spring and summer of 1792" (Tackett 2000:713).

Some scholars have begun to insist on the generalized impact of sentimentalist ideas. Both Denby (1994) and Vincent-Buffault (1986) have brought forward numerous uses of sentimentalist ideas and expressions in the early years of the Revolution. But so far no attempt has been made to explore the broader implications of this evidence.

To make progress in this area, it is simply necessary to keep firmly in mind the claims of Shaftesbury, that each one of us is possessed, at birth, of a moral sense that signals its perceptions to us through certain sentiments – love, pity, generosity, gratitude. In the passages from Shaftesbury quoted in Chapter 5, he, like Mme Roland and Saint-Just, compared animals favorably to human beings; both, he insisted, must be possessed of some modicum of "pity, love, kindness, or social affection" for his or her kind. But humanity was also capable of error; and "anything which teaches men" to deviate from natural affection toward their fellows "is not nor ever can be virtue of any kind or in any sense but must remain still horrid depravity" (Shaftesbury 1711:178–179, 175). It was optimistic to see goodness as natural, to be sure, but the same move made any deviation from goodness appear unnatural.

Revolutionaries, like many literate French men and women (and many illiterate ones who had learned such ideas from theater, painting, engravings, popular songs) thought along similar lines, although there were significant variations. It is not that they had read Shaftesbury in the original. They could have found the same ideas expressed in hundreds of essays and works of art. By 1789, the existence of a moral sensibility was simple common sense. It was quite possible, therefore, for one man to speak for a whole people without consulting them. If he looked into his heart (where he found the same natural sentiments anyone would find), if he ensured that he acted according to his heart's dictates, he could rest assured that he acted patriotically, that he applied the will of all.

Blum exaggerates the differences between Rousseau and his contemporaries and fails to recognize that he merely focused and enhanced an already prevailing emotional common sense. Rousseau's influence was great, but not everything can be laid at his door. Rousseau's celebrated falling-out with his fellow philosophes, and his solitary, even paranoid ways were the acts not of a loner but of a sentimentalist. It was not just Rousseau who affirmed the necessary infallibility of his own moral sense. He did do a great deal to propagate this idea; but by the time he did so, thousands of educated readers were prepared to understand and applaud. It was not just Rousseau who became paranoid, either. The very words of Shaftesbury, quoted in Chapter 5, encouraged stark moral judgments of others as either good or bad, natural or corrupt. Even Rousseau's loudest critics, such as Diderot or

Voltaire, were quick to identify evildoers and denounce them. Like Diderot, Voltaire, Suard, and (to a limited extent) Montesquieu and Condorcet – like Marivaux, Baculard, Riccoboni, Staël, and (to a limited extent) Beaumarchais – Rousseau's thinking bathed in an atmosphere in which ideas like Shaftesbury's were taken for granted.

Furet failed to recognize that such convictions easily underwrote the use of abstractions to justify political claims and political policies. The political power of empty words during the Terror had more than a merely institutional or political origin; it derived, as well, from sentimentalism. Higonnet fails to appreciate that, for Jacobins, as for any sentimentalist, individualistic and communitarian values were not at odds; the inborn moral sense, once individuals were free to follow its callings, would ensure the triumph of community. If there was disagreement, negotiation was not the first thing to occur to people of this period. Instead, each was called upon to check his heart again. If he was sure of the natural source of his feeling, then those who disagreed lacked morality. (What better way for Mme Roland to prove that the Convention ought to hear her than to hug a stray dog?) Once the Revolution began, Higonnet tells us, the new leaders became "addicted to self-criticism," and expected "to provide long autobiographies to prove that their conduct had been blameless from the start" (Higonnet 1998:81). This was their way of debating policy. To be blameless was to be in touch with the perceptions of the natural moral sense. To be blameless was to be right. We today expect politicians to seek compromise, to engage in the art of the possible – even to the point of inspiring cynicism about their commitment to values. In the 1790s, they checked their hearts, then embraced intransigence.

Hunt fails to appreciate that the Revolutionaries had their own psychological theories. Higonnet remarks,

Jacobins emphasized not just externally visible acts but inner emotion and character. They did not ask, "What did you do when you heard of the death of the king?" They wondered instead, "How did you feel when you heard this news?" and "Were you pleased to see that the nation had been restored to its rights when the goods of the clergy had been confiscated?" (p. 81)

Higonnet says such impulses were "reminiscent of prerevolutionary Catholic confessions" (p. 82); but they were far more reminiscent of epistolary novels or the judicial memoirs studied by Maza (1993). They were the direct application of sentimentalist doctrine. Hunt makes much of the Jacobins' ambivalence about violence, especially about the execution of the king. But they were perfectly aware of this ambivalence; they gloried in it (as Higonnet has noted). They understood the irony that, in fighting fire with fire, they were constantly called upon to act with brutality. But to be brutal could be itself a kind of sacrifice. As Danton put it, "Let us be terrible so that the people do not have to be" (quoted in Gueniffey 2000:85).[3] He accepted that every act of crowd violence was possibly, probably, an emanation of the human heart. The concern with family and images of family relationships Hunt found so prevalent in the period points back to the fundamental conception that there were natural sentiments guiding us toward benevolent and affectionate bonds – first of all toward those nature gives us as kin. The king should have been a "good father" to his people. The king betrayed his natural role. For many, it followed, he had to die. But that did not mean a good Jacobin felt no regret, no longing for a different outcome.

Tackett notes that the radical left developed "a deeply held sentiment that their version of democratic egalitarianism was profoundly true and right. . . . It was only one step further to the assumption that all who disagreed with the Jacobins' positions must of necessity be fools, dupes, or conspirators" (Tackett 2000:705). But these ideas did not come out of the air; they were not formulated opportunistically in the give-and-take of political conflict. This was sentimentalist ideology. One can hear the will of the people by listening sincerely to one's own moral sentiments; the capacity to listen in this way is confined to simple people, people who are without pride, aristocratic pretensions, or arrogance – people, literally, who live like animals, in tune with their own nature. Because they could consult this image by looking within, Jacobins had no need of votes, of opinion polls, or of compromise with opponents. "The image of 'the good people' rapidly became a leitmotif in the writings of many radicals," Tackett remarks (p. 705). Gueniffey notes that the Jacobins endowed an abstraction, "the people," with the same dignity and arbitrary power that the king had held before the Revolution (2000:81–110). But this was not the result of an unreflective adherence to Old Regime political habits. They firmly believed that the human heart spoke with one voice. Such a heart deserved the highest dignity and the fullest power. The power of emotives to shape feeling made such sentimentalist doctrine all the more believable because emotives often provided the confirming leaps of feeling within one's own heart, feeling that appeared to be the voice of nature.

---

[3] "Soyons terribles pour éviter au peuple de l'être."

The existence of an unspoken set of sentimentalist assumptions, a different emotional common sense from our own, is the missing link that can draw together all the recent efforts to make sense of the Revolution. That it has taken so long to realize its importance only tells us how profound was the reaction after 1794 that erased its memory.

THE EARLY YEARS OF THE REVOLUTION

The events of 1789 were shaped both by optimistic and by Manichean sentimentalist notions. The famous Night of 4 August, for example, during which the new National Assembly took its first step toward formulating the Declaration of Rights of Man and Citizen, has all the trappings of a sentimentalist gesture, an attempt to transform the nation itself into a kind of emotional refuge. The session went from 6:00 P.M. to 2:00 A.M., and during these hours, the delegates, by their own account, "abolished the feudal regime," that is, agreed to sweep away the whole vast and complex array of privileges that divided French citizens: privileges of the aristocracy, of the church, of towns, provinces, guilds, and seigneuries. As the older Marxist explanation had it, the driving force behind this sweeping set of reforms was the class interest of the bourgeoisie. Spurred by word of peasant insurrections and château burning, as well as passive resistance to taxes and dues, they sought to head off popular violence by an array of preemptive reforms. For more recent revisionist researchers, the Assembly's dismantling of privilege was a singular problem, because the revisionists showed, in study after study, that privileges were broadly shared by middle- and lower-ranking members of the society of orders. Guild masterships were privileges, as were the rights to engage in business enjoyed by Bordeaux merchants or Lyon manufacturers. The *cahiers de doléances* called for reform, not abolition, of privilege. The abolition of privilege was an ambitious piece of social engineering, an embarrassing difficulty for any explanation that attempts to view the Revolution as a merely political crisis.

But in the context of studies on sentimentalism, it is noteworthy that the Assembly's own official record of the debate treats the reform as an act of sentimental benevolence, rising up from natural sensitivities of the delegates (Hirsch 1978). The record speaks of "patriotic sacrifices" – where "patriotic" acts, as Maza has noted, were "selfless" and "humanitarian" – not narrowly nationalistic (Maza 1997:223). The procedure followed during the session was to favor reform proposals that came from a delegate who enjoyed the very privileges he proposed to abolish. Nobles offered to give up their tax exemptions, clergy their tithes, provincial delegates the privileges of their provinces, and so on. The night's work was widely described as a kind of sentimental cascade of reforms. Expressions of feeling often brought deliberation to a complete halt. The transcript, at one point, after mentioning proposals for the abolition of the church's tithe rights, notes that: "The signs of rapture and the outpouring of generous feelings which swept the Assembly, sharper and more animated with each hour that passed, hardly left time to specify the prudent provisions necessary to apply these beneficial measures" (Hirsch 1978:165).[4] Here is how the offer made by delegates to abolish provincial privileges was introduced in the official record:

After this observation [on the abolition of the tithe], which seemed to exhaust the extensive subject of reforms, *the attention and the sensibility of the Assembly were again awakened* and focused by an offer of an entirely new kind.

The delegates of the provinces called *pays d'Etats, yielding to the impulse of generosity, or counting on that of their constituents expressed in their cahiers, or simply presuming such generosity and offering themselves as guarantors, so to speak, of ratification,* offered to renounce the privileges of their provinces, to associate themselves with the new regime, which the king's justice, and that of the Assembly, were preparing for the whole of France. (p. 167; emphasis added)[5]

Both passages imply warm approbation of spontaneous acts of generosity that are accompanied by and stimulate feelings of benevolence

---

[4] "Les signes de transport et l'effusion de sentiments généreux dont l'Assemblée présentait le tableau, plus vif et plus animé d'heure en heure, n'ont pu qu'à peine laisser le temps de stipuler les mesures de prudence, avec lesquelles il convenait de réaliser ces projets salutaires."

[5] "Après cette observation, qui semblait épuiser le sujet si étendu des réformes, l'attention et la sensibilité de l'Assemblée ont été encore réveillées et attachées par des offres d'un ordre tout nouveau.

"Le députés des provinces appelées pays d'Etats, se livrant à l'impulsion de leur générosité, ou se prévalant de celle de leurs commettants, exprimée par leur cahiers, ou enfin la présumant, et se rendant en quelque sorte garants de leur ratification, ont offert la renonciation aux privilèges de leurs provinces, pour s'associer au régime nouveau, que la justice du Roi et celle de l'Assemblée préparaient à la France entière."

that border on the sublime. The flow of action and feeling – which is inherently pleasurable – is more important than working out the precise details of the legislation. Here reason is not just supplemented by feeling but, on this most important night of reform, is completely replaced by sentiment. At the same time, the transcript's wording suggests a certain uneasiness in the explanation offered for the delegates' motives. They are representatives; as such, they are duty-bound to act only according to the wishes of their constituents, a task that calls for care, deliberation, reserve. Yet prevailing expectations require that an act such as the renunciation of a privilege rise up from a natural wellspring of feeling. The tortured syntax of the rapporteur attempts to reconcile these two requirements.[6] The Assembly itself had acted much like the late eighteenth-century theater and opera audiences, described by Johnson (1995), that initially surprised Mercier (Baasner 1988:205). Like a theater audience, the Assembly expected to feel deeply, knew how to cry on cue, and believed that, in yielding to sentiment, they enacted natural virtue. Possessed of such legitimacy, they could afford to overlook the details of their mandates. Emotives that induced benevolence made them good lawgivers.

The fall of the Bastille on 14 July and the Great Fear that spread through the countryside in late July and early August were more Manichean in character. Whether sentimentalist ideas had been widely enough disseminated to influence the laboring poor in cities and in fields is an open question. There are indications that the topoi of sentimentalism were familiar far down the social ladder. Maza's evidence shows that thousands of lowly clerks and shopkeepers, at least in Paris, were avid followers of the celebrated affairs she examines. In addition, she shows that elite belief in the purity and sincerity of country people's emotions was conveyed to peasants in a variety of ways. Daniel Roche emphasizes how widely literacy had spread among the laboring poor of Paris by 1789, especially among the numerous domestic servants of the city. Among them, he notes "the frequent use of the sentimental, even erotic love letter" (Roche 1981:213). Arlette Farge's (1986) research on late eighteenth-century documents called "declarations of pregnancy" ("déclarations de grossesse") shows that unwed mothers often blamed their seduction on the adroit use of what we can easily recognize as a sentimentalist idiom. For example,

---

[6] Hirsch (1978) reports that the official transcript went through several drafts and took over three weeks to complete.

Madeleine Cougy, a cook, was hotly pursued by her lover. "He played mandoline for her; he threw himself to his knees, kissed her hands; he cried." The declaration of another young woman, Madeleine David, says that her seducer lent her novels to read, slipping love letters between the pages where she would find them, in a manner reminiscent of Saint Preux in *La nouvelle Héloïse* (Farge 1986:44–45; see also Vincent-Buffault 1986:31). Georges Lefebvre's careful research on the Great Fear showed that, in late July and early August, in thousands of villages, rumors of nonexistent bands of brigands and aristocrats bent on revenge sparked mobilization of recently organized militias to protect the peace. When word of these rumors came to Paris, they were denounced as part of an aristocratic plot. Ironically, notes Lefebvre, such opportunistic dismissals actually stoked the flames of fear (Lefebvre 1932). More to the point, both those who believed the rumors and those who blamed them on a plot may have been drawing on another sentimentalist cliché, that of the amoral aristocratic evildoer. Hardly consonant with the social reality of the time, this idea had been rehearsed in hundreds of novels and plays, from Molière's *Dom Juan* to Beaumarchais' *Le mariage de Figaro*.

It is understandable that participants in a revolution as profound and unprecedented as that of 1789 should feel intense emotions. The aim here is simply to point out three things: (1) that the dominant language of emotion available by that time was the language of late sentimentalism; (2) that this language, viewed in the light of the concept of emotives, was ideally suited for eliciting intense emotions, emotions of a kind that many novel readers, letter writers, and theatergoers had already trained themselves to feel; and (3) that this language was also well suited for raising doubts about the sincerity of these emotions – just because they were supposed to be, but never could be, "natural." This language had, for decades, encouraged the use of fiction and theater to educate and to instill virtue – the use, that is, of plot structures that, to our eyes, simplified social perceptions often to the point of caricature and depicted good and evil in constant combat. These plot structures also dealt with everyday characters and situations in defiance of traditional literary principles and were thus regarded at the time as especially realistic. It is an open question the extent to which the wide dissemination of this language and such plot structures shaped the astonishing hostility that the Third Estate was said to feel toward the privileged orders – clergy and nobility – in 1788–1789. A generation of detailed social research has demonstrated that the orders were becoming increasingly irrelevant to social practice. How they became so suddenly, so intensely meaningful is an issue that has vexed historians for some time now. The answer may lie in the history of emotions.

In the early years (1789–1791) as new networks of political clubs affiliated with the Paris club known as the Jacobins spread across the countryside, their leaders took pains to ensure that the meetings would be welcoming to all, serving as emotional refuges as well as democratic public spaces, just as the salonnières of the pre-Revolutionary days had done. Higonnet (1998) has found that

> the rules of many clubs were designed to make it possible for every member to have his say. At Moret, not far from Paris, the club set up a special committee at whose meetings members who feared to address a larger group might find the courage to speak up: "the only purpose of this committee . . . is to enable citizens to make those statements which they might otherwise not make because of their timidity or their inability to speak to a large audience." No one could speak a second time until all those who had something to say had spoken. Not allowed to interrupt, members were enjoined to listen to all speakers, who were under an obligation to speak politely, to the point, and not too often. At Ozoir-la-Ferrière the *clubbistes* adopted a procedure guaranteeing access to the podium because "it is evident that without this rule, it would not be possible for us to understand one another and for our society to reach the goal it has set for itself." To ensure fluidity and free access to the podium, presidents of clubs held office for one month only and, as a rule, were not eligible for immediate reelection. The Jacobins' increasingly intolerant stand after August 1792 was a definite break with their attitude in the first and more generous days of the Revolution. (p. 78)

Yet even the increasing intolerance Higonnet refers to had a sentimentalist basis insofar as it rested on a Manichean fear of the immorality of plotters (Tackett 2000).

Voices continued to be raised in favor of emotional moderation; but they were regarded with increasing suspicion. Condorcet, for example, urged representatives to be swayed by reason rather than passion; it was better, he said, "to enlighten than to move," and in a newspaper article as late as 31 October 1792, he denounced the use of passion in speeches (Aulard 1906:I, 265–266). But even those closest to him politically did not follow him in this. Brissot, defending Condorcet against his detractors in the Legislative Assembly on 25 April 1792, recalled Condorcet's long efforts, in partnership with the likes of Voltaire and d'Alembert, in the fight against fanaticism under the Old Regime: "Do you think that, if the glowing spirits of these great men had not, little by little, ignited our souls and shown them the secret of their grandeur and their strength, do you think that today the tribune would echo with your speeches about liberty?" (quoted in Aulard 1906:I, 252).[7] Condorcet's greatness is here assimilated to the forward march of sentimentalism.

For Brissot, the very essence of the eighteenth-century intellectual revolution was the discovery of natural feeling, as he stated in a kind of profession of faith in 1782:

Reason shows me only shadows, where the moral sense [*le sens moral*] enlightens and directs me. I leave reason behind, therefore, and follow only my moral instinct [*instinct moral*], the voice of happiness. I am happy when I work for the good of my fellow humans, when I do good for them. I am happy when I believe I am looked down upon by a Supreme Being, when I think I see him smile upon my feeble efforts and encourage them; I am happy when I call upon him, when I pray to him, and I only pray to him when driven by an irresistible need, by pleasure [*par un besoin irrésistible, par le plaisir*]: he is my master, I recognize this, we converse, and from that conversation, in the hope which it gives me, I draw new force, greater energy. (Quoted in Aulard 1906:I, 230–231)

This same belief in natural feeling guided Brissot's politics throughout his Revolutionary career, especially in his repeated speeches in favor of the war policy, in late 1791 and early 1792. In the eyes of sentimentalists like Brissot, the political reality of the summer and fall of 1791 was still not Manichean enough. After the king's failed attempt to flee France, and his forcible return from the town of Varennes, where he was recognized and dramatically captured on 20 June, the political atmosphere worsened dramatically (Tackett 2000). The king was held in the Tuileries Palace, still king, yet under a kind of house arrest. The new constitution, in preparation since the fall of 1789, was finally put into effect, three months later, on 14 September. It made the king head of state and chief of the executive branch of government. (His recent, treasonous flight had been called a kidnapping officially, but few were fooled.) Here was ambiguity sufficient to breed suspicion in the most

---

[7] "Croyez vous que, si les génies brûlants de ces grands hommes n'eussent embrasé petit à petit les âmes, et ne leurs eussent découvrir le secret de leur grandeur et de leur force, croyez-vous qu'aujourd'hui la tribune retentirait de vos discours sur la liberté?"

trusting mind. War would provide the ultimate, instructive melodramatic plot to clear away this fog; war, as Brissot preached it, was the ultimate blurring of fiction and reality into a didactic melodrama of patriotism. In his first discussion of this idea, during a speech of 10 July 1791, he insisted that soldiers of liberty would be moved by a generosity and a courage which no tyrant's army could resist.

The soldier of liberty fears neither fatigue, nor dangers, nor hunger, nor lack of money. He exhausts with joy the little money he has for the defense of his country . . . he runs, he flies to the cry of liberty. . . . If a patriotic army is destroyed, another is born at once from its ashes, because, under liberty, all are soldiers: men, women, children, priests, magistrates. (Quoted in Aulard 1906:I, 240)

Once individual liberty was granted, that is, a total communal solidarity followed naturally. War, Brissot urged in December of that year, was necessary to a revolution. "We need war to consolidate it, we need war to purge the vices of despotism, we need war to repel from its [the Revolution's] bosom the men who might corrupt it" (quoted in Aulard 1906:I, 247).[8] In his long and successful effort to bring the Assembly to declare war, Brissot was seconded by Germaine de Staël, who vigorously promoted the idea through her salon, and Jeanne-Marie Roland, who advocated this same plan among the circle of politicians around her husband (Gwynn 1969, May 1970). Both were enthusiastic sentimentalists of the post-Rousseau generation.

Brissot and his circle, the so-called "Girondins," including Roland and Staël, are known to history as moderates. But their more radical opponents were no different from them in believing that right political action could only derive from feelings of generosity and pity, natural feelings which moved the individual citizen both to anger against tyranny and injustice and to a willingness for self-sacrifice. Marat delivered daily diatribes in his paper, *L'ami du peuple*, always with this structure. When Marat, for example, sought to rouse the people of Paris against the government after the massacre of the Champs de Mars in July 1791, he evoked the scene following the National Guard's firing on a peaceful demonstration as follows:

---

[8] "Il faut la guerre pour la consolider; il la faut pour la purger des vices du despotisme; il la faut pour faire disparaître de son sein les hommes qui pourraient la corrompre."

The blood of old men, of women and children, massacred around the altar of the fatherland, still steams, it cries for vengeance; and the infamous legislator comes forward with praise and acts of public thanks for their cruel executioners, their cowardly assassins. . . . Cowardly citizens, can you hear of this without a shudder? They declare to be disturbers of the public peace any and every oppressed man who, to escape tyranny, makes a weapon of his own despair [*une arme de son désespoir*] and advises the massacre of his oppressors. (Quoted in Simond n.d.:101–102)

Violence against innocents, Marat claims here, has been justified by hypocritical mislabeling of the defenders of liberty as criminals. True citizens will "shudder" at this and will approve of him who "makes his despair a weapon." Emotion leads directly to embrace of political action. Marat ends with a call to feeling and a declaration of the profundity of his own feeling:

As for the friend of the people [i.e., Marat himself], . . . To save the fatherland, he would go at the head of the people to tear the heart out of the infernal Motier amidst numerous battalions of slaves; he would go and burn the monarch in his palace with all his lackeys. Just heaven! If only he could pass on to the souls of his fellow citizens the fires that devour his own! . . . Oh my fatherland! receive the signs of my pain and of my despair! (Quoted in Simond n.d.:101–102)[9]

Marat's idea of the relation between moral sentiment and action was no different from mild-mannered Marivaux's, who, in his *Spectateur français* early in the eighteenth century, defined sentiment as "that pain which softens [*cette douleur attendrissante*]," an "instinct which guides us and makes us act without reflection, by presenting us with something that touches us" (Baasner 1988:160). For Marivaux, too, there was an unbridgeable gap between those who developed such sentiment within themselves and others who did not.

These brief citations from Brissot and Marat suggest how the optimistic tenor of the early months of the Revolution turned increasingly Manichean, especially after the flight to Varennes. The problem was no longer the transformation of the nation, through benevolent generosity, into an emotional refuge; it was the salvaging, the rescuing, or the

---

[9] "Quant à l'ami du peuple, . . . Pour sauver la patrie, il irait à leur tête arracher le coeur de l'infernal Motier au milieu de nos nombreux bataillons d'esclaves, il irait brûler dans son palais le monarque et ses suppôts . . . Juste ciel! que ne peut-il faire passer dans l'âme de ses concitoyens les feux qui dévorent la sienne! . . . O ma patrie! reçois les accents de ma douleur et de mon désespoir!"

purification of those benevolent gestures already accomplished from the ruses of hypocrites who, like rakes and seducers, posed as generous patriots. Now generosity took the form of that willingness for self-sacrifice characteristic of the soldier.[10]

Although the war, declared on 20 April 1792, began badly, the sentimentalist creed of the pro-war party remained unshaken. The problem, they concluded, lay with the old, inherited structure of the army and its aristocratic officer corps. In a speech of 9 July 1792, as invading armies approached Paris, Brissot urged the Legislative Assembly to dispense with the normal rules of recruitment and advancement and open up the army to self-organized volunteer units. Patriotic citizens were ready to flood in. "You must electrify our souls!" he told them (Aulard 1906:I, 251). The creation of these volunteer units brought together the popular forces that ended the monarchy on 10 August 1792 and put a stop to the Prussian invasion force at Valmy in September of that year. Brissot's measure was thus the crucial first step in the building of that new army that would later sweep the Revolution's enemies out of France and bring Napoleon to European dominance.

When a newly elected Convention declared France to be a republic on 22 September 1792, everyone understood that this new regime was a product of the ardent patriotism expressed in, for example, one of the volunteer units' favorite songs, the so-called *Marseillaise*. Everyone understood that the Republic would rise or fall depending on its ability to continue inspiring such feelings.

THE TERROR

After Brissot and the other Girondins had been removed from the Convention and arrested in June 1793, and Marat assassinated by one of their supporters on 13 July, the new ruling faction, the "Mountain," often referred to simply as the "Jacobins," continued to draw upon the same complex of presuppositions about natural feeling to organize and justify their efforts to defeat civil insurrections and foreign invasion.

---

[10] That generosity was a characteristic of the soldier – or at least of the officer – was an established theme; see the work of Jay Smith (1996), who has examined the link between generosity and courage, in the context of seventeenth-century aristocratic notions of merit.

The papers of the Committee of Public Safety dating from that summer and fall of 1793 are filled with reports from the so-called *représentants en mission* that are imbued with the special sentimentalist style the Jacobins favored. These officials were elected members of the Convention, sent out to the provinces or to the armies with specific instructions from the Convention or the Committee. The idea was to achieve, rapidly, a measure of centralized coordination by putting members of the sovereign assembly directly on the scene. In practice, the wishes of a représentant en mission were law; one might appeal against their decisions by writing to the Convention or the Committee of Public Safety, but this was a slow, and highly uncertain, kind of check. If the reports of the représentants en mission were not satisfactory, they might be recalled. Otherwise, they returned to Paris on completion of their mission. The first of these officials was sent out in early March 1792; by the summer of 1793, there were well over a hundred of them in action throughout France. Some of the Terror's worst excesses were carried out on their orders. The storming of rebel cities Lyon, Marseille, and Toulon, and subsequent massacres, were carried out under their direction, as was the bloody campaign against the counter-Revolution in the Vendée.

Yet if one reads their reports, it would seem that their tasks were entirely emotional in character. Over and over, they claimed, by displaying the proper ardor, they inspired patriotic generosity and intimidated the enemies of virtue, that is, of the Republic.

Fouché, for example, sent a letter from Clamecy to the Committee of Public Safety on 17 August 1793 that is a perfect jewel of Jacobin sentimentalism.

Citizens, my colleagues,

Order and liberty, philosophy and fraternity, reason and nature have triumphed in the walls of Clamecy. A few words spoken in your name produced all the effect I ought to have expected. The hellish demon who is tearing into one part of the Republic had managed to divide citizens, friends, brothers, spouses and their unfortunate children. Sulfurous emanations enveloped the town of Clamecy. In an instant, they were consumed by the flame of liberty. All the citizens came together and embraced each other. Light-hearted songs, dances, patriotic sounds of a warlike music, artillery salvos, prolonged cries of "Long live the Mountain! Long live the Constitution!" announced to all the neighboring communes the happy festival of a general and fraternal reunion around the tree of liberty. All monuments that might recall hatred, re-ignite vile passions, divorces, hideous litigation, have been destroyed, trampled under foot, reduced to ashes, and everyone has drunk from the cup of equality the water of regeneration. Such sweet tears ran from every eye, because the love of the fatherland lives in every heart. Send arms to the citizens of Clamecy, they are ready to shed their blood in its defense. Fouché. (Aulard 1889–1923: VI, 17)[11]

Like Brissot and Marat, Fouché – who would later become Napoleon's feared minister of police – firmly and explicitly links the pleasurable emotions of mutual devotion – "light-hearted" and "happy" celebration, "sweet tears" expressing "love of the fatherland" – with violent action. For Fouché, the best words for the Revolution's opposition are themselves emotion terms, or terms for emotional situations: "hatred," "vile passions," "divorces," "hideous litigation." The language of the famous *levée en masse*, decreed a few days later, less colorful, nonetheless presupposed the same kind of unanimous, popular, natural love of the fatherland (synonymous with the cause of humanity) waiting to be tapped.

Philippeaux, a représentant en mission directing army action against the counter-Revolution in the west, wrote to the Committee of Public Safety on 3 September 1793 to apologize for a previous letter. He had learned, falsely, from a letter by Ronsin, that the Committee wanted to put a stop to a particular offensive he had planned.

Citizen collegues,
    I effectively put a great deal of bitterness in my last letter. I find, on calmly rereading it, that it must have wounded your generous hearts, and

---

[11] "Citoyens mes collègues, L'ordre et la liberté, la philosophie et la fraternité, la raison et la nature triomphent dans les murs de Clamecy. Quelques paroles portées en votre nom ont produit tout l'effet que j'en devais attendre. L'infernal génie qui déchire une partie de la République était venu à bout de diviser les citoyens, les amis, les frères, les époux et leurs infortunés enfants. Des exhalaisons sulfureuses enveloppaient la cité de Clamecy. Dans un instant, elles ont été consumées au feu de la liberté. Tous les citoyens se sont rapprochés, se sont embrassés. Les chants d'allégresse, les danses, les sons patriotiques d'une musique guerrière, les salves d'artillerie, les cris prolongés de Vive la Montagne! Vive la Constitution! ont annoncé à toutes les communes voisines l'heureuse fête d'une réunion générale et fraternelle autour de l'arbre de la liberté. Tous les monuments qui pouvaient rappeler la haine, rallumer les passions viles, les actes de divorce, les hideuses procédures, ont été déchirés, foulés aux pieds, mis en cendres, et chacun a bu dans la coupe de l'égalité l'eau de la régénération. De bien douces larmes ont coulé de tous les yeux, parce que l'amour de la patrie est dans tous les coeurs. Donnez des armes aux citoyens de Clamecy: ils sont prêts à verser le sang pour sa défense. Fouché."

that thought afflicts me. But put yourselves in my place. At that moment, I was facing all the tests that can exasperate an ardent republican. (Aulard 1889–1923:VI, 263)[12]

Instead, it turned out, the Committee had only called for further deliberation in a Council of War that brought Philippeaux together with other représentants in the area and the army generals involved. At that Council, Philippeaux had won the reluctant generals over to his plan. He explained in detail precisely which représentants and which generals opposed his plans and how he sought to bring them around. His report concluded as follows:

What would you have done, with a character as burning as my own, if, on the verge of seeing the Republic triumph, one had brought you a letter like Ronsin's? In any case, all the clouds have dissipated; the machine is back in motion this morning, after its temporary, ill-considered suspension. Those who vexed me, and who took you by surprise, will be my beloved brothers, if they will only, from now on, follow a path that equals mine in frankness.

As for you, citizen colleagues, do me the justice of believing that, even in my civic indignation, I can render homage to the purity of your hearts and to your generous virtue.

Philippeaux. (Aulard 1889–1923:VI, 264)[13]

Pure hearts, generous virtue, burning characters, republican ardor, civic indignation: these were the issues, not policy, not strategy or supply considerations, not the strength of specific factions or the likely outcome of votes. No word of alliance, maneuver, compromise. Philippeaux accepted the prevailing wisdom that had guided so many since the night of 4 August 1789: politics was emotional. A policy recommended by burning ardor for liberty was the right policy.

---

[12] "Citoyens collègues, J'ai mis effectivement beaucoup d'aigreur dans ma dernière lettre. Je trouve, en la relisant de sang-froid, qu'elle a dû blesser vos âmes généreuses, et cette pensée m'afflige. Mais mettez-vous à ma place. Dans ce moment, j'étais à toutes les épreuves qui peuvent exaspérer un républicain ardent."

[13] "Qu'eussiez-vous fait, avec un caractère aussi brûlant que le mien, si, au moment de faire triompher la République, on vous eût apporté une lettre aussi désespérante que celle de Ronsin? Au surplus, tous les nuages sont dissipés, la machine a repris de ce matin le mouvement qu'on avait mal à-propos suspendu, et ceux qui m'ont le plus vexé, en voulant vous surprendre, seront mes frères bien aimés, s'ils veulent désormais avoir une marche aussi franche que la mienne.

"Quant à vous, citoyens collègues, rendez-moi la justice de croire que, jusque dans mes emportements civiques, je sais rendre hommage à la pureté de vos coeurs et à vos vertus généreuses. Philippeaux."

One more striking example from the Committee's papers is the report of Couthon dated 5 September 1793 from Clermont-Ferrand. A member of the Committee himself, Couthon had been sent south in late August with two other représentants to aid with the organization of an army to put down the rebellion of Lyon. In his initial report, he spoke with wonder of the patriotic surge that had greeted his arrival.

This department [Puy-de-Dôme] has risen up in its entirety. Men, women, the old, the children, all wanted to march, and our only real trouble has been in moderating the ardor of these brave mountain people, and in obtaining from their boiling courage [*leur bouillant courage*] that they be reduced to the number we judged necessary. We could have sent *two hundred thousand men*. But we will send from *twenty to twenty-five thousand*. (Aulard 1889–1923:VI, 290; emphasis in original)

After reviewing details of assembly and provisioning, Couthon concluded as follows:

It would be impossible, citizen colleagues, to express to you the zeal, the enthusiasm, and the energy that all these brave Republicans have shown. Their example would have inspired the stupidest heart and electrified the coldest mind. The friends of liberty may rest assured; the people love it; they want it, they shall have it; and all those who dare to raise obstacles to the people's omnipotence will be annihilated. (p. 291)[14]

Local citizens, Couthon notes, "have overwhelmed me with marks of their affection and of their confidence." The Jacobins, it would seem, were attempting to transform a series of sudden, intense emotions: of generosity, affection, ardent indignation, boiling courage, into a veritable system of government. Such emotions were best elicited from "simple mountain people," from brave "sans culottes" (in other words, manual laborers), from "the people" who are "essentially good and just" (Thirion, to the Committee of Public Safety, 3 September 1793, in Aulard 1889–1923:VI, 259). In pursuing this strange goal, however, it must be remembered that they were doing no more than remaining faithful to the inspiration of the night of 4 August, to the lessons of

---

[14] "Il serait impossible, citoyens collègues, de vous exprimer avec quel zèle, quelle enthousiasme et quelle énergie tous ces braves républicains se sont montrés. Leur exemple eût animé le coeur le plus stupide et électrisé l'esprit le plus froid. Que les amis de la liberté soient bien tranquilles. Le peuple l'adore; il la veut, il l'aura, et toux ceux qui oseront opposer des obstacles à sa toute puissance seront anéantis."

Brissot's speeches in favor of war, to the whole legacy of the sentimentalist emotional style.

Faced with formidable threats, the Jacobins' legislation also placed increasing emphasis on flushing out its enemies from behind hypocritical masks. Harsh measures were necessary, not to force all to comply, but because some were insincere. Not mere obedience, but sincere devotion, was to be commanded by law, because, as André Dumont and Le Bon, représentants en mission at Amiens, wrote on 19 August 1793, "The people of Amiens are the same as everywhere else, they sincerely desire liberty; but the weakness of their magistrates exposes them to misfortunes and cruel divisions" (Aulard 1889–1923:VI, 30–31). Thus the legislation of the Terror, too, like the legal briefs analyzed by Maza or the Girondins' war policy, presumed that sincere natural feeling was intense, and that those who were insincere were likely to betray themselves by lack of intensity or by a misstep that true feeling never made. The law of suspects of 17 September 1793 designated for arrest "Those who, either by their conduct or by their relations, by their words or writings, have shown themselves to be partisans of tyranny . . . or enemies of liberty." Those who were relatives of émigrés who had fled the country were subject to an even higher, and vaguer, standard and were to be arrested "if they had not constantly shown their attachment to the Revolution."

This law, and others put into effect by the Mountain, were, in effect, laws about feelings. Down to Robespierre's final days in the summer of 1794, orators stood up before the Convention to demonstrate by the intensity of their expression the sincerity and virtue of their character. Grandiose rituals were designed, such as the Festival of the Supreme Being, to stimulate the benevolent patriotism of the simple and the unlearned. Saint-Just, Robespierre, and others even warned their fellow revolutionaries against "false pity." To have pity and spare the life of a convicted aristocrat, of a nonjuring priest, of a counter-Revolutionary peasant, endangered the larger acts of benevolence by which the Revolution had dismantled the Old Regime and restored to the people what they had lost.[15] False pity became itself suspect and grounds for the death penalty. Heads fell daily in the Place de la Révolution not to

---

[15] On new attitudes toward pity, and for more examples of sentimentalism in Revolutionary thinking, see Denby (1994:51–57, 140–164, 177, 200).

create a deterrent effect, but as a continual process of rescuing virtue in distress. Having fallen under suspicion, Brissot, Danton, and others made impassioned pleas on their own behalf before the Revolutionary Tribunal – intensity being one more proof of innocence – until the law of 22 Prairial, Year II (10 June 1794) simply deprived suspects of the right to legal counsel, witnesses, and evidence and allowed condemnation by "amalgams" (Aulard 1901:363).

Nowhere is the emotional dilemma of the Terror expressed more plainly than in the simple words of a recently discovered autobiography. Jacques-Louis Ménétra, a Parisian glazier, active in sectional assemblies and committees of surveillance under the Terror, was torn by concealed fear, and by grief over the execution of friends, in the very months he was carrying a heavy burden of successive offices and frequent service in the National Guard (Ménétra 1982). His support for the Revolution had been genuine and enthusiastic from the beginning.[16] But after May 1793, he recognized that, whatever misgivings he began to feel, he must maintain a good front or be sent to the guillotine. Twice he escaped attempts to raise suspicion about himself; he tried to save as many of his friends as he could. One was beheaded due to unguarded words spoken in a private conversation. The victim, Barbet Mathieu, a journeyman hatter, was from Lyon, a city in rebellion. "I warned you," writes Ménétra to his dead friend's soul, "you were Lyonnais, that was a mortal sin. They got you drinking, they got you talking. They arrested you." Those who, like Ménétra, remained active Revolutionaries, must have exerted great emotional effort to stifle their doubts and maintain a good front. Those who, like Ménétra, found that the prescribed emotives worked well enough to avoid arrest, were able to survive. Those less adept, like Barbet Mathieu, often went to the guillotine. But even Ménétra's successful effort was a kind of proof of insincerity and, therefore, a cause for increased, gnawing, internal doubt. As the Terror produced widespread induced emotional suffering, it may have assured greater conformity to government policy. But this induced suffering also began to sap the very power of those emotives that had rendered sentimentalism so persuasive in the first place.

Even after Robespierre's fall, Ménétra lacked an adequate vocabulary for talking about the ambivalence or mixed motives he felt.

---

[16] As early as July 1792, Ménétra signed a petition for the deposing of the king; see Ménétra (1982:265).

Instead, he speaks with perfect clarity about what went wrong with the Revolution. Its leaders were "unmatched prevaricators [*insignes prévaricateurs*]" (Ménétra 1982:259) seconded by wicked "monsters who made humanity groan" (p. 266). "Honest men," out of fear, did not oppose them (p. 262). "I saw many men," Ménétra laments, "whose physiognomy and whose manner announced their humanity . . . join in with those cannibals" (p. 264). He does not stop to ask if others – Brissot, Mme Roland, Vergniaud, Danton, Desmoulins – may have felt as he did, a mixture of things: political commitment and courage, based on principled acceptance of the ideal of liberty; fear and revulsion at indiscriminate political violence; grief at the deaths of friends and loved ones; a growing determination to survive, even through dissembling.

This reductionism, by which Ménétra explains and *condemns* the excesses of the Terror, is the same reductionism used by its supporters to *justify* the Terror, a campaign to rid the fatherland of monsters.

Had there been any such thing as the natural, universal, pleasurable generosity upon which the Jacobins were trying to build their new regime, their policies might have been more effective, more lasting. But if the concept of emotives is closer to the truth about human emotion, one would expect such laws to strike as much terror into supporters of the regime as they did into its opponents. Ménétra's text is a particularly compelling confirmation of this supposition. Because no one knows precisely what her emotions are, and because attempting to express them changes them, sometimes predictably, sometimes unpredictably, a requirement to have certain "natural" feelings or else face the death penalty is likely to inspire furtive doubts in most people. Am I being sincere? It is always hard to say.

By the vocabulary proposed in Chapter 4, the Terror, aimed at purging the Republic, inevitably spread induced emotional suffering across a wide swath of the population – suffering nowhere more intense than among the regime's activists themselves, who provided at least as many victims (counting the federalists) as the Republic's declared enemies. Such doubts, under the Terror, only helped feed an escalating spiral of suspicion, because everyone felt like a hypocrite in the face of such laws. The confirming power of sentimentalist emotives was thereby reduced. Targeting others was a means of deflecting suspicion; and it did not matter whom one targeted, since all were guilty.

Here is how R. R. Palmer describes the atmosphere in meetings of the Jacobin Club at the beginning of 1794:

The next great clash occurred at the [Jacobin Club] early in January. Collot d'Herbois assaulted the Dantonists on the 5th, vehemently opening a Hébertist counter-offensive. He accused Philippeaux of sowing strife by criticizing the generals in the Vendée, and Desmoulins of holding principles that were not those of the [Jacobin] society. Desmoulins jumped up, brandishing some papers, which, he said, proved that Hébert in selling copies of [his newspaper] the *Père Duchense* for the army had cheated the government out of 43,000 livres. Hébert tried to reply. Robespierre's younger brother interrupted, deprecating petty personal squabbles. Hébert stamped his feet and rolled his eyes, crying, "Do they wish to assassinate me? . . . Oh, God!"; and someone else shouted "Tyranny!" Then Maximilien [Robespierre] himself arose, rebuked his brother, supported Collot d'Herbois, said that the question must not be deflected, that the present inquiry was not against Hébert but against Philippeaux and Camille Desmoulins.

At the next meeting, on the evening of January 7, Robespierre tried to pacify the excited brethren. There are no more factions, he boldly said; only the French people against its enemies. To lift the level of debate he proposed a new subject as the order of the day, "The crimes of the English government and vices of the British constitution." . . .

But just as Robespierre's motion was carried Camille Desmoulins, arriving late, came into the hall. He sped to the tribune to answer the charges of Collot two nights before. He was vacillating, confused, gropingly contrite; he admitted perhaps having erred in supporting Philippeaux, whom he was now willing to forsake, for there was no mutual loyalty in the factions. (Palmer 1941:266–267)

As this fragment of narrative suggests, there is plentiful evidence that the leading Jacobins themselves were in the grip of gnawing anxiety about their own status, that they could not admit to such anxiety or address it directly, and that the safest response was often seen as the deflection of suspicion onto others. Far from providing an emotional refuge, the Revolution had turned into an emotional battleground, where everyone's sincerity was suspect, and where working to deflect suspicion, however essential it was to survival, was itself a proof of insincerity.

This may seem like an obvious point. But surely it is worthwhile having solid theoretical grounds for such a judgment. Neither the class analysis of the new social history, nor the elaborate social nominalism of the revisionists offered any grounds for such an insight. Richard Cobb long ago, and eloquently, complained of the lack of purchase of class concepts on the experience of the Terror (Cobb 1970). New cultural history was equally disarmed by the Terror; it could, at best, simply offer rich – and quite useful – explorations of the Jacobins' sweeping cultural ambitions and symbolic preoccupations. Hunt (1992) was right to try to move beyond it.[17] Furet's (1981) much discussed idea of "discourse" taking on a kind of independent political power in the early 1790s is important as far as it goes. What it does not address is the question of how real people could have lived such an abstraction. The history of the Revolution cannot be understood without an adequate theory of emotions.

THE ERASURE OF SENTIMENTALISM, 1794–1814

The Jacobin project, which carried on the project of the National Assembly of 1789, aimed, in its essence, to create a political utopia through the incessant repeating of a particular style of emotives. Of course, the Jacobins and those who lent their energies to the Republic engaged in intense practical activity and accomplished administrative, logistic, and military miracles. But they did so with a minimum of central planning, little centralized resource allocation, depending almost entirely on local initiative. They believed that patriotic emotions would ensure coordination, provide resources where needed, and resolve disagreements as to doctrine, policy, even military tactics. This faith was blind. Decentralization meant disorder; it meant représentants en mission acting like petty tyrants pursuing their own petty policies and settling scores, massacres of innocents, unnecessary destruction of monuments, suppression of local customs, and widespread theft of property. Yet this faith also brought remarkable discoveries. Not the least of these were the military implications of sentimentalism. Depending on the individual initiative and loyalty of soldiers (on their "burning courage"), it turned out, made the Republic's armies unbeatable in the field. Elevating officers from the ranks, too, it turned out, brought an extraordinary number of talented new generals to the fore.

The full implications of this military miracle were becoming visible by the spring of 1794. Meanwhile, the Revolution, like Saturn, kept eating its own children. Having gotten rid of the Girondins, the

---

[17] For cultural treatments of aspects of the Terror, see, e.g., Sewell (1980) and Hunt's own earlier work (Hunt 1984).

Jacobins had turned to purging their own numbers, most notably Hébert and his circle (13–24 March 1794) and Danton and his associates, including Desmoulins and Philippeaux (30 March–6 April 1794). But resounding victories on the frontiers and against the internal rebels had drained away the sense of emergency; doubts were raised about the continuation of the Terror policy. (Danton had died, in effect, for raising such doubts.) Attendance at the meetings of political clubs and local assemblies fell off dramatically. "For many weeks," Higonnet reports, "in June and July 1794 [Robespierre] stopped attending the meetings of the [Committee of Public Safety], as if unwilling to go either forward to more Terror or backward to the rule of law. Many Jacobins, we can wager, felt these same doubts" (Higonnet 1998:59). When, on 26 July, Robespierre made a speech intimating that further purges would, after all, be necessary, his initiative backfired. Within forty-eight hours he was arrested and guillotined on the grounds that he was attempting to set himself up as a dictator. Ménétra, like thousands of other sans culottes in Paris who had frequently supported Robespierre in the past, lifted not a finger to save him. Saint-Just and Couthon followed him to the scaffold.

In the subsequent days and months, it was as if the surviving Revolutionaries breathed a slow, collective sigh of relief. Executions stopped, prisons were opened, diversity of opinion and religious belief was again (for a time) tolerated. And soon, in some provinces, counter-Revolutionary lynch mobs began eliminating former Terrorists, settling scores of their own. Decentralization now meant that the country became almost ungovernable. But, since the armies were occupying foreign soil, and paying their own way out of booty and requisitions, it did not matter that the central government could not collect taxes, rein in local officials, or even so much as get clerks in the departments to answer questionnaires.

No one had known that Robespierre's death meant the end of the Terror; it only became obvious after the fact. Doubtless, no one realized, either, that his death meant the end of the quasi-official Jacobin brand of sentimentalism, indeed, the end of almost all attempts to establish a positive role for emotions in politics. But revulsion for the official emotives spread quickly. A new, disabused tone became prevalent in official and unofficial contexts alike. Unchecked corruption and the end of the Jacobins' puritan surveillance committees contributed to the rise of a cynical party atmosphere in the capital. Women began wearing red ribbons around their necks to the theater and to balls, frivolous reminders of those who had been guillotined. While little research has been done on the period after Robespierre's fall, the evidence we have suggests the kind of giddy pleasure that follows the end of difficult mental control efforts, like young French students who have just finished their baccalauréat exams. I would go further and claim that this was an atmosphere of frank disillusionment, not just with Jacobinism, but with emotional self-training of the type sentimentalism encouraged. At the same time, the parameters of political debate shifted rapidly.

Here is how François-Antoine Boissy d'Anglas presented to the Convention, on 23 June 1795, the constitutional law that would create the conservative Directory government, less than a year after Robespierre's death:

Absolute equality is a chimera. If it existed one would have to assume complete equality in intelligence, virtue, physical strength, education and fortune in all men. . . . We must be ruled by the best citizens. And the best are the most learned and the most concerned in the maintenance of law and order. Now, with very few exceptions, you will find such men only among those who own some property, and are thus attached to the land in which it lies, to the laws which protect it and to the public order which maintains it. . . . You must, therefore, guarantee the political rights of the well-to-do . . . and [deny] unreserved political rights to men without property, for if such men ever find themselves seated among the legislators, then they will provoke agitations . . . without fearing their consequences . . . and in the end precipitate us into those violent convulsions from which we have scarcely yet emerged. (Quoted in, and translated by, Hibbert 1981:282)

This brief sketch of the purposes and means of government contains not a whiff of sentimentalist ideas. Instead, it represents a reversion to classical republicanism (Pocock 1975). (For more discussion of this abrupt shift in the terms of political debate, see Aulard 1901: 543–579, Gauchet 1995:125–186.) Instead of natural moral sensibility grounding democratic enfranchisement of all, education, property, and the interests that property inspires are held up as the sole possible guarantors of order in the state. The granting of political rights to the poor is said to have been the principal source of the evils of the Terror. Simplicity had lost its luster.

As the leaders of the Directory struggled fruitlessly to solidify its tenuous hold on legitimacy, intellectuals closely associated with them gained control of the newly established Institut de France – a replacement for the old royal academies that had been abolished in 1793. One section of the Institut, the so-called Second Class, became a stronghold of a group of thinkers called the "Idéologues." Led by Antoine-Louis-Claude Destutt de Tracy and Pierre-Jean-Georges Cabanis, this group regarded Locke's and Condillac's sensationalist doctrines as the last word on the subject of human nature. All contents of the mind derived ultimately from mere sensations. For Cabanis, "life is a series of movements executed as a result of impressions received by our various organs; the operations of the soul or mind are also movements executed by the cerebral organ" (Cabanis 1802:34). Sensations entered the nervous system, causing reactions which led to the discernment of patterns. "There are no exterior causes for us except those which can act on our senses, and any object to which we cannot apply our faculties of sensation, must be excluded from our research" (Cabanis 1802:35). Individual organisms, the Idéologues taught, acted to maximize pleasure and minimize pain. Adam Smith's political economy, they believed, offered the key to understanding social life. Pleasure and pain were the source of all motivation, self-interest the thread of all social fabric, enlightened self-interest the sole grounds of morality. "Idéologie," quipped Destutt de Tracy, "is a branch of zoology" (quoted in Goldstein 1987:246).

Doubtless such resolute reductionism was music to the ears of Directory politicians who were seeking, by a combination of cajolery and intimidation, to shape an electorate capable of supporting them in the manner to which they had become accustomed. The Idéologues offered a multitude of ready arguments for anyone who wished to downplay the role of virtue or duty in politics. But the Directory did not last. The propertied men it most wished to rally to its support, when given the chance to vote, showed a marked preference for a return to monarchy. But many in the government, former Conventionnels who had voted to execute the king in 1793, could not tolerate such a step. As a result, the Directory tottered from crisis to crisis, kept alive by means of quashed elections and other extralegal improvisations, until it was replaced by Napoleon's coup d'état of 1799. It was left to Napoleon's regime to work out the finer details, and to entrench the habits of mind, that would establish the ascendency of an elite of propertied males.

Napoleon, when he came to power, showed only disdain for the Idéologues, abolishing their Class of the Institut in 1803. But he did not regard them as dangerous; they retained their posts and their salaries, and their privileged voice in intellectual affairs. Napoleon's strategy of rule, pursued with great success, was quite compatible with their doctrine. He ignored the past and accepted support from all quarters; former monarchists and émigrés were as welcome as former regicides and sans culottes. Superficial submission was quite sufficient; self-interested calculation was encouraged. Reconciliation with the church was pursued as a matter of pure convenience. Occasional conspirators were singled out for arrest and execution, not to "purify" the people of corrupt leaders, but to render the regime's insincere supporters firmer in their hypocrisy. This was a kind of repression fundamentally different in conception from the purifying terror of the Jacobin guillotine. Continued military victories were deemed essential to firming up the tepid, opportunistic support Napoleon counted on. Like Louis XIV, Napoleon sought to induce emotional suffering by the skillful manipulation of deterrents, strict bureaucratic control, and a glittering court. His success far surpassed the achievements of his predecessor, at least for a time. Compared to the Jacobin pursuit of sincerity, such a strategy is far more in tune with the givens of emotional life as the theory of emotives reveals them.

In the army, as new battlefield tactics became routinized and the hierarchy settled down, honor (frowned on by the Jacobins as an aristocratic value) rose again in importance. Duels, which had virtually ceased with the outbreak of the Revolution (Higonnet 1998:131), came back into vogue among the officer corps of the Napoleonic army, but democratized, no longer the exclusive preserve of nobles, as Robert Nye's research has found (Nye 1993). As Napoleon consolidated his power, the idea of honor was given new luster and new centrality with the creation of the Legion of Honor and the elaboration of a new, Napoleonic nobility. At the same time, the framers of the Civil Code, consolidating and refining the legacy of Revolutionary legislation between 1804 and 1807, confirmed and made explicit a new civil order based upon freedom of contract and the free play of competition. In addition, the writers of the code, under Napoleon's express direction, reinvigorated the patriarchal authority of husbands and fathers over wives and children, limiting access to divorce and firmly placing married women under the tutelage of men. In combination, these three Napoleonic trends tended to create an order in which the pursuit of honor, not virtue, was enshrined as the normative motive for action in the public service (military, administrative, and political) as well as in the private realm of the family, while interest was left to shape the sphere of commerce and contract. Sentiment was set aside, a private issue, purely a matter of individual inclination and consumer preference, implicitly feminine.

The sentimentalist interlude could not be simply expunged, however. The Idéologues' vision was resisted by Bernardin de Saint-Pierre, Grégoire, Sieyès, and others (Denby 1994:190–192). Staël repeatedly sought to win influence with the Idéologue group, as she did with Napoleon, but was rebuffed by both (Balayé 1979; Isbell 1994; Diesbach 1983). Her liberalism, crystallized in her remarkable essay of 1800, *De la littérature dans ses rapports avec les institutions sociales*, retained essential elements of the sentimentalist credo: (1) the idea of novels as educational tools (much of the book was devoted to tracing the history of the influence of literature on emotional experience); (2) the idea that feelings were necessary guides to political deliberation and decision making; (3) the idea that women had a special public role to play in guiding deliberation and educating the nation; (4) the idea that "friendship in love" was the highest form of social bond and the telos of historical change. Staël explained the Jacobin interlude as an outgrowth of the disastrous ascendency of the masses, the poverty and violence of whose existences rendered them insensitive to the impulses of natural feeling. Self-interest became, here for the first time, her bête noire: "The same creative force that pumps the blood toward the heart inspires courage and sensibility, two rights, two moral sensations whose governance we destroy in attributing them to self-interest, just as you deface the charm of beauty by analyzing it like an anatomist."[18] Pity, courage, humanity operate in us prior to calculation, she insisted (Staël 1800:378). But this essay was published at an inopportune moment; few republicans were prepared to admit, after 1795, that natural emotion should serve as a founding concept of their system. Staël was perfectly aware of this and pleaded with them to reconsider, but in vain. "People denounce eloquence," nowadays, she complained, because of the false ideas that have been defended since 1789. But "feeling [*le sentiment*] itself does not err; only the consequences which an argument derives from feeling can be in error" (Staël 1800:404–405). These explanations fell on deaf ears. The recent past was by this time

---

[18] "La même puissance créatrice qui fait couler le sang vers le coeur, inspire le courage et la sensibilité, deux jouissances, deux sensations morales dont nous détruisez l'empire en les analysant par l'intérêt personnel, comme vous flétririez le charme de la beauté, en la décrivant comme un anatomiste."

littered with the ruins caused when differing "consequences" were drawn from laudable sentiments.

A number of monarchist theorists were also hostile to the new prominence which the concept of self-interest was winning at the end of the 1790s. Notably, René de Chateaubriand, in two works, *Essai sur les révolutions* (1797) and *Le génie du christianisme* (1802), denounced the self-interest of the new age and glorified the honor and selflessness of the past. But the manner in which Chateaubriand resisted Idéologue thinking actually played into their hands. The sentimentalist trope of the hypocritical aristocrat had been circulated without challenge before 1789; but with the end of the Terror and the general revulsion against its excesses, it became possible to regard aristocracy as a principle of a lost, simpler past. In *Essai sur les révolutions*, Chateaubriand denounces the philosophes for their rationalism and their lack of understanding for practical politics. His review of Enlightenment developments says nothing of sentimentalist doctrine. He attempts to depict the philosophes themselves as libertines, condemning their extramarital liaisons (including Rousseau's ardent love of Mme Houdetot) as evidence of their indifference to morality – a claim hard to accept from any serious reader of d'Alembert, Diderot, or Rousseau. His extreme ambivalence toward Rousseau is evident in several remarks. With *Génie du christianisme*, five years later, one sees that his previous silence about sentimentalism has allowed him to relocate *sensibilité* on the side of the aristocracy and the monarchy, without acknowledging his debt to its eighteenth-century champions. Chateaubriand is thus able to glorify the honorable courage, religiosity, and patriotism of noble French warriors of the preabsolutist past. This was an important step in the process of relocation, by which feeling was gradually relegated to a secondary role, to a better past, or a utopian future, or a safe haven in the feminine space of the home.

Another important transformation of sentimentalism, which will be discussed in greater detail in Chapter 7, can be found in the intimate journal of Maine de Biran, whose opening pages date from May 1794, the days of the Jacobin endgame, when Robespierre sat at home pondering what to do next. In these pages, explicit sentimentalist emotives are conspicuous by their absence. But this absence seems to create a hole in Maine de Biran's self-awareness, at least by comparison with figures such as Rousseau, Mme Roland, or Staël. It is as if his introspection has slipped its anchor; new sources of sensibility are explored, and a new uncertainty about one's own self-worth is painfully evident.

Maine de Biran was prompted to begin his journal by a singular experience of happiness. Walking alone, in the Dordogne, far from Paris, he witnessed an unusually splendid spring sunset.

[E]verything that struck my senses brought to my heart a certain sweetness and sadness; tears were swelling under my eyelids. How many feelings followed each other. And now that I want to set down an account of it, how cold I feel! . . . If I could render that state permanent, what would be lacking to my happiness? I would have found on this earth the joys of heaven. But one hour of that sweet calm is followed by the ordinary agitation of my life. . . . [T]his unhappy existence is nothing but a series of heterogeneous moments with no stability; they go floating by, fleeing rapidly, without it ever being in our power to stop them. Everything influences us, and we change ceaselessly with our environment. I often entertain myself by watching the various situations of my soul flow by; they are like the currents of a river, sometimes calm, sometimes agitated, but always one following another without any permanence. (Maine de Biran 1954–1957:III,3)[19]

Maine de Biran is struck by a happy, sweet sadness on viewing a sunset; there is no one else present. He is not, like Mme Roland, reflecting on a good father bringing a stray dog home to his son. He is not, like Couthon, inspired by the burning courage of brave mountain people. All three were moved by visions of something they considered natural: affection between father and son, patriotism, a sunset. But by 1794 Roland's and Couthon's style of inspiration had been discredited by the highly ambiguous results it had produced, results that included both Roland's and soon Couthon's death on the guillotine. The ambiguity was heightened by general recognition that such deaths had been arbitrary; Couthon, as member of the Committee of Public Safety, had

---

[19] "[T]out ce qui frappait mes sens portaient à mon coeur je ne sais quoi de doux et de triste; les larmes étaient au bord de mes paupières . . . [*sic*] combien de sentiments se sont succédé. Et maintenant que je voudrais m'en rendre compte, comme je me sens froid! . . . Si je pouvais rendre cet état permanent, que manquerait-il à mon bonheur? J'aurais trouvé sur cette terre les joies du ciel. Mais une heure de ce doux calme va être suivie de l'agitation ordinaire de ma vie . . . ainsi cette malheureuse existence n'est qu'une suite de moments hétérogènes qui n'ont aucune stabilité; ils vont flottants, fuyants rapidement, sans qu'il soit jamais en notre pouvoir de les fixer. Tout influe sur nous, et nous changeons sans cesse avec ce qui nous environne. Je m'amuse souvent à voir couler les diverses situations de mon âme; elles sont comme les flots d'une rivière, tantôt calmes, tantôt agités, mais toujours se succédant sans aucune permanence."

acquiesced in Roland's death, and the death of many others whose beliefs and mode of expression seemed identical to his own.

Maine de Biran had never participated in Revolutionary politics; as a moderate noble he rode out the difficult years in provincial obscurity. But he was deeply imbued with eighteenth-century literature and with the sentimentalist idiom. What remains when Jacobin-style emotives are excised, out of revulsion against the emotional effort they entailed and the acts they justified? Happy sadness remains, the enjoyment of tears remains, a fascination with nature remains. But the discipline of emotives expressing generous affection, emotives that prove one's virtue, is gone. Learned in salons, Masonic lodges, opera houses, theaters; perfected in private letters and love affairs; transformed into a style of government and a required regime of emotional management between 1789 and 1792, sentimentalist emotives had proven extraordinarily successful but also extraordinarily deceptive. In the vacuum they left behind, engagement in the daily life of social commerce lost its direction. Happiness seemed now to derive from calm, not agitation, escape from society, rather than engagement with one's own kind. The soul becomes something one watches, changeable, unpredictable, like a river going by, instead of the warm wellspring of virtue. Maine de Biran's journal gives us a foretaste of important developments that will solidify in later years. His own role in those developments was not insignificant, as we shall see in the next chapter.

By the time Germaine de Staël intervened again, in 1810–1814, attempting to turn France away from its new course, the changes made since 1794 were irreversible. Napoleon's reign had brought the art, literature, and drama of seventeenth-century Versailles back into favor; new arbiters of taste worked to erase all memory of the late eighteenth century, of its sentimental novels, its lachrymose operas, its fashion for pathetic tableaux in paintings and engravings. This reorientation would survive Napoleon's fall; not surprisingly the restored Bourbons also preferred the art of Louis XIV. Staël's new book, *De l'Allemagne* (*On Germany*), completed in 1810, was banned by Napoleon and did not appear in Paris until 1814. But, through foreign editions, it had already begun to cause a stir with its bold challenge to the revival of seventeenth-century classicism in the arts. Staël initiated the debate that would continue with increasing intensity between classicists and romantics down to the production of Hugo's *Hernani* in 1830, and beyond. John Isbell's recent examination of Staël's essay underscores Staël's continuing devotion to sentimentalist doctrine (Isbell 1994).

Two points are worth stressing about Staël's argument. First, she attempts to fit German metaphysical idealism into a sentimentalist straitjacket, mistaking sublime contemplation of the limits of knowledge for a sentimentalist-style belief in the power of natural feeling. Of Kant's antinomies, for example – those intractable dichotomies between freedom and necessity, finitude and infinity that point to the limits of reason – she says that "he calls upon sentiment to tip the balance" (Isbell 1994:140). Kant was, as yet, little known in France; in any case, the book was read as an intervention principally in the debate over esthetics. The grand scope of Staël's subject matter was not noticed, or not taken seriously (since she was a woman author). Staël's repeated, vitriolic denunciations of the principle of self-interest were (rightly) taken as aimed at the French empire, and tied her to the likes of Chateaubriand.

Second, by focusing on Germany, Staël inadvertently reinforced the idea that France stood for strict classical (that is, seventeenth-century) esthetic tastes. This was certainly the case under Napoleon. But such a view failed to acknowledge the profound debt that German trends owed to English and French sentimentalism of the period before 1794. Staël's book was read as a celebration of something new and foreign. By 1820 Staël and Chateaubriand could be regarded as representatives of the same broad new movement in thought and the arts, called, following Staël's own initiative, "Romanticism." Its profound debt to sentimentalism was, ironically, obscured by the very work of sentimentalism's last great champion.

The erasure of sentimentalist origins and of the sentimentalist idiom, begun almost immediately after Thermidor, was, by 1814, virtually complete. A new, all-male Enlightenment was arising on the horizon of the past with the help not only of the Idéologues and Chateaubriand but of a new generation of liberal theorists, including Cousin and Guizot, and eventually Tocqueville. This Enlightenment was a product of reason and its fruit was the Revolution of 1789, establishing a constitutional monarchy that would ensure the rule of reason through public deliberation, debate, and voting, limited to men of merit. The Night of 4 August was understood as an application of the principle of equality, and its infusion with emotionalism was forgotten or brushed aside. The Terror was denounced as a deviation that could be regarded as an outgrowth of the unchained, uneducated political passions of the plebs; Staël herself believed this. Even Napoleon, after his death, was gradually rehabilitated as a great liberal.

EMOTIVES AND THE SENTIMENTALIST EPISODE

Sentimentalism's attack on the court ethos as artificial and hypocritical offered a slanted, exaggerated view of etiquette and *bienséance*, treating this ethos not as a system of emotional management but as a systematic falsity and hypocrisy. But sentimentalism equally denied its own status as a system of emotional management; by its own account sentimentalism opened the door for the true expression of certain (positive) natural feelings. However, such a doctrine was, in fact, a recipe for the formulation of emotives that would tend to heighten such emotions, and they did heighten them, to extremes in many instances.

The Jacobins spoke and acted as if their policy of Terror was aimed to purge the Republic, not to suppress dissent. That is, the Revolutionaries did not care what the designated traitors or criminals felt or thought; the ideal solution was simply to remove them, humanely, from the scene. The guillotine was designed to provide a painless death. The great problem of government they confronted was how to decide which persons had to be removed, which were good citizens. But, by the model elaborated in Chapter 4, the Republic's war waged against rebels, its summary executions, expropriations of émigrés, seizures of dissident newspapers, massacres of prisoners and suspects – all the machinery of violence the government and its wayward agents set in motion – was bound to create a powerful effect of induced emotional suffering. It is certainly the strength of this effect, as much as genuine patriotism, that must explain the remarkable successes of the Jacobin regime. However, fear of death, enhanced by the guillotine, was a feeling no patriot was supposed to feel. Quite the opposite, a patriot was "full of indignation, beyond all fear" in Jeanne-Marie Roland's words; carried away by "burning courage" according to Couthon. As a result, the more violence was used, the more every person found damning evidence of fear within him- or herself, and with that discovery came an urgent need to hide the fear, which itself increased one's danger. The induced emotional suffering, further, undermined the efficacy of sentimentalist emotives which, prior to 1789, had provided many with proof in their own hearts of the rightness of sentimentalist ideas. This was no accident. Sentimentalism as an emotional regime was bound to produce this effect. The greater its success as an oppositional idiom before 1789, the harder its fall was bound to be. Sentimentalism's conception of liberty was so far from real emotional freedom that, in the end, the contrast was patent to all, even if it could not be put into words. It was wrong, and by 1794 most knew it was wrong.

As an instrument of resistance, sentimentalism's critique of etiquette and *bienséance* was convincing and attractive, even if misconceived. As an instrument of rule, sentimentalism's insistence on true expression of natural feeling rendered it as inflexible as what it had supplanted, if not more so. Management of feeling was forced under cover, yet everyone sensed how common and necessary it was. Thus, all were made into traitors.

This is not to say that sentimentalism was responsible for the Terror in all its detail; that particular regime cannot be understood except in relation to many other circumstances, including food shortage and speculation, inflation, foreign invasion, military weakness, and domestic rebellion. The particular configuration of factions in the Constituent Assembly and in the Commune of Paris were equally decisive in shaping the Jacobin regime. However, sentimentalism, viewed as a mistaken understanding of emotional expression, can help to explain (1) the extremes of feeling that were frequently expressed, (2) the tendency to couch political decisions in terms of feeling (the "terror") and to justify policy as arising out of feeling, and (3) the extreme frustration, and anxiety, produced by the unintended, but intense, induced emotional suffering created by the Terror policy. The resulting emotional efforts to sustain feelings which, everyone knew, were supposed to be natural and spontaneous made everyone a traitor. The attempt to govern on the basis of sincerity, and to govern in such a way as to produce sincerity, even when using instruments of pure coercion – the whole idea, that is, of a republic of virtue – was sentimentalist in conception and therefore both self-contradictory and unworkable. Again, this may seem like an obvious point. But it is a point that neither class analysis nor cultural interpretation alone can provide any grounds for.

CHAPTER 7

Liberal Reason, Romantic Passions (1815–1848)

In July 1816, two Parisian notables came to Maine de Biran's door. M de Castel Bajac and the duchesse de Rohan, both friends of his, asked him for the traditional contribution for the poor in honor of Saint Sauveur. In response he offered them six francs,

believing that this would be the average amount offered by the well-off sort. But the duchess told me of persons who had given twenty or forty francs. Her words upset me, and I experienced at once an agitation of the mind and a regret as sharp as if I had committed the most malign and most dishonorable of actions.[1]

Maine de Biran was struck dumb with chagrin, and the duchesse and her escort left without further conversation. Afterward, he rehearsed the situation obsessively.

From that moment, I could not think of anything else: What would the Duchess of Rohan think of me? What of my colleague [M de Castel Bajac] who held only the most benevolent feelings for her? . . . Wouldn't I become the laughing-stock of that whole group? Wouldn't they view a contribution so out of proportion with my position, as shabby, selfish, and this single gesture would it not reveal a character that was narrow and small-minded? (Maine de Biran 1954–1957:I, 186–187)

He attempted to dislodge the episode from his mind with the distraction of a ride on his horse, to no avail. He walked to the duchesse's house, thinking to add more to his contribution, but feared making

---

[1] "Cette parole m'a bouleversé, et j'ai éprouvé à l'instant une agitation d'esprit et un regret aussi vif que si j'avais commis la plus mauvaise et la plus déshonorante de toutes les actions."

another blunder. Fear of humiliation drove him to the point where he found himself in "that state bordering on dementia" ("cet état voisin de la démence") of talking and gesticulating to himself when no one was present. "What he finds in himself," remarks Pierre Pachet, "is neither purity of soul nor turpitude, but mediocrity; and the way he entangles himself in describing it suggests a strange kind of candor." "One asks oneself," Pachet concludes, "in reading such passages, if they were not written, involuntarily, to illustrate the 'misery of the soul without God'" (Pachet 1990:43). What is sure is that Maine de Biran had penetrated a typically nineteenth-century type of internal space, a space where moral uncertainty and ambiguity has supplanted the fervent clarity of late sentimentalism, and where shame has a new power, greater perhaps than it had even at the court of Versailles. In such a space, as Pachet implies, the old Christian doctrine of original sin could find a new cogency, a factor which played no small role in the religious revival of the post-Revolutionary years.

But along with ambiguity had come a substantial increase in richness and mystery. "Who knows," Maine de Biran exclaimed at one point, "what concentrated reflection can do, and if there isn't a new *inner* world which may be discovered one day by some *Columbus of metaphysicians*" (Maine de Biran 1954–1957:I, 176, emphasis in original; quoted by Pachet 1990:43). Late in life, he concluded that the human soul was – not, as so many eighteenth-century thinkers had thought, inherently good, but – "ineffable." "The interior man is *ineffable* in his essence, and how many degrees of depth, how many points of view on the interior man have not yet even been seen" (Maine de Biran 1954–1957:II, 244; emphasis in original; quoted by Pachet 1990:44). In Maine de Biran's simple enthusiasm over this inner mystery can be found summed up the characteristic shift in attitude that separated the generation of Romanticism from their sentimentalist predecessors. Beginning from an attempt at scientific introspection, aimed at pure observation of the "physical and moral" phenomena of consciousness, Maine de Biran had found both emotional frailty and a necessary spiritual dimension, whose nature and extent remained unclear.

Because Maine de Biran was as involved in Restoration politics as he was in the period's academic circles, it is significant that his journal also expresses a new, characteristically nineteenth-century attitude toward political activity and politicians. Napoleon's conclusive defeat at Waterloo had paved the way for a return of the Bourbon dynasty to its former throne. Louis XVIII hoped to solidify his hold on power by granting a fairly liberal constitution, called the Charter, which established a Parliament based on a very limited suffrage. In 1816 and 1817, as the Restoration regime sought to discipline a rowdy ultraroyalist majority in the new Parliament, Maine de Biran expressed consistent dismay about Parliament's deliberations and the personalities that dominated it. Maine de Biran himself served as a deputy from the Dordogne, until his defeat by an ultraroyalist in 1817. Shortly thereafter he was appointed to the Council of State. The great question of the day, whether to impose royal authority on a recalcitrant people, or win them back to monarchy by slow and temperate measures, was beyond the Parliament's capacity to handle.

It is impossible to examine such questions calmly, and everyone takes sides according to his character or his particular affections. We have no statesmen capable of embracing a whole. These little spirits think only of what suits their locality and support the opinion that will win them the most partisans in their department of origin. Passions face each other and clash, and passions are always connected with small ideas, never with principles or general or regulatory concepts. (I, 101)[2]

Electoral politics, Maine de Biran feared, far from facilitating rational deliberation and statesmanlike behavior, only encouraged particularism and passion. Here emotion's effect on politics is entirely detrimental. Maine de Biran conceded the necessity of an assembly as a voice for public opinion but was profoundly pessimistic about its chances of acting wisely. His journal registered, again, the failure, and the erasure, of that late sentimentalism which had sought national salvation through the expression of emotions in politics.

Maine de Biran's pessimistic remarks about the life of the new Restoration Parliament are constantly interlaced with discouraging observations about his own state of mind, and it is difficult not to see the affinity that existed between these two trains of thought. Just like the Parliament, so Maine de Biran's own constitution was weak, subject to the influence of nerves and passions. He saw physical circumstances,

---

[2] "On n'examine pas ces questions de sang-froid, et chacun prend son parti suivant son caractère donné ou ses affections particulières. Nous n'avons pas d'homme d'état, qui embrasse un ensemble. Ces petits esprits songent à ce qui convient à leur localité et soutiennent l'opinion qui leur fera le plus de partisans dans le département d'où ils sortent. Les passions se choquent et sont en présence, et les passions ne sont jamais en rapport qu'avec des idées particulières, jamais avec des principes ou des idées générales et régulatrices."

physiological symptoms, and emotional states as closely intertwined. Constantly, he notes the effects of weather on his mood – recalling for us the recent researches of Clore and Parrott (1991), discussed in Chapter 1. In a typical passage, from the entry of 29 February 1816, he anxiously diagnoses the linked shifts of what he called, following the Idéologue Cabanis, the physical and moral dimensions of his being:

I feel in a peculiar state both physically and morally. I pass not a day, not even an hour without suffering: my mobile, diseased nerves make themselves felt most painfully in the region of the stomach; that is the source of my ill-ease and my habitual concentration. A bit of gastritis can help make me more somber, more fearful, more discontent with myself; my instincts would now push me towards solitude, and I find it cruel to be obliged to live among men who don't seem to feel any benevolence for me. (I, 108)[3]

Maine de Biran's accute self-observation did not always focus on the emotional effects of gastritis or the weather, however. He was also fascinated, if dissatisfied, with the sheer mobility of his thoughts.

I always need to attach my ideas to a fixed point and firmly enchain them from there; otherwise, if I don't hold onto the thread, I find myself as if lost in a chaos, and feel no confidence in my own ideas. There are advantages and disadvantages to this. The disadvantages are more obvious for me, who cannot compose the shortest essay without great effort and suffering. *I have carried out some new experiments on myself in this last fairly long bit of work.* Truth is within, and comes out of the fog that our inner organization surrounds it with, only when there is an equilibrium among our faculties. (I, 118; emphasis added)[4]

---

[3] "Je me sens dans un état particulier au physique comme au moral. Je ne passe ni un seul jour ni guère une heure dans la même journée sans souffrir: mes nerfs mobiles et malades se font sentir péniblement dans la région de l'estomac; c'est là qu'est la source de mon malaise et de ma concentration habituelle; un peu de gastricité contribue encore à me rendre plus sombre, plus craintif, plus mécontent de moi-même; mon instinct m'entraînerait maintenant vers la solitude, et je trouve cruel d'être obligé de vivre au milieu d'hommes en qui je ne trouve presque plus de sentiment de bienveillance."

[4] "J'ai toujours le besoin de rattacher mes idées à quelque point fixe et de les enchaîner assez fortement; sans cela, si je ne tiens pas le fil, je me trouve comme perdu dans un chaos et je ne prends aucune confiance dans mes propres idées; il y a à cela des inconvénients et des avantages. Les inconvénients sont pour moi qui ne puis faire la moindre composition sans de grands efforts et sans souffrir. J'ai fait de nouvelles expériences sur moi dans ce dernier travail d'assez longue haleine. La vérité est intérieure et sort des nuages où notre organisation l'enveloppe, lorsqu'il y a équilibre dans nos facultés."

But the happy equilibrium that allowed truth to emerge from the fog came for him, as for most people, all too rarely.

All the blind and involuntary passions or emotions have their seat [*siège*] in our organic life; all that is voluntary and intellectual has a different seat. The will does not directly influence the passions, it cannot generate a single emotion; nor do the passions have any direct influence on the will which can always, except in certain extreme cases, hold itself at a height where it is not touched. There are some who are so organized that the two sorts of life, the superior and inferior parts of man, are more separate and each plays its separate role, the superior part retaining all its activity even when the inferior part is troubled. Bonaparte was blessed with such an organization, if one believes those who examined him. That's just the way of it: the most divine model of all the perfections applied to one of humanity's greatest scourges.

One must simplify oneself to be the most perfect and the happiest possible. My great unhappiness here is to be too complex [*composé*], too multiple. (I, 111)

By comparison with the psychological theories of Charcot or Freud, Maine de Biran's view of the interaction of appetites, emotions, and will is underdeveloped, but it is no less firmly anchored in physiology, no less diagnostic in form, no less gloomy in its conclusions.[5] Maine de Biran's gloomy outlook and his closely associated sensitivity to humiliation, I will argue in this chapter, are keys to understanding the greater stability of the French social order of the nineteenth century by comparison with the period of late sentimentalism (1760–1800).

The nineteenth-century political scene was sometimes tumultuous, it is true, punctuated by revolutionary ruptures in 1830, 1848, 1871. Nonetheless, Napoleon's great work of consolidation, represented by the law codes, the judicial system, and the administrative bureaucracy, survived all the surface tumult intact. The law codes established civil society as a realm of contractual freedom and (relative) freedom of expression. Patriarchal family law and partible inheritance encouraged relatively free competition among adult males for wealth and office. Through a century of rapid growth and technological change, urbanization, and changing social relationships, these basic principles and practices were not subject to serious challenge. What was the source of this stability? An earlier historiography (both liberal and Marxist)

---

[5] On Maine de Biran's direct contribution to the development of French psychiatry, see Goldstein (1987:258–260).

concluded that this was the "bourgeois century," a period in which the interests of the commercial and industrial classes dominated government, society, the arts, and thought. But as class analysis has become more refined, the precise identification of classes has proved impossible, and the idea of class interest has lost its explanatory power. More recent poststructuralist and culturalist accounts have offered no explanation for the sudden shift, in 1815, from relative turmoil to relative stability. As was noted in Part I of this study, these interpretive methods are not well equipped to account for change, whether they are wielded by historians working on nineteenth-century France or anthropologists studying emotions on Pacific islands.

Can the theory of emotives improve our understanding of this stability? In this chapter I will sketch an overall picture of the period, emphasizing the sustained refusal to remember or come to grips with sentimentalism, as well as the development of related liberal and Romantic conceptions of emotion. In the following chapter, I will explore a set of cases derived from primary documents that allow a close-up look at the emotional sense of the new regime, a picture of the compromises and sufferings it entailed for individuals navigating their way through life. Together, these two chapters will provide a counterpoint to the chapters on Enlightenment and Revolution. We will see how a new set of emotional norms, just as erroneous in their own way as those of sentimentalism, nonetheless rendered navigation easier, caused less emotional suffering, tolerated greater diversity of responses to normative emotives, and thus generated less political resistance.

EMOTIONS IN LIBERAL SOCIAL THOUGHT

In the late eighteenth century, reason and emotion were not seen as opposed forces; in the early nineteenth they were. In the late eighteenth century, natural sentiment was viewed as the ground out of which virtue grew. In the early nineteenth, virtue was regarded as an outgrowth of the exercise of the will, guided by reason, aimed at disciplining passions – much as it had been from ancient times up to the seventeenth century. In the late eighteenth century, political reform was deemed best guided by natural feelings of benevolence and generosity. In the early nineteenth century, while some would have continued to grant benevolence and generosity a role in politics, much more importance was attached to personal qualities such as commitment to principle, soldierly courage, a willingness, if necessary, to resort to violence, and, above all, a proper understanding of justice and right. In the early nineteenth century, the very enunciation of this list of differences would have surprised most people. The most authoritative interpreters of the Enlightenment for French general readers after 1815 – figures such as François Guizot, Victor Cousin, Théodore Jouffroy, Jean-Philibert Damiron – attached little importance to the emotionalism of the previous century, depicting it as an age of dawning rationality and science whose promise was betrayed by a revolution gone astray. Not only were sentimentalist ideas rejected, then; their very importance in the prior age was lost from view.

But the early nineteenth century, some will object, was a period with just as many ardent love affairs as the late eighteenth, just as many intense friendships, just as much passion and utopian zeal in politics. The Romantic movement in literature and art was just as concerned with understanding the place of emotions in personal life as sentimentalism had been (see, e.g., Houbre 1997:146). Melodramas and tempestuous operas continued to pack theaters in Paris and the provinces. Like the Revolution of 1789, some will note, the Revolution of 1848 began with a flood of optimistic enthusiasm and followed the same inexorable course toward factional mistrust and repression – only it went much faster. How, then, can it be claimed that the period 1794 to 1814 brought an "erasure" of something? How can it be claimed that important possibilities and important avenues of thought and practice were cut off, to remain shut down for a long time?

All these observations are true, as far as they go. I am not claiming that the people of early nineteenth-century France were without emotions, nor that they were without a past. It would have been impossible to completely eliminate the intellectual legacy of the sentimentalist period, just as it would have been impossible to recast personal, familial, and public practices in a form completely devoid of sentimentalist features. But this legacy and these features of practice were set in a new intellectual framework and put to new uses. When the new thinking and new practices of the early nineteenth century are viewed as elements of a normative emotional management regime – which I will here refer to as the "Romantic" management regime – it is possible to understand how a constitutional monarchy could be more stable than the Jacobin republic of virtue.

A New Kind of Introspection: Maine de Biran and Cousin

If Marie-François-Pierre Maine de Biran (1766–1824) was not the first to navigate emotional life in the new way we have examined, he was certainly one of the earliest. His intimate journal, written at various times between 1794 and 1824, is considered to be the very first of this now common modern genre (Pachet 1990). According to Pachet, Maine de Biran, in starting his journal, took his cue from a desire expressed by Rousseau. Rousseau had proposed to write an account to be called "Moral Sensitivity, or the Sage's Materialism," which would track the effects of everyday circumstances "on our machine, and on our soul" (quoted in Pachet 1990:36). Such circumstances would include the weather, colors, light and dark, food, noise, movement, rest – all the impressions, however minute, of daily existence. Maine de Biran's journal began, therefore, as a kind of naturalist's notebook, tracking the impact of environment on feelings, brimming with observations about the weather, his health, his reasoning powers, and his mood swings.

During the Napoleonic years, Maine de Biran wrote several influential treatises on the nature of consciousness, including *L'influence de l'habitude sur la faculté de penser* (*The Influence of Habit on the Faculty of Thought* – 1802), *Mémoire sur la décomposition de la pensée* (*An Essay on the Decomposition of Thought* – 1805), *Mémoire sur les perceptions obscures* (*An Essay on Obscure Perceptions* – 1807).[6] Maine de Biran shared with his contemporaries, the Idéologues, the ambition of finding a truly scientific approach to human behavior, and these early essays won him election to the Institut de France, at the time an Idéologue stronghold.

As noted in Chapter 6, this group, led by Cabanis and Destutt de Tracy, defended a highly reductionist view of human nature. Soon after 1805, Maine de Biran became dissatisfied with the simplistic approach of the Idéologues. Just as Shaftesbury, Diderot, and other sentimentalists criticized Locke's sensationalism, Maine de Biran began to find more going on in his own interior than the Idéologues could account for. Unlike the sentimentalists, however, he did not believe that these additional facets of consciousness could be considered a kind of inner moral sense. He found no evidence of that *sensibilité*, that natural wellspring of moral goodness, that the sentimentalists had so fervently believed in. Instead, Maine de Biran was insisting by 1807 that con-

---

[6] On the complex chronology of Maine de Biran's writings, see Funke (1947:336–338).

sciousness possessed, among other things, a rational and therefore free will as well as a remarkably complex and sensitive connection with the body.

The date of this shift in attitudes is significant. A number of intellectual figures, including Philippe Pinel, Pierre-Paul Royer-Collard, and Pierre Laromiguière, began moving away from strict Idéologue doctrine after 1805, suggesting that prior allegiance may have been motivated more by the political climate than by conviction. The development of Pinel's "moral treatment" of the insane, the clinical approach that launched French psychiatry, has been carefully traced by Jan Goldstein (1987). Pinel seemed to draw substantially on sentimentalist ideas, even though he failed, perhaps purposefully, to acknowledge them in the first edition of his *Medico-Philosophical Treatise on Mental Alienation or Mania* (*Traité médico-philosophique sur l'aliénation mentale ou la manie*, 1801). Moral treatment meant, first of all, gentleness, and, secondly, the use of a "theatrical apparatus" to break down the delusions of the patient. Pinel understood theater in precisely the same terms as Diderot, as a mimetic illusion capable of circumventing reason by working directly on the imagination. In the second edition of his treatise, published in 1809, Pinel added substantial new discussion of the emotional features of his clinical case studies. In addition, he affirmed that the return of the patient's *sensibilité* – of his or her regard for and generosity toward family and friends – was the sure sign that a cure had been effected (Goldstein 1987:117–119).

Pinel and others may have drawn on sentimentalism, but their general outlook on human nature had none of the old optimism or confidence. Before the Terror, in 1790, Pinel had predicted the Revolution would bring a great reduction in insanity. By 1795, however, he was claiming the opposite, that the political instability that had afflicted France since 1789 greatly increased vulnerability to insanity (Goldstein 1987:101). Just as the Terror and its failure had rendered the problem of curing insanity more pressing for Pinel, we sense in Maine de Biran that political and social turmoil reinforced a sense of fragility and uncertainty.

By 1818, the young Victor Cousin (born in 1792) was already presenting at the Ecole normale, to vibrant acclaim, a philosophical synthesis built around a critique of the Idéologues. His critical stance toward their sensationalism drew directly on Maine de Biran, with whom he was in frequent contact, as well as his own mentors, Royer-Collard and Laromiguière, and was supplemented by his reading of

the history of philosophy. Cousin's thought was destined to be extraordinarily influential – through his teaching, in the first place, and then
after 1833 through the policies of the ministry of public instruction that
he headed for a time and that enshrined his system in the official cur-
riculum of the nation. (On Cousin, see Spitzer 1987:71–96; Billard 1998;
Brooks 1998.) It is therefore important to dwell for a moment on his
carefully constructed vision of humanity's emotional fragility.

It was reasonable for Cousin to concentrate his fire on the Idéologues. They firmly held the institutional high ground throughout the
Napoleonic era, and several held onto their posts into the Restoration.
To Cousin's generation they seemed to epitomize all that was good and
bad about the Enlightenment and the Revolution. But this critical focus
allowed Cousin to brush past sentimentalism with only occasional gestures in its direction.

Looking across the Enlightenment legacy in philosophy from the
vantage point of 1818, Cousin saw only, on the one hand, the sensationalists – Locke, Condillac, Cabanis, and the Idéologues – and on the
other, their critics, especially Thomas Reid and Kant, who affirmed the
independence of reason from sense impressions.[7] He had nothing
whatever to say of Shaftesbury; he knew that Hutcheson and Adam
Smith attached a certain importance to natural sentiments, but mentioned this only in connection with esthetics. Cousin found all these
thinkers wanting. He sided with Reid and Kant, against the sensationalists' effort to reduce human consciousness to the recognition of patterns in sense impressions. But he was also impatient with Kant's
insistence on the limitations of human reason. Following Maine de
Biran, Cousin's method was "psychological" in the sense that he began
with what he hoped was a kind of scientific introspection. Looking
within himself, and within others, he found that ideas such as those of
truth, liberty, justice, beauty, and the good – universal in their occurrence – pointed to capacities we all possess, the capacity to reason, the
capacity to make judgments, and the capacity to choose. Our capacity
to reason, which underlay all our other capacities, linked us to a realm
quite beyond the empirical world of sense impressions. Cousin exalted
reason, insisting on its power – not merely to provide an a priori structure (that we could never verify) to sense impressions, as Kant claimed

---

[7] Here I am following Cousin's presentation in *Du vrai, du beau, et du bien*. First published in 1836, this book is explicitly presented as an account of Cousin's course at the
Ecole normale of 1818. I use the twenty-first edition of 1879 (Cousin 1836).

– but to give us access to truths such as the existence of God (following a trail similar to that blazed by Descartes). Cousin's doctrine was therefore aptly dubbed "rational spiritualism." Because he claimed to draw on the whole history of philosophy, he also called it, at times, "eclecticism."

Emotions played an important, but subsidiary role in Cousin's view of human consciousness. In a lesson devoted to the refutation of various forms of mysticism, Cousin denied that sentiments could offer us a direct link to a spiritual realm; only reason had that power. Here he defined emotions succinctly as follows:

We carry within ourselves a profound source of emotions [*une source profonde d'émotions*] at once physical and moral, which express the union of our two natures. Animals do not go beyond sensation, and pure thought belongs to the nature of angels alone. Sentiment [*le sentiment*], which compounds sensation and thought, is the birthright of humanity. Sentiment is, to be sure, only the echo of reason; but this echo sometimes makes itself better heard than reason itself, because it reverberates in the most intimate and most delicate parts of the soul and shakes the whole man. (Cousin 1836:106–107)

There is much here that is merely traditional; man the "rational animal" has a dual nature and is subject to, not just pure thought, not just appetite, but also a lower form of conscious event, a kind of hybrid, called emotion or passion. Animals, accordingly, have been downgraded from the high status they enjoyed in sentimentalists' eyes. Original to Cousin is the close partnership he sees between reason and certain "sentiments" which "echo" reason (elsewhere, he says, they "envelop" it, they serve as its "faithful companion" – see Cousin 1836:265, 318).

In his discussion of morality and of the morally good, it is easy to see how he arrived at this thesis of sentiment's subsidiary role. He first shows at length that neither pleasure, nor even enlightened self-interest, could serve as an equivalent of the good, as the Idéologues had argued. Then, in a section entitled "Other Defective Principles," he takes a few pages to refute the core doctrines of sentimentalism. This is the only point in his teachings of 1818 where he comes to grips explicitly with its legacy. It is certainly true, Cousin concedes, that we derive pleasure from accomplishing an admirable action, an act of benevolence or generosity. It is also true that, when we see others suffer, we may feel "pity," or "sympathy," a form of suffering of our own that

urges us to act to help them. But, if we do good solely because it brings
pleasure, or if we help others solely to avoid the pain of pity, then we
are actually only pursuing our own interest, maximizing our own pleasure. However, Cousin has already argued at length that morally good
action must be based on disinterested motives. If we look more closely
at what is going on, he says, we find that esteem or contempt toward
our own or others' actions are judgments. The accompanying sentiments, "admiration" or "indignation," are feelings that "derive from
intelligence" and surround it.

This move will be familiar to many present-day psychologists
working on emotion, especially to those who followed the well-known
debate of the 1980s between Zajonc and Lazarus over the question
whether cognitions (judgments) preceded the accompanying emotions
or followed from them (for a summary, see Parkinson & Manstead
1992). This issue was considered closely in Chapter 1, where I argued
that it is the existing emotion/cognition distinction that is at fault. This
was an important step in arriving at a view of emotion as a type of activated thought material too broad to fit into attention all at once.

What Cousin has done is recognize that any "moral sentiment" must
have a cognition at its core. He reclaims for reason a function that the
sentimentalists had attributed to *sensibilité*. Thus he praised sentimentalism for coming closer to the truth than the sensationalists, while at
the same time setting it aside and exalting reason. Training our ability
to feel pity or generosity, Cousin conceded, is a useful part of our moral
education. Moral sentiment, Cousin concluded, is "a kind of sign of the
presence of the good, and renders doing what is good easier" (Cousin
1836:318). But at the core of morality was a certain kind of "natural and
instinctive judgment." "It is only after this judgment that our *sensibilité*
is aroused" (p. 319).

Sentiment alone could not serve as a foundation for morality, Cousin
insisted, because it was too changeable. The tumultuous Revolutionary years as well as the glory and misery of the Empire period made
this point an easy one to carry.

It is far from the case that all men are made to taste the pleasures of the
heart with the same delicacy. There are coarse natures and elite natures. If
your desires are violent and impetuous, will not the idea of the pleasures
of virtue be conquered in you by the force of passion more easily than
if nature had given you a tranquil temperament? The state of the weather,
health and illness dissipate or revive our moral sensibility. [*L'état de
l'atmosphère, la santé, la maladie émoussent ou avivent notre sensibilité*

morale.] Solitude, delivering a man over to himself, allows remorse all its energy; the presence of death redoubles it. But worldly affairs, noise, involvement, habit, although they cannot smother it, daze it [*l'étourdissent*], so to speak. The mind breathes when it wants to. One is not every day capable of enthusiasm. Even courage has its ups and downs. We all know the famous quip: He was brave for a day. Mood [*l'humeur*] has its vicissitudes which influence our most intimate sentiments. The purest, the most ideal sentiment depends in part on our physical organization. The poet's inspiration, the lover's passion, the martyr's enthusiasm all have their lassitude and their failings [*leurs langueurs et leurs défaillances*], which often have the most petty material causes. Can one possibly establish a legislation equal for all on these perpetual fluctuations of sentiment? (pp. 321–322)

These observations are remarkably reminiscent of Maine de Biran's journal entries of the same years. How could such a shaky foundation as sentiment provide an "equal legislation for all," Cousin asks, using a political metaphor loaded with meaning. Just thirty years before, the Old Regime had been swept away, and the very principle of equality before the law established by an assembly which, every witness agrees, was caught up in a single profound sentiment of generosity. Cousin's lectures were shutting the door on such folly, without fanfare, without need of argument.

In Cousin's system, the true, the beautiful, and the good were each discerned by means of a different type of judgment. Each type of judgment was associated with a distinct sentiment. The true inspired love and a desire for more truth. The good inspired admiration. Beauty inspired "a delicious emotion . . . you are attracted to that object by a sentiment of sympathy and love"; you feel "an exquisite interior enjoyment" which is "profound without being passionate" (p. 141). Cousin found it easy to dismiss the Idéologues' attempt to equate enjoyment of beauty with "pleasure" in general. If pleasure was the sole measure of beauty, then the "Hottentot Venus would equal the Medici Venus. The absurdity of the consequences demonstrates the absurdity of the principle" (p. 139). In addition, before a truly beautiful woman, one's desire for sexual pleasure is in fact "reduced by an exquisite and delicate sentiment, even replaced by a disinterested cult" (p. 143).

Cousin had next to nothing to say about the very different approach to art championed by the sentimentalists. The idea that sentiment was responsible for our recognition of beauty was, he believed, an improvement over the sensationalist's dependence on the narrow concept of pleasure. However, Cousin dismissed Diderot as a disorganized mind, marked by flashes of genius, but devoid of principles. Diderot "abandoned himself to the impression of the moment," Cousin charged; "he had no concept of the ideal; he was satisfied with a certain naturalness, at once vulgar and mannered" (p. 133). This is an unfair caricature of a figure whose thinking was both coherent and powerful. As Fried (1980) has shown, Diderot's theory was just that the observer ought to abandon himself to the impression that a work of art, or theater, or music had on him, so that the artistry could work directly on our innocent, inborn moral sense. Art's purpose was to train us in virtue. Beauty and the good were fused, as were art and life. This fusion, for Cousin, was merely incoherent.

Judgment of the beautiful was a distinct activity of reason; beauty required its own separate realm of discussion and reflection. Cousin's system would thus provide strong support for the Romantics' new doctrine of "art for art's sake." His dismissive attitude toward Diderot reinforced the general sense that the art of the previous century was deeply flawed, vulgar, intolerably didactic and exaggerated.

It is easy to see how attractive Cousin's synthesis must have been to many educated French men and women in the years after 1815. On the one hand, he painted a vision of human nature very close to traditional Aristotelian and Christian notions, but completely secular and scientific. It was not difficult, reading Cousin, to understand how the disasters of the Revolution could have occurred, nor to appreciate that the remedy lay in bolstering the institutional power of those few who could reason well. There were even grounds for a renewed faith in God. On the other hand, for those who retained a lively sense of their own inner emotional constitution, Cousin cautioned them strongly against trusting sentiments; they were not sure guides. Still he invited them to value emotions as signs, supports, aids to reason. Properly trained, emotions could tip the balance in favor of right thinking, good action, proper esthetic judgment. Observation of what lies within was an important part of the search for truth and opened up a vast field of exploration.

The New Emotives of Powerlessness

Both Cousin and Maine de Biran expressed nagging fear of the effects which the cold light of reason might have, when turned on one's most treasured hopes and enthusiasms. Cousin, in words that bear witness to the birth of a nineteenth-century preoccupation, warns of the power of reason, and of its necessity, as follows:

One must be very sure of one's attachments before putting them to the test of reflection. O Psyche! Psyche! respect your happiness; don't sound the mystery too deeply. Don't bring the fearful light to bear on the lover your heart has chosen. At the first ray of the fatal light, love wakes and flies away: a charming image of what happens in the soul, when the careless and serene confidence of sentiment is replaced by reflection with its sad train. This is also, perhaps, what one may understand by the biblical story of the Tree of Knowledge. Before science and reflection come innocence and faith. Science and reflection engender first doubt, disquiet, disgust for what one possesses, the agitated pursuit of what one does not know, troubles of mind and soul, the hard work of thought, and, in life, many mistakes, until innocence, lost forever, is replaced by virtue, naive faith by true knowledge, and, after so many vanished illusions, love finally arrives at its real object. (Cousin 1836:110)

Compare this passage with the following, from Maine de Biran's journal entry of 1 January 1817, in which he sums up the developments of the previous year:

Overall, I lose many advantages in advancing, without any compensation in the form of wisdom or the force of reason. I am disillusioned about many prestigious positions, but I no longer feel those sweet and happy impressions that embellished my existence now that I judge more coldly. I feel less interest in examining them at their true value; and, becoming indifferent, in the end, towards all the objects that used to attract me, I also feel less stimulated to study and think. I no longer give my active and intellectual faculties any strenuous employment, and I waste my moral life with a mass of petty cares, petty occupations, which use up each separate moment without tying these moments together, without leaving any continuous trace. (Maine de Biran 1954–1957:II, 3)[8]

---

[8] "En tout, je perds beaucoup d'avantages en avançant, et sans compensation du côté de la sagesse ou de la force de raison. Je suis désenchanté de beaucoup de prestiges, mais je n'éprouve plus ces impressions douces et heureuses qui embellissaient mon existence en jugeant les choses plus froidement. Je mets aussi moins d'intérêt à les examiner sous les véritables rapports et devenant indifférent sur le fonds de presque tous les objets qui m'attiraient auparavant, je me sens aussi moins stimulé pour étudier et penser. Je ne fais plus de fort emploi de mes facultés actives et intellectuelles et je laisse gaspiller ma vie morale par une foule de petits soins, de petites occupations, qui employent chaque moment séparé, sans lier la suite de ces moments, sans laisser de trace continue."

It was during this period, and not before, that a modern type of Cartesian dualism gained the undisputed upper hand in French thought, a type of dualism familiar in our own time, discussed at length above in Chapter 3. In its nineteenth-century configuration, this dualism included a diagnostic attitude toward the self, an accute sensitivity to humiliation sometimes coupled with a longing for "benevolence" from those around one, a hopelessness about politics, because passion seems to prevail easily over the deliberative reason that ought to reign.[9] The psychological introspection which served as the central method of rational spiritualism was, according to Cousin, the fruit of the efforts of Descartes, the sensationalists, and their opponents; it was the one thing they all had in common. It was the distinctive feature of modern philosophy, the procedure that endowed philosophy with the same power and dignity as modern science. As Cousin later explained it, this method consisted of "analysis applied to the soul," that is, "the slow, patient, minute observation of facts hidden in the root of human nature": "We have observed, described, counted the real facts that we have found in the soul, without omitting nor presupposing a single one; then we have observed their relationships, relationships of resemblance and of dissimilarity; finally we have classified these relationships."[10] He continued: "The consciousness that applies itself [to this observation] is an instrument of extreme delicacy, it is a microscope applied to the infinitely small" (Cousin 1828:Lesson 2, pp. 5–6).[11] It was only natural that the belief one could find "facts" by means of introspection would lead to discovery of the "fact" that human nature was dualistic, consisting of one part (reason or consciousness) capable of identifying and classifying facts and another (the physical) serving as a kind of residuum or support for the first part. It was only natural, as well, that, in such a scheme, emotions would be difficult to locate; beyond the reach of volition (as Maine de Biran insisted), they were nonetheless (according to Cousin) hybrid phenomena, the special possession of the "rational animal."

Maine de Biran's journal is a precious indicator of the kind of emotives that such a dualistic scheme was likely to give rise to and the

---

[9] I have explored these issues extensively in Reddy 1997b.
[10] Each lesson in Cousin (1828) is paginated separately; this quote is from p. 5 of lesson 2.
[11] "La conscience qui s'y applique est un instrument d'une délicatesse extrême: c'est un microscope appliqué à des infiniment petits."

likely self-altering effects such emotives would have on feeling. Moods, sentiments, emotions, for Maine de Biran, were to be observed in the same way that a naturalist observed the forms of a flower or a chemist the pressures of a gas in a tube. But were not such "observations," which were actually emotives, likely to increase Maine de Biran's sense of helplessness over feeling? Helplessness is precisely the impression that emerges most strongly from reading his entries. Here are two more examples from early 1817.

6 January, rain continues, storms. I passed the whole morning quite peacefully at home; and so long as the time allowed, reading and medi- tating. I made several forays into the domain of metaphysics but without enthusiasm, without success, and with the sole advantage of passing time without boredom. Left home after 4 pm, in the rain. I went to the Chamber of Deputies where I listened with interest to the discussion of the law on elections. Even in the best speeches from the rostrum there is a tone of char- latanism that disgusts me, and seems contrary to reason. Eloquence is mis- placed when it is a question of proposing the principles of a law. I feel that nature has called me to think, to reflect, distancing me from the art of oratory.

Returned home at 5:30 pm. I found M Ampère waiting to dine with me; I was expecting others, but they did not come. I felt moody and sad, feel- ings not dissipated by a conversation on metaphysics that I followed only halfheartedly. I went out again at 8:30 for some distraction. Evening at Suard's.

Sixth [February]. – Rain and wind. I passed the whole morning peace- fully without occupying myself with business. I had a few visits, especially that of M. Mounier, with whom I chatted about the business of [the Com- mission for the] Liquidation [of Foreign Debts]. At 4:30 pm, I climbed in my carriage to go dine at the abbé Morellet's, where I found Mme Chéron and M Auger, both feeling ill. I passed a calm evening. I took the foolish step of stopping after 9 pm at Mme de Staël's where there were many guests, and where I cut a rather sad figure [*où j'ai montré une triste figure*]. Returned home feeling ill at ease and dazed. Perspiration and coughs less strong during the night. [*Rentré avec du malaise et de l'étourdissement. Transpiration et toux moins forte dans la nuit.*] (Maine de Biran 1954–1957:II, 8, 16)

Psychologist Daniel Wegner's research (discussed in Chapter 1) has shown that emotional expression easily gets caught up in the ironies of mental control; I am arguing here that emotives (i.e., all emotional expressions) have both self-exploratory and self-altering effects, that they can be used, via a kind of fugitive instrumentalism, to shape feeling, to train it, that feelings may, however, sometimes defy such efforts, even terminate them. But what happens when emotives are formulated purely as observations, in the way Maine de Biran intended them? In that case, they are intended neither to shape or change feeling nor to find out if the feelings expressed are really there. If such emotives have the very common effect of confirming and enhancing what they express (i.e., to use the language of contemporary cognitive psychology, if they activate the thought material they purport only to describe), then the "observer" will sense that he or she is indeed quite removed from her feelings and quite without control over them. And he or she may indeed feel sadness or fear as a result. This is an error. While our "control" over emotions is far from perfect it is far from the case that emotions are beyond willful manipulation, as Maine de Biran believed they were. Thus, his journal would have constituted a training in helplessness. A heightened sense of one's own delicacy and fragility, of one's own changeableness and unpredictability may well have been inherent in this type of "observation." Cousin recognized this necessary corollary of his method with as much acuity as did Maine de Biran. Both regarded mental fragility as a genuine discovery, rather than as a side effect of their method. And doubtless for many, as for Maine de Biran, this sense of fragility increased concerns about honor. How could one predict that, in all the trying day-to-day social interactions of public life, one's fragile nature would never betray one into a slip, a humiliating gesture, an inadvertent insult? Maine de Biran was constantly aware of this danger.

Nonetheless, Maine de Biran's and Cousin's conception of emotions as too changeable and too weak to ground moral or political judgment lowered expectations. By lowering expectations, Maine de Biran and Cousin, in turn, gave greater free play to emotional activations and reduced the level of vigilance required of mental control. Increased emotional freedom was purchased at the price of a generalized sense of distance from feelings, of helplessness, fragility, even melancholy. Here was an erroneous formula capable of framing a polity that demanded much less of the individual than the Jacobin Republic – or even Napoleon's empire of hypocrisy – and could thereby win a greater measure of consent or of acquiescence.

Denis Bertholet's recent research into the autobiographies of this period suggests that Maine de Biran was far from alone in regarding his mind as weak and changeable, and far from alone in struggling against discouragement with the help of pen and paper (Bertholet 1991). Bertholet suggests this mind-set was a byproduct of the sudden changes of fortune of the 1790s and Napoleonic years. But these sudden changes of fortune cannot be separated from the failure of sentimentalism. Bertholet finds melancholy and nostalgia, to be sure, but also a sense of the inner as an uncharted realm, full of the unexpected, of deception, and of disillusionment. As in Maine de Biran's life, journal or memoir writing itself becomes, in other lives, an instrument for restoring partial continuity and keeping hold of the threads that provide integration. For example, in Chateaubriand's *Mémoires d'outre-tombe* (*Memoirs from Beyond the Tomb*, 1849–1850), as Bertholet shows, the great novelist and publicist sees himself as split between at least two selves.

In my interior and theoretical existence I am a man of dreams, in my exterior practical existence a man of realities. Adventurous and orderly, passionate and methodical, there never was a being more chimerical and more positive than me, more ardent and more icey, bizarre androgyne, shaped by various bloodlines from my mother and my father. (Quoted in Bertholet 1991:46)

But both dreamer and realist were sometimes overcome by pessimism: "In the last analysis, is there anything worth getting out of bed for? We go to sleep to the noise of kingdoms falling during the night, which they sweep up, each morning, in front of our doors" (quoted in Bertholet 1991:47). At other times, he recognized this discouragement as one of his great weaknesses and sought consolation, firmness of purpose. "In life weighed at its lightest, measured at its shortest length, devoid of all cheating, there are only two true things: religion with intelligence, love with youth, that is, the future and the present; the rest is not worth the trouble" (quoted in Bertholet 1991:47). In the end, he came to see his memoir itself, which he worked on continuously from 1803 until his death in 1848, as his "alter-ego."

Bertholet also considers the memoirs of Charles d'Haussez (1778–1854). Ardent royalist in the 1790s, proscribed under the Directory, d'Haussez rallied to Napoleon, then with greater conviction to the Restoration. After 1815, he served as député, préfet, member of the Council of State, and finally minister of the marine at the time of the Revolution of 1830, which cut short his career and sent him into exile until 1839. In his later years, he praised the writing of his memoirs as an exercise that protected him from the worst self-loss and the worst suffering, even if it could not bridge the gap between past and future, imaginary and real.

I write to give myself an accounting of what I think, to persuade myself that I remain in communication of ideas with a world from which I have been separated. . . . I throw words to the wind, as if it might carry them beyond this retreat where I am forgotten: useless return towards a past forever closed, impotent aspiration for a time, indeterminate in its duration, but which could not be called the future. . . . [This habit of writing] neutralizes the annoyances that, at times, trouble my repose. If it cannot turn away from my heart the deeper grief that tends to penetrate, at least it prevents grief from taking root. A topical medication applied on deep wounds, it leaves to time the business of providing scar tissue. (Quoted in Bertholet 1991:52)

Examples of this sort could easily be multiplied. In his memoirs, Edmond de Lignères, comte d'Alton-Shée, for example, remembers how, as a young page in the court of Charles X, in 1826–1828, he arranged to have forbidden literature delivered to him at Versailles: including *Le Journal des débats, Le Globe*, the published university lessons of Guizot and Cousin. His outlook on life and human character is thoroughly imbued with the clinical reserve and pessimism of the period. He apologizes for saying little about his own private life, for example, as follows:

Sheltered behind the thick ramparts of society's morality, of received ideas and social fictions, men defend themselves against the truth. How many, in the secrecy of their thoughts, are capable of looking truth in the face? Even fewer have the courage to say it. No one would dare to write it except masked behind the pomp and ornaments of an artificial style. It is, in any case, difficult to be sincere about oneself without being the same about others. Outside of political issues, I don't think I have the right to do that. (Alton-Shée 1869:I, 84)[12]

This passage expresses the same sense of personal fragility, linked to a concern to avoid humiliation, that we have already seen in Maine de

---

[12] "A l'abri derrière l'épais rempart de la morale mondaine, des idées reçues et des fictions sociales, les hommes se défendent contre la vérité; combien dans le secret de leur pensée sont capables de la considérer en face? Moins encore, ont le courage de la dire, et nul n'oserait l'écrire autrement que défigurée sous la pompe des ornements et des artifices du style. Il est d'ailleurs difficile d'être sincère sur soi, sans l'être aussi sur les autres, et, hors de la vie politique, c'est un droit que je ne me reconnais pas. . . ."

Biran. Alton-Shée's portraits of others showed the same keen sense of weakness and the same concern for honor. Although a member of the Chamber of Peers, Alton-Shée, by 1831, had been won over to republicanism, and offered his services to Armand Carrel, at that time the charismatic leader of the republican faction. To his surprise, Carrel told him not to bother offering help and launched into an angry outburst on the state of the party. "Fools, impotent idiots, full of envy!" he claimed. Alton-Shée refrains from repeating the specific charges and excuses Carrel's tone in words that recall Cousin's and Maine de Biran's remarks on mood. He was only "pouring out unjust reproaches based on the bitterness and disgust of the moment," Alton-Shée explains. "There is no character, however strong its fiber, which is safe from a momentary lapse." But Carrel's warnings had a decisive impact on Alton-Shée, turning him away from politics entirely (p. 76). Alton-Shée also saw Carrel the night before Carrel's fatal duel with Emile de Girardin in 1836. The duel, Alton-Shée observed, was only a pretext for Carrel, seeking outlets for his exasperation. Talking with friends as his last evening wore on, Carrel decried, again, the state of the republican party.

The men I appear to direct are not ready for the republic; no understanding of politics, no discipline. We commit one error after another. In effect, I am reduced to the role of hammer. They use me to strike. Hammer for breaking, I can build nothing. The future is too far away for me to reach it. (pp. 162–163)

Carrel, Alton-Shée explains, had been educated as an officer under Napoleon and conserved a military outlook on politics. His ardor, his spirit inspired the republicans, but he was not their deepest thinker. Other memoirs, too, speak of duels as disasters forced on individuals by a kind of psychological weakness, rather than as worthy proof of honorable self-regard (see, e.g., Musset 1836:46–50; Pontmartin 1885–1886:I, 111–118).

Like Chateaubriand, Alfred de Vigny in his journal, begun in 1836, observed himself from a certain distance and saw himself as split in two. "There are in me two distinct beings, the *dramatic self* who lives with violence and activity, and the *philosophic self* who separates itself daily from the other, disdains the other, and judges it" (emphasis in original; quoted in Pachet 1990:105). His powers of self-observation were, he believed, great. "Nothing in me can suspend, stop, or trouble that invincible interior *attention* of my mind for sounding, interrogating, analyzing, studying what I do, what is done to me, what happens to me, what is said to me" (p. 103). But this invincible capacity for self-observation found a self that was weak and that had to cover up its weaknesses. "I felt within myself from my birth an abundance of unbelievable tenderness; and the broadcasting of its too ardent signs, of its too vivid emotions escaped in spite of myself all the time. I had to take up, at age sixteen, the cold mask of society. I was educated in its use by a woman who loved me (Madame de M.)" (p. 104).[13]

It was a long distance indeed from the confident assertions of sentiment in the letters of Marie-Jeanne Phlipon to her fiancé, or the domineering claims of suffering that fill the love letters of Germaine de Staël, to this new, solitary type of writing, as if dipping the pen like an oar into the fearful ocean of the mind.

Emotions in the Liberalism of the Globe Group

From its inception in 1824 to its sale and transformation in 1830, a newspaper called *Le Globe* defended, with a remarkable unity of conception, a new sort of "liberalism" that drew on all the major thinkers of the post-Napoleonic period, helping to consolidate their orientations into a new common sense. In a recent study, Jean-Jacques Goblot (1995) has painted a remarkable collective portrait of the group of young intellectuals who came together in Restoration Paris to found *Le Globe*, and his study makes it easy to appreciate the central role they played. The term *liberalism* had first come into wide currency after 1815, to refer to the opponents of the ultraroyalists in the Parliament. Liberals were those who accepted the necessity of constitutional government and equality before the law; some went further, hoping for the establishment of a democratic republic, others did not. The *Globe*'s version of this new ideology was destined to become a kind of landmark.

Early in the life of the periodical, Théodore Jouffroy published an essay, "Comment les dogmes finissent" ("How Dogmas Meet Their End"). When it appeared as a supplement to the 24 May 1825 issue of *Le Globe*, it was widely admired and commented on. It was embraced as a manifesto of the younger generation whose voice *Le Globe* hoped to become (Spitzer 1987:113–115; Goblot 1995:291–293). Jouffroy, in formulating the group's view of recent history, followed Guizot's think-

---

[13] "Je sentais en moi dès l'enfance une abondance de tendresse incroyable et l'expansion de ses témoignages trop ardents et de ses émotions trop vives s'échappait malgré moi en toute occasion. Il me fallut prendre à seize ans le masque froid du monde. Il me fut enseigné par une femme qui m'aimait (Madame de M.)."

ing closely. Both understood the failure of the Revolution in terms of the negative character of its inspiration. Sentimentalism simply dropped out of the picture. The progressive forces of the eighteenth century had failed for two reasons, in Guizot's view; first, the thinking of the period only wanted to "eliminate its contrary." Second, eighteenth-century philosophy, Guizot believed, "only examined man in relation to his material dimension" (here the reference was certainly to the Idéologues); reason, as a result, "had not reached its own logical limits" (Billard 1998:32–33).

According to Jouffroy, the eighteenth century had developed a skeptical rationalism, a pure "esprit d'examen," well suited to undermining the moldering dogmatic structure of the old monarchy and its religion. The faith of the Revolutionary generation had no positive content; it was merely

the belief that the old faith was not sound. But this conviction is vibrant because unexpected, it is vibrant because it is the awakening of human intelligence after centuries of numbness, and because truth, always beautiful in itself, exalts those who feel it for the first time; it is vibrant, finally, because one senses that it implies a revolution. (Jouffroy 1825:60)

The emotionalism of the Revolution's beginning and the violence of its radical period reflected only the vivacity of a newly discovered, negative conviction. Called upon to substitute something for what they destroyed, the Revolutionaries fell to fighting among themselves; the people lost faith in them; and the forces of the Old Regime were able to regain the upper hand. But this restored Old Regime, Jouffroy assured his readers, could not last.

Jouffroy's essay voiced both the discouragement and the hope of many of his contemporaries, but it offers at best a myopic vision of the Revolution. The special ardor and optimism of late sentimentalism, as well as its Manichean fears, were entirely lost from view, and so was the Jacobins' agonized pursuit of a republic of virtue. Salient, instead, in Jouffroy's thinking, although he makes no explicit reference to it, is the atmosphere of compromise and accommodation that characterized the Napoleonic years, the crises of the end of his empire and the disappointments of the Restoration. To young men arriving at maturity in the 1820s, many of the older generation appeared to be sanctimonious Pharisees who would serve any master. They are the butt of Jouffroy's constant references to a "game of perjury and fraud," to a regime based only on "fear," and "interest," to the "corruption" and "cunning" of its leaders. Far, indeed, from Jouffroy's mind, if he even knew of it at all, was that special atmosphere of the Night of 4 August 1789.

In philosophy, *Le Globe* embraced the new dualism of Maine de Biran and Cousin. Philosophy, the paper assured its readers, was a science like any other; its truths, just as those of physics or chemistry, must be based on observation. The individual, observing within himself discovered "rational facts" just as the scientist, observing nature, discovered "sensible facts." These rational facts included the elemental categories of substance, duration, and cause and the ideas of the true, the beautiful, and the good. From these observations it was possible, by a process of induction, to conclude that man possesses a threefold nature, combining the capacities to feel, to think, and to will. As a sensible being, man is "purely passive and totally submitted to the laws of the material world." As a thinking being, he is subordinate to "the laws of reason." Endowed with a will, he becomes "a person, a moral agent" and, as such, is free (Goblot 1995:220). The *Globe* group was in perfect accord with Cousin's hesitant admiration of new German trends. Rather than emphasizing the limits of reason, as Kant had done, or the transcendental character of the dialectic as Hegel wished to do, they celebrated the confirmed power of reason within its proper sphere. To mark their disagreements both with sensationalism and what they called the "sentimental school" or "dreamy school" of the eighteenth century, *Le Globe*, following Cousin, tagged its approach "rational spiritualism" (p. 217). Man had a soul, he was not a mere machine; but as a spiritual entity, his business was reason, not feeling or sublime contemplation.

With these straightforward conclusions about man's nature, the *Globe* group could easily justify their enthusiastic commitment to liberty. Submissive to the laws of reason, and, as a moral agent, possessed of freedom of the will, the individual must necessarily enjoy the greatest freedom to reason and to decide for himself. The group's motto, "La vérité est au concours" – "Truth is in the contest" – enunciated a common sense they applied in every domain. Religious freedom, freedom of speech and of the press, free competition in commerce and industry, as well as in literature and the arts, were requirements of human nature, they insisted. Thus, a social order which honored these requirements was itself natural. The slow advance of liberty in European history, as Guizot and Jouffroy argued, was not an effect of civilization softening custom and rendering individuals more (emotionally) sensitive and more inclined to benevolence, as Voltaire or Suard had argued (Baasner 1988:149). Instead, liberty advanced with time because, just as Cousin insisted, reason was humanity's highest source of authority, and reason could only achieve its function when it was freely exercised (Rosanvallon 1985:67, 87–94; Billard 1998:66–70).

The present government and laws of France were a good approximation of this natural order. The group's greatest concern was therefore that the king's current ministers, the church, and the ultraroyalists in Parliament opposed this natural political order and sought to undo it. Expounding their commonsense liberal philosophy, therefore, weighed on the group as an urgent duty.

Freedom in intellectual debate and political deliberation, in the *Globe*'s vision, were necessary to the emergence of truth. In the economy, freedom was necessary to the emergence of innovation and efficiency. Greatness in all of these realms consisted in seeing clearly the single, true road forward. Only the realm of art was set apart, as an arena where the endeavor was to be true to oneself, rather than submitting to the discipline of reason, interest, or science. Being true to oneself meant attending to emotions. The *Globistes* agreed with Cousin that moral truths could not be founded "on the uncertain basis of some sort of sentiment." But artistic truths, it seemed, must have such a foundation. Charles de Rémusat, in the pages of *Le Globe*, demanded that the poet "be himself," that is, "translate and embellish a true movement, a real affection" (Goblot 1995:396).[14] In the realm of art, the *Globe* group followed the sentimentalist dictum, above all to avoid affectation. (On the eighteenth century's aversion for affectation, see Fried 1980.) There is nothing worse, Saint-Beuve insisted, than a work of art produced "with the aim of bringing triumph to a literary theory" (Goblot 1995:408). However, unlike sentimentalists, the *Globe*'s literary critics admitted that achieving naturalness and being true to self were difficult in the extreme. Rémusat insisted "that the true poet is a child without reason, sublime by instinct" but admitted "that the time is past," if it ever existed, when poets could actually write this way (quoted in Goblot 1995:399).[15] To approximate this state, it was necessary to follow an arduous path; necessarily one looked to the work of

---

[14] "Etre soi-même . . . traduire, en embellissant, un mouvement vrai, une affection réelle."

[15] "que le vrai poète soit un enfant sans raison, mais sublime par instinct, j'y consens: mais je dis que le temps est passé où il en était ainsi, supposé que ce temps ait jamais existé."

prior generations, one imitated great models; but this was never
enough. To be dominated by these models was certain death. Thus, the
Globistes believed, art was the special endeavor to give form to explorations of that fascinating inner space Maine de Biran had found while
writing his journal, to give form to those exquisite and delicate sentiments that accompanied esthetic judgment according to Cousin.

The *Globe* critics insisted that, in literature, the novel had finally been
elevated to equal dignity with the traditional genres of tragedy and
poetry. However, it was not the rambling sentimental masterpieces of
the eighteenth century – *Pamela, Clarissa, Marianne, Julie* – but the brilliant historical fictions of Walter Scott which had brought the genre this
new status. The critics had little patience with the older novels, or their
present-day imitations, which mixed "the artifices of a melodramatic intrigue" with "interminable dissertations" on social or political
matters (Goblot 1995:458). Their attitude toward contemporary
poetry was complex. On the one hand, many of them admired the
new Romantic style of Byron and Lamartine. Rémusat, for example,
acknowledged that modern civilization deprived the poet of the
resources of the marvelous; but "There still remained in the human
heart an inexhaustible fund of passions and sentiments, eternal fuel of
enthusiasm and of dreams. Thus modern poetry has as its dominant
characteristic that it is interior, reflective, meditative" (quoted in Goblot
1995:442).[16] But *Globe* writers also expressed a certain dissatisfaction
with poetry's new mission; they could not bear to see it deprived of
subject matter dealing with history, the nation, morality. They were prepared to rate Béranger's patriotic songs higher than Lamartine's
"melancholy and vaporous" lyricism (p. 443). Goblot concludes they
were frustrated by the implications of their own philosophy, by
which the institutions of modern society "resituate man in private
relations, and return him to his individuality," giving rise to "a new
poetry, totally interior, where the unity of man and citizen is broken"
(p. 449).

Essential to the liberalism of the *Globe* group, then, was a sharp
distinction between reason and sentiment and a desire to relegate
the latter, sentiment, to a private realm of personal reflection, artistic
endeavor, and interior, noncivic spaces. This sharp division between

---

[16] "Il n'en reste pas moins dans ce coeur humain un fond inépuisable de passions et de
sentiments, aliment éternel d'enthousiasme et de rêverie. Aussi la poésie moderne a-
t-elle pour caractère dominant d'être intérieure, réfléchie, méditative."

reason and sentiment licensed their equally sharp division between those who were capable of civic action and others who were not. The former group consisted of adult French men (to which were added, in one article, the adult men of Germany and England); the latter, all others: women, children, non-European men. (Here, they followed Guizot; see Rosanvallon 1985:95–104.) This distinction was central to the group's vision of esthetics, religion, politics, the family, and world history. By this outlook, emotions had no place in the public sphere (except in the safe realm of art).

It is remarkable how closely the *Globistes* adhered to the teachings of their two principal guides, Guizot and Cousin. Dismissed from their official positions during the backlash of 1820–1822, these two thinkers were part of an adventurous, illicit, intellectual avant-garde during *Le Globe*'s early years. Both Guizot and Cousin would return triumphantly to university teaching during the thaw of 1828. Guizot, like Cousin, would go on, under the July Monarchy and thereafter, to play leading roles in government and in the shaping of France's educational institutions. They jointly fashioned the education act of 1833, authorizing the creation of public schools in every village (although these institutions were not yet free or compulsory). Cousin served as minister of public instruction in Guizot's 1840 government; for a long period, Cousin's system of thought was taught as the official doctrine of the school system (Billard 1998; Brooks 1998). Insofar as *Le Globe*'s liberalism was a distillation of their thought, it represented a set of dominant tendencies of the period.

Filling Sentimentalism's Shoes: Nascent Socialism

At least a brief note must be appended here on the emergence of socialism in the decades after 1815. Like other members of the post-Revolutionary generation, the early socialists in France saw themselves as bearers of a grave historic mission. Free of the work of destruction, untainted by compromises and betrayals, they saw themselves, very much like Jouffroy and the *Globe* group, as endowed with an unusual creative capacity and as charged with the task of moving history on to the next stage (Spitzer 1987:171–205; Prochasson 1997). They did not, in other words, anymore than the liberals, see the Revolutionary era as marked by a peculiar loss or about-face, as I have argued that it was. They did not see sentimentalism as its first inspiration, as the hidden source of both optimism and terror before 1794; its erasure was as effective for them as for their liberal opponents. They did recognize, and reject, the extraordinary leap of faith that equated freedom of contract in civil society with the rational use of society's resources. They rejected the whole architecture built upon the notion of interest. It is surprising that Victor Cousin and his disciples had so little to say about this matter. Highly critical of self-interest as a motivation for rational, moral, or esthetic judgment, Cousin implicitly accepted it as the shaping principle of civil society. The *Globe* group, in designating Tanneguy Duchâtel to summarize the lessons of political economy in its pages, and to report on the ideas of Malthus and Ricardo and the debates they had inspired (Goblot 1995:310–325), complacently accepted the compatibility of the new gospel of rational spiritualism with the laissez-faire economy. A good number of artists and novelists, including Victor Hugo and Eugène Sue, would eventually see the problem. The sublime cannot be packaged; yet the new production methods and technologies enslaved individuals and packaged their substance in the form of mass-produced, often shoddy merchandise.

Even before this frightening recognition began spreading in the 1830s, however, a number of young intellectuals had begun searching for alternative organizing principles that could replace "interest." Like their liberal contemporaries, they gathered around select leaders, of an earlier generation, whose words acquired an almost religious authority. One group was drawn to the aging Henri de Saint -Simon and, after his death in 1825, attempted to propagate his vision of history. Saint-Simon believed that industrialists, intellectuals, and artists must come together in the new age and, by their collaboration, reduce politics to a set of technical competences. These new leaders would be inspired to carry out this transformation by a refurbished Christian ethic; in the name of the vast majority, they would set aside the petty dictates of interest, and a new selfless sense of mission would inspire the whole of society. Another group drew inspiration from the reclusive autodidact Charles Fourier. In a variety of texts, Fourier had proposed concrete alternative principles of motivation that could replace interest as the drive behind economic behavior. He insisted that he had identified, among others, a butterfly passion – the desire to change tasks every couple of hours or so – and a cabalistic passion – the desire to conspire with others. As a kind of parallel to the laissez-faire marketplace, he proposed the founding of "phalansteries," ideal communities designed to harness the potential of these and other hitherto unknown passions rooted in human nature. The phalanstery would make it easy to change tasks; the phalanstery would harness cabals to increase output. The result would be more happiness for less work. Just as sentimentalists imagined there were moral sentiments that rendered generosity pleasurable, so Fourier taught that there were passions that might render productivity pleasurable. But the obvious kinship of this way of thinking with the earlier ideas of the sentimentalists was apparently unknown to Fourier.

Both Saint-Simon and Fourier were true visionaries; their writings were often obscure, fragmentary; their thinking was protean. Fourier elaborated a remarkable cosmology to go along with his social doctrines: an astonishing system which few of his admirers seem to have taken at face value. He also believed that sexual desire was a legitimate need that a good society ought to respect; the ideal phalanstery would include persons inspired by the duty to answer to this universal need. Almost nothing was said by his disciples about this dimension of Fourier's system. There was both cross-fertilization as well as mutual jealousy and acrimony between the two camps of socialists. By 1830 a number of Saint-Simonians, lead by Prosper Enfantin, had recognized that private property and the family would have to be abolished. Before they were broken up by the police and laughed into silence by the daily press in 1832, Enfantin's faction had gone so far as to proclaim the unique superiority of women and the need for their liberation. This was not a form of feminism, however. Enfantin and his followers advocated looser sexual mores because they endowed women with a special spiritual function. Shifting his group toward a kind of millennialism, Enfantin even predicted the arrival of a "mother" from the East who would serve as the spiritual focus of a new kind of community. Enfantin's initial talks about gender reform drew excited crowds, including many women; but the doctrinal disputes, personal conflicts, and rapid disillusionment of converts would have torn his sect apart soon if the police had not done it first. The Fourierists were able to hold together somewhat longer; but repeated efforts to establish a working phalanstery all failed for a variety of reasons, including, notably, an inability to agree on just how far to take Fourier's prescriptions in the actual organization and management of a farming community.

Without any apparent direct filiation, the early socialists, in effect, occupied something like the same conceptual space in post-Revolutionary social thought that sentimentalism had in the thought of its era. What united them was their critical stance toward a strict, mechanistic form of sensationalist philosophy and its ready corollary, that self-interest was the universal motivating force of the machinery of the mind. Few were prepared to defend such a doctrine in its unadulterated form. As we have seen, Guizot, Cousin, and the liberals of the *Globe* group insisted on the higher motivations that derived from universal principles of reason, justice, and beauty. However, only the socialists were prepared to recognize the new order's dirty secret. To them it was obvious that the practical workings of the civil order thrown up by the Revolution, and systematized in the law codes, assumed that self-interest did prevail, and ought to prevail, in the everyday business of life. Society was being run as if the mechanistic view of human nature were right. Only the socialists were prepared to offer practical alternatives. The force of their core recognition was sufficient to propel them to extraordinary visibility and influence in spite of their often incoherent, even delusionary, excesses. After the end of the July Monarchy, cooler heads – including Louis Blanc, Pierre-Joseph Proudhon, as well as Marx and Engels – would develop a sense of the politically possible that helped to turn socialism into the dominant left force it became later in the century. But, in doing so, they paid a heavy price. Later socialism too often dispensed with speculation about human nature and human motivation in favor of a cynical appreciation of power politics. Yet, even their more realistic dreams were doomed without something to fill the conceptual space that sentimentalism's erasure had left vacant. (Good entrées into the extensive bibliography on early socialism include Beecher 1986, 2000; Carlisle 1987; Spitzer 1987:145–170; Grogan 1992; Prochasson 1997.)

THE NEW DISPENSATION IN THE REALM OF ART

Art in the Romantic era marked its distance from the art of sentimentalism first of all, as has been noted, by refusing to play a didactic role, and by refusing all blurring of genres. For the new post-1815 generation, art declared its independence. Art was not life, its effects on one were not the same as those of the real; precisely here lay its power, as a refuge, as a superior realm of the sublime, the imaginary. The artist marked the independence of his realm by harnessing art's representational powers to depict the fantastic, the exotic, the impossible. Myth, legend, history, pagan symbolism, the Orient, the Middle Ages, the far away, the forgotten – such were the subjects that allowed the beautiful to impress itself on the observer, just because it leapt out from the unexpected, the unfamiliar. In thus declaring its independence, art put itself in an ambiguous relation with the new order. On the one hand, freedom of expression and freedom of contract – the very foundations of the much maligned "bourgeois" order – were the legal warrant for the artist's new mission. Yet, the new competitive marketplace represented a threat as well as an opportunity. That art might now be bought and sold like any other commodity raised the danger of philistinism and required the artist to renounce exterior signs of success, to avoid ostentatiously even the appearance of pandering to uninformed tastes. The artist had to be independent, as well, with reference to conventional morality; in pursuit of inspiration, in pursuit of the pure forms that could embody beauty, no barriers could be admitted in choice of subject matter (Cassagne 1906; Seigel 1986; Hemmings 1987; Spitzer 1987; Bénichou 1992).

Art's "independence" was thus based on a conception of art that was entirely new and unthinkable except in the context of the post-Revolutionary social order. The artist of the new era retained great interest in, if not to say fascination with, human sentiments and passions; but, more often than not, these were now conceived of as either constituting (along with imagination) a separate realm, or else as best harnessed to certain higher goals (just as Cousin would have recommended). Already, in 1818, as Cousin gave his riveting lectures at the Sorbonne, Charles Nodier was defining Romanticism as a movement aimed at exploring the unfathomable depths and subtleties of human feeling, recalling Maine de Biran's belief in the vast, unexplored inner world of the self. In the first of a series of articles on Staël's *De l'Allemagne* (discussed in the last chapter), published in the *Journal des débats* in 1818, Nodier ventured to characterize the "magic" which the new kind of writing worked on the reader. Was it, he asked,

a result of a vague quality which can be explained only through means which are themselves unexplainable? Facets of things hitherto unseen, an order of perception new enough to be bizarre. I don't know what secrets of human emotions which individuals have experienced but never attempted to convey to others, yet when the reader comes across them he knows he is meeting an old friend. I know not what mysteries of nature – which have not escaped us but which we have never analyzed all at once – strike us because the writer, thanks to a happy coincidence, has suddenly placed them in harmony with memories and feelings; above all, the art of speaking to the imagination by inviting it to dwell on the first emotions of childhood, by evoking those fearful, early superstitions which advanced societies have relegated to the domain of foolishness and which succeed in being poetic only in the poetry of the new school; those are some of the traits of romanticism. (Quoted in, and translated by, Oliver 1964:99)

By cutting art off so firmly from the rest of social life, Romantics did authorize themselves to create emotional refuges. Artistic salons, and the intimate groups called "cénacles," characterized their new way of life; Nodier, Hugo, Gautier, Flaubert, Baudelaire, and many others poured sometimes intense energy and devotion into the life of such circles. Yet this vast esthetic prospect that opened up often led artists away from the center of civil society. Sentimentalism had pushed them in the opposite direction.

Examination of a few works of art will reveal the extent to which sentimentalist conceptions were lost from view in the realm of art as much as they were in the realms of political life and social thought. Novels, plays, poetry, and painting of the new century displayed both a preoccupation with honor and the primacy of a certain type of inner exploration.

Walter Scott's works were extraordinarily popular in France in the 1820s; his novels were rapidly translated and they routinely outsold all new domestic titles.[17] He had a profound impact on young French writers, as well. We have seen that the *Globe* hailed Scott as having lifted the novel genre to the dignity of great art. Yet he also achieved unprecedented popularity. One novel in particular, *Quentin Durward* (Scott 1823), deserves a close look because it was set in France, contained a thinly veiled, harsh commentary on the French Revolution, and sold extremely well in France in the late 1820s (Rosanvallon 1985:200; Lyons 1987:86).

Quentin Durward is the story of a Scottish knight who comes to France in search of honorable employment. He finds his way to the court of France and is engaged in an elite company of Scottish mercenaries who serve Louis XI (reigned 1461–1483). Scott depicts Louis as governed by interest rather than aristocratic honor. He thinks like a merchant; he surrounds himself with commoner advisors of vile origin and narrow outlook, instead of depending on the advice and support of his great vassals. His chief rival, Charles the Bold, Duke of Burgundy, is depicted as a true knight and his court as truly chivalric. Louis's indifference to honor is summed up in his warning to Quentin

---

[17] On the popularity of Walter Scott, see Pontmartin (1885–1886:II, 2–3); Lyons (1987:129–144).

Durward, "I have bought thee body and soul" (Scott 1823:167). But Durward thinks otherwise; no pay could induce him to act dishonorably; and it is on this grounds that he eventually will disobey his employer's orders. Commanded to guard the princess Isabelle, he falls in love with her and she with him. But both realize that this love cannot be expressed until and unless honor permits. Here, the departure from sentimentalist convention is sharpest. Love is not set against honor, as in hundreds of eighteenth-century novels and plays, but treated as an outgrowth of devotion to honor. Tension derives not from the problem of arranging rebellion against family or rank, but from the problem of finding honorable means of expressing one's feelings.

Scott dwells at length on the uprising of the people of Liège against their bishop. They are "unwashed artificers" (Scott 1823:261) whose wealth has gone to their heads; their leaders are demagogues who find that it is easy to fool "a multitude whose eager prejudices have more than half done the business" (p. 266). This deluded crowd loves Louis XI. Thus Louis's defeat of the Burgundians and successful consolidation of his realm is here treated as the fatal step on the road to absolutism that will also lead to Revolution, and to a world turned topsy-turvy, in which self-interest and the blindness of the mob rule, crushing honor, deference, devotion to duty, and love.

This is worlds away from, say, Voltaire's *L'écossaise* (1760), a play whose chief character, a West Indies merchant, wins the hand of the Scottish woman he loves by selfless acts of generosity. In this play as elsewhere, Voltaire contrasts the harmless, even beneficial character of commercial self-interest when compared with the slavish court etiquette of Versailles – elements which Scott, with his very different historical agenda, attempts to fuse.[18] It is also worlds away from Germaine de Staël's highly successful novel *Corinne, ou l'Italie* (1807), in which the young Scottish lord, Oswald, refuses to marry Corinne despite his profound love for her, because his (dead) father regarded the match as dishonorable. Oswald's inner turmoil, his suffering in a disastrous marriage dictated by family considerations, and Corinne's affliction and early death all result from this misguided Scottish devotion to honor.

---

[18] Baasner (1988:145) quotes the following comment from one of Voltaire's letters: "Je ne sais pourtant lequel est le plus utile à un état, ou un seigneur bien poudré qui sait précisément à quelle heure le roi se lève . . . ou un négociant qui enrichit son pays, donne de son cabinet des ordres à Surate et au Caire, et contribue au bonheur du monde."

Corinne's very attractions, her talent as poet and performer, render her an unworthy match because she is a woman too much in the public eye. Yet she readily compromises her own reputation for Oswald. What good is reputation, she asks, if my heart is broken? But in the end she loses both honor and love.

Scott's vision of French history is, on the other hand, close to Chateaubriand's. Both conspire to relocate love and generosity on the side of a preabsolutist aristocratic honor code, and to forget (rather than refute) the sentimentalist interlude of the eighteenth century. Scott's view of the compatibility of love and honor is also close to that of Eugène Scribe, perhaps the single most prolific and successful playwright of the Restoration and July Monarchy eras.

Scribe's 1827 play *Le mariage d'argent*, for example, offers a typically convoluted plot which turns on the tension between considerations of love and honor. The tension is only apparent, however, just because those who act honorably end up free to choose (and be chosen by) those they truly love. A young woman waits loyally for her man to return from the army so that they can be married. However, her father, on the verge of bankruptcy, pleads with her to marry the rich M de Brienne, so that his fortune can cover their debts. In anguish, she sacrifices happiness to family honor. Her lover, Poligny, on his return from the army, is in turn offered a rich heiress in marriage. Mme de Brienne, his true love, is suddenly widowed, but once again she decides to sacrifice her own happiness, this time to save the honor of a friend. That friend, a married woman, is having an illicit affair. Her husband discovers a compromising letter during one of Mme de Brienne's visits. Mme de Brienne claims the letter was intended for her, not for her friend. This claim saves her friend from discovery, but when word of this letter reaches Poligny, he is outraged. Mme de Brienne is, in turn, offended by his lack of faith in her. Poligny decides to proceed with his plans to marry for money, telling Mme de Brienne (falsely) that he does not love her any more. Finally, a penniless young painter, Olivier, who also has secretly loved Mme de Brienne for years, and who knows that Poligny still loves her, tells Mme de Brienne of Poligny's continuing affection, urging her to induce him to break his engagement to the heiress and return to her. During this encounter, however, Mme de Brienne recognizes Olivier's genuine devotion to her; she also sees that money is very important to Poligny, in fact, too important. Her heart warms to Olivier. As the play ends, these two selfless persons, who have proven their willingness to sacrifice for others, are united in a happy and comfortable marriage. Poligny is left with the bitter fruits of his lack of faith and his desire for the glamor of wealth.

As in Scott's *Quentin Durward*, so in this tangled love story, neither love nor friendship can be incompatible with honor just because concern for others cannot be true unless it includes concern for their honor as well as one's own. Scribe's notion of love owes much to the sentimentalist legacy; but in this play, as in others, he gives that legacy a surprising twist when Mme de Brienne's generosity takes the form of a sacrifice of the object of her (sexual) love, Poligny. She sacrifices him, first, to save her father's honor, second to save the honor of her friend. In sentimentalist fiction, it is the father whose honor must not pose an obstacle to the son's or daughter's generous devotion of the self to the one he or she loves. The sentimentalist hero or heroine sacrifices obedience, duty, family honor to the necessity of acting according to the dictates of natural sensibility. This is what Mr. B. finally agrees to do in *Pamela*, and what Oswald fails to do in *Corinne*. Rousseau's twist on this conventional scenario in *Julie, ou la nouvelle Héloïse* cannot be compared to Scribe's. Rousseau defies his readers' expectations in order to advance the idea that there is a difference between natural feeling as a foundation of virtue, on the one hand, and the mature virtuous action that grows out of the education of such feeling. Scribe, by contrast, simply makes old-fashioned family honor a good that cannot be questioned.

Scribe's opportunism may help explain both why critics have never taken him seriously and why he was so popular in his time. In effect, Scribe's plays were safe. One could bring a wife, son, or daughter to such a play without fear, but also with some hope they would be entertained. Even better, Scribe depicted not legendary Scottish knights but simple people of the present day, showing they were just as capable of honor and self-sacrifice as heroes of yore. *Le mariage d'argent* is laced with commentary on the reign of money and self-interest in the new era. Says Olivier to Poligny at the beginning of the play, "The top financiers now play a grand role in high society; the rich are also powerful, and their brilliance has not failed to seduce you. Unable to be like them, you attempt, at least, to come closer to them." Poligny responds: "In this century of money, those who possess great fortunes are the happy ones" (Scribe 1827: I, 303). Olivier, however, is not tainted by such considerations. Poor, he wins a scholarship to study art; by hard work and creativity he makes his way as a painter. Mme de Brienne's modest fortune will allow him to continue.

Even the high art of Victor Hugo's *Hernani*, a verse tragedy of a new type, performed to great acclaim (and great censure) in the spring of 1830, respected the new rule, that love and honor must not conflict. In this celebrated play, Hugo set out to display his contempt for the classical forms of tragedy as they were still defended by well-placed luminaries in the Académie française, the university, and the press. By these rules, revived during the Napoleonic years as part of the erasure of sentimentalism, a tragedy had to preserve unity of time, place, and action; it had to deal with elevated subject matter and elevated personages; it had to be written in *alexandrins* (twelve-syllable lines). Hugo spread the action out over a whole year and across western Europe. His star was a bandit. The sublime, the quotidian, the grotesque are consciously blended on every page. King Charles of Spain, in Act One, Scene One, hides himself ignominiously in an armoir in order to spy on a woman. At several points, secondary characters comment in degrading fashion on the sexual appeal of the heroine. There is also a sustained intensity of emotion in every line entirely at odds with the dignity and composure that are supposed to mark tragic figures. The *alexandrins* are pushed and stretched to the breaking point to allow character and action greater immediacy.

The play appears to do homage to the esteem which Shakespeare had gained in the Romantics' eyes. The plot appears to pit love and honor against each other; as in *Romeo and Juliet*, the play ends with a dual suicide, when two lovers find that the route to honorable marriage is blocked. However, on closer scrutiny, one recognizes that the bandit lover, Hernani, never swerves from obedience to the prevailing honor code, in contrast to Romeo, who was eager to toss family and name aside if they proved obstacles to his love of Juliet. At the end of the play Hernani takes poison to honor an oath he made earlier to one of his rivals for the love of Doña Sol. She, however, loves only Hernani and, taking the vial of poison, joins him in death. But Hernani's act (unlike Romeo's) is not presented as an error; it is, rather, an inevitability, a necessary consequence of Hernani's very admirable manhood. The same is true of his bandit status. The lowly status of protagonists in many sentimentalist novels is intended to show how honor and status are at odds with virtue. But Hernani is a bandit because of honor; his father was put to death by the king, and thus his family

name requires that he rebel against royal authority. He thinks nothing
of stealing a woman away from an impending marriage to one of the
king's great lords. Still, but for his father's (unjust) execution, he would
be a worthy companion for this young countess. When he dies in order
to respect an earlier pledge, nothing in the play invites the audience to
judge this action harshly or to draw the lesson that honor leads to
wasted lives. Honor blocks true love in this case, but honorable action
is still a necessary condition of true love's fulfillment, even if sometimes it leads the other way. Scott, in his historical novels, Scribe, in his
bourgeois melodramas, Hugo, in his famous Romantic tragedies, were
all thinking along the same lines, lines pointing 180 degrees away from
the position sentimentalism had taken on conflicts of love and honor.

When Balzac's great novels began pouring out in the 1830s, his new
style of realism, which was to influence fiction writing through the rest
of the century, concerned not conflicts between love and honor of
the sentimentalist type, but conflicts between honor and interest. I will
briefly mention just two examples. *Les illusions perdues* (1837–1843)
recounts the decline of the innocent but intensely ambitious provincial
Lucien de Rubempré, come to Paris to make his name. Blocked from
advancing as poet or writer by the fierce competitiveness of the Paris
literary scene, he turns to journalism as an easier path. What he does
not fully appreciate is that work as a journalist, while it pays well,
requires one to sell one's convictions, along with one's pen, to the
editor. Young Rubempré makes rapid progress thanks to the facility of
his pen and his willingness to adopt the political cause of whatever
paper hires him. But in the end he goes too far. Switching political
camps in order to maximize his income, he dishonors himself and is
chased from Paris.

Père Goriot (1834) is the story of a retired grain wholesaler willing to
impoverish himself in order to provide additional gifts to his already
generously dowered daughters. Their self-interest makes them blind to
his well-being; to avoid dishonor, they pretend not to know him, as he
is gradually reduced to rags by their constant requests for additional
money. His aristocratic sons-in-law, their fortunes inflated by his
dowries, would rather not acknowledge a mere merchant as kin, in any
case. Gradually, an ambitious young provincial, Eugène de Rastignac,
becomes aware of Goriot's generosity and of his daughters' mistreat-
ment of him. Eugène also falls in love with one of the married daughters, and she with him. Yet this is a love mixed with no small amount
of self-interest, just because Eugène has set out in search of conquests

among the wealthy women of Paris as a quicker route to riches than the study of law could ever provide. Eugène himself, Balzac tells us, is not really aware how much self-interest still tinctures his feelings for Delphine. Yet Eugène restores the daughter, Delphine, to a proper relationship with her father, Goriot; and Goriot, as a final act before his death, blesses their illicit union. This extramarital liaison is depicted as a kind of cynical, yet fulfilling, resolution of all the conflicts in play. Eugène now has money; Delphine is now safe from the hostility of her wheeler-dealer real-estate magnate husband. Honor is also preserved, in the limited sense that such liaisons, if they are not too public, are widely tolerated in Parisian high society.

Balzac's attitude toward his characters is not that of the Romantic artist, to be sure, but it is still easy enough to situate in the new nineteenth-century configuration. It is that of the disabused philosopher who is all too cognizant of Cousin's warning, not to subject feelings to the withering light of reason. Balzac's novels beam withering light into the dark corners of contemporary life. Even his heroes and heroines come in for harsh judgment. Innocence is no excuse for embracing illusions, especially those dictated by self-interest and ambition. Arranged marriages seldom work, to be sure; but love matches are just as fragile. Money is a universal solvent; it is no sooner received than it flows through one's fingers. Self-abasement, as common as air, is no guarantee of success. This new literary "realism," which was to be taken to even greater heights by Flaubert and Maupassant later in the century, was yet another way in which the intellectual and artistic outpourings of this era worked to reduce expectations about one's own feelings and those of others. Reduced expectations meant greater emotional freedom, but in this case coupled with an erroneous cynicism about the human capacity for "rational" (and therefore, moral and beautiful) action.

SAND'S SENTIMENTALIST CRITIQUE

This brief overview of post-Revolutionary attitudes toward emotions and the self cannot do justice to the variety of practices to which the period gave rise, including significant, if inconclusive, contestation of existing norms. In literature, the sentimentalist tradition did not simply die out, although use of its conventions was increasingly confined to the less serious genres. But even this rule had its exceptions.

One exception worth mentioning is the work of George Sand, who burst upon the literary scene in 1832 with a stunning first novel called *Indiana*. This masterpiece was defiantly sentimentalist in conception. Sand's pen reveals a mastery of the resources of Romanticism, but she deploys that mastery only to condemn the new masculine world that the post-Revolutionary generation was busily building. The text is replete with references to Bernardin de Saint-Pierre's 1789 bestseller, *Paul et Virginie*; the plot itself is a form of homage to that earlier novel, which represented a kind of high-water mark of late sentimentalism. Like Bernardin de Saint-Pierre's characters, Sand's hero and heroine come from a distant island, the Île Bourbon (today the island is called Réunion), off the coast of Madagascar. Like them, Sand's characters must engage in the "grand and terrible struggle of nature against civilization" (Sand 1832:272). Like them, Sand's lovers, called Ralph and Indiana, are inseparable friends during their childhood on the island, but family honor and fortune decree that they be married advantageously, in Europe: Ralph to a rich Englishwoman who shows only disdain for him and dies before the action of the novel begins, Indiana to a coarse veteran of Napoleon's army, now engaged in a manufacturing venture. But, unlike Paul and Virginie, Sand's pair, through courage and inner strength, eventually come to understand their love for each other and find the freedom to reunite, living out their lives back on the island, where they spend their fortune purchasing and liberating deserving slaves.

The greatest obstacle to their happiness comes, not from Indiana's brutal husband, but from a slick young Parisian gentleman who seduces first Indiana's beloved maidservant, Noun, then Indiana herself. Through this young seducer, Raymon de Ramière, Sand vilifies the educated elite of her time. Besides being dashing, eloquent, and entertaining, he is one of the young figures of the "eclectic salons" (Sand 1832:78, see also p. 261, where he is referred to as "the young eclectic") – "eclecticism" being one of the names for Victor Cousin's influential philosophy. Raymon is also a liberal monarchist who, during the Martignac government of 1827–1828, argues for a reconciliation between constitutionalism and legitimism. He is, in other words, a member of the same generation as the *Globe* group, a young Charles de Rémusat or Duvergier de Hauranne, gifted, wealthy, well educated, with a brilliant political career opening before him. Raymon is no lying rake, no "Lovelace" – villain of Richardson's *Clarissa* – Sand makes this clear. Instead he suffers from the very weaknesses that we have already seen displayed in Maine de Biran's journal. Sand goes after the Achilles' heel of the new sense of self, that consciousness of inner vastness, accompanied by a sense of the difficulty of achieving integration. Ramière truly loves both Indiana and her maidservant Noun, insofar as he is able; but his variability of intention, the instability of even his deepest feelings, betrays him and leads him to betray these two innocent island women. Here is how Sand describes him:

M de Ramière was, however, neither a fop nor a libertine. . . . He was a man of principles when he stopped to reason with himself; but vagabond passions often pulled him out of his systems. Then he was no longer able to reflect, or else he avoided appearing before the tribunal of his conscience: he committed wrongs as if unknown to himself, and the man of the night before struggled to fool the man of the morning after. (p. 72)[19]

Significantly, Sand compares him more than once to a barrister pleading a case, to a preacher, to an actor:

[H]e expressed passion with art, and felt it with warmth. It was just that passion did not render him eloquent; it was eloquence, instead, that rendered him passionate. If a woman pleased his taste, he became eloquent attempting to seduce her and in love with her in the act of seducing. This was sentiment as barristers and preachers create it, the ones who cry hot tears the moment they start working up a sweat. (p. 83)

Or, again:

With the effort of thinking over his project of seduction, he became passionate like an author for his subject, like a barrister for his client, and one could compare the emotion he felt on seeing Indiana to that of an actor absorbed in his role who finds himself in the presence of the principal character of the play and no longer distinguishes the fictitious impressions of the stage from reality. (p. 143)

In contrast, both Noun and her mistress are natural; each offers Raymon that first, innocent, intense love of one's life, that "leap of generosity that was a need of her nature" (p. 275). Noun cannot even spell

---

[19] "M. de Ramière n'était pourtant ni un fat ni un libertin. . . . C'était un homme à principes quand il raisonnait avec lui-même; mais de fougueuses passions l'entraînaient souvent hors de ses systèmes. Alors il n'était plus capable de réfléchir, ou bien il évitait de se traduire au tribunal de sa conscience: il commettait des fautes comme à l'insu de lui-même, et l'homme de la veille s'efforçait de tromper celui du lendemain."

correctly, knows nothing of eloquence, but when she pleads with Raymon not to break off with her, she finds "the secret of that eloquence that reveals itself all at once to an ignorant and virgin mind in the crisis of a true passion and of a profound grief" (p. 103).[20] This is just the kind of eloquence Mme Roland believed herself capable of on 31 May 1793, as she contemplated going before the Convention to defend her husband.

Ralph, likewise, is hesitant in speech, often tongue-tied; he is viewed as of inferior intelligence. But he watches over Indiana with an unwavering loyalty that we gradually learn is based on the same kind of innocent first love which draws her mistakenly to Raymon. Ralph's politics are at the opposite pole from Raymon's; Ralph pities France's weakness when, in 1815, finally freed from the tyrant, France was forced to accept Louis XVIII's Charter, that poor scrap of liberty (p. 168). Ralph looks forward to the reestablishment of a republic (p. 170). He hates society's vices, dreams of generous new systems, and feels only sharp impatience for the day when new laws and new customs will reign (p. 174). Without using the word, Sand gives us the portrait of a Jacobin, a man with the same generosity and optimism, as well as something of the same rigidity. And nature acknowledges her own. When Ralph and Indiana played as children in their usual haunts on the island, even the waterfowl recognized them, "because they hardly bothered to disturb themselves on [the children's] approach" (p. 257).

As a result, we have no doubt that Indiana speaks for Sand, when, addressing her husband, she denounces with ready irony the laws of marriage then existing in France.

I know that I am the slave and you the lord. The laws of this country have made you my master. You can bind my body, tie up my hands, govern my actions. You have the right of the greater force, and society confirms it. But over my will, monsieur, you can do nothing. Only God can curb it or reduce it. So search out a law, a cell, an instrument of torture that will give you a hold on me! It's as if you reached out for air, grabbed a vacuum. (p. 232)

To resist such illegitimate authority, Indiana demanded from her lover equal devotion. "You must be prepared to sacrifice everything for me,"

---

[20] "le secret de cette éloquence qui se révèle tout à coup à un esprit ignorant et vierge dans la crise d'une passion vraie et d'une douleur profonde."

she said to Raymon, "fortune, reputation, duty, politics, principles, family; everything, monsieur, because I put the same devotion into the balance and I want it to be equal. You see perfectly well you cannot love me that way!" (p. 148). This was not just a nascent nineteenth-century feminism; this was also sentimentalist doctrine. What Indiana insisted on was no different from what Richardson's Pamela demanded from Mr. B., or Choderlos de Laclos's Mme de Tourvel expected from Valmont. As in the eighteenth-century novels, so in *Indiana*, society provides a backdrop of corruption and illegitimate authority waiting to be reformed, to bring it into tune with natural virtue. The difference is that this society is a far more ambiguous, far more uncertain target. Raymon de Ramière's weaknesses and self-centeredness are understandable; much like Balzac's young heroes, he seems constantly on the verge of recognizing the need to reform himself, constantly on the verge of sinking into the swamp of compromise society imposes on him. It is only in the heat of crisis that we learn how he will jump; each time, he falls back on a preoccupation with honor (e.g., p. 218), justifying his own perfidy with platitudes about the weakness of woman's nature.

Sand's insightful characterization of her own period can help me to articulate, at least in a preliminary way, why I see that period as capable of more stability than the late eighteenth century. She contrasts the purity and profundity of Indiana's and Ralph's feelings with the hesitancy and fluidity of Raymon's. But the theory of emotives suggests that the latter is closer to the truth about us, that we are all somewhat like barristers warming up to our cause. Like Raymon, we are apt to be drawn by our own eloquence into passionate feelings we did not know we had. Like him, and like Maine de Biran, we must expend effort, we must master the ironies of mental control to one extent or another, if we are to maintain steadiness of purpose. This is not to detract from her critique of the social order of her time; its rigidities were quite as unjust and inequitable, especially in regard to marriage, as she suggests. If males were more forgiving toward their own foibles than they were toward women's, still, at least there was the beginning of a forgiving attitude. If males of the time were preoccupied with honor, imposing its impossible rules, sometimes risking life and limb in duels to protect their impossible reputations, still, at least the honor code allowed them to be weak and changeable, so long as they concealed their lapses effectively. Sentimentalism allowed no such foibles, insisted on a complete, unalloyed, and equally impossible virtue. Emotional navigation is difficult and unpredictable; by comparison with the late eighteenth century, the social order of the years after 1815 offered better weather and wider channels.

CONCLUSION

Sand's *Indiana* won its author instant fame, even if it made few converts among male literati. The press and the well-established literary critics were quick to denounce her sexual politics, even if many men (e.g., Balzac himself, see Houbre 1997:332) secretly admired her courage. Journalist Nestor Rocqueplan summed up the official attitude when he dubbed her "that apostle of adultery," and noted with sarcasm that all the modern kept women, if asked, would insist that they had "read George Sand, and had loved deeply" (Roqueplan 1853:21, 29). From this kind of comment, and from the enduring popularity of her novels, one can guess that there was a substantial female readership who had different opinions about the merits of her ideas from those of Roqueplan and company. Ronsin (1992:77) provides some interesting confirming evidence. From facts such as that *Paul et Virginie* went through fifty-seven editions between 1815 and 1850, outselling virtually all other novels, or that Germaine de Staël's *Corinne, ou l'Italie* was reprinted in the 1830s and enjoyed brisk sales (Lyons 1987:89, 103), one may also guess that many literate women believed both their love and their judgment to be undervalued by men, and their life chances harmed by prevailing attitudes.

Was marriage undergoing a crisis beneath the surface calm that protected reputations and family honor in this period? It is difficult to say; there is only anecdotal evidence. With divorce outlawed in 1816, and legal separations available only with difficulty, most marriages did remain intact. But there were many arrangements possible that resulted in de facto separations, and these arrangements were often accepted without comment as a routine facet of married life (Reddy 1993, 1997b).

Bertholet's (1991) evidence emphasizes the inordinately high expectations marriage was made to bear in the early years of the century. In the nascent industrial era, he argues, social identity could no longer come from privilege, guild membership, or lifelong residence in an established neighborhood. Hopes of a sweet, limitless intimacy with someone of the opposite sex, he suspects, helped fill the gap. The residual impact of sentimentalism in literature and art encouraged such hopes. Yet land remained the most common form of wealth, and marriage and inheritance the most common modes of access to land. In many minds, therefore, marriage had to provide access to property as well as satisfy desires for intimacy.

We saw in Chapter 4, in the case of the Gogue-Picard marriage and separation of 1839, that the husband appears to have harbored just such broad expectations. He wanted a wife who stood to inherit vineyards from her mother, a wife whose social position was respectable and equivalent to his own, but also a wife who could make his life a "garden full of flowers." Bertholet suggests that many husbands of the period either found their garden, or else, like Indiana's ill-matched husband, swore eternal hatred against the woman who did not fit their expectations. Marie-André-Laurent Odoard, a justice of the peace, for example, wrote in 1812 to his bride of one year, after a brief separation, "I would never have expected, my dear friend, that a separation of two weeks would seem so long; it seems to me as if a year has passed since I had the pleasure of embracing you – except in imagination, for I can tell you that not a minute passes without a thought of my beloved! Oh, how I embrace you with my heart in all those moments!" Twenty years later, during another separation, he wrote, "If I had the misfortune to lose you, I could not survive you for very long" (Bertholet 1991:22). In 1826, a certain Brosset sang the praises of his arranged marriage. "If the happiness [of marriage] comes from love, if love is necessarily founded on esteem, if esteem can only be born and strengthen through the exact appreciation of the desired object, then one has the right, it seems to me, to expect that a [carefully] prepared union will be happy." Once married, Brosset's wife, Elisa "made it her law, from that moment forward, to renounce her own being forever, and to model herself for good on the will of her spouse" (p. 23). "The other is not denied," remarks Bertholet about this period "but annexed" (p. 27) – the other in all these cases being the woman.

Houbre (1997) has found fascinating details about the sexual mores of elite Parisian salons that confirm certain aspects of Sand's critical portrait of Ramière. In his memoirs, *Globiste* Charles de Rémusat, for example, recalled the indulgence with which the aristocratic salons of the Restoration regarded affairs, so long as they were properly conducted. He admitted that he took advantage of this tolerance. "It was in a milieu a bit below my own that I sometimes found distractions for my heart. I say 'heart' but in fact it was rarely engaged with any force" (quoted in Houbre 1997:329). But Houbre also remarks an aspect of the situation that Sand overlooked. Young men such as Rémusat, Jean-Jacques Ampère, Hyppolyte Auger, or Frédéric de Carcy were all initiated into the sexual mores of salon life by older women who made them temporary protégés. For these women, they felt a heady mixture of sensual desire and uplifting emotional devotion. Ampère took his flirtation with Mme Récamier with the utmost seriousness, even though she held him at a distance. "Last night," he confided to his journal in 1824, "I held the humid hand of Mme R., and at last, very late, I embraced her. I covered her hands with kisses. I understood the difference between the fulfillment of the soul and the enjoyment of the senses"[21] (p. 327). When other, younger women attracted him, he struggled over his response. "I will only fall for her if it is a true passion," he decided. "Girls degrade you; a little affair would soil the beauty of my love for Mme R. But against true love, I can do nothing."[22] (The words could have been written by Raymon de Ramière himself, struggling with his changeable enthusiasms.) Rémusat, too, found a first love in the arms of the brilliant baronne de la Barante. "I was very young; I had always dreamed of a respectful and plaintive love, profound and unbroken, high-minded, imbued with the most disinterested devotion, warmed by the passion of duty, of honor, and of truth" (p. 328).[23]

Yet these same young men were often fearful; Ampère, of his feelings toward Récamier remarked, "Of course, it made me look like an idiot."[24] Frédéric de Carcy vaunted his use of a lover to gain access to exclusive salons, but admitted, indirectly, to the sensitivity of his heart and his fear of other men. Rémusat excused his idealism by insisting on his youth and noting how quickly it passed. Certainly, elite members of the Old Regime had roughly parallel experiences of the salon world of their time: idealistic beginnings, more jaded and less memorable mature experiences. But these young men of the early nine-

[21] "J'ai tenu la main humide de Mme R. Enfin, dans la nuit, je l'ai tenue embrassée. J'ai dévoré ses mains de baisers. J'ai compris la différence qu'il y aurait entre la jouissance de l'âme et celle des sens."
[22] "C'est seulement quand j'aurai une passion que j'admets de m'y livrer. Les filles dégradent . . . Une amourette souillerait la beauté d'aimer Madame R. . . . Mais contre un amour il n'y a rien à dire."
[23] "J'étais fort jeune; j'avais toujours rêvé un amour respectueux et plaintif, profond et contenu, uni aux pensées les plus hautes, au dévouement le plus désintéressée, échauffé par la passion du devoir, de l'honneur et de la vérité."
[24] "Cela [. . .] me fait paraître comme un niais."

teenth century swung more rapidly, and more helplessly, I would argue, from the sublime to the shameful, precisely because they were learning to look at themselves with that clinical distance Cousin identified with "psychological" introspection. The reign of such self-observation, the withering effect of the cold light of reason, learned in adulthood, and expressed in so many journals and memoirs, as well as novels, may help explain the special interest that came to attach to adolescence as well. Houbre has provided a range of evidence suggesting that, for both boys and girls, the years from age ten to age sixteen were a time of extremely close friendships, often passionate attachments to a brother or sister, and intense imaginings of the future. The closed world of wealthy households and austere boarding schools to which adolescents were often confined helped to render this a distinctive period of illusions and hopes. But much of Houbre's evidence, drawn from retrospective accounts, also suggests that adult disappointment and impotence charged reminiscences with a special fervor.

While one can only cheer George Sand's condemnation of this type of shifting, insecure, opportunistic self, nonetheless, my argument here is that the rise of such a self helped render post-Revolutionary society more stable. As we will see in detail in the next chapter, the challenge for us, looking back, is to find a more adequate conceptual approach to those types of performance Sand most readily condemned: those of lawyers, preachers, actors. The moral extremism that requires us to be always perfectly sincere and always to make irreversible pledges leads us astray not because we are so imperfect, so decadent, so in need of reform. Quite the contrary, we are incapable of such simplicity because of the very richness of the thought material that arrays itself around attention. We navigate emotional life with extraordinarily odd charts, whose contours change, sometimes very substantially, whenever we make a course correction.

CHAPTER 8

Personal Destinies: Case Material of the Early Nineteenth Century

On 26 January 1826, Mlle Anna de Favancourt signed a will making over her whole fortune (about fifty thousand francs) to her fiancé, Lieutenant Frédéric Descoutures. She was seriously ill. On that same day she wrote to Descoutures begging him to get leave and come to see her in Paris as soon as he could.

I send you all that I desire; no friendly hand will close my eyes; your poor little sister will pronounce your name; you will hear her no more. . . . The leaves will be reborn, nature will come alive again, and I will leave life! I will walk no more leaning on your arm. I will see you smile at me no more. My happiness will have evaporated like a dream. My friend, you will still be happy. Don't torture yourself too much, I want you to console yourself. Adored Frédéric, you whom I cherish more than life, soul of my soul, sole link that holds me still to existence, you are the only thing I will regret of the life that I will leave so young; never forget that your poor little woman loved you well. . . . I would be so happy if you could come! I want it! You cannot imagine how much. That thought occupies me night and day. Could it be impossible! Don't think that I'm deceiving you [about how ill I am]; nothing I take passes. If you were here, I would be so happy to see you. Come if you can. If that is not possible, write me often to console me. Remember your little one who lives for you alone, thinks only of her love. I embrace you a thousand, thousand times, as I love you, that is, more than everything on earth. Yours alone for life. Your little wife, Anna.[1]

---

[1] "Je t'envoi tout ce que je désire; aucune main amie ne fermera mes yeux; ta pauvre petite soeur prononcera ton nom; tu ne l'entendra plus. . . . Les feuilles vont renaître, la nature se ranimer, et moi je vais quitter la vie! Je ne me promènerai plus appuyée sur ton bras. Je ne te verrai plus me sourire. Mon bonheur se sera évanoui comme un songe. Mon ami, tu seras encore heureux. Ne t'afflige pas trop, je désire que tu te consoles. Frédéric adoré, toi que je chéris plus que la vie, âme de mon âme, seul anneau qui m'attache encore à l'existence, toi seul que je regrette de la vie que je vais quitter

In a civil action following her death, the relatives of Anna de Favan-court argued that she was suffering from dementia when she wrote this letter and signed her will. Even Descoutures's lawyer did not defend Favancourt's generosity or intense love as morally good. Instead he simply argued that a strong passion, while it might be deplorable and might lead one astray, was not dementia. Therefore the court should not intervene. The arguments deployed in this case are one index of the distance that had been traveled by 1826 from the emotional common sense of the pre-Revolutionary era. As the letter itself suggests, the sentimentalist idiom had not entirely disappeared; but the lawyers' arguments – so different from those Maza (1993) examines from the 1770s and 1780s – show how sentiment itself is coming to be seen as a kind of affliction or weakness, rather than the source of all virtue.

The three previous historical chapters have offered panoramas, aerial photography, aimed at showing that the theory of emotives can provide an explanatory framework within which we can work out understandings of the trajectory of historical change. In this chapter, we take a closer look at part of the terrain.

In the French case, I have argued, the power of emotives to shape feeling had a decisive impact on the opening and the outcome of the Revolution. The eighteenth-century rise of sentimentalism gave the Revolution both its initial impetus and a strong bias toward extremism. As the monarch came increasingly to be seen as a traitor to the cause, many Revolutionaries nurtured utopian hopes that an inborn moral sensibility could provide the foundation for radical democracy. These hopes were based on their own success in finding what they thought was the inner wellspring of benevolence and compassion within themselves. In reality, unwittingly, they had used emotive rehearsal – encouraged by novels, paintings, theatrical and political dramas – to train themselves to have such feelings. When sentimentalism became a reigning ideology, however, it inspired the Jacobins to

si jeune, n'oublie jamais que ta pauvre petite femme t'aimait bien. . . . Que je serais heureuse si tu pouvais venir! je le désire! tu ne peux t'en faire une idée. Cette pensée m'occupe nuit et jour. Serait-ce donc impossible! Ne crois pas que je t'abuse; rien de ce que je prends ne passe. . . . Si tu étais ici je serais si contente de te voir. . . . Viens si tu peux. Si cela ne t'est pas possible, écris-moi souvent pour me consoler. Souviens-toi de ta petite qui vit pour toi seul, ne pense qu'à son ami. Je t'embrasse mille et mille fois comme je t'aime, c'est-à-dire plus que tout sur la terre. A toi seul pour la vie. Ta petite femme Anna."

think in terms of purging the Republic of its enemies, setting up, again inadvertently, powerful induced emotional suffering that undermined the credibility of sentimentalism's central doctrine. (The logic of this undermining effect went something like this: True republicans ought not to fear death; but the guillotine frightened everyone, making everyone feel insincere in their protestations of republicanism.) The consequence, in the aftermath of Robespierre's fall, was a widespread and deep aversion for certain kinds of emotional claims. The prevailing conception of politics shifted quickly toward classical republicanism, with its emphasis on honor; male competition based on merit became the new cornerstone of liberty. Introspection of the type many had learned during the sentimentalist era slipped its anchor. No longer believing they could find that once comforting moral sensibility within, many of its former devotees began a kind of exploration of new terrain. This exploration, however, was shaped, and its proper terrain limited, by the likes of Pinel, Maine de Biran, and Cousin. They tried to make it scientific, founding it on a refurbished Cartesian dualism that remains familiar to this day. Those who preferred a less clinical approach were exiled to the realm of esthetics, where new, quite imperialistic claims were made for the power of art, as a kind of compensation.

The new age that dawned after 1815 was thus one that made a sharp distinction between reason and emotion. This distinction in theory of course failed to apply in practice, for the simple reason that emotions are an omnipresent and inevitable element of human motivation. Or rather, emotion and thought are not really different phenomena. But the failure of the distinction to apply to practice was understood as evidence for a highly pessimistic evaluation of the human capacity to reason. Here also, Maine de Biran and Cousin showed the way; they regarded themselves (and others) as highly susceptible to environmental and physical influences, full of illusions, capable of rationality only intermittently, fearful of its effects on their affections and their hopes. A sense of fragility heightened concerns for honor, but fragile men also sought refuge in the flexibility of honor, in its ability to heal by concealment.

The new pessimism, in conjunction with the refurbished honor code, created a much more resilient order, because more tolerant. Expectations were radically lowered by comparison with 1792–1794. At the same time, Napoleon's codification of the law provided substantial support for the power of male family heads over wives and offspring, a power that could only be justified on the grounds that men – fragile as they might be – were far more rational than women or children. In the critical gaze of someone like George Sand, the fragile male was a danger made worse by his legal powers; the whole course of history since 1794 represented a slide into systematic, self-serving self-deception. But, against Sand's sentimentalism, we must note that lowered expectations, even if pessimistic in character, were more in tune with the reality of human emotional experience. The problem was not that Raymon de Ramière did not know his own mind, it was that he enjoyed unfair privileges and influence. In particular his power over women, his ability to move at will into and out of their lives, his ability to use them without hindrance or accountability, made his own frailty appear all the more egregious. The problem of the new era was, in a word, its pessimism. Against this pessimism, it is not enough to liberate all the subjugated categories – women, laborers, non-European males. The solution can only come from a reconception of human flexibility in a positive light, a goal that remains to be achieved.

This, in a few words, is the picture these three chapters have given us of the history of emotions in France between 1700 and 1848. In this chapter, I will try to fill in this picture with a ground-level exploration, using evidence from systematic research into primary documents. The aim is twofold: (1) to show how the theory of emotives can frame such detailed primary research, and (2) to explore how real individuals navigated the pessimistic realm of the Romantic emotional regime.

SOURCES AND METHOD

The choice of judicial archives for this type of research was obvious. Judicial archives have become a common source for practitioners of the new cultural history in the last twenty years. Their use was pioneered by such figures as Carlo Guinzburg, Natalie Z. Davis, and Christine Stansell. Sarah Maza's important work (Maza 1993), discussed in Chapter 6, relied on them. Like Maza, I chose to concentrate on civil, rather than criminal, cases. The civil courts handled everyday conflict, and cases found there are less susceptible to the distorting effect that working with criminal cases can introduce. Civil litigation, in addition, was in this period a realm dominated by men competing on an equal basis for honor and advancement, including, notably, the lawyers whose interesting emotional skills inspired such mistrust in Sand.

Documents on civil litigation contain abundant expressions of emotions, as well as homilies and heated debates about the proper expression of emotion. An advantage of the courtroom over the realm of art is that courts were involved in enforcing norms; when interpreting the law, attorneys and judges attempted to take into account unwritten presumptions and attitudes, as well as to clarify moral and civic norms. Thus, when emotions do come up, there is a good chance of getting information on norms. This is both a strength and a weakness for the utility of judicial records. The courtroom is a place where ambiguity must be resolved. The danger of using judicial sources is that they may misrepresent the degree of deviance and the level of toleration that prevailed in practice as well as the possible existence of countervailing informal systems of norms (see Morrill 1998).

To correct for this built-in bias, I turned to two sources for evidence on civil litigation, a printed source that is well known to historians and an archival source of a type that has been little exploited. These two types of sources both complement and correct each other. The printed source, the *Gazette des Tribunaux*, a daily newspaper which began publishing in 1825, aimed at a combined audience of lawyers and educated readers. Interest in courtroom dramas had a long history in France already (Davis 1983; Maza 1993) and had only increased after Revolutionary legislation opened the doors of the courtrooms and made them public. The editors of the *Gazette des Tribunaux* hoped to exploit this interest and chose cases for in-depth coverage on the basis both of potential utility to specialists and of potential attraction for a larger public. When a case was deemed worthy of popular attention, the paper often provided verbatim transcripts of the pleadings of attorneys, of the view of the state's attorney (which was always expressed in civil cases), and of the court's ruling. The abundance of evidence – especially in the form of transcriptions of oral statements, frequently adorned with descriptions of audience reactions – makes the *Gazette* an invaluable source. But its preference for high-profile cases and famous litigants, and, even more, for famous attorneys, whose rhetorical skills were widely admired, creates a problem. Its editorial choices – which cases to cover and at what level of detail – introduce an element of bias for which there is no remedy. This is all the more the case in that the *Gazette* lavished attention on the Paris courts; most Paris court records have been destroyed, and there is, as a result, no way to check *Gazette* coverage against the official records of cases. However, the *Gazette's* editorial policy is itself a form of evidence of great interest. The paper was very successful and sparked imitators. It responded to a genuine hunger for information.

In the period 1825–1829, the newspaper's index allows one to identify all articles about cases tried in first instance (rather than on appeal). From 1830 on, cases are indexed only according to the type of dispute or criminal offense involved. Arguments in first instance were broader and the evidence brought forward more revealing, whereas, on appeal, arguments focused on specific points of law, some of them technical or obscure. Therefore an initial sample was made of all civil cases covered between November 1825 and October 1829 at the level of first instance. Of these, a subset were chosen of cases for which the *Gazette* offered three or more articles. (Where there were three or more articles, the *Gazette* was more likely to provide extensive quotes from, or verbatim reports of, pleadings, as well as a full account of the court's judgment.) This resulted in a sample of forty-six cases.

The other source exploited here was the archives of the Tribunal civil de Versailles, a source which I had used in an earlier project (Reddy 1993, 1997b). The archives contain a full record of the court's judgments for this period, but in most cases, filings and depositions are lost. (Judicial archives contain no records of oral pleadings.) Without knowing the initial complaints, the depositions, or the pleadings, it is difficult to make any useful inferences from a simple register of judgments. However, from these archives, dossiers of 1840 and 1841 preserve full sets of depositions deriving from twenty-eight civil cases. These depositions, some containing testimony of as many as twenty witnesses, are sufficiently rich to allow one to make useful inferences about both witnesses' attitudes and the court's conclusions. Unlike trained barristers, witnesses have no special preparation to express themselves for the record; often they are not personally involved in the outcome of the case. Their responses to questions therefore allow one to look beyond the official, normative postures defended by barristers, and to glimpse how people viewed things from street level, instead of from the floorboards of crowded courtrooms. Because no editorial policy intervened between the researcher and this set of cases, their mix and level of interest provides, as well, a check on the sample taken from the *Gazette*. One case from the Versailles archives, the marital separation of Gogue and Picard, was briefly discussed in Chapter 4, offering a preliminary sense of the potential richness of this kind of source.

FOUR SALIENT CASES

The period of the Directory (1795–1799) and of Napoleon's ascendency (1799–1814), according to the reading I offered in Chapter 6, had brought an erasure of sentimentalism, the assignment of emotion and sensitivity to women and to the private realm, and the devaluation of sincerity in public action. I therefore expected initially that the civil cases in my samples would display a simple pattern. Cases involving women and families – such as disputed wills, marital separations, disputes over paternity, dowries, or power of attorney – would contain discussion of emotions and expression of emotions. Cases involving public action or commerce – such as debt repayment, property ownership, foreclosure, or contract fulfillment – would, by contrast, be dry and contain few references to emotion. But this initial expectation proved to be surprisingly wrong.

It is true that emotions were more often directly at issue in the familial cases. A disputed will might have been written at a time when the testator was in an extreme emotional state rendering her incompetent. A marital separation case could turn on whether the husband was guilty of "cruelties" (*sévices*), a concept that entailed interpreting both his intentions (his emotions) and the effects of his actions on his spouse's feelings. However, not all familial cases turned on such issues, and in many, reference to emotion was rare. Further, in commercial cases, attorneys frequently judged that the emotional states of their clients were relevant to their pleadings. Public and commercial action, as examined in the light of the courtroom, was supposed to derive, not simply from the exercise of reason, but from certain morally appropriate emotions. Expression of such emotions was not necessary in day-to-day affairs; nonetheless, when relationships went awry and disputes arose, it could easily become important to establish that one's actions were motivated by laudable sentiments. Proof of such sentiments might cast doubt on an opponent's factual claims, for example. In addition, clients caught in the glare of publicity expected their attorneys not just to win the case but also to protect their reputations, to exonerate them from slanderous charges, or to weave a plausible narrative of their feelings and their actions that would minimize damage even if they lost in court. Attorneys also strove to express as vividly as possible feelings they attributed to their clients – of outrage or regret, of calm or resolution – to the court or to public opinion. For attorneys, therefore, as for flight attendants, or the Balinese, or Paxtun women, expertise in the expression of certain emotions was inherent in their activity.

Exploration of this evidence must satisfy three aims: (1) We must map out the complex conceptions of sentiment, reason, public, private, morality, gender, honor, and interest that are deployed in the texts that survive. (2) We must examine how this complex terrain of conceptions can be better understood as a moment in history if it is viewed as part of an emotional "management regime," that exploited, with greater or lesser efficacy, the limited shaping power of emotives, and provided some understanding, however flawed, of the mishaps of emotional navigation. (3) We must attempt an evaluation of the kinds of induced emotional suffering and the forms of emotional refuge that characterized this regime, in the hope this may help to explain its greater stability than the sentimentalist configuration.

I will begin with a detailed discussion of four cases from the *Gazette* sample, two intrafamilial disputes, one emotional and one dry, and two commercial disputes, one emotional and one dry. The sketch of the terrain of emotion derived from these cases will then be checked against the whole range of cases from both samples.

1. Lallemand et al. v. Descoutures, 1827

The Lallemand v. Descoutures case, reported on by the *Gazette* in seven articles in January, February, and March 1827, contains more explicit discussion of emotion, and explicit expressions of emotion, than any other case in either sample. In this case, relatives of Mlle Anna de Favancourt, who died in March 1826 at the age of twenty-two, requested the court to set aside her will. In that will, which was only one sentence in length, she left all her property, evaluated at roughly fifty thousand francs, as noted above, to her young fiancé, Lieutenant Frédéric Descoutures. Fifty thousand francs was a modest fortune for the time; at 5 percent interest, such a sum would have produced an income (twenty-five hundred francs per year) equivalent to that of a successful butcher or mason or a junior executive in the civil service – honorable, but necessitating strict economies (Reddy 1997b). As a supplement to an income from office or employment, it offered an ample margin of security and comfort.

The relatives (an uncle, an aunt, and her husband) stood to inherit if the will were invalidated. Their attorney, the eminent barrister Antoine Hennequin, advanced three arguments for overturning the will. First, because the relationship between Descoutures and Anna de

Favancourt had included sexual intimacy outside wedlock, the will itself represented an affront to public morality and ought to be set aside on that ground alone. (Hennequin obviously regarded this approach as weak, in view of the slight time and energy he devoted to elaborating it.) Second, Anna de Favancourt's love for Lieutenant Descoutures had been so extreme that it robbed her of her reason, causing dementia (*démence*), and therefore rendering her incompetent to sign a will. Third, Descoutures had cynically set out to elicit Anna de Favancourt's extreme passion for him, repeatedly promising to marry her with no intention of fulfilling the promise; and, in her final illness, he had pressured her to sign a will and then prevented her from changing it. He was thus guilty of *captation* – that is, fraudulent misrepresentation aimed at obtaining an inheritance. Two of Hennequin's arguments, however, involved interpretation of Anna de Favancourt's emotional state at the time she signed her will on 26 January 1826, and the last one also involved interpretation of Descoutures's feelings and intentions. Thus, emotions were at the center of Hennequin's version of events and were the focus of the counterattack devised by Descoutures's attorney, the equally eminent François Mauguin.

The seven articles in the *Gazette* provide nearly complete verbatim reports of each attorney's opening statement, first rebuttal, and second rebuttal. The king's attorney's opinion is given verbatim, as is the Tribunal's final judgment. We do not have any of the documents that were submitted in evidence; but the pleadings include direct quotations from sixteen different private letters written by Descoutures, Mlle de Favancourt, her mother, her father, and her uncle.

The *Gazette*'s coverage of the case attracted widespread attention. Both attorneys refer to the publicity its articles were generating as the case unfolded; in addition, the *Gazette* offers repeated descriptions of the crowds of men and women who struggled to get into the courtroom starting with the second hearing on 12 January. In twenty-one different instances, as well, the *Gazette*'s account includes descriptions of audience reactions: including moments of laughter, tears, heated applause with "bravos" from many voices, sometimes requiring reprimands from the presiding judge. Starting with the second hearing, the Paris bar was well represented in the audience (special chairs were set up for barrister spectators inside the railing); and colleagues swarmed around both Hennequin and Mauguin when their pleadings ended, offering warm congratulations. The *Gazette* commented that two such displays of talent would be long remembered in Paris courtrooms.

On sixteen different occasions in the pleadings, and in the opinion offered by the king's attorney, Bernard, general statements were made about emotions, reason, and human character to support the varying interpretations of the case. In many other instances, specific interpretations were offered that drew upon a shared common sense about emotions. Also, the attorneys' pleadings were themselves highly emotional, as may be judged by the choice of vocabulary, by the more than ninety exclamation marks which the *Gazette* inserted to suggest their tone of voice, and by the fact that Hennequin had to stop twice during his first rebuttal because he was reportedly overwhelmed with emotion. Given the prominence of the two attorneys, the high visibility of the case, and the widespread approval both attorneys' arguments elicited, these views of emotion and expressions of emotion are of great interest.

Hennequin's narrative of the case was, in brief, as follows: In 1821, Lieutenant Descoutures met seventeen-year-old Mlle de Favancourt and her mother in one of the fashionable venues of Nancy, where he was stationed. Their mutual attraction met with the mother's approval. She allowed them to meet each other frequently and, when Descoutures was posted to Stenay, she allowed them to exchange letters. (What Hennequin did not say, but everyone knew, was that the exchange of letters between a single young woman and a single young man was either based on an implicit commitment, or else was highly improper.) One letter by Descoutures of this period shows that the lieutenant was engaging in subterfuge to heighten Favancourt's passion for him, according to Hennequin. In this letter, Descoutures claimed that a mysterious young woman had visited him, had charged that Favancourt was no longer interested in him, and had offered him stolen letters as proof; he claimed that he burnt the letters without even looking at them. In another letter from Stenay, he asserted that enemies were stealing his letters to her, so that many did not get through. Attorney Hennequin heaped derision on these colorful claims, lies, he said, designed to heighten Favancourt's anxiety and inflame her fragile imagination.

Later, Descoutures fell ill. Favancourt was desperate and raged against her mother until the latter agreed to accompany her to Stenay. After Descoutures was posted to Metz, they made many visits there, as well; one visit lasted four months. With the mother's consent, the lovers had many hours alone, and during at least one visit Favancourt succumbed to the lieutenant's advances. When Favancourt and her mother returned to Nancy, they found that the father disapproved of the mother's conduct; as word spread of the daughter's visits to Metz, she and her mother were also shunned by respectable society in their home town. Favancourt and her mother fled Nancy, traveling first to Bethune, then to Paris, against the father's wishes. The father cut them off financially, and in Paris mother and daughter experienced real impoverishment. During this time, Lieutenant Descoutures was in Spain, part of the invading French force of 1823; he wrote to Favancourt making exaggerated claims about his bravery under fire; he offered her no financial aid whatever.

Descoutures promised to marry Favancourt, Hennequin said, but kept coming up with excuses for putting it off. An officer had to have permission from the ministry of war to marry at that time, and marriage might negatively affect his advancement. He had a rich uncle (his parents were dead) who, he claimed, opposed a marriage to Favancourt, because he had heard of her lack of virtue. These were flimsy pretexts; that Favancourt accepted them only showed how deeply her passion had deformed her thinking. Compared to the sacrifice she had made for him, Hennequin insisted, Descoutures should have happily set aside career and fortune in order to render her honorable.

By 1825, Favancourt and her mother were back in Nancy; but her father's health was deteriorating. Weakened by the terrible suffering his daughter's conduct had caused him, he died soon after their return. Her mother, also weighed down by suffering over her daughter's compromised position, died a few months afterward. Back in Paris, Favancourt languished with her passion for Descoutures – who came occasionally to see her from his garrison, but who still would not marry her. Gradually, weakened by longing and disappointment, she lost her mind between December 1825 and February 1826. Increasingly frequent episodes of dementia led her relatives to intervene; she was ruled incompetent by a justice of the peace in mid-February 1826, and committed to the hospital at Charenton, where she died three weeks later. But on 26 January 1826, before the family could intervene, Descoutures had convinced Favancourt to write a will naming him sole heir. Descoutures's business agent had provided the model will; Descoutures himself had spelled out his name in pencil for her to copy. He had prevented her from seeing a notary when she asked for one. With the will in his hands, he had abandoned her as her insanity worsened. Thus, Hennequin concluded, the cynical Descoutures's seduction of Favancourt had brought three members of the family to

their graves, and now he hoped to harvest the fruits of his depreda-
tions. The relatives of Favancourt did not care about the money,
Hennequin insisted, they wished only to prevent this criminal from
enjoying his booty, and to restore the good name of their niece and
cousin by showing that she was a victim of a calculated plan of seduction and entrapment.

Mauguin disputed many facts in this narrative. First of all, Descoutures was from the beginning as passionately attracted to Favancourt
as she was to him. Favancourt's mother, in a surviving letter, identified
the mysterious woman who visited Descoutures at Stenay as probably
the chambermaid of a relative she hated (one of the very parties in the
case), who wished to damage her daughter's prospects. Favancourt,
her mother, and her father had all hated the relatives who now were
attempting to break the will; numerous statements in letters submitted
in evidence proved it. This was one reason Favancourt had written a
will, to prevent the relatives from inheriting. In Metz, it is true, both
Favancourt and Descoutures yielded to their weakness for each other.
But Descoutures fully intended to marry her. Without fortune, dependent on his pitiful lieutenant's salary, he felt he had to wait for his
inflexible uncle to die. Doubtless this was wrong, but it was a mistake,
not a crime. In Spain, his bravery had been genuine, as a letter from
his commanding officer attested. On his return, he was hoping to
receive a medal of honor for his battlefield exploits, and thus had to
remain in the army, and single, a while longer. Then, Favancourt's
father died of gout (blessing his daughter to the end); her mother of
smallpox. And Favancourt herself became ill with a lung disease that
eventually altered her sanity. During this time, Descoutures, stationed
in the north of France, begged for frequent leaves to rush to Paris for
brief visits with his stricken fiancée. He saw to her every need through
his business agent. He was not even in Paris when she signed the will;
a letter she wrote on the same day showed her to be completely lucid
at that time. Descoutures was guilty of mistakes but not of deceit or
entrapment. Favancourt had a great passion for him, but such a passion
does not render one incapable of signing a contract, or a will.

At the conclusion of his initial statement, Mauguin read a dramatic
letter from his client. In it, Descoutures offered to turn the money over
to his opponents, provided only that (1) they admit that he was the
legitimate heir and that they had defamed the memory of their relative, Anna de Favancourt; and (2) they allow him sufficient funds to
bury Favancourt as she had requested in a letter, as well as to carry out

certain other "secret" wishes she had expressed. This unprecedented offer caused a furor.

Hennequin, the following week, referred to it as the now "famous" offer which, "in a brief moment of surprise and illusion, had been viewed as a noble gesture of disinterest and generosity." It was nothing of the sort; only further evidence of Descoutures's cleverness at making offers he had no intention of fulfilling. No honorable French family, Hennequin protested, would admit to calumny when it was untrue. Descoutures knew this, and knew his offer would be refused; it was merely a maneuver aimed at deceiving the public, cooked up with the help of a talented attorney.

Although extremes of emotion are frequently expressed or claimed in this case, the differences between the emotional common sense assumed by both sides and the assumptions of eighteenth-century sentimentalism described in the last chapter are stark. It is particularly revealing to contrast the emotional ideology that Maza has discerned in famous court cases of the 1770s and 1780s with the Restoration ideology implicit in the Lallemand et al. v. Descoutures case. The eighteenth-century sentimentalist ideology, as applied to civil litigation, could be summarized in six interlinked propositions: (1) The nation, or public opinion, is a higher tribunal that stands above and beyond the existing royal courts. (2) Publication of trial briefs allows barristers to appeal directly to this higher tribunal, despite the secrecy of judicial proceedings (Maza 1993:115–121). (3) Sincere confession of one's feelings and actions is proof of one's innocence and one's virtue; lying about feelings is very difficult, and the guilty, as a result, never speak openly of their sentiments (Maza 1993:274). (4) Honor, with its concern for appearances and preference for secrecy, favors injustice, inequality, aristocratic privilege, and despotism (Maza 1993:118). (5) Society ought to be bound together in the same way as a family (or lovers), by ties of benevolent, sincere, generous affection (Maza 1997). (6) So bound together, society (in the form of the nation, of public opinion) deploys these same feelings to evaluate cases, acting as the ultimate court of appeal (Maza 1993:161; 1997).

Against these six propositions, both attorneys in this case would have opposed something like the following contradictory assumptions:

1 and **2.** Not the public, but judges only are competent to rule, because they are lifted above human passions. Mauguin, for example, apologized for discussing passions in such detail in their presence: "Excuse me for speaking to you this way, you, who must be strangers to human passion; yet you must judge their effects, necessarily, you must understand them." Later, in his final rebuttal, Mauguin insisted that all women favored Descoutures in the dispute, because they feared losing the power to pass on property to the ones they loved. But, in the midst of this implicit appeal to public opinion, he stopped suddenly: "But I see that I am arguing as if . . . before a court of love. Because I am in the presence of judges, let me return to my role of legal counsel." Women's feelings are not serious; to discuss them is almost a literary pursuit, an allegorical one, as before a "court of love." Only from male judges, lifted above feeling, can understanding, and therefore justice, flow. Hennequin, likewise, referred to the influence of public opinion on the case as troubling; his opponents, he insisted, were trying to fool the public; but the judges would be able to see through their stratagems.

3. Both Mauguin and Hennequin agreed that expressions of sentiment can be easily feigned and can easily fool people, especially impressionable young women, and that emotions are no guide to reality. The stronger they are, the more deluded one becomes. Each attorney targeted the emotional intensity of his opponent's performance for attack. Hennequin, in his first rebuttal, deplored that Mauguin had managed "by one of those inexplicable creations of the art of oratory" to present Descoutures as passionately in love. Mauguin came right back in his rebuttal: "My adversary, exhausting all the resources of the art of oratory, may have overwhelmed your consciences for a moment, moving you with alarming images." Both attorneys condemned "seduction" and the sorrows which it brought in its train, Hennequin more forcefully, because he charged Descoutures with a deliberate plan to "excite Anna's imagination, in order to acquire absolute empire over her."[2] Mauguin argued that the seduction was mutual, although this did not make it benign; far from it. His client, "infected by one of those passions which have their moments of intoxication, but which bring so many tears," was little better off than Anna de Favancourt.[3] The distance traveled from the precepts of sentimentalism could not have been further; in the sentimentalist idiom, a stronger feeling was a truer feeling, and the passionate love that bound a man and a woman, in or out of wedlock, was

---

[2] "exalter l'imagination d'Anna pour prendre sur elle un empire absolu."
[3] "atteint d'une de ces passions qui ont leur moment d'ivresse, mais qui font verser tant de larmes."

the highest form of human relationship. Thanks to the Christian tradition and the modern novel, Staël rhapsodized as late as 1800, men and women had learned to have new feelings about each other, and family life had thus received "the imprint of that divine alliance of love and friendship, of estime and attraction, of merited confidence and involuntary seduction" (Staël 1800:180).[4] By 1827, however, the word *seduction* had lost again any positive connotation that it might have briefly carried.

4. Protecting the honor of individuals and of families is the highest good, Mauguin and Hennequin agreed. Both insisted repeatedly that their clients had no other motive. The king's attorney Bernard, in his opinion, attacked both parties on the grounds that their true motives were monetary. Both sides insisted forcefully that keeping up appearances, or repairing appearances as soon as possible, was the best way of reacting to any breach of honor. Hennequin condemned Descoutures's refusal to marry Favancourt after their liaison became public knowledge, because only marriage could repair her reputation. Mauguin countered by citing, with triumph, a recent ruling of a Rouen court, that it was better not to scrutinize a man's seamy private life after his death (and thereby scandalize public opinion), even if a few relatives lost their share of his fortune as a result. "The noise and the scandal" read the Rouen ruling, "will be much more damaging to society than the loss, for a few collateral heirs, of a fortune, which the testator may have disposed of in an abusive or injudicious way." This was a very far distance indeed from the views of late eighteenth-century sentimentalist attorneys such as Pierre Firmin Delacroix who, in a frequently cited battle cry of 1775, asserted: "Are you seeking, in a nation where honor means everything, and virtue is counted for nothing, to put a break on iniquity? Threaten to unveil it, to expose it to daylight in all its ugliness" (quoted in Maza 1993:118, Maza's translation).

5. Both attorneys agreed that society was bound together, not by sentiment, but by contracts, and that contracts could only be properly concluded if the parties were possessed of reason, not driven by a strong emotion. "Society could not exist without contracts," Hennequin noted, and contracts had to be the expression of a free will. But a last will and testament was a special kind of act, almost

---

[4] "l'empreinte de cette divine alliance de l'amour et de l'amitié, de l'estime et de l'attrait, de la confiance méritée et de séduction involontaire."

like a law, and, even more than with a contract, "one must have the full exercise of one's moral faculties to make such an act." The added freedom to dispose of one's property at death granted by Revolutionary legislators, Hennequin mused, may have reflected a long-standing national esteem for liberty. "But what does the liberty of a people have in common with the independence of passions?" His opponent, he charged, in defending the validity of Favancourt's will, was attempting to make an "impossible alliance" between public liberties and seduction. Mauguin countered that everyone is affected by passions.

Where would we be, if we adopted a system of incapacity founded on the passions! I don't deny the blindness they can cause. Avarice, for example, does not recoil from any act, however vile [here, Mauguin might have looked pointedly at the plaintiffs]; but must we therefore drag before the courts the wills of all the dead?

Here, again, a sharp contrast with the late eighteenth century, when, according to Maza, "Writers ranging from luminaries to obscure scribblers obsessively promoted ideals of deep social unity. Under the rubric of what they called *les moeurs*, they proposed a system of social morality that negated class difference and sought to bring the French together in a moral community called *patrie*, which was itself a sentimental family writ large" (Maza 1997:225).

6. With passions so strong and reason so fragile, both attorneys agreed, the court must substitute its own reasoning powers for those of the public and, if necessary, even for those of private individuals. "It is for you, judges," Hennequin insisted, "to revise this will, as Anna would have if, more enlightened, she could have seen clearly whom she was benefiting." Mauguin begged the judges' indulgence for his client's weaknesses. "Grand passions, if sometimes they blind us, they also, sometimes, lift us up." He cited Orestes, Sappho, and Tasso as examples, to repeated "bravos" from the audience. But Mauguin's client did not turn to the public for understanding; he turned to the judges. "Your honors, it is you he implores; he was weak, but not guilty; if he has need of your indulgence, he has a right to your justice." Not a public possessed of strong feelings, but only a panel of judges lifted above the passions of daily life, both attorneys agreed, was competent to excuse, to rectify, to chastise. The king's attorney, Bernard, agreed; he and the judges would bring "the simple and severe language of reason and of the law" to bear on the case.

In its final judgment, the court castigated the "odious means Descoutures employed to seduce Anna de Favancourt" but concluded that her passion "even though pushed to the highest degree of exaltation"[5] did not incapacitate her. Hence the inheritance went to Descoutures. The judges accepted the terms in which the attorneys had cast the case, siding, reluctantly, as had Bernard, with Descoutures.

The Restoration was a conservative regime; ambitious lawyers were not likely to pursue lines of argument inimical to its political doctrines. But Restoration courts were sufficiently free to serve as arenas of genuine political debate over issues of press censorship, religious practice, and public morality. Hennequin and Mauguin both served as deputies in the Parliament; the former was a political moderate, but Mauguin was a member of the Carbonari conspiracy in the early 1820s; he served as a member of the provisional government during the Revolution of 1830, and remained an associate of the republican general Lamarque until his death in 1832 (Cormenin 1842:419–432; Caron 1991:259, 307).

Mauguin's task in the Descoutures case was the defense of sentiment. It is easy to imagine how George Sand might have spoken in favor of Favancourt's devotion, denouncing the false sense of honor that justified Descoutures's uncle in refusing to permit the marriage, and Descoutures's in hesitating to resign his commission. But there is no indication that Mauguin even harbored mental reservations along these lines. Instead, both Mauguin and Hennequin operated entirely within the new liberal worldview. Like Cousin and Maine de Biran, both saw the individual as weak, prone to irrational illusions and emotions. Mauguin began his first statement of the case with this warning: "In tossing us onto the earth, the supreme being gave us neither strength nor wisdom whole and entire; he created us weak, and submitted us to all the consequences of our weakness."[6] Like Romantic theorist Charles Nodier or poet Victor Hugo, Mauguin insisted on the sublime and uplifting character of true passion. Mauguin invites us to forgive, not condone, Descoutures by recognizing ourselves in his understandable lapse. "Who among us is without passion?" he

---

[5] "même poussée au dernier degré d'exaltation."

[6] "En nous jetant sur la terre, la suprême puissance ne nous a donné ni la force ni la sagesse en partage; elle nous a créés faibles, et nous a soumis à toutes les conséquences de notre faiblesse."

demands to know. "Those strong passions, imperious, as irresistible as fate, which make us cry in the theater over the suffering of *Phèdre* or *Zaïre*, soften our hearts when encountered in the world; we deplore their effects on others, as an evil that could have befallen ourselves."[7] Grand emotions, Mauguin insists, are never contemptible; a great love inspires only "compassion." He comes very close to saying that the strength of love might excuse, or lift the burden of shame from, actions it commands, but prudently avoids going this far. Other Romantics would struggle with this idea, some embraced it. But no Romantic asserted that sentiment was the foundation of social bonds, the sure guide to right knowledge and virtuous action, partner to reason and source of legitimacy for government and law. Inescapable like a disease, grand like a storm, and like a storm sometimes destructive, emotion was natural, but dangerous. Transgression in the name of emotion was often considered justifiable, but seldom without fateful consequences.

Furthermore, Mauguin pointed out that the tenor of our private affections ought not to invalidate signatures on legal documents. Here he was on firm grounds. If one could not dispose of one's wealth according to one's desires, the pursuit of wealth itself would be meaningless. Hennequin's argument for dementia, while drawing support from the new pessimism about human nature, ran afoul of Mauguin's repeated reminders that we are all weak.

Mauguin's strongest evidence that Favancourt was sane when she signed her will came from the letter she wrote to Descoutures that same day, quoted at the beginning of the chapter. Ironically, this text is itself suffused with sentimentalist overtones. Hennequin claimed these expressions of love were too extreme, proof of Favancourt's unbalanced mental condition. He focused on another letter, written a few days later, in which Favancourt told Descoutures how she wanted to be buried:

May the earth of your country, oh my Frédéric, not reject the poor orphan after her death, who died for having loved. I would so love to have seen those places where you spent your childhood! Because my eyes will not have seen them, at least let my ashes mix with the dirt you walk on! . . . If

---

[7] "Ces passions fortes, impérieuses, irrésistibles comme la destinée, qui nous font pleurer au théâtre sur la douleur de *Phèdre* et de *Zaïre*, nous attendrissent aussi dans le monde; nous les déplorons chez les autres, comme un malheur qui aurait pu arriver jusqu'à nous."

you knew how much I love you! I die a thousand times at the thought I must leave you. Oh, come if you can, calm my despair![8]

In this morbid desire for self-immolation, Hennequin intoned, lay proof of Favancourt's derangement. This was tantamount to claiming that sentimentalism itself, of the kind championed by Roland, Staël, Bernardin de Saint-Pierre, and others, was a form of insanity.

As noted in Chapter 5, Daumas's (1996) study of love letters through the end of the eighteenth century reveals an ideal of love that has a stable core of features: (1) the loved one is placed above the self; (2) fidelity; (3) equality between the partners; (4) reciprocity of giving and receiving; and (5) exclusivity. What changed, in Daumas's view, is the relation between this ideal and surrounding cultural values. By the eighteenth century, love is reconceived, not as a deviant and dangerous passion, but as a natural sentiment that fashions its own morality. Women no longer overcome an inherent weakness to achieve love, but instead display their true nature by loving. Love is no longer seen as dangerous to marriage, instead it is the proper foundation of marriage. The affectionate marriage was one of those newfound emotional refuges of the eighteenth century (where before marriage had been conceived as a family alliance, and partners as bound by contractual obligation and honor).

Favancourt's letters conform perfectly to Daumas's description of the eighteenth-century sentimentalist configuration. Her point of reference is not God, but nature. In the coming spring, she laments, leaves will return, but she will no longer be able to walk with her loved one. Implicitly, her love is a natural thing of beauty, like a leaf. Her love is more important than life; it is what attaches her to life. Propriety and honor have little importance in comparison. She would rather die unhappy than cause the slightest chagrin to her lover. She calls him her "friend"; she calls herself his "sister" and his "wife." The assertion of a fundamental similarity among all such roles was central to sentimentalism (Daumas 1996:178–186; Maza 1997:225). She foresees marriage as the natural outcome of her love, an outcome which death will deprive her of.

---

[8] "[Q]ue la terre de ton pays, ô mon Frédéric, ne repousse pas après sa mort la pauvre orpheline, qui meurt pour avoir aimé. J'aurais tant aimé à voir ces lieux où tu as passé ton enfance! Puisque mes yeux ne les auront pas vus, qu'au moins mes cendres se mêlent à la terre que tu fouleras! . . . Si tu savait combien je t'aime! Je meurs mille fois de la pensée que je vais te quitter. O viens, si tu le peux, calmer mon désespoir!"

Mauguin, and the court, implicitly recognized that Favancourt's letters expressed a coherent and well-known conception of love. About the letters of 26 and 31 January (both quoted above), Mauguin waxed ecstatic: "What truth! what profundity of feeling! And in the second one, do you not remark that delicacy that only women feel. She fears her Frédéric's pain, she consoles him." The judges agreed that "it is apparent . . . from the letters written by Anna de Favancourt, at the same time [as the will], that she was in full possession of all her intellectual faculties."

Only three of Descoutures's letters to Favancourt were quoted in court. Mauguin charged that members of Favancourt's family had destroyed all the rest because they could have been used to demonstrate the sincerity of Descoutures's attachment. Of the three, only one can be properly said to be a love letter; it was written during the Spanish campaign. In it, Descoutures tells Favancourt, "In battle, when a clutch of the enemy pressed upon me too closely, I pronounced your name, Anna, and at once I emerged victorious." This brief fragment, all that remains, suggests that Descoutures may have matched Favancourt in the unlimited rank accorded to love. In his letter to Mauguin, offering to give up the inheritance, Descoutures referred to his love for Favancourt only in passing, on two occasions: "As for Mlle Anna, whose name I cannot write without pain . . ." and "Now I am accused of having begged for the inheritance of her whose days I would gladly repurchase at the cost of my own." This reserve stands in sharp contrast to the voluble emotional claims typical of male litigants in the late eighteenth-century cases studied by Maza.

The evidence of this case thus suggests that sentimentalism, although its doctrines had been discredited and were no longer admissible as public justifications for action or norms of judgment, lived on as a private code of behavior, available to shape affective ties within the family, between lovers. It could still provide a guide to the creation of emotional refuge, but only in the private sphere. This was a limited, somewhat tamed sentimentalism, devoid of its politically charged appeals to public opinion and of the related claim that sentiment was the foundation of civil society and legitimacy. Descoutures made only muted references to feelings in a public letter, but, disciplined as they were, they suggested powerful undercurrents. At the same time, its continuing availability tempered efforts to revive pre-eighteenth-century notions of the self – the whole vocabulary of faculties, the glorification of reason. Behind Mauguin's highly circumspect admiration for the "strong passions" that inspire only compassion in observers lay a past whose erasure could never be fully accomplished.

It remains to be seen whether other cases in the sample confirm, alter, or enrich this preliminary picture.

2. Baron D*** v. Mme H***, veuve, 1827

The *Gazette* devoted five articles in June and July 1827 to the case of a certain Baron D*** who, alleging that the widow H*** was his wife, was asking the court to order her to return to the conjugal domicile. (The *Gazette* often masked the names of private persons in marital or family disputes.) The Civil Code empowered the husband to require the wife to live in his home; Baron D*** wished only to exercise this right. Mme H*** alleged in response that the marriage celebrated between the two in Scotland in 1821 was not valid under French law and that therefore they were not married. This was a family case and one apparently involving some strong feeling, to judge by certain statements of the attorneys, but also a case that turned purely on a single technical issue, whether the specific Scottish marriage ceremony was valid under French law. The attorneys disputed whether the ceremony was valid in Scotland and whether the French code required only that a marriage be valid in the place in which it was celebrated. These issues involved interpretation of Scottish law and of the wording of certain articles in the French Civil Code. The range of emotions expressed or alluded to was, therefore, extremely limited.

Hennequin, arguing for Mme H***, claimed that she had resisted Baron D***'s initial proposal of marriage. She feared the legal consequence of a marriage, because it would have entailed the loss of control over her son's fortune, which was considerable. But Baron D*** convinced her that a marriage celebrated in Scotland would allow her to retain her control. He deceived her, Hennequin maintained, knowing that such control would be retained only if the marriage were invalid in France. After the ceremony they returned to France and lived together there for five years. But, beginning in 1824, Mme H*** began to "conceive fears as to the sincerity of his [Baron D***'s] marriage" in view of his dissipated lifestyle, which was beginning to threaten her son's fortune. She went to Scotland to investigate and returned convinced that their marriage was not valid. In the course of 1826, therefore, Mme H*** moved out of the baron's home and broke off relations with him.

Crousse, arguing for the baron, noted that his own resources provided an annual income of forty thousand francs. The baron "had always had the delicacy to allow her to handle all" her son's money. Crousse was astonished that Mme H*** could have forgotten the import of the ceremony, performed in her presence and with her full consent, or the years of cohabitation. "As a mother, ought she not give her son an example of complete virtue? What imbalance has carried her away [*quelle vertige l'égare*] to inspire such conduct!" As for the baron's alleged dissipation, Crousse challenged his opponents to cite a single documented fact. Baron D*** "only wants one thing, that his wife come back and live with him."

Both attorneys thus constructed contradictory narratives that put their clients in the best light, depicting each as motivated only by socially approved feelings, and challenged the sincerity and virtue of the opposing party. Both attorneys came to moments of high outrage in their expositions. Hennequin denounced with rich irony the Scottish officer who had performed the marriage, "this Robert Elio, high priest of matrimonial happiness" whose ceremonies had been contested before in English courts. Crousse deplored that a woman should seem to want to "claim for herself the title of concubine" and to have "lost the memory and the sentiment of all her duties." But, in marked contrast to the Lallemand et al. v. Descoutures case, neither attorney pursued these interpretations of feeling and motivation very far, knowing that the case would turn on the question whether the Scottish ceremony fit the definition of a valid marriage provided by the Civil Code. The court, in ruling that the marriage was not valid, said nothing of the parties' feelings or intentions, simply noting that, given the size of the son's fortune, the protection of the minor's interests made the legal requirement of prior publication in France all the more imperative.

This example suggests that the dividing line between the simplified realm of public reason and the realm of private sentiment had to be drawn within the family, in order to constitute the family. The validity of this marriage did not depend upon the intentions or emotions of the persons who celebrated it, but only on whether the ceremony's form satisfied behaviorally defined rules. These rules included a statement of intent, a vow, but did not require that the statement be sincere. They required publication as a means of testing this sincerity, since publication allowed those who knew of an impediment to step forward. But, if publication were carried out, then, sincere or not, the vow was still valid. Unlike the knotty issue of Mlle de Favancourt's mental competence, the second thoughts or mental reservations of Baron D*** and Mme H*** did not require special investigation by the courts. The laws of marriage and contract were designed to relieve the courts of such onerous investigations as far as possible. Marriage was a relationship which ought to be founded on private intent (and therefore on feelings). But it was also a contract that conveyed property and endowed husbands with authority; law had to define it in such a way that private intent and feelings became irrelevant.

This kind of artificial dividing line between behavior and feeling was, like the concept of self used in the Lallemand et al. v. Descoutures case, an age-old tool, as old as the idea of the signature as a binding sign of intent (see, on medieval evolution of the signature, Fraenkel 1992). It differed strikingly from judicial presumptions employed during the Terror, however; in that period, sincerity was deemed a requirement of all patriots and a panel of Revolutionary judges was presumed capable of distinguishing sincerity from aristocratic hypocrisy in relatively short order (Higonnet 1998:79). Under the Terror, as noted in Chapter 5, even actors were regarded as intending what they said on stage (Johnson 1995:121). (If they said what they did not intend, that was just as bad as intending something unpatriotic.) Saint-Just had suggested that men who had no friends ought to be tried as traitors (Vincent-Buffault 1995:110–111). The formal separation of public and private allowed the private sphere to be variable, even deviant, up to a point.

But this separation did not prevent the attorneys in this case from applying sentimentalist norms to private feeling. Crousse could not admit that his client had married out of a desire to gain access to wealth, and insisted, in good Rousseauvian fashion, that a mother ought to be a model of virtue for her son. Hennequin showed great solicitude for his client's feminine sensitivity, which Baron D*** had cynically exploited. She was right to be afraid, but easily fooled by "this shadow of a marriage which might indeed calm the anxieties [*inquiétudes*] of a woman, but offered no solidity, no legal engagement." As in the Descoutures v. Lallemand et al. case, sentimentalism, pushed out of the public realm, no longer allowed to influence law or contract, seems to have continued to set standards for private, weak feminine emotion.

3. La Caisse hypothécaire v. le duc de Raguse, 1828–1829

The attorneys in the Caisse hypothécaire's suit against the duc de Raguse for breach of contract, when it came to trial in December 1828, unleashed a storm of emotionally charged mutual recriminations. Even though the question was a technical one, the contract involved was faulty and ambiguous; each attorney strove to denigrate the motives and feelings of the opposing party, in order to undermine that party's credibility. The duc de Raguse was a friend of the king's and enjoyed his protection; he was Marshall of France, member of the Conseil de guerre, commander of the Paris garrison. (In July 1830 he would be charged with the defense of Paris against the insurrectionaries.) Early in the 1820s he launched an ambitious industrial enterprise on his family estate. But by the mid-1820s the operation was in difficulty, and the economic slump of 1826–1828 finished it off, forcing the duc to cease payments on his debts in January 1827.

The Caisse hypothécaire, a mortgage investment bank, was one of his major creditors. Beginning in October 1824, the Caisse had allocated a credit of 3.7 million francs to the duc, to be paid in five installments spread out over the period 1824 to 1834; most of the money was to become available at once. The duc was to pay the loan back in twenty yearly installments of 333,000 francs, beginning at once. The effective interest rate is difficult to calculate, because we are not told the precise schedule by which the Caisse was to make the loan money available; but the rate was certainly over 7 percent, at a time when 3 to 5 percent was the normal rate paid on government bonds. Of the loan amount, 2.8 million was secured by liens on the duc's property; an additional 900,000 was allocated to the duc on condition that he use 500,000 of this amount to purchase five hundred shares of stock in the Caisse hypothécaire; the Caisse would retain these five hundred shares as security for the initial payments due from the duc. Once the duc had paid off the additional 900,000, so that his debt was reduced to an amount secured by liens only, he was to gain full control of the five hundred shares he had purchased.

But by November 1824, within two months of the conclusion of the agreement, the duc was requesting an alteration. He wished to be granted control of the five hundred shares immediately, and in return he offered to cede to the Caisse the proceeds of a number of sources of revenue: (1) a 50,000-franc-per-year rent in the form of Austrian government bonds; (2) a Legion of Honor pension of 10,000 francs per year; (3) a sum of 30,000 francs per year paid him by the city of Paris, in his capacity as Governor of the First Military Division. These sums, totaling 90,000 francs per year, were signed over to the Caisse. However, technically, the pension and the city of Paris payment could not be the subject of liens, ceded to third parties, or garnered; therefore the Caisse required the duc to promise, in writing, "on his honor," that he would continue to turn over these sums as long as they were due.

After the duc ceased payments in January 1827, he began signing over the very same sources of income listed above (as well as others) to unsecured creditors, in return for their agreement not to pursue him for payment in the courts. By December 1828, the Caisse hypothécaire and the duc de Raguse had already done battle in court over the question of how the duc's estates should be parceled out for sale, to satisfy the Caisse's liens. In the litigation examined here, the question was whether the duc had broken his agreement of November 1824 to cede to the Caisse, from the three sources mentioned above, the 90,000 francs per year. The Caisse maintained that he had. The duc's attorney, however, noted that, at the time the duc ceased payments, he had only received 2.9 million francs of the total promised him by the Caisse. Therefore, under the original contract, the duc immediately gained control of the five hundred shares and was no longer bound to make payments set up to substitute for control of these shares. His salary, pension, and rent reverted to him, and his use of them to cover unsecured debts only demonstrated his solicitude for creditors who stood to lose if he were forced into bankruptcy court. The court, in the end, sided with the duc, and ruled the Caisse's claims to be without merit.

The attorneys were ruthless. The Caisse's counsel, Crousse, drew a picture of a faithless, fickle aristocrat, who traded on his social prominence to wring sums out of the Caisse he had no intention of repaying. Repeatedly, Crousse said, the duc had come back to the Caisse asking additional credits. Each time, he assured the Caisse's officers of his personal gratitude. Crousse cited several letters of the duc, thanking the Caisse for "yet another favor," "a favor I will never forget." Crousse read out the duc's promise "on his honor" to continue the 90,000-franc payments in the absence of liens. Crousse said he was "astonished, in the presence of an engagement contracted *under the bond of honor*, that a marshall of France would dare to oppose" (emphasis in original) the Caisse's rights.

Parquin, the duc's attorney, fired back with equally heavy artillery. The Caisse was nothing but a bunch of "usurers" who had "plotted a most revolting speculation."

Not content to make secured loans at a rate never below 8 and sometimes higher than 16 percent per year, they wanted to acquire for themselves at a depressed price the properties of their client. This client has managed to frustrate their plans. The efforts they made before the courts to overcome his resistance have not borne fruit. A frightful resentment has since descended on their souls; they promised a trial of hatred and of anger, and they have kept their word. [*Un affreux ressentiment est alors descendu dans leurs âmes; ils ont promis un procès de haine et de colère; ils ont tenu parole.*]

Knowing their client to be a prominent military official, Parquin charged, the Caisse inferred that honor must be especially dear to him. The Caisse reasoned, according to Parquin, as follows: "Well then! Let's accuse him before the courts, before all France, of being a debtor of bad faith, of violating engagements contracted under the seal of honor, of breaking solemn promises; and, as we do, let's lie with rare effrontery; let's deform the facts, and present them in the most perfidious colors." Here, as in the other cases we have looked at, there are some quite traditional elements. Honor, good faith, generosity, gratitude are contrasted, by one litigant, with disregard for promises, poor management of resources, and exploitation of social inferiors; and, by the other, with grasping, profit-hungry deceitfulness and resentment. Parquin's counterattack, that the Caisse officers were vile usurers, drew on a theme that went back to the Middle Ages.

However, in Crousse's pleading, sentimentalist elements may be easily detected, even if they are somewhat muted. With his implicit attack on aristocratic mismanagement, Crousse was sounding a theme dear to sentimentalist lawyers of the late eighteenth century. As the attorneys studied by Maza had frequently done, although less explicitly than they, he made insinuations that Raguse was using his connections with the king to cheat his creditors with impunity. But the presiding judge ordered both attorneys to cease mentioning the "august person."

Crousse defended the Caisse against the charge of usury by pointing out that its methods of operation had been approved by the government, that its shareholders included peers of the realm, even judges, of unimpeachable character. The duc de Raguse himself had attended stockholder meetings and verified accounts after he had become an owner of five hundred shares. The duc had even intervened with the prime minister, Villèle, to help get the Caisse's stock listed on the Paris Bourse. Obviously, Crousse concluded, the duc "did not believe that he was dishonored to be associated with [the Caisse's] stockholders."

Against this background, the tone of the duc's letters to these officers, quoted repeatedly by Crousse, took on additional meaning. In a letter of 19 September 1825, during the initial negotiations with the Caisse, the duc had praised them warmly: "*The loyal and kind manner* in which you have behaved in all the relations we have had together, permit me to hope that, understanding my situation, you will be so good as to greet with favor the request I now send you" (emphasis added).[9] When he wrote in November of that year, requesting control of the five hundred shares, he was equally effusive in his protestations of appreciation: "It will be a great pleasure for me, who have already had occasion to put to the test the helpfulness of all [the board of directors'] members toward me, to have yet another reason to express my gratitude, for a favor that is rescuing me from the necessity of a very disadvantageous and, in effect, ruinous operation."[10] The duc de Raguse understood that the Caisse had to make a profit, and to operate according to prudent rules, but called on its officers' kindness to find a way. "I hope that you will find some means of reconciling my desires with the Caisse's interests," he urged with confidence.

The duc addressed equals; his manner was devoid of the condescension of an Old Regime aristocrat, and his words promised undying gratitude for their loyalty, their understanding, their concern. From these words, and from Crousse's approval of them, there emerges an image of an implicit normative substructure of feelings undergirding commerce. However impersonal and rigorous in principle, business transactions involved, and became, personal emotional connections (see, on this, Hirsch 1991). These normative emotions were not without a certain sentimentalist imprint; they included generosity, benevolence, gratitude, kindness, loyalty. These emotional norms could go unmen-

---

[9] "La manière obligeante et loyale avec laquelle vous vous êtes conduits dans toutes les relations que nous avons eues ensemble, me fait espérer, qu'entrant dans ma situation, vous serez assez bons pour accueillir favorablement la demande que je vous adresse."

[10] "Il me serait bien agréable, à moi qui ai déjà fait l'épreuve de l'obligeance de tous [les] membres [du conseil d'administration] à mon égard, d'avoir à leur exprimer ma reconnaissance pour un nouveau service qui me délivrera de la nécessité de faire une opération extrêmement onéreuse, et pour ainsi dire ruineuse."

tioned, or be mentioned only in passing, when contracts were carried out as planned and business was good. But when difficulties arose and blame had to be assigned, it became necessary, as in this case, to discuss these norms openly.

Crousse's muted evocation of sentimentalist norms recalls Cousin's treatment of the proper role of moral sentiments. In the realm of business, men are driven by the rational pursuit of profit, but their calculations must be enveloped in, or echoed by, moral sentiments appropriate to relations among equal citizens.

4. *Mlle Mars v. Mlle Thélusson, MM Trobriant, Constantin, and Forster-Grant, 1827*

A final case from the *Gazette* to be considered in detail is a commercial dispute that involved only passing reference to feelings. The issue in the case was the precise nature of the obligations that tied together the members of a partnership (a "société"). The issue was both technical and obscure. Doubtless the *Gazette* would not have reported on this case at all if the plaintiff, Mlle Mars, had not been a famous actress, reigning queen of the Paris stage for over twenty years.

In April 1824 Mlle Mars sold a building located on the rue Saint Lazare to a partnership organized by a friend named Constantin. She had paid 300,000 francs for the building, and sold it for 550,000 francs, a substantial profit; she received 200,000 francs in cash when the deal was concluded, of which she paid 66,000 to Constantin as a commission for arranging the deal. (However, the Constantin commission took the form of a loan until the balance of the purchase price had been paid.) All of the down payment was put up by Mlle Thélusson, who, we are told, had just turned twenty-one and just gained control of her fortune. None of the subsequent payments due from the partnership were ever paid. Apparently, they had planned to buy a neighboring building and to create a "passage," that is, an indoor walkway lined with shops to be rented out. Several such passages had met with commercial success in the early 1820s. However, the partnership was unable to acquire the second property and thus unable to begin the construction work. When cash became due from the other partners to pay their part in the purchase price, they failed to provide it. Complicating matters was the fact that Mlle Mars herself purchased from M Trobriant his one-thirteenth interest in the building. She had originally loaned him the money to join the partnership, but he had been unable to meet his scheduled payments to her. After numerous promises to pay from the partners, all broken, Mlle Mars had proceeded to attempt a legal seizure and sale of the property.

In court, dispute centered on the question whether her purchase of Trobriant's portion of the property made Mlle Mars a partner, and also whether, as a partner, she was required to collect debts it owed her only through dissolution of the partnership. Several attorneys for members of the partnership complained that a legal seizure and forced sale would reduce the proceeds considerably, and that a mutual agreement for a private sale would satisfy Mlle Mars while protecting the partners. But Mars's attorney responded that she was not interested in pursuing out-of-court arrangements with them any longer. The court ruled that she was not a partner, and also ruled that, even if she were a partner, this did not deprive her of the right, as seller at a time prior to joining the partnership, to pursue the partnership for nonpayment.

The three articles which the *Gazette* devoted to the case in December 1827 contain so few references to emotions, they can easily be listed. There is a reference to Mlle Mars's initial confidence in the members of the partnership, another to her goodness (*bonté*) in bailing out her friend, M Trobriant. There is a reference to the reassurance she ought to feel at the good credit enjoyed by one of the partners and another to the attractiveness of the initial offer. None of the attorneys expressed surprise or outrage, contempt or pity.

Like most actresses, Mars had never married, for the usual reasons: (1) actresses could make substantial incomes from gifts and pensions provided by admirers or lovers; (2) acting was a dishonorable profession, for both women and men, placing them outside the prevailing norms and sanctions that shaped elite behavior, as well as the different ones that governed plebeian conduct; (3) as a single adult woman, Mars enjoyed the same powers to own property and to enter into business transactions and contracts as men. Married, Mlle Mars would have lost even her power to decide which plays she would be in. Stars of the stage such as Mlle Mars generated a great deal of curiosity; they were successful and independent, in a society where most women depended entirely on their husbands for both status and fortune; they displayed their attractions across the public stage, while most women were expected to display them discreetly, and only in private homes. Doubtless such curiosity was considered sufficient by the editors of the *Gazette* to justify coverage of a story that revealed Mlle Mars capable of toughness, as well as of generosity, in her private business dealings.

The very dryness of the case, given what readers already knew of her – her special talent for the lofty tragedies of the seventeenth century, her famous lovers – added a new dimension of understanding. If it were not already clear, readers were reminded that the new laissez-faire marketplace was a ruthless environment, that friendships could be dangerous and costly, and that at least some women could negotiate this environment's impersonal forces with skill.

Preliminary Conclusions

Attorneys' emotives, judging from these four cases, suggest that these professional orators had developed a certain emotional plasticity that was an essential facet of their skill. They displayed mastery, not just of the law, not just of the age-old art of oratory, but also of a certain emotional availability, a capacity we all share, to feel in response to, or in conjunction with, utterances. The limits they placed on their own plasticity were as important to their mastery as was the plasticity itself. They were held, and held themselves – when the issue arose – to be "genuinely" convinced of the positions they defended. (On this point, see the interesting remarks of Cornut-Gentille 1996:144.) However, this presumption had little resemblance to the strict expectations of sincerity applied during the Terror. It was tacitly accepted that attorneys had broader plasticity than the untrained, that their ingenuity consisted of an ability to conciliate social norms and the letter of the law with the desires of their clients, and an ability to demonstrate normative feelings about breaches of written and unwritten codes.

Hennequin, for example, defended wives in four of the marital separation cases sampled in a prior study (Reddy, 1993, 1997b); in each instance he showed himself eloquent in demanding better treatment and greater freedom for women within the institution of marriage. In his defense of Mme H***, one of the four cases discussed here, he insisted that there was no shame for her in discovering that her marriage was invalid and that she had lived with a man for several years without being properly married to him. In another case that turned up in the current sample, however, Hennequin defended a husband against a marital separation suit, even though the husband had repeatedly abandoned his wife and publicly insulted her more than once (Chabannes de la Palisse, 1826). And in the Lallemand et al. v. Descoutures case, he stoutly defended paternal authority, deplored the fragility of female imagination, and denounced the dangerous indulgence of personal preference. That Hennequin and Mauguin were both applauded and praised for their performances in the Descoutures v. Lallemand et al. case, by their colleagues, as well as by the *Gazette*, indicates a broad acceptance of a certain public emotional flexibility. The *Gazette* recalled, with approval, a legend concerning Henri IV (1595–1610), that, after hearing two talented attorneys argue, he had exclaimed, "By God, they are both right!"

Unlike actors or traveling salesmen, however, who were regarded with mistrust in this period, attorneys could not properly allow themselves to represent any position at all.[11] Attorneys were admired for harnessing their emotional plasticity to the convincing architecture of a legal argument. Their plasticity was prestigious, because it was subservient to the adversarial pursuit of truth. The public exercise of this skill was one of the fruits of political liberty and essential to the right conduct of political deliberation. Mauguin, Hennequin, and numerous other prominent attorneys (Berryer, Odilon-Barrot, Chaix d'Est-Ange, to name but a few) became members, and often leaders, of Parliament. Their finely balanced capacity to resonate with the concerns of others and to find emotional coherence in legal and unspoken social norms was fundamental to the political order, and even gave shape and sense to the political upheavals in this period. This capacity consisted of insight into the multiple connections that might link particulars with generalities, into the multiple pathways of activation that might stir their audiences to feel and to think in surprising new ways.

These cases allow a refinement of our conception of the line that was drawn in that period between public and private. Men displayed emotions, weak and strong – joy, sorrow, outrage, pride, gratitude, loyalty, love – constantly in the public sphere of the Restoration and July Monarchy eras. When they did so, it was in the service of a publicly designated, "rational" end: the pursuit of a profession, of prestige, of profit; and, regulated by this pursuit, such emotional expression rose out of, and testified to, a carefully cultivated emotional plasticity. In the realm of the private, men were understood to have many other emotions they would never express, or would express only among select intimates or refer to only in passing (as Descoutures did in his public letter to Mauguin). In the private sphere, men might relax from the emotional effort their flexibility required; their emotional orientations could be both more steady and more capricious than publicly produced

---

[11] On traveling salesmen, see Beecher (1986:93–94); see also two contemporary novels: Balzac, *L'illustre Gaudissart* (1831), Louis Reybaud, *Le dernier des commis voyageurs* (1845). On actors and actresses, see Brownstein (1993).

emotions. More steady, because they did not have to change with the shift from one client to the next or one employer or superior to the next. More capricious, because they could change according to internally generated goals and activations. Hence the private realm was one of less rationality; women were judged to lack the capacity for public flexibility that men cultivated, that is, to lack rationality, and thus to be both more capricious and more genuine. The private realm was their proper sphere of activity. This was why it could serve as a refuge for sentimentalist practices.

These norms were both widely accepted and widely recognized to be only approximate. Many writers insisted, either humorously or in earnest, that private feelings were often as "false" and as mercenary as those displayed in public and commercial venues. (See the popular writings on male-female relations by the humorist J. P. Cuisin, or Balzac's wry *Physiologie du mariage* [1828].) But such observations were seldom presented as grounds for a reformulation of the prevailing common sense. Instead, they were presented under the umbrella of the fashionable new, scientific pessimism about human nature. Hence the popularity of references to the naturalist Buffon in social satire (e.g., Roqueplan 1853), and of descriptions of social types as if they were distinct species or had special "physiologies."

Thus Hennequin's charge that Descoutures had brought mercenary motives into his displays of love toward Favancourt suggested he was no better than a traveling salesman, worse because he deployed in the private realm deception that was dishonorable even in public venues.

We can now see that George Sand's denunciation of lawyers' emotional plasticity (discussed in Chapter 7) took aim at the new emotional regime's Achilles' heel. Only through such plasticity were the needs of public institutions and the requirements of public "rationality" reconciled with the simple fact that emotions are an inevitable dimension of all thought and action. Only through such plasticity were lawyers able to show how one could breathe the life of feeling into behaviors required by law, honor, or interest. Such plasticity, in turn, implicitly instructed individuals how they, too, could reconcile their divergent and often deviant feelings with normative requirements. This plasticity was admired, but also regarded with pessimism, even cynicism, as a sign of human frailty. (Daumier's caricatures of lawyers are particularly expressive of this standpoint.) This ambivalence provided Sand with her target and enabled her to hold up the older norms of sentimentalist sincerity and naturalism as inherently superior. But Sand was hardly in a position to undo the failure of Jacobinism and sentimentalism's subsequent discrediting and erasure.

However, Favancourt's letters suggest that Sand was not alone. There are a number of ways of reading Anna de Favancourt's letters. It seems likely that she was in the grip of one of those sentimentalist spirals, discussed in Chapter 5, in which expression of intensity elicited increased intensity, confirming the sense that the expression was sincere, true, and natural. That a young woman might be prone to this kind of spiral effect, in view of the life chances typically available to them, seems understandable. Favancourt, like most elite adolescent women, was carefully guarded by her family and introduced into social activities in the homes of other respectable families about the age of sixteen to eighteen (Houbre 1997). It was exceptional, however, that her mother allowed, even fostered, a close relationship with a young man in the absence of definite prospects, definite promises, or at least the preparation of a marriage contract. Favancourt's sense of self, in terms of available norms and the ambiguities they carried within them, could go either of two ways: (1) She could condemn her mother and herself for the severe lapses of decorum that had sullied their reputation in Nancy. (2) She could embrace the sentimentalist idea that love was a natural feeling, the ultimate source of virtue, capable of overriding and neutralizing social norms (especially those associated with honor). Such sentimentalist ideas were still widely disseminated. Many novels of the eighteenth century continued to be read, as noted in Chapter 7. Certainly, once Favancourt had broken with decorum to pursue Descoutures, from that point on, she had every reason to seek to intensify and to glory in her love for him, a saving grace that offered a heroic alternative to pariah status.

This is not to say that Favancourt was driven by ulterior motives. The point is merely to recognize that the coexistence of strict norms of decorum and respectability appropriate to a system of arranged marriages, on the one hand, and of the norms of sentimentalism, on the other, might easily predispose a young woman to intensity. Her allegiance to both sets of norms recommended that only passion could exonerate, justify, beautify her conduct of her life. Romantic attitudes toward emotions might strengthen this orientation. Many prominent women of the period, as well as other women caught up in famous trials, displayed emotional intensity like a badge of honor: Flora Tristan, George Sand, Marie d'Agoult, Emily Loveday (Ford 1994), Marie Lafarge (Adler 1985), Marie de Morell (Cornut-Gentille 1996).

There is a closeness, too, between shame and longing for another who is far away; thought activations that could bear these labels would share a devaluation of the self. Both Hugo's famous play *Hernani* (1830) and George Sand's *Lélia* (1832) are suffused with a similar intensity of longing in conflict with shame. The very lucidity of Favancourt's enunciation of a sentimentalist style of love suggests that something like this did happen to her.

Applying the concept of emotives, I contend that Favancourt was displaying emotional flexibility every bit as much as the attorneys in the courtroom, but it was a flexibility that no one recognized. The attorneys defended starkly opposing theses about her: either she was in the grip of a powerful passion or else she was demented; the court opted for the former interpretation. No one suggested that she might have played an active role in shaping her emotional configuration, in line with a culturally sanctioned strategy of self-valuation. A woman involved in a private tragedy, she was deemed to be a victim, passive, weak. In addition, the private realm was deemed as a whole to be a sphere of weakness to, and victimization by, feelings. Emotional management informed by this notion reinforced its credibility. But she appears to have been pursuing that peculiar emotional refuge promised by affectionate marriage; the more her pursuit subjected her to public disapproval, the more desperately she longed for its safety.

These cases taken together suggest that the tacitly applauded public flexibility of males was paired to a private flexibility, displayed by both men and women, not recognized as an outcome of emotional management but treated as an expression of true, inner private feelings before which the will was weak. The line between public and private (and between feeling and reason) did not run along the boundary separating men and women, or that separating family relationships from contractual relationships. Instead it ran along the boundary that separated public flexibility (admired when properly deployed) and private flexibility (where emotions were treated as not flexible at all, but emanations of a truer self).

Commercial and familial disputes remained emotionally flat if the issue before the court involved interpretation of a law, or a decision about the legality of a certain procedure, or about the wording of a contract, rather than the intentions (and thus emotions) of the actors in the case. Commercial disputes were as likely as family ones to become occasions of intense emotional expression if and only if the issue of the parties' feelings became relevant to the legal judgment that had to be made. When one or the other party's "true" feelings had to be determined, attorneys' own emotional flexibility met its highest challenge, as they mapped out detailed patterns of action, made damaging inferences about their opponents (or flattering ones about their clients), and expressed emotions appropriate to the defense of public norms. With the complicity of the courts they pursued a phantom truth about the private feelings of their clients, giving such truths a commonsensical concreteness.

In this limited sense, the Restoration courts were like the courts of the Jacobin republic of 1792–1793, with the difference that the Revolutionary tribunals sent suspects to the guillotine on the basis of sneers or mannerisms, choice of clothing or vocabulary, on the basis of offenses such as playing an aristocrat on stage or being a former priest, as if knowing true feeling were easy, as if there were no private obscurity they could not look into. Post-Revolutionary courts only penetrated with difficulty the place where true feelings resided, only occasionally, after lengthy, difficult deliberation. Hence, belief that there was a single true private thing that each person felt on each issue was far less damaging than had been the sentimentalist optimism of the Terror.

PATTERNS IN THE SAMPLES AS A WHOLE

If the patterns discerned in these four cases held true for the sample as a whole, one would expect to be able to sort it into two types of cases, according to whether the issues in the case were technical or emotional, that is, involved interpretation of law or contract (technical) or intentions (emotional). The expectation is that oratorical displays and debates about character and sentiment would be frequent in cases that turned on a person's motives, and infrequent in those that turned on the meaning of a statute or of the wording of a contract or the status of a certificate. By and large, both the *Gazette* sample of forty-six cases and the Versailles sample of depositions in twenty-eight cases of 1839–1841 do bear out this expectation. The sample from the Versailles archives required slightly different treatment because the content of depositions is quite different from that of the pleadings that dominate *Gazette* coverage.

1. Overview of the Gazette Sample

Table 1 offers a rough categorization of the *Gazette* cases in terms of three parameters: (1) whether the dispute involved a public,

TABLE 1. Emotional Tenor of Debates in Forty-Six Civil Cases Sampled from the *Gazette des Tribunaux*, 1826–1829

Case No.	Date of First Article	Plaintiff	Defendant	Cause	Sphere of Conflict	Point of Contention	Tenor of Debate
1	November 13, 1825	Serpinet héritiers	Vérac et al.	inheritance	F	T	dry
2	December 17, 1825	Chabannes de la Palisse, Mme	Chabannes de la Palisse, M	marital separation	F	M	emotional
3	December 18, 1825	Charvet, enfants	not given	validity of a will	F	T	dry
4	January 12, 1826	Desjardin de Ruzé héritiers	Delamarre	validity of a debt	P	M&T	emotional
5	January 12, 1826	Syndics de la faillite Sandrié Vincourt	Compagnie des agents de change de Paris	liability in a bankruptcy	P	T	*mixed*
6	January 15, 1826	Milon	Bridieu	validity of receipts for payment	P	T	*mixed*
7	January 25, 1826	Parker	Rapp héritiers	validity of a sale of property	P	T	dry
8	February 10, 1826	Chevrier	Bourbon, duc de	loss of a note of indebtedness	P	T	dry
9	February 18, 1826	Thésignies héritiers	Desmares enfants	disavowal of paternity	F	M	emotional
10	February 24, 1826	Merlo héritiers (of Paris)	Merlo héritiers (of Genoa)	inheritance	F	T	dry
11	June 11, 1826	Schellings, Mme de, née Saint-Morys	Moligny, marquis de	validity of a marriage	F	T	*mixed*

292

#	Date				F	T	*emotional*
12	June 13, 1826	Leroy	Bidaut	question of paternity (inheritance)	F	T	emotional
13	July 30, 1826	Thierry héritiers	Thierry héritiers	inheritance	F	T	dry
14	August 15, 1826	Collange héritiers	Laferté-Sénectère	inheritance	F	T	dry
15	August 8, 1826	Desprez, Mme	Desprez, M	marital separation	F	M	emotional
16	November 16, 1826	Guerinot	Lemoine, Geslin	copyright infringement	P	T	dry
17	November 23, 1826	Viard	Cayla, comtesse du	validity of a gift (inheritance)	P	T	dry
18	January 6, 1827	*Lallemand et al.*	*Descoutures*	validity of a will	F	M	emotional
19	April 19, 1827	Boulanger	Viallane, Mme veuve	validity of a loan	P	M	*mixed*
20	April 21, 1827	Mainvielle-Fodor	Sosthènes de la Rochefoucauld and the Théâtre Italien	terms of a contract	P	T	dry
21	May 17, 1827	Viard	Cayla, comte du, and his children	liability for repayment of a debt	P	T	dry
22	May 26, 1827	Planès, Mme de, née Montlezun	Lagarde, de, and Montlezun, her aunts	eligibility for indemnity	F	T	dry
23	May 31, 1827	Laprée et héritiers Valette	Raguse, Mme la duchesse de	seizure of movables for debt	P	T	dry
24	June 27, 1827	*D***, baron*	*H***, veuve*	validity of a marriage	F	T	dry
25	June 30, 1827	Franceschetti	Mme Bonaparte, comtesse de Lipano, widow of Joseph Murat	validity of a debt	P	T&M	emotional
26	July 6, 1827	Rellot	Girolet	existence of a partnership	P	T	*mixed*

TABLE 1. (*cont.*)

Case No.	Date of First Article	Plaintiff	Defendant	Cause	Sphere of Conflict	Point of Contention	Tenor of Debate
27	August 4, 1827	Jacquinot héritiers	Gravier, Chabaud, et Garillon	validity of a will	F	T	*mixed*
28	August 9, 1827	Aubertin	Dehamel	validity of a will	F	M	emotional
29	August 18, 1827	Muller	Durfort, comte de	copyright infringement	P	T	dry
30	December 6, 1827	Morteuil, Mme de	Morteuil, M de	martial separation	F	M	emotional
31	December 7, 1827	*Mars, Mlle*	*Thélusson, Mlle, MM Tobriant Constantin et al.*	collection of a debt	P	T	dry
32	December 8, 1827	Charuel héritiers	Lenchère héritiers	validity of a will	F	M	emotional
33	December 26, 1827	Aumont, duchesse d'	Comte, Mme	fraud by a business agent	P	M	emotional
34	December 29, 1827	Raguse, duc de, and his creditors	Raguse, duchess de	liquidation of marital community	P	M	emotional
35	December 7, 1827	Savard, Mme	Savard, M	marital separation	F	M	emotional
36	February 9, 1828	Bidet, veuve, et fils	Labourdonnaye-Blossne, comte de	validity of a debt	P	M	*mixed*
37	March 1, 1828	Viotte	Violette	validity of a debt	P	M	dry
38	March 13, 1828	Les théâtres secondaires (Paris)	Académie royale de musique	legality of a government fee	P	T	dry

294

					F	T&M	
39	March 15, 1828	children of K***, Mme, née Bailly	G***	question of paternity	F		emotional
40	April 18, 1828	L***, Mme	L***, M	marital separation	F	M	emotional
41	May 27, 1828	L*** Mme Dumonteil	Esnée	marriage of a priest	P	T	*mixed*
42	December 18, 1828	*Caisse hypothécaire*	*Raguse, duc de*	terms of a contract	P	M	emotional
43	January 3, 1829	Sannejouant	Paris, ville de	damages for property loss	P	T	dry
44	April 23, 1829	Choiseul	Théâtre Feydeau	ownership of a theater box	P	T	dry
45	August 8, 1829	Bouchers de Paris	Préfet de la Seine	legality of government fees	P	T	dry
46	August 13, 1829	Prévost et al.	Intendant général de la maison du Roi	nonpayment of salaries	P	T	dry

Notes: **Boldface italic** type indicates names of the plaintiffs in the four cases discussed in detail. **Boldface *underlined* italic** type in the "Tenor of Debate" column indicates anomalous cases discussed in the text and in Appendix A.

F – familial or private relationship.
P – public, contractual, or commercial relationship.
T – technical issue in interpretation of code, contract, will, etc.
M – issue requiring interpretation of motives.

commercial, or contractual relationship or a familial or private relationship; (2) whether the issue was technical or involved the interpretation of motives; (3) whether the tenor of the debate was emotional or
dry. The hypothesis is, simply, that parameters (2) and (3) should vary
together, and independently of parameter (1). It was found necessary
to introduce a third category for parameter (3), besides "emotional" or
"dry," called "mixed." As noted above, attorneys often used multiple
arguments in their pursuit of victory by any means; and in three cases,
these multiple arguments included both technical claims and claims
about motives. In each of these, the motivational claims gave attorneys
ample grounds to discuss emotions, and they did so. In a number of
other cases, the interpretation of motives only came up in the course
of rebuttals, or was discussed in tandem with other matters or in
an ancillary way. The tenor of debates in all these cases was therefore
designated as "mixed."

In nine cases out of forty-six (19.6 percent), the tenor of debates did
not fit the hypothesis. Of these, debates in one technical case (no. 12 in
the table) were markedly emotional in character. In the remaining eight
cases, debates were mixed, either involving considerable emotional
discussion in spite of the apparently technical nature of the issue, or
involving less emotional discussion than the centrality of motives to
the case would appear to warrant.

A closer look at these nine apparently anomalous cases (see Appendix A) shows that some of the technical cases raised fears about
reputation, or turned on documentary proof found only after the trial
got under way. As a result, despite the technical nature of the judgment,
motives did come into play in the pleadings, at least for a time. In the
two anomalous cases involving motives where the debate was mixed
in tenor (cases 19 and 36), technical interpretation of documentary
records offered a way of avoiding the interpretation of motives, if the
court wished to take it. But it was not clear what point of departure the
court would choose to take; thus one or both attorneys made both technical and emotional arguments. Therefore none of these cases require
reformulation of the interpretation that has been developed so far. A
careful examination of these anomalous cases, provided in Appendix
A, demonstrates the process by which this determination was made.

2. Evidence from the Versailles Sample

Archival evidence on civil litigation differs markedly from the evidence available in the *Gazette des Tribunaux*. The newspaper reported

pleadings; pleadings were publicly available because carried out in an open courtroom. But only rarely does the *Gazette* enter into the details of the supporting documents, such as the *requêtes* – written complaints that request court action – or the *enquêtes* containing depositions of witnesses. In the archives, to the contrary, there are no records of pleadings, no trace of the feats of eloquence by which attorneys sought to sway the court to their way of seeing things. Even the *requêtes*, *enquêtes*, and supporting documents are often missing. The twenty-eight cases sampled in this study were selected because, in each, *enquêtes* – collections of depositions from witnesses – had been carried out and survived. Final judgments were located in the register of judgments for most of these cases. (Cases dropped or settled out of court did not yield final judgments.) In *enquêtes*, the witnesses were guided by questions; usually their opinions were of no interest; they were only asked about the actions and events they claim to have seen. As a result, there is much less use of emotion terms, much less discussion of emotions, than in the records of pleadings by famous barristers in the *Gazette*.

These differences make the archival sample an important corrective to the *Gazette* evidence. Witnesses being deposed do not attempt to display eloquence or learning; they do not attempt to provide a neat interpretive package that demonstrates how the case fits into prevailing normative scenarios. But if the testimony concerning emotions is sparse, there is enough to provide the contours of a structure of presumptions about emotion and motivation quite similar to that found in the *Gazette* cases.

In these cases, too, the frequency of discussion of emotion by witnesses in these depositions was closely related to whether the case involved a technical legal issue or a question of motivation. Of the twenty-eight cases in the sample, only six cases (21 percent) varied from this pattern. These cases are listed in Table 2.

Cases that typify the pattern include Barat v. Santerre (case no. 52, familial, involving motives, frequent mention of emotions); Chavannes v. Parturier (case no. 69, familial, technical, no expression or discussion of emotions); Lebaudy v. Sureau (case no. 51, public, involving motives, frequent mention of emotions); and Hembuisse v. Compagnie La Dorade (case no. 65, public, technical, no expression or discussion of emotions). Each of these four cases will be briefly examined to indicate how an emotional configuration similar to that found in the *Gazette* sample came up in the context of deposing witnesses.

TABLE 2. Presence of Testimony on Emotions in Twenty-Eight Civil Cases from the Archives of the Tribunal civil de Versailles, 1840–1841

Case No.	Date of First Enquête	Plaintiff	Défendant	Cause	Sphere of Conflict	Point of Contention	Testimony on Emotions
47	September 11, 1840	syndics de la faillite Lepeltier	veuve Lepeltier	ownership of movable property	P	T	none
48	March 23, 1840	Cloud	Boutillier	personal injury	P	T	none
49	January 22, 1840	Louvet	Leroux	liquidation of succession	F	T	none
50	May 20, 1840	Bonert and Haguenier	Gruter	real estate boundary line	P	T	none
51	February 11, 1840	*Lebaudy*	*Sureau*	unpaid medical bill	P	M	frequent
52	April 18, 1840	*Barat*	*Santerre*	marital separation	F	M	frequent
53	January 2, 1840	Pelletier	Gabet	marital separation	F	M	frequent
54	June 23, 1840	Bezier	Lebreton	real estate boundary dispute	P	T	none
55	June 26, 1840	Charon and veuve Souillard	veuve Tierce	mental competence	F	M	*infrequent*
56	March 19, 1840	Mailan	Lesine	marital separation	F	M	frequent
57	June 26, 1840	Picard	Gogue	marital separation	F	M	frequent
58	September 1, 1840	Druet	Barbedette	marital separation	F	M	*infrequent*
59	December 17, 1841	Malingre	Delarue	marital separation	F	M	*infrequent*
60	September 15, 1841	époux Berrurier	Laporte, et époux Paulmier	fulfillment of an out-of-court settlement	P	T	*infrequent*

No.	Date			Issue			
61	November 16, 1841	Leguiene	Meunier	marital separation	F	M	frequent
62	December 20, 1841	héritiers Vincent		disappearance of a family member	F	T	none
63	March 24, 1841	Schneider	Lamaure	marital separation	F	M	frequent
64	March 19, 1841	Lallemant	Herbert	marital separation	F	M	*infrequent*
65	February 24, 1841	*Hembuisse*	*Cie. La Dorade*	boat accident	P	T	none
66	January 8, 1841	Daniel	Collet	marital separation	F	M	frequent
67	January 8, 1841	Bouyer	Godefroy et al.	dispute over a payment	P	T	none
68	July 22, 1841	Barat	Santerre	payment of alimony (provision)	F	T	none
69	June 2, 1841	*Chavannes*	*Parturier*	marital separation	F	T	none
70	July 26, 1841	Par	Masselin	marital separation	F	M	frequent
71	September 10, 1841	Marehais	Blavat	collection of a debt	P	T	none
72	November 3, 1841	Blain	Aumont	marital separation	F	M	frequent
73	June 29, 1841	Duton	Nezan, veuve, et al.	validity of a gift	F	M	*infrequent*
74	August 18, 1841	Beauchamps	Jacob	right of way across a property	P	T	none

Notes: **Boldface italic** type indicates names of the plaintiffs in the four cases discussed in detail. **Boldface *underlined italic*** type in the "Testimony on Emotions" column indicates anomalous cases discussed in the text or in Appendix B.

F – familial or private relationship.

P – public, contractual, or commercial relationship.

T – technical issue in interpretation of code, contract, will, etc.

M – issue requiring interpretation of motives.

Source: Cases 47 to 58 are from dossier 3 U 0246[48], cases 59 to 74 are from 3 U 0246[53]. Both dossiers in the Archives de l'ancien département de Seine-et-Oise.

CASE NO. 52. *BARAT V. SANTERRE*. In this instance, Thérèse Agathe Barat, widowed and remarried to René Auguste Santerre, was seeking a separation from her spouse, a café operator. Both spouses had been authorized to seek depositions, but only the husband actually did so. Subsequently, the court ruled against Barat, who had failed to appear. The husband's eleven witnesses painted a remarkable, if elusive, picture of a highly unconventional marriage. All agreed that Barat and Santerre had lived in separate dwellings since their marriage, Santerre in rooms above his café in central Versailles, his wife a few blocks away in a rented room. All agreed that Mme Santerre visited her husband from time to time for a few days and that, when she did so, "good harmony" appeared to reign. The couple retired to bed together; they addressed each other lovingly as "mon ami(e)," "ma bonne amie"; they used the familiar "tu" when speaking to each other and were "full of consideration [*égards*] for each other." Mme Santerre's brother was among the witnesses, and he indicated that she had also kept a separate dwelling in her first marriage. One witness had seen Santerre visiting her room frequently to care for her when she was ill. Although the law of the period required a wife to live with her husband, and required the husband to provide her with shelter, there was nothing illegal about the Santerres' unusual arrangement so long as the husband acquiesced, permitting the wife to stay outside his home, and so long as he did not shut her out when she came to his home. Husbands had great legal discretion to allow their marriages to vary from the norms of law and social custom.

While there are no emotion terms in a strict sense in this testimony, one must nonetheless accept that such expressions as "good harmony," "mon ami," "full of consideration" have an emotional significance. Because each witness repeats these terms (doubtless there was some coaching involved), their depositions provide frequent evidence on emotions, as is appropriate to a case in which the husband's motives were at issue.

CASE NO. 69. *CHAVANNES V. PARTURIER*. In this case, Fidèle Auguste Chavannes, a clerk, sued his wife, Adrienne Eulalie Parturier, a dressmaker, for a separation, on the grounds of abandonment and serious insult. Witnesses in the case – including a theatrical booking agent, and an actress, both from Paris, as well as a Versailles voice instructor – testified that Parturier had traveled to Metz about six years earlier and taken up residence there with an orchestra conductor on tour. The two had met earlier when the conductor's troupe was playing in Versailles. Since that time she had lived with the conductor and had even taken to using his name. This unauthorized departure was illegal, and living openly with another man, besides being illegal, was also severe public insult. There was no need to enter into fine-grain interpretations of Parturier's motives or sentiments. Chavannes was readily granted a separation.

CASE NO. 51. *LEBAUDY V. SUREAU.* In this instance, M Lebaudy, a Parisian doctor, sued M Sureau, a landowner of Herblay, for nonpayment of a large bill incurred for treatment of Sureau's wife. This public, commercial affair came to turn on emotional expression as a result of the testimony of the curé of Herblay, François Bertrand, and his friend, Denis Trou, another priest who was a vicar in Pontoise. Both priests testified that they had believed Lebaudy was treating Sureau's wife for free as an act of benevolence. Lebaudy was a good friend of curé Bertrand who, along with Trou, had been visiting Bertrand about the middle of 1838. Because the curé's courtyard was too small to accommodate Lebaudy's carriage, Sureau, who lived across the street, allowed the carriage to be parked in his own courtyard. Because of this "neighborly" act, the priests had mentioned to Lebaudy that Sureau's wife was gravely ill, and that Sureau himself was near bankruptcy and unable to provide her with proper care. Lebaudy had gone across to talk to the man and subsequently, the priests said, had agreed to treat Sureau's wife. Neither priest had actually witnessed the negotiations between Lebaudy and Sureau; however both spoke of the great "désintéressement" displayed by the doctor. This term, which could be translated as "altruism" or "unselfishness," clearly pointed to Lebaudy's emotional state at the time. He showed great "piety," according to Bertrand. Lebaudy had questioned Bertrand carefully about Sureau, as Bertrand recounted it:

"Does M Sureau merit interest?" Lebaudy asked.
I responded, "Overall, he does."
"Does Mme Sureau merit interest?"
I responded, "She does in every respect."
"What is M Sureau's religious situation?"
I responded, "It is quite deficient."
"What is M Sureau's financial situation?"

Bertrand responded that it was in bad shape, either due to speculation or poor administration. Some days, Bertrand said, he does not even have a five-franc piece in the house.

Then M Lebaudy said, "I've made up my mind; it is providence that has brought me here. If I have the good fortune [happiness, *bonheur*] to cure Mme Sureau, he must understand that it is God who has sent me."

Later, after Mme Sureau had undergone an amputation and been fully cured, her husband told Bertrand that he was "enchanted" with Lebaudy's "benevolence." Subsequently Sureau and his wife, who had been married in a civil ceremony only and who had not baptized their child, were married in the church across the street from their home and had their child baptized by Bertrand. The court ruled that Lebaudy had agreed to treat Mme Sureau either for free or at a very minimum price, and ordered Sureau to pay 400 francs to cover Lebaudy's expenses only; the parties were to split the court costs. The priests' testimony about Lebaudy's emotional demeanor was decisive.

CASE NO. 65. *HEMBUISSE V. COMPAGNIE LA DORADE.* This case involved a collision that occurred on 4 October 1840, between a steamboat named *La Dorade* and a horse-drawn barge in the Seine just off Conflans-Ste.-Honorine. Hembuisse, the barge owner, sued *La Dorade*'s owner, a company that operated a fleet of steamboats on the lower Seine. Hembuisse brought sixteen eyewitnesses of the accident into court, including members of his own crew and people who had been on the shore: a woman washing clothes, three different men who had been fishing along the shore, another man who had heard the crash from inside his café. The defendants brought in five more witnesses, crew members of the steamboat. Almost all of the plaintiff's witnesses had seen the accident coming, many had cried out trying to warn the steamboat. But the captain was not on the bridge at the time, and the noise of the engine and the paddle wheel prevented the pilot from hearing the warnings. After ramming the barge, the steamboat had repeatedly reversed its engine, trying to shake itself free, causing further damage to the barge, which sank immediately thereafter. Doubtless everyone who witnessed the accident had some emotional reaction to it; there was a long moment of suspense, the crash, the crew of the barge swimming to safety, then the damaging efforts of the steamboat to shake free, stretching over fifteen minutes or so. But none of the twenty-one witnesses who deposed referred either to their own emotions or to those of any other actor in the case. The only point at issue was whether the crew of the steamboat exercised appropriate caution; clearly they had not, and they had failed to respond to repeated warnings. The court ordered the steamboat company to pay damages.

These cases conform perfectly to the pattern found in the *Gazette* sample.

As with the *Gazette* sample, a small number of cases – six in the Versailles sample – were anomalous. Two of these six were marital separation cases in which the husband's pattern of violence toward his wife was so well established and so widely known in the community that the witnesses provided little more than a dry description of his acts (case no. 59, Malingre v. Delarue; case no. 64, Lallemant v. Herbert). Bare descriptions were enough to establish "cruelty" as defined by the law when a husband, habitually drunk, threw rocks at his wife, threatened her with a pistol, stole money from her stall in the market, dragged her across the floor by the hair, or threw her out of the house at night. Marital separation was by far the most common type of case to give rise to depositions in the Versailles records of 1840–1841. Of the thirteen separation cases in the files, ten involved extensive evidence of violence by husbands. Nine included some discussion of emotions; one did not. All ten cases provide important evidence of a logic of intimate violence, closely related to concepts of emotion, that will be considered in more detail later.

The four other anomalous cases are considered in detail in Appendix B.

There is nothing in the anomalous cases from this sample that contradicts the overall interpretation offered here: that emotions were associated with the roots of motivation and, therefore, especially with ulterior or conflicting motivations. As a result they came up in cases in which motivation had to be established in order to render judgment, where motivation was alleged to have broken with norms in some respect. In such cases, emotions were discussed openly or, often, in a slightly veiled manner by witnesses, in spite of the general preference that witnesses avoid interpretation of motives or states of mind. They had to discuss them in such cases, because evidence about motives was precisely what the witnesses were called on to provide. The frequency of marital separation cases in a sample based on the survival of depositions is suggestive; separation rulings required that motives be established; if they were contested, it was highly likely that an *enquête* would be ordered.

TRACES OF SENTIMENTALISM IN THE TWO SAMPLES

In the experiences of private life, as depicted in civil litigation, sentimentalist plot structures frequently appeared. The private realm, like art, was now conceived of as a space where emotions and emotional performances held sway. Examining cases that offer such plot structures suggests, however, that the idea of an inborn moral sensibility was entirely gone, replaced by a conception of the individual as weak. Susceptibility to intense emotion gave private life its special meaning, but also its tendency to run off course. Women, viewed in the eighteenth century as morally superior to men, now ranked lower than them. Their emotional sensitivity required male guidance and sometimes the special protection of the court. Thus sentimentalism provided a kind of collection of concepts for giving order to some parts of that vast terrain of weakness where emotions now lived. The Descoutures case offers a vivid illustration of how this reuse of sentimentalist conventions could take place. Many other cases follow the same plan.

I will briefly discuss eight cases in which attorneys or witnesses employed one or more of the following sentimentalist plots: (1) public acts of generosity; (2) virtue in distress; (3) true love versus arranged marriages; (4) the good father versus evil relatives.[12]

(1) Public Acts of Generosity

In the Lebaudy v. Sureau case, no. 51, from the Versailles sample, both priests testified that Dr Lebaudy had intended to make a public act of generosity toward the Sureau family in order to bring them back to the church. As Agulhon (1970) has shown, the church found itself in a novel position in post-Revolutionary France. After many centuries as the official cult of the community (despite the challenge of Protes-

---

[12] For discussion of eighteenth-century examples of each of these types of plot structure, see, for type (1), Denby (1994); for type (2), Barker-Benfield (1992) and Brissendon (1974); for type (3), DeJean (1991) and Daumas (1996); for type (4), Hunt (1992).

tantism between 1536 and 1685), the church had become a sect; membership was now optional, a question of personal choice. But many still desired the church to fulfill its traditional role as public cult. Thus angry crowds protested when parish priests refused to bury the bodies of nonpracticing persons in church cemeteries. Lebaudy's gesture was aimed at converting Sureau; he and the priests were taking a page from the sentimentalist book (albeit one which bore significant Christian influence). Charity reestablished membership. Benevolence could now serve sectarian aims, rather than natural or political ones.

In case no. 25, Franceschetti v. veuve Murat, from the *Gazette* sample, a retired general was suing the widow of Joseph Murat, son-in-law of Napoleon and former king of Naples. The general alleged that, during Napoleon's hundred days in 1815, Franceschetti had sheltered Murat on his Corsican estate, and then aided Murat in attempting to gather a small fleet to return to Italy and reclaim his throne. The venture had ended in Murat's death. Franceschetti claimed he had spent eighty thousand francs of his personal fortune on Murat's orders, and that reimbursement was owed him from Murat's estate. This claim was far-fetched, had only the slimmest legal basis, and was not one that Restoration judges were likely to smile upon. The general's attorney, Gilbert-Boucher, made much of Franceschetti's poverty – and here was the sentimentalist twist. He evoked the prospect of Franceschetti's openhearted loyalty, his worries over heavy debts incurred, his unmarried daughters deprived of dowries. Men of every party, he intoned, could not help but be moved by the prospect of this loyal general's plight. Gilbert-Boucher, in effect, called on the judges to make a public act of generosity toward the defendant by granting his request.

In case no. 66, Daniel v. Collet, a suit for marital separation, from the Versailles sample, the wife was the object of numerous acts of generosity on the part of neighbors and passersby. The mayor of Néauphle-le-Château, the deputy mayor, the commissaire de police, and a local doctor all testified about an incident in which they had found her and her young daughter wandering in public, about 10:00 P.M., crying. They stopped to ask her what was wrong. She explained that her husband had beat her and put her out of the house. They went to the couple's home; the mayor lectured M Collet, who appeared drunk, about his behavior. The mayor compelled him to readmit his wife. On another occasion the commissaire de police took Mme Collet in to stay overnight and his wife treated her bruises. On another occasion a sawyer found Mme Collet lying in an alley after a beating. He took her to a nearby home for help. A porter and his wife testified to having helped Mme Collet on numerous occasions. He and his wife intervened to stop beatings, gave Mme Collet shelter, and finally escorted her back to her father's house in Versailles. M Collet threatened them with guns; he threw ignited gunpowder into the face of the porter's wife, causing burns to her hair and her skin. While many separation cases involving violence provide information about help extended by neighbors and relatives, what makes this case distinctive is that most of the help was elicited when passersby found Mme Collet wandering, or lying, in public. While the testimony is unemotional, one senses a certain zest in the narratives that suggests self-conscious appreciation of the witnesses' public generosity.

(2) Virtue in Distress

Case 25 and case 66, just discussed, might as easily have been placed in this category – the two are closely linked in sentimentalist thought. In case no. 30, Mme de Morteuil v. M de Morteuil, from the *Gazette* sample, Hennequin, arguing for Mme de Morteuil's request for a separation from her husband, followed a common strategy for this kind of case. (See, for further examples, Reddy 1997b.) While emphasizing that only her wounded honor had brought the wife to the last resort of seeking court protection from her husband, Hennequin nonetheless noted Mme de Morteuil's sensitivity and deplored her extreme emotional suffering. Hennequin describes Mme de Morteuil as having lived an exemplary life; widowed in a first marriage, she remained single until her son from that union had come of age. Then, in 1800, still young, she had remarried and had four children with M de Morteuil. Hennequin insisted he would not go into the details of her life with this man. "It is enough for you to know," he assured the court, "that up until 1817 Mme de Morteuil faced great suffering; that she had suffered with patience and that she would still be suffering without having raised the slightest objection, if the interests of her children had not made it her duty, and if intolerable humiliations had not added the last straw to her grief." As in the sentimentalist vision, here it is the woman's very sensitivity that is the foundation of her devotion to duty. Love of her son keeps her single; then her ability to love leads her to a new union. From her heightened sensitivity comes her ability to submit to suffering when that is appropriate but also the determination to brave public scrutiny when it becomes necessary to end "intolerable humiliation."

(3) True Love versus Arranged Marriages

This theme plays a role in the pleadings in the Lallemant et al. v. Descoutures case discussed above. It is also present in the Picard v. Gogue case discussed in Chapter 4; Gogue, who hoped to find a "garden" in his marriage, is counseled against such high expectations both by his father and his new in-laws; disappointment fuels his violence. Mme Druet's escape to Italy with a false passport (case no. 58 – for discussion, see Appendix B), following an elaborate plan she and her lover developed, fits the sentimentalist prescription to place true love above marriage; whether or not she and M de la Jariette were influenced by sentimentalist conceptions or practices, the witnesses' (and the court's) readiness to conclude against her demonstrate their influence.

In the case of Schellings v. Moligny (case no. 11), a niece and her uncle were disputing possession of an inheritance; the case turned on the validity of the niece's marriage. Mme Schellings's attorney, somewhat diffidently, attributed his client's legally dubious marriage to her strong romantic involvement. M Schellings had been among certain Prussian officers, during the conflict of spring 1815, who had been given quarters in the château of a M de Saint-Morys. The daughter of the family was forced to share her home with these representatives of the occupying force.

The effect which the presence of armed strangers must have produced on her solitude was soon succeeded by a very different sentiment. She was treated with the greatest respect and tenderness. She was not insensitive to it. A marriage was planned [with M Schellings], discussed by the family, but rejected by M de Saint-Morys, who married his daughter to a neighbor in the country, M de Gaudechart. Soon she was widowed. It was about that time that M de Saint-Morys died in a duel.

Fifteen months later the widowed Mme de Gaudechart received a letter from M Schellings, who said he was a prisoner in the fortress of Vesel, "that he retained for her the liveliest affection," and who asked *"if she was happy!"* (*"si elle était heureuse!"*; emphasis in original). "That was all that was necessary to turn the head [*tourner la tête*] of this still very young woman." Here, her own attorney seems to condemn her ardent feelings. M Schellings had been convicted of embezzling funds from his regiment, but was soon granted a royal pardon, rejoined his beloved, and went with her to Scotland to be married. During this period he traveled under a false name because, the attorney assured the court, he was wanted in Prussia in connection with a duel. (This was, perhaps, the only honorable excuse possible for falsifying one's identity.) Therefore the Scottish marriage certificate listed him as "Theodore Albert Schellings" instead of "Inglebert Schellings." The uncle's attorney charged, however, that Schellings had lied about his origins, concealing that he was an illegitimate child. The pleadings on both sides in this case, as well as the king's attorney's pointed views, all condemned the deleterious effects of sentimental attachment on family honor. Implicitly, they identified both Mme Schellings and her husband as motivated in accord with sentimentalist doctrines, and therefore weak and shortsighted. The character of the case, in this sense, strongly resembles that of Lallemant et al. v. Descoutures.

Case no. 39, from the *Gazette* sample, pitted the children of Mme K***, née Bailly, against a M G***. The uncle of the defendant (also referred to as M G***), a high navy official in 1789 (premier commis de la marine), fell into political difficulties during the Revolution, was imprisoned for a time, then escaped from France and, in 1794, took ship with his family in Hamburg on a Dutch vessel sailing for New York. But the ship ran aground in a storm off Cork, Ireland; and its passengers sought refuge in that town. As the plaintiffs' attorney, Mérilhou, put it:

This family consisted of the father, the mother, a daughter, and a nephew who is today our adversary. Apart from his former functions in France, and his wealth, M G*** had a special claim on the benevolence of all those to whom he addressed himself [*avait un titre particulier à la bienveillance de tous ceux à qui il s'adressait*]. He came from the prisons of the Terror and fled a country in the grip of endemic warfare to find a refuge in the land of liberty; he was welcomed with concern [*intérêt*] and his stay lengthened into the middle of 1795.

M K*** soon got to know the family, and soon began to feel the most tender affection for Adélaïde G***, who was everywhere introduced by her father as his dearest daughter.

K*** followed the family to New York, there offered his hand in marriage to Adélaïde, and was welcomed into the family with open arms. Only on the steps of the altar did he learn that his bride was not the real daughter of the G***s, but a foundling they had taken into their care, without a legal adoption. The offer of a fifty-thousand-franc dowry was maintained, but given the form of a loan (for which repayment was never demanded). Now, the children of that union were suing for their share in the fortune of the G*** couple, which had, in the meantime, passed to the nephew. The court ruled, however, that the plaintiffs had no claim on the inheritance of M and Mme G***. In his pleading, Mérilhou consciously played up the colorful nature of the story, and explicitly likened the G***s' welcome in Cork (and by M K***) to an act of public generosity. In addition, K***'s decision to go ahead with the marriage is treated as an outgrowth of his noble feelings: "But the sentiments of M K*** forbade any hesitation that might have passed for an insult of the one he loved."[13] Mérilhou's story ends like a Scribe play: K*** marries out of an affection that binds honor, setting interest aside.

(4) The Good Father versus Evil Relatives

In one final, complex case (Charuel héritiers v. Lenchère héritiers, case no. 32, from the *Gazette* sample), attorneys for both sides in an inheritance dispute depict their clients as the loyal and devoted children and grandchildren of a good father, and depict their opponents as betrayers of paternal trust. François Lenchère, a merchant of Metz, had made a fortune in military supply, when, at age seventy-five, he was struck with a partial paralysis in 1804. His family at first sought to have him declared incompetent, then dropped the plan. His eldest son, with whom he had had many legal wranglings over business matters, decided to make a last-minute reconciliation. Now, twenty-three years later, the son had died, and the validity of his inheritance from his father was in dispute. The heirs of merchant Lenchère's married daughter, Mme Charuel, through their attorney Hennequin, charged that her brother had hypocritically made up with his father in order to cheat his siblings out of substantial portions of their rightful inheritance back in 1804. Keeping others away from the sick bed, he told his father that he "bitterly regretted" the effort to have him declared incompetent. It was the other children who had pushed the idea, he falsely claimed. The elder Lenchère agreed to sign a note acknowledging a fictitious debt of 448,981.50 francs to his son – payable

---

[13] "Mais les sentiments de M K*** lui défendaient une hésitation qui aurait pu passer pour un outrage à celle qu'il aimait."

only after his death. In addition, he revised his will, granting 400,000 francs to his sister, a Mme Dubois. Hennequin charged that this sister had an agreement with her nephew to divide up this sum between them after the merchant's death. Finally, when he heard that death was near, this same son rushed to his father's bedside, and while pretending to lavish affection on his dying father, stole 120,000 francs' worth of bills of exchange from a purse tied around the man's neck while his body was still warm. In response to these charges, attorney Mollot, for the defendants, paid the plaintiffs back in their own coin.

One part of the family takes pleasure in tearing apart the other. You have, it seems, conceived against us a profound hatred! What? It is not enough that Lenchère's eldest son had to die regretting that he had never been able to have his just claims heard? It is not enough that you have reduced him to leaving his family nothing but penury and grief while all of you are swimming in riches? It is not enough to have rejected the laments of his children who have begged you to grant them at least a small pension? None of that is enough, you must still further stir up his cold ashes.

Nothing Hennequin had said was true, Mollot insisted. Mme Charuel's father had been extremely generous with her at her marriage; her mother's immense fortune had gone largely to her. The 120,000 francs in billets were given to his son before the moment of death, as witnessed by the doctor and the dying man's wife. Subsequently, Lenchère's son, whose life had been nothing but "a long series of misfortunes, as a result of the vindictiveness and the cupidity of our present adversaries," left at his death a wife and children in poverty.

The case pitted one melodrama against another; but the court dryly pronounced the merchant's 1804 will valid. By 1827, melodrama had been drained of all but a modest residue of persuasive power. Emblematic of sincerity and realism in the days of the celebrated court cases of the 1770s and 1780s, the conventions of sentimentalist plots had entered daily life. Lawyers used them routinely if selectively. They might serve the clergy in search of conversions. Women might furnish their private spaces with sentimentalist images and goals. But now they were signs of weakness, of the breakdown of rationality. A young girl's head might be turned by love, a remarried widow might become anxious about her husband's intentions. But such feelings were not guides to right action, they were problems; not moral imperatives, but illusions.

CONCLUSION

These cases reveal a number of new norms in operation. In the post-Revolutionary regime, a unitary self imbued with clear motivations strove for distinction in the public sphere, fulfillment in the private. None of this is surprising in itself; the construction of such an order was the stated aim of reformers, at least from 1794 on. But what the cases also suggest is (1) that emotions, far from being simply relegated to the private sphere, played a central role in all motivation and came under scrutiny whenever motivation was deemed to be at fault; (2) that courts were, however, reluctant to judge motives if they could avoid it and preferred to do so only if private letters or witnesses provided support; (3) that deployment of emotional flexibility in the service of public deliberation (in courtrooms, newspapers, parliament) was highly prestigious, even though in other contexts it tainted the performer (traveling salesmen, actors); (4) that a great range of individual variation in conforming to these norms was tolerated. Sentimentalism still played an important role in the understanding of emotions, but not in the estimation of their public utility. Virtue could no longer rise up from natural simplicity; sincerity could not be easily discerned; sentiment could no longer guide the polity. Yet tales of benevolence, generosity, virtue in distress, and romantic love were still considered to have special plausibility and to be morally edifying. Generosity and mutual esteem enhanced contractual relationships and supported credit. For a great number, affectionate love was essential to a good marriage. And some continued to cling to the idea of love's higher moral standing, whenever it came into conflict with custom, propriety, or family honor.

Toleration of difference and frank acceptance, even admiration, of emotional flexibility (at least in public deliberation) eased the task of emotional navigation in this social order, by comparison with the period of sentimentalism's "trivialization" and the Terror. Ironically, it was the new democratized code of honor that, in particular, enhanced toleration of difference. It did so by insisting that variation from norms be kept secret. Closely allied with male honor was a notion of male rationality that was equally flexible. Male superiority in reason was coupled to a new scientific appreciation of human frailty that made a great deal of male deviance acceptable, if not laudable.

Greater ease of navigation was therefore purchased at the price of a pervasive malaise, a sense of shame about the new "bourgeois" society that found expression in myriad ways. Diverse forms of emotional refuge remained available within the new order. Affectionate marriage and friendship remained important sources of relief from effort for many; and the evidence of civil litigation confirms what Vincent-Buffault (1995) and Houbre (1997) have found, suggesting that sentimentalist ideas, stripped of their public and political implications, continued to shape private practice. Other studies of sociability, for example, those by Agulhon (1970), Gauthier (1992), and Gasnault (1986), show that the period was not without innovation in this regard. What they point to is a type of refuge made possible by the commodification of leisure. Public dance halls, new dance fashions (such as the waltz), and a new enthusiasm for Carnival celebration suggest many were pursuing relief from the stiff discipline imposed by concern for appearances. None of these forms of refuge, whether new or old, drew coherence from a fashionable new ideology with political implications (as those inspired by sentimentalism had in the eighteenth century). Moralists and government officials were prepared to denounce them, but none of them posed a direct threat to the status quo.

The kind of emotional flexibility attorneys and others were expected to show in the new contract-based social order, even when limited by professional standards, contributed to the widespread sense of malaise about the post-Revolutionary order of things. Journalists and salaried civil servants in the period after 1815, as I showed in an earlier study (Reddy 1997b), struggled to reconcile their duty of submissiveness to superiors' decisions and to superiors' political allegiances with a sense of honor that required independence and truth speaking. This submission, as with attorneys' commitment to their clients, differed substantially from the kind of submission cultivated in the patron-client networks of early modern states (such as at the court of Versailles). The civility and loyalty of the courtier was to a single lord and was also contingent on that lord's recriprocal services. These were the relationships targeted by sentimentalists in the eighteenth century as incompatible with individual liberty and sincerity. Sentimentalism had not anticipated the kind of contractual emotional availability that became an essential feature of civil society after 1815. Its necessity was widely denounced and inspired outpourings of cynicism and satire throughout the first half of the nineteenth century. But the new sense of a generalized human frailty took much of the bite out of this cynicism. It was no surprise that things were going badly. There was grudging acceptance, driven in part by the belief that another reign of terror was the likely alternative. This reluctant acceptance gradually sank roots and made it possible for the contract-based order to survive.

In addition, in the private sphere, individuals were expected to have clear feelings and preferences and to pursue them in an orderly fashion. Those who fell short of this individualistic ideal could find little help navigating the shoals of the new order. We find ample traces of deep ambivalence about marriage: Descoutures, M and Mme Santerre, young M and Mme Gogue, the widow H*** who married in Scotland – all showed their uncertainty, all improvised idiosyncratic arrangements, not without difficulty and pain. Morteuil and the widow Tierce (see Appendix B), each in a different way, struggled against the loneliness of old age. Many men simply failed to find anything fulfilling in the private sphere and turned to alcoholism and violence. But over all, this was a more flexible, and more survivable, regime than that which the sentimentalists had attempted to build.

Not the least of its strengths was the linkage of contractual relationships with emotional flexibility. Critics of the regime were quick to point out that a society based on freedom of contract was a society based on the competitive pursuit of gain, and that the motive of gain was imposed on all, despite its spiritual shallowness, despite the fact that many were ill-equipped to join the fray. But compared with the Terror, when norms required the patriotic selflessness of all, the post-1815 regime of contractual freedom and competition allowed those operating in the public or the marketplace a wide margin for exploring and adopting emotional postures, without embracing them absolutely. At the same time, it allowed retreat into the private sphere, where motives and emotions were less subject to scrutiny. It must be said that this margin for emotional maneuver was much more readily available to the wealthy than to the poor, to men than to women. Nonetheless, critics who wished to undo the evils of the profit motive continued to call for transformations that would entail greater emotional discipline, and such calls continued to inspire, for many, only fear of a return to the Terror.

From the 1820s down to the present, and not just in France, debates over capitalism have continued to fall into the same confusion. Restriction or elimination of contractual relationships in favor of other forms of reciprocity have continually been conceived as entailing greater, rather than lesser, emotional control by the state, to supplement a "natural" or just emotional commitment that has been corrupted by capitalism. This is the very essence of what has been called "totalitarianism" in the twentieth century, a label which, however inadequate in some regards, is sound in targeting excessive state encroachment on the self. The concept of emotives will have served its purpose if it contributes even slightly to the rethinking of this false dichotomy. The challenge is to conceive of emotional management regimes that are less strict, less dependent on civic coordination, virtuous selflessness, perfect public sincerity, rather than more.

Conclusion

As this case study of the French Revolution and its aftermath shows, the theory of emotives makes possible a new kind of historical explanation. The differential effects of emotives can explain the success of some emotional regimes, the failure of others, and therefore help us to understand how real states and real social orders come and go. I have shown that there is a great deal at stake in the emotional regimes that come to govern our lives and our sense of self. Some may provide a measure of emotional liberty that renders them tolerable, even when they treat emotional flexibility as a sign of weakness and expect individuals to conceal deviations that are, in practice, ubiquitous. Others, which aim at universal liberation, may require an inflexible regimentation of emotions that ensures their downfall. The concept of emotional liberty gives political meaning back to history and allows us to discern, in the past, the trail of a succession of experiments with emotional regimes.

EMOTIONS IN WESTERN COMMON SENSE

Embrace of this theory means moving far from the prevailing Western common sense about emotions. But such movement, after a long period of blockage, already appears well under way in many fields of research. Why have emotions come on the agenda only now? What is at stake in the working out of a proper theory of emotions? Emotion is a constitutive feature of the Western conception of the self. Like thought, memory, intention, or language, emotion is something the self has by virtue of being a self and without which it would not be a self. In the Western conception, emotions are involuntary, inherently pleasant or unpleasant, and thus they orient the self to perform certain actions or to maintain certain dispositions. The involuntary character of emotions and their inherent "valence" (pleasantness or unpleasantness) are associated with the role they are assigned in motivation. In Western common sense, strong emotions are linked to a person's high-priority goals, and it would be difficult to conceive of a person having high-priority goals without at the same time having strong feelings about those goals. The involuntary character of the emotions supporting a high-priority goal and their inherent pleasant or unpleasant quality ensure that the goal is not neglected (Frank 1988). The involuntary character of emotions is the basis of their polyvalent quality, their mystery. From one vantage point, our emotions are that which we most deeply espouse as our own; yet at times they appear to be external forces that rob us of our capacity for reflection or action. The power of emotions to overcome will is sometimes attributed to their biological roots: like pain, cold, or the desire to breathe, emotions override our current plans because, it is said, evolution has programmed strong emotional responses into the organism for its own safekeeping. In other cases a quite opposite explanation is put forward. Emotions are said to be involuntary because of their sublime origin, emanating from a core of authenticity that is not available to consciousness. In countless modern stories, of love or of coming of age, a feeling – of love, anxiety, determination, or despair – guides hero or heroine, often against his or her better judgment, toward a spiritually significant, or life-fulfilling choice.

In view of their importance in our commonsense conceptions of self, it is curious that emotions have received so little attention from scholars in the social sciences and the humanities until very recently. For a long time, our common sense supported a certain division of labor among the disciplines that assigned emotions to the sphere of psychology. But this is not the whole explanation for their neglect. In psychology itself, emotions drew little attention. Behaviorists and later cognitive psychologists working in the lab did not, until after 1970, see any way to approach them. Clinical psychologists, following Freud's lead, regarded emotions as relatively unimportant in themselves. Freud was ambiguous about their exact role, but was widely read as regarding emotions as of only surface significance. A fear of elevators, for example, might result from a childhood experience of being trapped in a closet. The resulting belief that elevators were a trap, although combated and partially repressed by the conscious mind, is nonetheless powerful enough to enter consciousness at the sight of an elevator and there to elicit fear reactions. Fear itself, by this view, is not unconscious, only the belief about elevators and its "irrational" source in early experience are. (For discussion of Freud's views, see Ortony, Clore, & Collins 1988:176; Erdelyi 1990, 1992; Clore 1994; Zajonc 1994:294; Chodorow 1999.) Clinical psychologists' interests were absorbed by such unconscious beliefs, the processes by which they were masked or expressed, and their contribution to the dynamic development of personality. Emotions in this context appeared to be straightforward in their operation, possibly biological responses to conscious or unconscious content, and not worthy of investigation in their own right. As a result, even the discipline to which emotions seemed to belong had little to say about them (Gergen 1995).

The disinterest of clinical psychologists may help to explain why emotions were also neglected by cultural anthropologists until the late 1970s. Cultural interpretation drew on psychoanalysis in the early stages of its development; like clinical psychologists, anthropologists such as Malinowski, Mead, Bateson, or Lévi-Strauss focused on the ideational structure of symbolic systems. Affect did not emerge as a theme in its own right (Levy 1984:214–215). The few ethnographies before 1975 that dealt with emotion tended to consider only whether emotions were highlighted or muted by cultural norms. Briggs (1970) demonstrated that anger played no role in Inuit family life. Likewise Levy, in his pioneer work on the Society Islands (Levy 1973, 1984), suggested cultures might render specific emotions either prominent ("hypercognized") or suppressed ("hypocognized"). The impression was that emotions themselves were a fixed factor, lying outside the purview of ethnography. Geertz (1973:360–411) demonstrated that Balinese symbolic systems for naming persons and situating them in time and space denied individuals any reason to feel, and Balinese rules for interpersonal conduct offered them no acceptable way to express feeling. The only feeling he found evidence of was what he called "stage fright," a fear of making a slip in performance. However, Geertz's work was important in suggesting that emotional experience was perfectly malleable, perhaps itself constituted by culture. M. Rosaldo (1980, 1984), following out the implications of Geertz's work, proposed one of the first, fully constructionist views of emotions.

The broad influence that poststructuralist theory achieved in a number of disciplines beginning in the late 1970s, and peaking around 1990, brought little change to the general picture of neglect of emotions.

In retrospect, this is rather surprising. Posing as a root-and-branch critique of the Western conception of the subject and of subjectivity, poststructuralism denied the existence – except as a byproduct of certain discursive structures – of intention, experience, choice, perception, and desire. Even the presence of other persons was a metaphysical illusion, by Derrida's accounting. To Foucault, the "self" was not something that could be free or imprisoned but a product of certain discursive and disciplinary orders – the self was the prison to be escaped from. But to make such a radical attack on Western common sense while saying nothing of emotions is peculiar to say the least.

To be sure, by the late 1980s, Harré (1986), Abu-Lughod (1986), Lutz (1988), and other anthropologists (e.g., Lynch [1990]; Grima [1992]) had stepped in to fill the gap. They drew explicitly on Foucault to justify a strong constructionist stance vis-à-vis emotions. Like everything else about the Western self, emotions, they insisted, were merely discursive in origin and constituted yet another site where power was surreptitiously exercised over us. Among these new anthropologists of emotion, the strongest constructionists took a feminist stance. M. Rosaldo, Abu-Lughod, Lutz, Grima, and others focused on emotions for two reasons. (1) The peculiar constraints and advantages that women faced in the field often gave them privileged access to evidence about this neglected topic. (2) Demonstrating the cultural origin of emotion made possible a critique of the prevalent Western common sense that women were inherently more emotional than men – historically one of the most important justifications for the exclusion of women from public life and for their domination by men within the family.

Among historians and literary critics, as well, feminist concerns were at the root of a relatively independent discovery of emotions. As in anthropology, without the new probing of the history and cultural construction of gender, the issue of emotions might well have remained in the shadows. By the mid-1990s, however, as the review of eighteenth-century sentimentalism in Chapter 5 shows, recent work had placed emotions at the very top of the agenda in many fields. (See, in addition to citations mentioned in Chapter 5, Stearns & Lewis [1998], for a broad sampling of work in U.S. history.)

In the meantime, a reaction against theory in general has set in; and even among those who still uphold the importance of explicit theoretical discussion, many have drawn back from the constant generation of formalisms and coining of new terms that went along with the poststructuralist struggle to dismantle and replace a corrupted Western common sense.

There is considerable irony in this trend. One element of Western common sense about the self cries out for special theoretical treatment in its own right. This is the one element that has been most neglected – and neglected not only in the twentieth century, not only by post-structuralism, but since the erasure of sentimentalism at the beginning of the contemporary era. Yet emotions are no sooner placed, at last, on the research agenda, than a cloud of suspicion falls across everything new and innovative. Vincent Crapanzano in a short essay of 1992 recognized the need to treat emotions differently from other features of the self such as language or behavior; but he immediately dismissed the idea of a theoretical formulation to satisfy this need:

> I do not claim that such utterances as "I love you" or "I am angry at you" are explicit performatives ... but they do have considerable illocutionary force. They do bring about through their very utterance a change in the context of that utterance. . . . Their very utterance is taken as a manifestation, a symptom, of the condition – the emotion – they are said to be describing, in a way which is simply not true of the third person propositions. It is as though their referentiality looped over onto itself and became at once its own object and yet, through some sort of topological contortion, other than itself. Were we not appalled by the idea of creating yet another linguistic category, we would call such locutions "symptomatizers." . . . It is as though their presumed referentiality – in Peirce's terms, their symbolicity, their semanticity slips into a sort of symptomatology – into, again in Peirce's terms, an immediate indexicality. (Crapanzano 1992:234–235)

Here Crapanzano glimpsed the whole project of this study. Rather than being "appalled by the idea of creating yet another linguistic category," however, I insist that emotion is the one concept that has most needed theoretical interrogation, that has most – and most mysteriously – suffered from theoretical neglect in our long Western examination of the self (see Meyer 1991). Emotional expression does have a "looped" sort of referentiality; but, unlike performatives, the loop is not direct. It does indeed pass through "some sort of topological contortion." Furthermore, I contend that what it passes through (i.e., activated thought material and attention, as described in Chapter 3) represents a door out of the poststructuralist dead end, an emergency exit, that allows us to refound and reconceptualize the self, not in the form of "subjectivity," not by means of a Cartesian dualism between mind and matter, but in the form of an extraordinarily rich "double-anchored" field (Wikan

1990), a field in which agency finds its proper place and in reference to which freedom (and historical change) again become meaningful.

THE THEORY OF EMOTIVES

Mental control is an inescapable facet of thought, because attention has limited capacity. So recent research in cognitive psychology would suggest. Individuals may marshal any of a wide array of processing strategies depending on the kind of cognitive task that is before them. Accomplishment of cognitive tasks equally depends on the exclusion of possible competing tasks or thoughts, to avoid the degradation of performance that results from cognitive "load." Exclusion of thoughts from attention is, however, an ironic process. Outside attention, thought material may lie in states of greater or lesser readiness to enter attention, levels of "activation" that offer attention ways of moving forward. The current strategies that guide attention, including mental control strategies, determine which of the overwhelming array of currently activated thoughts will gain access to attention's intense transformative activity.

While I acknowledge the force of the many critiques of dualism that have been made in the last century, including the poststructuralist critique, I still believe that the findings of psychological research can be highly instructive. It is quite possible to restate these findings in terms free of dualistic implications by drawing on the notion of "translation" as it has been developed by philosophers including Quine, Davidson, and Alcoff. Viewed in this way, the notions of activation, attention, and mental control refer to the ways in which a formidable, multiply-parallel work of translation is carried out in the waking life of every human being. Such translation remains indeterminate. But, because it is happening *within* the individual rather than between individuals, the indeterminacy involved gives back to the individual richness and creativity. Navigating the sea of activated thought material involves agency, making possible the acceptance of interpretations of the world and goals to go with them, as well as conversions, when those interpretations and goals are traded for others.

In poststructuralist theory, the relation between *langue* (language) and *parole* (utterance) is dialectical. An utterance is endowed with the capacity to reveal structure by a deferral, a delay that gives the utterance unity, from beginning to end, and allows parts and their relationships to emerge from this unity. An utterance can, in this way, seem to convey meaning or to be driven by an intention. But both the unity and the structure are arbitrary. It is this arbitrariness that serves as the foundation of the poststructuralist critique of the "subject." The Western sense of subjectivity, of being an individual with subjective perceptions and experiences is, in the poststructuralist critique, neither right nor wrong, merely one arbitrary way of determining the unity behind utterances.

In my view, the poststructuralist concept of the sign, because it entails operating with only one code at a time, is by far inferior to the concept of translation (developed to address the same difficulties that preoccupied poststructuralists). An utterance occurs not just in the context of a single background code, but also in the presence of material available in many other codes: not just sensory codes (visual, aural, etc., "inputs"), but also procedural codes. Languages may be viewed as one important type of procedural code; others include social or relational codes, such as codes of propriety, rank, dress, hairstyles, gesture, command. Translation is indeterminate in that it always involves the reduction of material in one code to the terms of another. But attention is never prisoner of these reductions; attention can decide that a translation is inadequate, for example, a translation of visual material into (say) a linguistic code involving only two color terms. Attention can revise translations; it can devise new codes.

Research in cognitive psychology has also shown that emotions are virtually indistinguishable from cognition itself, just as they have shown that cognition is not made up of a single pathway of successive "automatic" processes. To make sense of this confusing but abundant research, Barnett and Ratner (1997) have begun speaking of "cogmotion." I propose that emotion lexicons actually offer ways of talking about, of "describing," the landscape of activations that currently presents itself to attention. Cognitive states, the tasks of translation under way, the array of activations that are resulting, the relative successes or failures of ongoing mental control efforts – these are what we talk about when a person asks us "How do you feel?" Our answers have immediate rebound effects on what they "describe"; as we hear ourselves speak them, or rehearse them in our speech center (by laying out possible utterances in an appropriate code), they give rise to yet further, new activations. The ironies of mental control, as described by Wegner and his associates (Wegner 1994, 1997; Wegner & Smart 1997; Wegner & Gold 1995), make it highly likely that statements about how we feel will activate thought material that conforms with the statement (and therefore confirms the statement). However, if such statements are used to produce appropriate activations, when such activations are inherently weak, mental control may easily fail, as when the "deep activation," as Wegner and Smart (1997) call it, of contradictory material makes it readily available to attention.

Statements about how we feel deserve a special term; I have proposed the term "emotives." Like the "performatives" of speech-act theory, they do things to the world. However, the world they operate in is richer than J. L. Austin's world. Austin, to understand performatives, had to allow the existence of social contexts that determine whether performative utterances are happy or not. To say "I do" happily, one must be at a proper wedding, in the presence of someone authorized to say, happily, "I now pronounce you man and wife." The world emotives operate in includes more. This world includes attention; activated thought material; and translation as the fundamental task of attention. In this sense the concept of "emotives" is quite a departure from speech-act theory.

Use of emotives makes possible a kind of fugitive management of one's states. It offers attention a kind of feedback loop, an external means of influencing activated thought material that often enhances the effectiveness of internal strategies of mental control. When one makes an emotion claim in the presence of another, one hears the words, one sees the other's reception of the claim, one feels one's face contracting in suggestive ways. These social and proprioceptive "inputs" create or alter activations, often in ways that confirm or enhance the state that is "described." Emotives can thus be used as tools for arriving at desired states. However, their effects are unpredictable; they represent an attempt at translating that is always inadequate. Rather than confirming the state described, they may produce the opposite effect or no effect. Rather than facilitating the achievement of current goals, they may result in activations that force the revision or rejection of those goals. (One can easily imagine a scenario like the following: A friend asks, "Do you feel guilty about leaving your spouse?" One answers, "No, I don't feel guilty," and immediately the claim backfires, activating intense remorse, leading to a decision to stay with the marriage.) Because of the unpredictable effects of emotives, it is better to think of them as allowing a kind of navigation, but that special kind of navigation in which changes of course can alter the charts, that special kind of navigation in which the port we seek may, as a result, change its position.

Anthropologists have shown that emotion lexicons, emotion claims, and scenarios for acting out emotions are ubiquitous features of social life. Many anthropologists employ a constructionist method (whether or not they espouse a fully poststructuralist theory of emotions). Such methods have allowed them to appreciate the extraordinary variety of affects humans have created. However, even the most constructionist ethnographies contain evidence that communities systematically seek to train emotions, to idealize some, to condemn others. Emotions are subjected to normative judgments and those who achieve emotional ideals are admired and endowed with authority. This evidence offers strong confirmation of the theory of emotives. The shaping power of emotives is so significant that no human community can afford to ignore it. Emotives are therefore of the highest political significance. To make sense of how communities tend to shape the emotional management of their members, I propose a series of corollary concepts, the concepts of emotional liberty, emotional suffering, emotional effort, induced goal conflict, emotional regime, and emotional refuge.

High-priority goals and emotions are closely related because a goal that is deeply espoused has many associations; it may be closely connected with other important goals as well as with subsidiary and short-term goals of various types. Emotional claims are often made in contexts of goal conflict. One wants to go camping, but bears have been seen in the woods. "I'm not afraid of bears" – the claim, if it is effective, will facilitate proceeding with the plan. If it is only marginally effective, the goal conflict remains activated. Emotional suffering results. To sustain pursuit of one goal in the face of such suffering requires effort. Emotional liberty is a capacity to respond to emotive effects, wherever they lead, to drop goals or espouse new ones as appropriate, so as to minimize emotional suffering. Emotional norms are often enforced by induced goal conflict. On Nukulaelae, fear of gossip will induce goal conflict when one wants to express anger. On Bali, fear of black magic will induce goal conflict when one contemplates expressing grief. In Paris, under the Terror, fear of the guillotine would have induced goal conflict in any person inclined to display arrogance in a sectional assembly. The complex of practices that establish a set of emotional norms and that sanction those who break them

I call an "emotional regime." Most emotional regimes, it would appear, offer venues where norms are relaxed, where the ironies of mental control can be allowed to hold sway; these emotional refuges may or may not provide staging grounds for historical challenges to existing regimes. An ideal emotional regime would be that which allowed the greatest possible emotional liberty.

EMOTIONS IN THE BIRTH OF MODERNITY: FRANCE, 1680–1848

There has been a great deal of discussion in recent years of early modern European civility or etiquette. (See, e.g., Elias 1978; Greenblatt 1980; Gordon 1994; Martin 1997; Muchembled 1998.) While many issues remain in dispute, there is a sufficiently clear chronology already in place. The new standard of "civility" emerged in the princely courts of Renaissance Italy as a terrain of emotional compromise between the liberty of urban citizen (or feudal vassal) on the one hand, and the new power to command of the Renaissance despot on the other. The multiplicity of skills and the ready obedience that rulers required of their immediate servants at court were displayed with a facade of nonchalance (*disinvoltura*), ease, and grace that symbolized the freedom and self-determination, in the last instance, of the otherwise obedient courtier. This facade was more than a facade, however. Many, including the influential Baldassare Castiglione, embraced nonchalance as, in effect, an uplifting standard. Infused with nonchalance, elaborate court ceremonial and etiquette and the elaborate tasks imposed by high office or diplomatic missions became a liberated way of life, a moral ideal. The skills and obedience of the courtier appeared as a freely chosen "self-fashioning," an ideal that could, as in Thomas More's case, lead on to martyrdom. Thus, the requirement of nonchalance entailed invisible but real limits on the kinds of ceremony and the extent of obedience a ruler might impose.

These limits were, perhaps, pushed as far as they could go – or even further – at the court of Versailles and in those many courts of the so-called absolute monarchs where Versailles was imitated, toward the end of the seventeenth century. The failure of the English monarchy to develop in this direction as well as the emergence of new types of emotional refuge in France after 1660 set the stage for the elaboration of the new emotional style of sentimentalism.

Sentimentalism achieved the status of a kind of political and personal common sense by the 1780s. New emotional practices took shape at the same time as new ideas about emotions. The egalitarian salon, the Masonic lodge, the intense friendships and correspondence networks of the "republic of letters" offered direct, practical relief from the hierarchical, honorable comportment of court and public ceremonial. Shaftesbury's critique of Locke, insisting on the existence of an inborn moral sense that made itself felt as virtuous impulses of sentiment, was quickly taken up in England and France alike, by thinkers as diverse as Hutcheson, Marivaux, and Diderot. With the appearance of the novels of Richardson and Rousseau in mid-century, the elaboration of the new "drame bourgeois," and the new styles of painting and opera popularized by Greuze and Gluck, sentimentalist ideas and practices gained a prominence and popularity of unprecedented scope. In the context of the aristocratic or gentry household, as depicted in hundreds of novels from *Pamela* to *La nouvelle Héloïse* to *Paul et Virginie* or *Sense and Sensibility*, sentimentalism constituted a liberatory political and emotional ideology. The emotional suffering of spouses in arranged marriages, the emotional suffering of domestic servants raped with impunity by their masters, of young educated men and women without fortune, of lovers separated by a gulf of wealth or birth, of young women consigned to convents by their parents, of orphans, widows, and aging spinsters – all these political evils were explored and denounced before an expanding and avid reading public. Similar messages were conveyed by painting, song, opera. Sentimentalism began to transform the personal relationships of a narrow elite of insiders, such as Jeanne-Marie Phlipon and Jean-Marie Roland, and to have effects (difficult now to gauge) on a broader public.

In the context of the absolutist state, as well, sentimentalism delivered a clear, liberatory political message. In France, the king's extrajudicial powers, as embodied in, for example, *lettres de cachet*; his favoritism; his exorbitant luxury; his debauchery – all compatible with the old facade of aristocratic etiquette – were decried in novels, plays, libelous pamphlets, and lawyers' briefs. The sentimentalist ideal of simple sincerity and egalitarian empathy offered one of the most important standards by which the monarchy was judged and found wanting in the years before the Revolution. By this time, Rousseau had shown how to combine sentimental emotionalism and civic virtue; even Louis XVI and his ministers began to portray themselves as both publicly accountable and empathetically benevolent.

But the great weakness of sentimentalism was its naturalism, the doctrine that emotional sensitivity constituted an inborn moral sense. Those who espoused this doctrine often used emotives to train themselves to feel intense, "natural," and morally good sentiments. Their success seemed to confirm the new doctrine. Tears of empathy, transports of friendship and love, a studied simplicity of dress and manner became so many badges of moral worth. Novels, plays, operas, letters between friends became so many occasions for tearful display of natural sensitivity. Of course, some devotees of this style were better than others at conforming to its norms, and those who were less convincing came to be regarded with contempt or suspicion. Both among those who embraced this style of emotional management and among those who found it distasteful, concern with insincerity, as a result, became a growing preoccupation after 1770 or so. Belief in the natural origin of good feeling resulted in oversimplified and overly optimistic hopes for political reform. Simple peasants came to be seen as possessing a natural capacity for civic virtue. In general, reform seemed to involve the sweeping away of impediments to natural feeling, rather than the establishment of protective norms. At the same time, suspicion of the insincere gave a tinge of Manicheism to the political thinking of the period, a sense that goodness was locked in conflict with evil. After the French Revolution got underway and sought to establish the rule of natural sentiment, its leaders had great difficulty distinguishing between reasonable dissent and evil, dissembling opposition. The Manichean tendency that can be glimpsed here and there in the pre-Revolutionary years multiplied a hundredfold. After all, natural sentiment ought produce perfect consensus among good citizens (as Couthon claimed it did in Puy-de-Dôme in August 1793). Dissent was inevitable in a time of sweeping change of government and civil legislation. But, thanks in part to the illusions of sentimentalism, dissent could only find expression in the form of civil war, just as war came to be promoted by some as a stimulant to citizens' natural, patriotic benevolence. In this somber context, even Revolutionary leaders who agreed on fundamentals, and who shared laudable records of political heroism, could not refrain from executing each other over minor differences of interest or policy. The Terror was, in this sense, just as much an expression of sentimentalism as were the lachrymose operas of Gluck or the tear-stained letters of Julie de Lespinasse or Jeanne-Marie Roland. However, by 1792 the induced emotional suffering caused by the guillotine and the rising tide of civil conflict began undermining the ability of sentimentalists to believe in themselves. It was in response to this failure, to this rapidly spreading recognition of insincerity, of ambivalence, of uncertainty, that the Terror was brought to a close. In 1794–1795, a failure of translation came to be broadly recognized. A certain sentimentalist "discourse" came to be seen as wrong or false. Use of this discourse in political contexts was abruptly terminated. Here was a discourse that could not construct its world, an effort at "self-fashioning" that broke down, spectacularly.

The end of the Terror and the rise of the Napoleonic dictatorship brought a new emotional regime no one could have foreseen. Sentimentalist doctrines were proscribed; their defense by Staël, Bernardin de Saint Pierre, and a few others was regarded with ill-concealed distaste. In their place a new democratized code of honor was rapidly elaborated – and hastily reconciled with Adam Smith's invisible hand of self-interest – to create a vision of a new, male sphere of public endeavor and private enrichment. The rapid erasure of sentimentalism may, in fact, reflect efforts at mental control, attempts to remove from attention disappointed beliefs and feelings too painful to remember. If so, the success of these attempts has left its (negative) trace on the historical record down to this day.

The Civil Code of 1804 provided a legal framework for this new male sphere of action. But, almost before the ink was dry on the law books, Maine de Biran and others were beginning to challenge the narrow conception of self-interest that the Code enshrined in favor of a spiritual, yet secular conception of human reason. If reason was the uplifting element in human nature, they believed, its rather limited influence on human history reflected the large, countervailing impact of physiology, environment, appetite, imagination, and passion. Reason was weak; the human constitution was frail. Careful "psychological" introspection revealed a disordered terrain of impulses, moods, bodily influences, fears, and illusions. This terrain could be explored by artists. Illusions of happiness might be pursued (prudently) in private life. But practical affairs, involving property, commerce, politics, and honor, went better if reason held sway, aided (not supplanted) by certain "echoing" moral sentiments. By the 1820s, this sort of thinking was being taught in the universities, promulgated in newspapers like *Le Globe*, used by barristers arguing cases before the courts, and widely applied by memoirists and diarists in their private contemplations. The emotive training that (inadvertently) resulted encouraged them to see themselves as weak, changeable. Weakness,

when confirmed, easily led on to sadness, melancholy, fear of humiliation. The history of the Enlightenment and the Revolution was recon-
ceptualized with sentimentalism left out. The emotional flexibility of
certain male public actors – notably barristers and politicians – con-
ferred prestige and authority, but also attracted the cynical gazes of
those imbued with the new, pessimistic vision of human possibilities.
In the private realm, sentimentalist conceptions often lived on, especially among literate women who continued to read the masterpieces
of the previous era. Although deprived of their intellectual grounding,
sentimentalist emotives continued to shape many lives. George Sand's
effort to mount a latter-day sentimentalist challenge against the new
conception of human frailty was admired but persuaded few. For many
men, doubtless, recognition that their claims to special authority were
poorly grounded only deepened their sense of personal fragility and
their nagging fear of humiliation.

The advantage of the pessimistic outlook was that it lowered expectations and tolerated greater deviation from norms. The advantage of
the new democratized honor code was that it seconded this toleration
with its own indulgence toward any deviation that was properly concealed. The new order was in this way, at least, more in line with our
real, our great, natural legacy, that is our plasticity – the very hallmark,
not of weakness, but of intelligence itself. The theory of emotives gives
a logic, a coherence to the curve of events, a partial answer to the
question why.

The theory of emotives also allows us to appreciate both the new
regime's strengths and its shortcomings. Civil litigation records reveal
some of the kinds of emotional suffering that the Romantic management regime systematically inflicted. The economy of the time was still
based largely on exploitation of landed property. Management of marriage and inheritance remained the most important avenue by which
the young acquired wealth and status, even mere access to gainful
work. There was ample occasion, as a result, for marriage contracts and
wills to run roughshod over emotional norms that required mutual
affection and love among family members. The new democratized code
of honor provided heads of families great freedom to make private
arrangements that violated public norms, on condition that they maintain a discreet secrecy about them. Married men and women often lived
apart and even acquired new, stable love relationships, quietly and
without scandal. But it was essential that the husband at least acqui-
esce in such arrangements. Law endowed him with the power to dis-

cipline his wife, as well as to dictate her place of residence, whereas women enjoyed no say over their husbands' sexual practices, so long as they were performed outside the home. If a married woman wanted to make a new life for herself, over her husband's objection, she had only a few difficult options: (1) pursuit of a grounds for separation (such as proof of cruelty or of public insult by the husband); (2) absolute secrecy; (3) flight. The records reveal cases of women who tried all three of these unpalatable options, with greater or lesser success. Inheritance disputes uncover the intense dislikes, fears, and jealousies which the sharing of property among family members often provoked. The stakes could be very high and the disappointments and animosities intense.

Emotional suffering in the world of commerce and public affairs also left its traces in the records. Disputes over contractual and employment relationships reveal the extraordinary power one party often exercised over the other. An estate agent's years of loyalty, even amidst Revolutionary upheavals, might win him nothing, or even public denunciation, from his former masters. The mutual trust necessary to property or debt transactions rendered the parties vulnerable to sudden, sharp setbacks. This was as true of small property owners as it was of large-scale merchants, stockbrokers, and financiers.

The kinds of suffering revealed by civil litigation can hardly be considered a complete catalog; too many segments of the population were effectively excluded from using the courts, not only by high costs, but also by fear of damage to their reputations. A tailor to the rich could not afford to sue one of his customers, for fear of losing all the others. Nor could a sharecropper contemplate suing her landlord, not if she hoped to find another. Records of special courts set up to deal with worker complaints reveal that plaintiffs seldom if ever stayed on with the same employer, whether they won or lost (Reddy 1984). Still other forms of suffering, such as those of young children in elite boarding schools and colleges, can only be accessed by means of memoirs and letters (Houbre 1997; Reddy 1997b:31–32; Caron 1999).

There can be little doubt that the new, laissez-faire society of the nineteenth century, because it was more tolerant, more flexible, offered greater emotional liberty than either the Old Regime or the Revolutionary period. At the same time it was a harsh and discouraging order for many, if not most, of its citizens. The individual freedom on which this social order based its legitimacy was only a rarefied abstraction for them, a reproach that rankled, an ideal which social practice travestied rather than approximating. The new order's stability was only relative. Nearly constant repression of political expression, broken by occasional episodes of revolutionary conflict and rapid change, yielded grudgingly to a gradual easing of rigid standards as the century grew old.

WIDER IMPLICATIONS

Just as the concept of emotives and the related notion of emotional liberty can shed new light on the history of one society's transition to modernity, so they can open new perspectives on problems of great current concern.

The concept of emotives makes it clear why human beings live in a perpetual state of uncertainty about themselves. Emotion claims can be neither true nor false; instead they are more or less successful attempts to alter or stabilize, explore or pledge. The reach of attention is small. The activity of translation it can carry out is limited and indeterminate, while the scope of a linked array of thought material – thoughts that may be activated together as a "feeling" – can be much broader. The scope of material not currently activated is broader still, and the range of codes in which it is stored or received is staggering, while the thoughts that serve as current goals are inherently beyond the reach of attention. There is necessarily a sense of open-endedness, of lack of resolution, in being a "double-anchored" self. Communities, for the same reason, are characterized by diversity first. Likeness, similarity, the capacity to mutually comprehend – these are accomplishments which must be constantly revised and renewed. Such accomplishments emerge against the ever-present background of unpredictability and peculiarity constituted by a collection of selves viewed in isolation from each other, viewed in terms of their own unpredictable, incorrigible resistance to emotional management styles. Such incorrigibility is not weakness; it stems from the indeterminacy of translation. Community life must constitute not only a process of ongoing negotiation and pursuit of consensus (not because of conflicting interests, but because of the open-endedness of selves). It must also include a collective effort to prescribe, or at least to establish models of, emotional management. By sharing management styles, those for whom the prescribed emotives are effective constitute a core of mutually comprehensible actors capable of superior cooperation and coordination of effort. History leaves no doubt that such styles empower those who share them and who find them effective. The stakes are often very high; the very survival of a community is frequently at issue. This was surely the case in the spring of 1792, for example, when Brissot rose before the French National Assembly to call for the reconstruction of the army on the basis of patriotic volunteer units. There can hardly be any doubt that, by one means or another, the precepts of sentimentalism were widely enough shared by 1792 that raw volunteers could coordinate their actions with the help of an emotional style, even though they had had virtually no training as units and little knowledge of each other. Such styles are best communicated by means of sensory-rich participatory performances: ritual, predication, theater. But they may also be conveyed, or suggested, by literature, art, music, iconography, architecture, dress. All such practices and products can be viewed as emotive in character. The subject matter of virtually all the disciplines of the humanities and social sciences can fruitfully be analyzed from this perspective.

In view of the high stakes of achieving collective emotional management styles, it is not surprising that such styles almost always employ induced emotional suffering as a tool to enhance conformity to one degree or another. Emotional suffering, derived from goal conflict, affects all those who might be subject to a penalty, not just those few who are singled out for coercion, imprisonment, exile, torture, or death. Such suffering will, for many, enhance the confirming effect of official emotives. Emotives are therefore essential to understanding the political significance of ideology, law, state ritual, coercion, and violence. The legitimacy of a specific regime may, in turn, be measured in terms of its openness to the full character of selfhood, openness to its unpredictability, to its always unfinished quality. A regime that is so open is one in which a greater number of individuals will feel at ease. At the same time, there are obviously many stable intermediary points. History offers many examples of management styles that combine a judicious mixture of coercion and liberty, that have allowed generations of adherents to navigate life with adequate stability, that have allowed the development of marginal refuges for deviance, and that therefore constitute landmarks on the terrain of the past.

The prospect of the French Revolution and its subsequent ramifications suggests that emotional liberty cannot be achieved by any disconnect between means and ends; emotional liberty is emotional liberty; only emotional liberty propagates emotional liberty. This is not to say that public action, contestation, or resistance have no role to play in the pursuit of emotional liberty. It is important to recognize, however, how quickly emotional suffering can propagate within a movement aimed at liberation, when loyalty and violence come into play – that is, when induced emotional suffering becomes a tool for organizing the movement itself – as occurred in France in 1789–1793, with disastrous results.

CLOSING THE CIRCLE

This study has traced out the greater part of a circle, not quite closed. We began by noting that a certain conception of emotions as physiological in character has broken down; we ended by examining the consolidation of the modern form of this conception almost two centuries ago. The gap from the "psychological" introspection Victor Cousin described in his lessons of 1828 to the current research in cognitive psychology examined in Chapter 1 is in some ways vast, in others, relatively minor. I have tried to show that an entirely new conception of emotions can be built in a space opened up once we confront the weaknesses both of modern Cartesian dualism and of its principal critics, the poststructuralists. This space is constituted by the indeterminacy of translation and the recognition that translation is the principal activity of "cognition," *within* the individual. It is the space between attention's limited capacity and the vast array of thoughts in various codes, in various states of activation, available to attention at all times, a space we must navigate by means of the imperfect strategies of mental control. Here "emotions" come to life, to vex, enlighten, guide, encumber, to reveal goal conflicts we have overlooked, to aid us in overlooking others. When we speak of such matters, we inevitably alter their configuration. When we "describe" this space through which we are obliged to navigate, we change its map. This is a frustrating, paradoxical sea whose shape is of the utmost importance. It is central to individual identity and, therefore, to community life and to politics. I have tried to show how a certain conception of emotional liberty can help us to evaluate the emotional styles that communities and states attempt to impose on their members. These emotional "regimes" may make navigation easier or more difficult; minimizing human suffering inevitably entails that we seek ways to make navigation – which will never be a simple matter – as easy as we can. From this perspective, it is possible to judge the political merits or demerits of any regime.

Examining the political history of emotional regimes in France across the Revolutionary divide reveals that many French in the eighteenth century believed sentimentalism would guide them to a new and unprecedented kind of emotional liberty. This belief went to the scaffold with Robespierre, Couthon, and Saint-Just on 28 July 1794. The modern dualist conception of emotions, formulated in reaction against this stunning failure, lowered expectations, allowing greater flexibility, but at the cost of imposing a painful burden: a systematic, pessimistic underestimation of our capacity for self-determination. Poststructuralists revealed this pessimistic dualism to be a mere construct, but they threw out the baby with the bath water, selfhood along with subjectivity. The theory of emotives recovers for us a vast (if limited) sphere of endeavor, through which we may navigate with a full set of sails.

APPENDIX A

Detailed Review of Anomalous Cases
from the Gazette des Tribunaux *Sample*

Note: *Case numbers refer to the listing of the sampled cases in Table 1.*

CASE NO. 5. *CREDITORS OF SANDRIÉ-VINCOURT V. THE GOVERNING BOARD OF THE PARIS BROKERS ASSOCIATION.* Sandrié-Vincourt, a licensed broker (agent de change) of the Paris Bourse (stock and bond market), ceased payments on his debts in 1823 after illegally trading on his own account, with the backing of a number of private lenders who were promised huge profits. The brokers' Governing Board (Chambre syndicale) stepped in to prevent legal proceedings, took control of Sandrié-Vincourt's assets, and began making what payments it could to his creditors. But Sandrié-Vincourt fled the country, and not long afterward, the Governing Board dropped its role in his affairs, forcing creditors to sue in the courts, with little hope of collecting. The creditors therefore sued the Governing Board as well as Sandrié-Vincourt, claiming that the Board had implicitly accepted liability for the bankrupt broker's debts. But the court ruled that the Governing Board, chartered by the state, did not represent, or engage the liability of, the members of the brokers' association, and was not itself a legal entity capable of incurring debts. The debates focused at times on this technical issue, at times on the feelings of betrayal of the creditors when the Board dropped its involvement in the affair, at times on the question of the honor of the Paris brokers' association, and at times on the morality of speculation. Dupin, arguing for the Board, denounced the calumnious charge of bad faith leveled by the creditors. They were nothing but usurers. "Renounce," he ordered them, "your mad accusation, you creditors, or rather you unbridled gamblers who were the cause of the ruin of your debtor" ("Renoncez-donc à votre folle accusation, créanciers ou plutôt joueurs effrénés qui avez été la cause de la ruine de votre débiteur"). Hennequin, arguing for the creditors, decried the "distressing contrast" ("affligeant contraste") between the Board's moralistic stance against gambling and its agents' practices, "enriching themselves in this new palace which the genius of the arts has raised to the genius of man" ("s'enrichissant dans ce nouveau palais que le génie des arts vient d'élever au génie de l'homme"). These points might have carried some weight if the Board had been found to be a contractual agent, acting in the collective name of the brokers. In that case, the issue to be decided would have been the implicit commitment the Board made by intervening, and the faith it inspired in the creditors, who temporarily agreed not to go to court.

CASE NO. 6. *LE COMTE DE MILON DE MESME V. LE MARQUIS DE BRIDIEU.* Under the Jacobin republic (1792–1794), émigrés who had fled the Revolution forfeited all property rights within France; thousands of estates were seized and auctioned off. On 27 April 1825, the Restoration parliament passed an indemnity law to partially repay former émigrés for lost property; the law triggered many lawsuits, resurrecting disputes over events of the 1790s. In this case, the comte de Milon, a high government official (préfet of the Doubs), sued the marquis de Bridieu for nonpayment of the purchase price of a piece of land sold in 1790 for 115,000 francs. The marquis de Bridieu's mother had made the original purchase, which was to be paid off over the following three years. But both Milon and the marquis de Bridieu fled into exile before the final payment was due. Mme de Bridieu remained behind, but in 1793, the government seized her lands and sequestered her papers (which were later lost), after a new law targeted even the parents of émigrés. Now that her son stood to receive compensation, Milon came forward with the allegation of nonpayment in order to claim a share of the government money. But the marquis de Bridieu claimed that his mother had paid Milon in full and received receipts. As it turned out, after the trial got under way, as a result of extensive searches in the files of notaries his mother had used, the marquis finally located these receipts, which his mother had deposited before the land was seized. The pleadings then focused on whether the receipts were valid. But prior to this point, with only Mme de Bridieu's register to indicate payment had been made, the attorneys' rhetoric had been heated. Fontaine, arguing for Bridieu, called down the court's "indignation" and "contempt" on the comte de Milon's "guilty hope." Crousse, for Milon, insisted on the purity of his client's intentions and expressed his astonishment that Bridieu did not come forward with the whole truth. Even after the receipts were found, Crousse claimed they were false, produced by a business agent of Milon's who had been charged with protecting his interests in France. Thus the availability and meaning of documents from a thirty-year-old transaction of the Revolutionary decade, although a technical matter, generated heated emotional charges and countercharges, because documentation had gone astray.

CASE NO. 11. *MME SCHELLINGS V. MARQUIS DE MOLIGNY.* In this case, the indemnity law again played a role; but the dispute was not over events of the 1790s, it was over the validity of Mme Schellings's marriage. She had married a Prussian officer in a Scottish ceremony (as in the case of Mme H*** discussed above) in order to circumvent her mother's opposition to the marriage. On her return to France, her mother and her uncle had contested the validity of the marriage. But a lawsuit was dropped out of fear of public scandal (according to the family's attorney, Berryer fils). The 1825 indemnity law excluded French women who had married foreigners, however; and after its passage, ironically, Mme Schellings's uncle, M de Moligny, sued to block payments of the indemnity to her. In court, he and her mother now insisted on the validity of her marriage, which they had earlier denounced, whereas Mme Schellings herself at first asked the court to pronounce its annulment. In the opening hearing, Mme Schellings changed her position slightly, however; Lavaux, her attorney, recoiling at the idea of publicly arguing for his client's dishonor, only asked the court to say, once and for all, whether or not she was married. "She would happily sacrifice the indemnity," he said, "provided that the court puts an end once and for all to the doubt that surrounds her civil status" ("Elle fera de bon coeur le sacrifice de l'indemnité qu'elle a droit d'obtenir, pourvu que le jugement du Tribunal fasse cesser à jamais les incertitudes de son état"). Thus, the question of the marriage's validity was entirely technical, but the attorneys of both parties expressed their embarrassment at the position they had taken, and each heatedly charged the other side with greedy, self-interested scandalmongering. Miller, speaking for the state, noted that a technicality prevented the court from ruling on Mme Schellings's marriage; at present, he noted, no party had approached the courts to request an annulment, and as a result no annulment could be pronounced. (The *Gazette*'s report on the judgment in the case was not found; it is highly likely the court followed the opinion of the king's attorney, M Miller.) In this instance, what caused the heightened emotional tone of the pleadings was not the legal issues in play, but the embarrassing reversal of positions each party had made, taking stands that appeared incompatible with their family's honor. Protecting reputation, not persuading the court, drove the emotional outbursts.

CASE NO. 12. *MLLE LEROY V. BIDAUT*. In this case, a young woman who had always been known as "Betzi Leroy" claimed that her true civil status was Betzi Bidaut, daughter of a certain Bidaut who had died leaving property worth eighty thousand francs. Bidaut's brother disputed her pretensions, hoping to claim the inheritance for himself. Here, as in the previous case, the issue was strictly technical, but its implications in terms of public reputation encouraged attorneys to make emotional charges against their opponents. Mlle Leroy's mother had married Bidaut in 1793; not long thereafter he abandoned her, pursuing a career as military supplier that required extensive travel and yielded healthy profits. The daughter was born in the Year 10 (1802–1803) and inscribed in the civil register as the daughter of M and Mme Leroy; she and her mother resided in M Leroy's house until the mother's death in 1825. However, it turned out that Leroy had been married to someone else in 1793, and neither he nor Betzi's mother had ever been divorced from their absent spouses. As a result, under law, Betzi was the daughter of M Bidaut, unless Bidaut himself had legally disavowed her within a certain delay, or unless it could be shown that Bidaut had been wholly ignorant of her existence. Bidaut's brother did not even try to show that he was wholly ignorant; Bidaut may well have known of his abandoned wife's whereabouts. Mlle Leroy's attorney, Chaix d'Est-Ange, charged the brother with scheming to keep the husband and wife separate. "This man, who feared a reconciliation, and had formulated the plan to inherit from his brother and alienate his child, induced him to settle in Salins" ("Celui-ci, qui craignait un raccommodement, et avait apparemment fait le projet d'hériter de son frère et d'éloigner son enfant, l'entraîna avec lui à Salins, où il le détermina à se fixer"). Mauguin, arguing for Bidaut, charged that Mlle Leroy had hired a business agent to help her pursue the inheritance and had proceeded, fraudulently, to induce witnesses to help her win a correction in the civil registration of her birth. Chaix d'Est-Ange countered, according to the *Gazette*'s summary, by recalling a letter Mlle Leroy had sent to her alleged uncle, noting "in dramatic and touching terms" how she "deplored the loss of her mother and begged for Bidaut's pity" ("L'avocat rappelle ici, dans des termes dramatiques et touchans, la lettre de la demoiselle Leroy, qui déplore la perte de sa mère et invoque la pitié du sieur Bidaut."). The court ruled that the only issue to be resolved was whether Mlle Leroy's mother was indeed the same woman who married Bidaut in 1793, and authorized Mlle Leroy to seek depositions establishing this identity. In this case, a technicality did promise to designate as legal heir a young woman who was, in all probability, the illegitimate daughter of Mme Bidaut and M Leroy. Much of the emotional intensity of the debates derived from this tension between law and presumption. The fact is that the civil code, in the name of family honor, offered powerful protections for the children of married women. It was quite difficult to deny them the status of legitimate offspring of the marriage. (It was, by the same token, impossible for single women to sue men to recognize their paternity, a measure also aimed at protecting family honor.) Mauguin tried desperately to get around this bias, but in vain. Railing against Mlle Leroy's alleged avarice was to no avail.

CASE NO. 19. *BOULANGER V. MME VEUVE VIALLANE.* In this case Boulanger claimed ownership of a rente sur l'état (state debt) worth eighteen thousand francs per year which, according to Mme Viallane, belonged to the estate of her late estranged husband. On 7 June 1826, Boulanger and Viallane had signed a contract by which each party contributed rentes worth nine thousand francs per year to form a single bundle; Viallane was to receive all the interest as a life annuity. On his death, Boulanger was to acquire sole title to the whole. Viallane died two months later on 3 August 1826. Under their marriage contract, M and Mme Viallane had made each other sole heir, and this provision was not invalidated by their legal separation. Mme Viallane's attorney, Hennequin, claimed that the contract with Boulanger represented a vindictive effort by Viallane to deprive his wife of her rightful inheritance. He knew he was dying, Hennequin insisted, having undergone five operations for a kidney disease; and he knew, as did Boulanger, that the life annuity was next to worthless. The case therefore turned on the intentions of the retired general at the time he signed the contract with Boulanger. Hennequin made much of what he called Viallane's "hatred" for his wife, demonstrated by "outrages" and "violence" during the marriage, as well as by purposeful mismanagement of their fortune during the separation proceedings. Persil, for Boulanger, made no mention of emotions; he confined himself to a careful examination of Viallane's finances, the losses caused by his wife's spendthrift habits, the need, after the separation, to repair his annual income. Persil documented Viallane's efforts to find some kind of life annuity with statements from notaries and brokers. The court found in favor of Boulanger, ruling that life annuities, by law, could not be invalidated unless the signatory died within twenty days, and that Mme Viallane had not gathered sufficient evidence to prove fraudulent intent. What made this case "mixed," then, in Table 1, instead of "emotional" was the choice made by Persil to depict Viallane's financial decisions as reasonable and prudent. He countered claims of vindictiveness with dry detail.

CASE NO. 26. *RELLOT V. GIROLET.* Champonnière, Rellot's attorney in this case, offered a gripping, if peculiar story. Rellot, he claimed, was a simple farmer who owned about thirty thousand francs' worth of property in 1801. At that time, a promise of marriage was exchanged between Rellot and Girolet's sister. Girolet, a parish priest who lived near Saint-Denis, north of Paris, was poor. From 1801 on, however, Rellot and Girolet pooled their resources; Rellot paid for a new house, he farmed land, leased land, paid taxes, made purchases of land – all in partnership with Girolet, even though the projected marriage did not take place. In 1824, suddenly, Girolet came with a justice of the peace to command Rellot to stop pretending he was co-owner of Girolet's property. A legal seal was placed on Rellot's room; but, Champonnière charged, all his papers, kept outside the room, were stolen by Girolet and destroyed. Subsequently, Rellot was evicted from the property and was now living in dire poverty. Champonnière offered records of property holdings Rellot had inherited or sold in the late 1790s; and he cited numerous records in which Rellot had signed leases or paid taxes for land now claimed by Girolet. Girolet's attorney, Colmet-d'Aage, countered that Rellot was an impoverished domestic servant when Girolet hired him in 1801. There had never been any thought of a marriage between this servant and his sister. Over the years, he had depended on Rellot as a faithful agent, whose name appears on numerous contracts and receipts signed for him, but always with acknowledgment of his status as agent. In 1824, when Rellot had tried to sell a plot of Girolet's land as his own, Girolet had reacted by firing him. Rellot's claims then escalated, and it was necessary to bring in a justice of the peace to assist in removing him from their shared residence. The court ruled that Rellot's written evidence was insufficient to prove that he still owned property in 1801, that he had given it to Girolet, or that he had acted as a partner, rather than an agent, in the numerous cases where his name appeared on a contract or receipt. The court rejected the claim that papers had been stolen and dismissed Rellot's suit. The emotional dimension of the case derived from Champonnière's effort to depict the simple, trusting Rellot's long reliance on Girolet's good faith, and the latter's sudden, perfidious renunciation of him. As in Boulanger v. Viallane, the defendant's attorney, Colmet-d'Aage, confined himself to a recitation of facts, except for expressing a desire to "master my indignation" ("maîtriser mon indignation") and the concluding remark that in Rellot's suit "Ingratitude is joined to the odious reproach of looting" ("L'ingratitude vient ici se joindre à tout l'odieux d'un reproche de spoliation"). Had the court chosen to look beyond the paper trail, Champonnière's melodramatic narrative might have been relevant.

CASE NO. 27. *JACQUINOT HÉRITIERS V. GRAVIER, CHABAUD, AND GARILLON.* This case turned out to be technical in nature, but that was not apparent before the court ruled. The Paris solicitor Jacquinot, on his death in 1823, left a large portion of his fortune to his former caretaker, a Mlle Jeoffroy, small sums to his brothers and sisters, and the remainder to three men who, his will stated, would doubtless use this wealth to further charitable goals which Jacquinot approved. These three men negotiated with the collateral heirs for months to ensure that the latter would not contest the will, offering small additional sums as inducements. In the end, one nephew held out and sued. He charged that the three men, whom his uncle had hardly known, were actually acting in the name of a secret, and illegal, religious association of Jansenists. The law forbade the willing of property to secret or unnamed persons or entities, or to persons acting secretly as agents for unnamed parties. In reality unauthorized religious orders and associations did seek to control property and receive gifts through the intermediary of trusted persons. The trusted person had simply to assert that she saw herself as true and sole owner of the property and that she intended to use it however she saw fit. Cases of this kind thus often turned on arguments about the intentions of both the testator and the named heirs. The nephew's attorney, Liouville, who noted that this was the first case he had ever argued, cited evidence of a complex scheme for passing property among trustworthy persons. Jacquinot had himself received numerous inheritances from persons outside his family, and, Liouville claimed, so had the three defendants. He then denounced them heatedly, as inspired by a "false zeal more damaging in its consequences than a shameful passion whose excesses are condemned by reason" ("un faux zèle plus funeste dans ses conséquences que les passions honteuses dont la raison condamne les excès"). The spirit of religion, Liouville intoned, did not condone their conspiracy. "Around her march faith, piety, horror of lies and of dissimulation, charity's ardent heart, the love of justice, respect for the property of others" ("Autour d'elle marchent la foi, la piété, l'horreur du mensonge et de la dissimulation, la charité au coeur ardent, l'amour de la justice, le respect pour la propriété d'autrui"). Barthe, representing the three defendants, an experienced and skilled attorney, belittled Liouville's high-flying rhetoric. "It is in man's nature to wish to do good to his fellows. To help the unfortunate is a need which Providence put in every heart. . . . Interest can dry it up; but there are privileged natures who ceaselessly rekindle it, who are exalted by it as it becomes the sweetest habit" ("Il est dans la nature de l'homme de vouloir faire du bien à ses semblables. Secourir les malheureux est un besoin que la Providence a mis dans le coeur de tous. . . . [L]'intérêt peut le dessécher; mais il est des natures privilegées qui le réchauffent sans cesse, chez lesquelles il s'exalte et devient la plus douce habitude"). Barthe saw no association among the defendants; perhaps they had similar religious beliefs, but that was not a matter for the courts to concern themselves with. The court ruled for the defendants, noting that written proof was required by law to demonstrate the existence of an illegal association or of the testator's intention to bestow property on one. The plaintiff had not even proposed to find such proof; presumptions on the basis of a network of inheritance provisions were insufficient. In this case, both attorneys attempted to pursue the technical side, but, out of prudence, also sought to deal with the question of motives, using emotional claims and expressions of outrage and indignation.

CASE NO. 36. *BIDET VEUVE ET FILS V. LE COMTE DE LABOURDONNAYE-BLOSSNE.* This case, another in the series inspired by the indemnity law, pitted the widow and son of an estate agent against the agent's former employer. Labourdonnaye-Blossne had fled into exile in 1791, leaving his agent Bidet in charge of managing his estates. He had even left his children in Bidet's care. Bidet's heirs claimed that the agent had gone to considerable risk and expense in his efforts to preserve Labourdonnaye's property and to save it from confiscation during the period of Jacobin rule. Bidet had himself spent 3,500 francs to purchase movable property sold off by the government and preserve it for his employer. He had incurred many other expenses. After the end of the Terror, Bidet had sought and won a court order recognizing he was owed 17,123 francs, but he died in 1809 without receiving a sou. That same year, Labourdonnaye returned from exile; under the Restoration he was named to the Chamber of Peers. But he refused to recognize the debt which now, with interest, was put at 50,000 francs. The issue was a technical one because it was simply a question of the court's estimation of the validity of written records; both Bidet and Labourdonnaye had preserved accounts and documents for the court to examine. But the Bidets' attorney, Bonnet, drew a touching picture of the "devotion" of the estate agent and the disdain and indifference of the aristocratic employer. Labourdonnaye's attorney, Lavaux, countered that Bidet, far from being a hero of devotion, had been out to rob his client, a "man of honor" ("un homme d'honneur"), who had had some difficulty finding all his records. The furniture purchase of 1793 was itself just an instance of looting. Lavaux responded angrily that such language was a despicable effort to avoid the obligations which Bidet's devotion had created. The court, after examining the accounts, found for Bidet's heirs. In this case, as in many others, the passage of time since the Terror and the unusual circumstances those days had created gave added significance to even technical disputes and cast doubt even on clear records. Hence the emotional assertions about motive.

CASE NO. 41. *DUMONTEUIL V. ESNÉE.* In this case a priest who had been relieved of all duties by the church, including the administering of sacraments, and who had renounced his membership in the church, sued a notary who refused to register the required legal publication of his intent to marry. The case raised the ticklish question whether the priest's vows had any effect on his civil status. This was an entirely technical issue, the parties' motives had nothing to do with the matter. There were no grounds in the law for preventing Dumonteuil from marrying since the Civil Code did not recognize religion as having any effect on citizenship. However, the Charter of 1814 recognized Catholicism as the religion of the state. The king's attorney, Dammartin, argued that, by this bare statement, all the disciplinary canons of the church gained legal status, including the requirement of celibacy for the clergy. This claim was forcefully disputed by two different attorneys who argued, pro bono, on the priest's behalf and who took this opportunity to express an avid Voltairian anticlericalism. Here is a sample from Duverne's initial pleading for Dumonteuil:

The mad fakir who vows to spend his life immobile with his arms in the air and his face turned toward heaven, the Indian wife who vows to burn herself on the funeral pyre of her husband – they obey ardent convictions; their faith sustains them, they would feel only horror at the idea of retracting. But, if a purer light falls on them, if a benevolent religion comes to dissipate their delirium, they would reject their mad vows. Would you call them perjurers? Would you rebuke them in the name of morality?

(Le faquir insensé qui fait voeu de passer sa vie immobile, les bras en l'air et la face tournée vers le ciel, la suttie indienne qui fait voeu de se brûler sur le bûcher de son époux, obéissent à des convictions ardentes; la foi les soutient, ils auraient horreur de se rétracter. Mais qu'une lumière plus pure vienne les éclairer, qu'une religion bienfaisante vienne dissiper leur délire, ils repousseront leurs sermens insensés. Les appellerez-vous parjures? les réprouverez-vous au nom de la morale?)

Dumonteuil's attorneys were seconded by public statements of colleagues; the liberal wing of the Paris bar was, in effect, mobilized by Dumonteuil's suit. The emotional charge of the case was due entirely to its political character; the Charter's implications had never been spelled out and the regime's constant efforts to enhance the status and power of the church were deeply and widely resented. The court, putting political prudence before the positive import of the law, ruled in conformity with the government's view; Dumonteuil was not allowed to marry.

Detailed Review of Anomalous Cases from the Tribunal Civil de Versailles Sample

Note: Case numbers refer to the listing of the sampled cases in Table 2.

CASE NO. 55. *CHARON AND VEUVE SOUILLARD V. VEUVE TIERCE.* This case involved the mental competence of an aging widow. Witnesses described many of her acts of "madness" without using emotion terms, although the clear intent was to indicate that these acts went beyond what could be counted as normal expression of fear or anger. When collecting personal property from a M Maugart, for example, she claimed she had not received all that was her due and refused to give him a receipt. She sat in the doorway to his courtyard for two days and nights, ignoring the admonitions of her lawyer who was summoned to talk to her; then she went away leaving all of her things behind. On another occasion, she was seen standing in the rain outside the courthouse for a long period, but refused help. When a *huissier* (process server) came to her apartment, she threw a pot of soup at his head, then threatened him with an iron. When he returned with the commissaire de police, she locked herself in and refused to answer. The commissaire got a locksmith to open the door; they found her seated with her arms crossed, holding a knife. Neighbors heard her making speeches to herself inside the apartment; one night she made a hole in the ceiling by banging on it with a piece of wood. The depositions in this case resemble those in anomalous cases involving violence by husbands: emotional terms are not necessary because witnesses deem the actions described to speak for themselves – about abnormal emotions *and* intentions.

CASE NO. 58. *DRUET V. BARBEDETTE.* In this case a retired banker was suing his wife for separation on the grounds of abandonment and public insult. She had disappeared about six months earlier, but there was no direct evidence of where she had gone or with whom. There was abundant circumstantial evidence that she had run away to Italy with a lover, but this evidence entailed interpretations of the nature of her relationship with a former employee of her husband's, a M de la Jariette. Witnesses managed to convey their firm conviction of the couple's illicit attachment without using emotion terms. Before M Druet had closed his bank in Paris, the Druets lived in an apartment adjoining the bank offices. Mme Druet and M de la Jariette, a bank clerk, "chatted frequently" together, especially when Druet was out of the office, according to one witness. "She concerned herself with his moves to new apartments, his problems, and his affairs." Frequently he went into Mme Druet's bedroom, the witness said. "When he was needed, the husband was so blind that he said 'Don't disturb him, he's working on correspondence.' It was well known in the office that M de la Jariette was courting, at the very least, Mme Druet."

When Druet closed his bank and retired to Meulan, a town on the Seine northwest of Paris, M de la Jariette moved there soon after, taking rooms in a contiguous building. He and Mme Druet saw each other almost every day, said one witness, who said he knew from the way she talked that "intimate relations" existed between the two. They called each other "mon ami, mon bon ami." (This is the closest any testimony in the case comes to actual expression of emotion.) On 16 April, Mme Druet left for Paris, saying she had to have a tooth pulled, but would be back by evening. That same day, M de la Jariette moved out. He had sold his furniture and arranged for a deposit of the proceeds to be made at the Laffite banking house. Neither was seen in Meulan again; however, M Druet's brother, a notary, said he had gotten reports that de la Jariette was seen traveling with a woman as far south as Avignon. According to other witnesses, M de la Jariette was married; he had left his wife in Paris, working at the counter of a grocery store, when he moved to Meulan. During July 1840 (three months after the couple's disappearance) Jariette's brother paid Jariette's wife an unknown sum of money to acquire (and turn over to him) a passport for travel to Italy. Presumably, Mme Druet used this passport to cross the border with her lover. Witnesses kept to their role, attempting to describe with minimal interpretation actions whose meaning was beyond doubt. But, because no witness had seen the couple cohabiting or traveling together, evidence on the tenor of the relationship was essential. Hence the use of phrases such as, "M de la Jariette was courting Mme Druet" ("M de la Jariette faisait la cour à Mme Druet") – used twice; they had "intimate relations" ("relations intimes") – used twice;

she "concerned herself" ("s'occupa") with his affairs. Such evidence readily swayed the court; the separation was granted.

CASE NO. 60. *BERRURIER HUSBAND AND WIFE V. LAPORTE, A NOTARY, AND PAULMIER HUSBAND AND WIFE.* The plaintiffs charged that Laporte had used undue intimidation and threats to compel them to sign a settlement arising from a disputed foreclosure sale. Both the Berruriers and the Paulmiers were farmers in the village of Herblay near Versailles. Paulmier and his wife had been obliged to sell land at auction in order to satisfy their creditors. In the public auction, Paulmier claimed, Berrurier had bid a sum sufficient to cover his debts (about eight hundred francs); later, in the notary's office, Berrurier and his wife were shocked at the amount they were expected to pay. But Laporte pressured them to sign the deed, saying that they would be saddled with huge court costs and a possible prison term for fraud if they reneged on their public bid. After Berrurier finally agreed, a witness refused to cosign, stating afterward that he viewed Laporte's conduct as improper. Subsequently the Berruriers sued Laporte and the Paulmiers. The case was purely technical in one sense: Did Berrurier risk court costs and prosecution for backing out on the deal? The mayor of Herblay supported Laporte's assertions, but indicated his knowledge of the case came strictly from Laporte himself. In another sense, the case was not technical: Did Laporte overstep the bounds of proper conduct as an official with a public charge? This issue brought emotions into play. The witness who refused to cosign the agreement in the notary's office said Laporte was motivated more by a desire to intimidate than a desire to conciliate. One witness said that Berrurier "cried out in amazement" ("s'est récrié") when he first heard the amount he was expected to pay. After a few moments he stormed out of the office, leaving his wife to talk with the notary. However, several witnesses spoke of the "contentment" of all parties after the signing, noting that the Paulmiers and Berruriers dined together afterwards to celebrate. Laporte told a witness he forgave Berrurier for the insults. No final judgment was found in the case; it may be that the Berruriers dropped it after the *enquête* was completed.

CASE NO. 73. *DUTON V. VEUVE NEZAN.* Mme Duton and her husband, in this case, were disputing the validity of a deathbed *donation* (a gift confirmed in writing) by René Nezan, to his wife, of his entire fortune. Law limited the proportion of one's property one could freely dispose of at death; the act was intended to ensure that this disposable fraction went entirely to the widow. The donation was contested by Mme Duton, Nezan's daughter – apparently by an earlier marriage – and her husband. They claimed that Nezan was not competent at the time, ill health having weakened his mental functioning. In the two *enquêtes* carried out, thirteen witnesses testified as to Nezan's state of mind in his last days without using any emotion terms. Two doctors testified that Nezan, although dying and very weak, remained of sound mind ("ses facultés mentales ne m'ont pas paru dérangées," as one put it). The notary who drew up the donation and the two witnesses who agreed to cosign it described a scene that was doubtless fraught with tension, as a "violent" knocking was heard at the door of the bedroom just as the notary was beginning to draw up the document. The notary, René Jacques Boucher, said he went to the door to see what the disturbance was; when he saw it was Nezan's daughter who had knocked, he invited her in.

And before her Nezan, interrogated by me, repeated that he had the intention to make a donation to his wife. I asked Mme Duton to retire, and I proceeded to draw up the act. M Nezan appeared to me to dispose of all his intellectual faculties. I remember that, during the drawing up of the act, he recalled that he owed the postman (one of the witnesses asked to cosign the document) for two letters from Orléans he had delivered a few days before.

Several witnesses said that they had seen Nezan during his final days, and he had not even recognized them. Although no one in the case spoke of emotions, two circumstances point to the strong undercurrents that were present in the room when Nezan confronted his daughter. First Mme Duton and her husband fought the donation vigorously; they carried out a separate *enquête*, and during both *enquêtes* their attorney repeatedly interrupted witnesses to interrogate them about Nezan's state of mind. Second, one witness said that he had seen the postman shortly after Nezan had signed the donation. The postman said, "I have just been the witness of an act of purification; Nezan has just made a donation to his wife." But we get no hint as to what sort of "purification" ("épuration") was meant.

References

Abu-Lughod, Lila. 1986. *Veiled Sentiments: Honor and Poetry in a Bedouin Society.* Berkeley: University of California Press.

Abu-Lughod, Lila. 1990. "Shifting Politics in Bedouin Love Poetry." In *Language and the Politics of Emotion.* Edited by Catherine A. Lutz and Lila Abu-Lughod, pp. 24–45. Cambridge: Cambridge University Press.

Abu-Lughod, Lila. 1991. "Writing Against Culture." In *Recapturing Anthropology: Working in the Present.* Edited by Richard G. Fox, pp. 137–162. Santa Fe, N. Mex.: School of American Research.

Adler, Laure. 1985. *L'amour à l'arsenic: Histoire de Marie Lafarge.* Paris: Denoël.

Agulhon, Maurice. 1968. *Pénitents et francs-maçons de l'ancienne Provence.* Paris: Fayard.

Agulhon, Maurice. 1970. *La république au village.* Paris: Plon.

Alcoff, Linda Martín. 1996. *Real Knowing: New Versions of the Coherence Theory.* Ithaca, N.Y.: Cornell University Press.

Alton-Shée, Edmond de Lignères, comte de. 1869. *Mes mémoires.* 2 vols. Paris: A. Lacroix.

Appadurai, Arjun. 1990. "Topographies of the Self: Praise and Emotion in Hindu India." In *Language and the Politics of Emotion.* Edited by Catherine A. Lutz and Lila Abu-Lughod, pp. 92–112. Cambridge: Cambridge University Press.

Argyle, Michael. 1991. "A Critique of Cognitive Approaches to Social Judgments." In *Emotion and Social Judgments.* Edited by Joseph P. Forgas, pp. 161–178. Oxford: Pergamon Press.

Asad, Talal. 1997. "On Torture, or Cruel, Inhuman, and Degrading Treatment." In *Social Suffering.* Edited by Arthur Kleinman, Veena Das, and Margaret Lock, pp. 285–308. Berkeley: University of California Press.

Aulard, Alphonse, ed. 1889–1923. *Recueil des actes du Comité de Salut Public.* 28 vols. plus supplements. Paris: Imprimerie Nationale.

Aulard, Alphonse. 1901. *Histoire politique de la Révolution française: Origines et développement de la démocratie et de la République (1789–1804).* Paris: Armand Colin.

Aulard, Alphonse. 1906. *Les orateurs de la Révolution: La Législative et la Convention,* 2 vols. Paris: Edouard Cornély et Cie.

Austin, J. L. [1962] 1975. *How to Do Things with Words*, 2nd ed. Cambridge, Mass.: Harvard University Press.

Averill, James R. 1985. "The Social Construction of Emotion: With Special Reference to Love." In *The Social Construction of the Person*. Edited by Kenneth J. Gergen and Keith E. Davis, pp. 89–109. New York: Springer Verlag.

Averill, James R. 1994. "Emotions Unbecoming and Becoming." In *The Nature of Emotion: Fundamental Questions*. Edited by Paul Ekman and Richard J. Davidson, pp. 265–269. Oxford: Oxford University Press.

Baars, Bernard J., Michael R. Fehling, Mark LaPolla, and Katharine McGovern. 1997. "Consciousness Creates Access: Conscious Goal Images Recruit Unconscious Action Routines, but Goal Competition Serves to 'Liberate' Such Routines, Causing Predictable Slips." In *Scientific Approaches to Consciousness*. Edited by Johnathan D. Cohen and Jonathan W. Schooler, pp. 423–444. Mahwah, N.J.: Erlbaum.

Baasner, Frank. 1988. *Der Begriff 'sensibilité' im 18. Jahrhundert: Aufstieg und Niedergang eines Ideals*. Heidelberg: C. Winter.

Baker, Jane E., and Shelley Channon. 1995. "Reasoning in Depression: Impairment on a Concept Discrimination Learning Task." *Cognition and Emotion* 9:579–597.

Balayé, Simone. 1979. *Madame de Staël: Lumières et liberté*. Paris: Klincksieck.

Balota, David A., and Stephen T. Paul. 1996. "Summation of Activation: Evidence from Multiple Primes That Converge and Diverge Within Semantic Memory." *Journal of Experimental Psychology: Learning, Memory, and Cognition* 22:827–845.

Barker-Benfield, G. J. 1992. *The Culture of Sensibility: Sex and Society in Eighteenth-Century Britain*. Chicago, Ill.: University of Chicago Press.

Barnett, Douglas, and Hilary Horn Ratner. 1997. "Introduction: The Organization and Integration of Cognition and Emotion in Development." *Journal of Experimental Child Psychology* 67:303–316.

Barrett, Karen Caplovitz. 1993. "The Development of Nonverbal Communication of Emotion: A Functionalist Perspective." *Journal of Nonverbal Behavior* 17:145–169.

Battaglia, Debbora, ed. 1995. *Rhetorics of Self-Making*. Berkeley: University of California Press.

Beecher, Jonathan. 1986. *Charles Fourier: The Visionary and His World*. Berkeley: University of California Press.

Beecher, Jonathan. 2000. *Victor Considerant and the Rise and Fall of French Romantic Socialism*. Berkeley: University of California Press.

Behar, Ruth, and Deborah A. Gordon, eds. 1995. *Women Writing Culture*. Berkeley: University of California Press.

Beik, William. 1985. *Absolutism and Society in Seventeenth-Century France: State Power and Provincial Aristocracy in Languedoc*. Cambridge: Cambridge University Press.

Bénichou, Paul. 1992. *L'école du désenchantement: Sainte-Beuve, Nodier, Musset, Nerval, Gautier*. Paris: Gallimard.

Berlin, Brent, and Paul Kay. 1969. *Basic Color Terms: Their Universality and Evolution*. Berkeley: University of California Press.

Bertholet, Denis. 1991. *Les français par eux-mêmes, 1815–1885.* Paris: Olivier Orban.

Besner, Derek, Jennifer A. Stoltz, and Clay Boutilier. 1997. "The Stroop Effect and the Myth of Automaticity." *Psychonomic Bulletin and Review* 4:221–225.

Besnier, Niko. 1990a. "Conflict Management, Gossip, and Affective Meaning on Nukulaelae." In *Disentangling: Conflict Discourse in Pacific Societies.* Edited by Karen Ann Watson-Gegeo and Geoffrey M. White, pp. 290–334. Stanford, Calif.: Stanford University Press.

Besnier, Niko. 1990b. "Language and Affect." *Annual Review of Anthropology* 19:419–451.

Besnier, Niko. 1993. "Reported Speech and Affect on Nukulaelae Atoll." In *Responsibility and Evidence in Oral Discourse.* Edited by Jane H. Hill and Judith T. Irvine, pp. 161–181. Cambridge: Cambridge University Press.

Besnier, Niko. 1995a. "The Politics of Emotion in Nukulaelae Gossip." In *Everyday Conceptions of Emotion.* Edited by J. A. Russell, J. M. Fernández-Dols, A. S. R. Manstead, and J. C. Wellenkamp, pp. 221–240. Dordrecht: Kluwer Academic Publishers.

Besnier, Niko. 1995b. *Literacy, Emotion, and Authority: Reading and Writing on a Polynesian Atoll.* Cambridge: Cambridge University Press.

Billacois, François. 1986. *Le duel dans la société française des XVIe–XVIIe siècles: Essai de psychosociologie historique.* Paris: Editions de l'Ecole des hautes études en sciences sociales.

Billard, Jacques. 1998. *De l'école à la république: Guizot et Victor Cousin.* Paris: Presses universitaires de France.

Bless, Herbert, Gerald L. Clore, Norbert Schwarz, Verena Golisano, Christina Rabe, and Marcus Wolk. 1996. "Mood and the Use of Scripts: Does a Happy Mood Really Lead to Mindlessness?" *Journal of Personality and Social Psychology* 71:665–679.

Blum, Carol. 1986. *Rousseau and the Republic of Virtue: The Language of Politics in the French Revolution.* Ithaca, N.Y.: Cornell University Press.

Bornstein, Robert F. 1992. "The Inhibitory Effects of Awareness on Affective Responding: Implications for the Affect-Cognition Relationship." *Review of Personality and Social Psychology* 13 *Emotion.* Edited by Margaret S. Clark, pp. 235–255. Newbury Park, Calif.: Sage.

Bougerol, Christiane. 1997. *Une ethnographie des conflits aux Antilles: Jalousie, commérages, sorcellerie.* Paris: Presses universitaires de France.

Bourdieu, Pierre. 1977. *Outline of a Theory of Practice.* Translated by Richard Nice. Cambridge: Cambridge University Press.

Bower, Gordon H. 1992. "How Emotions Affect Learning." In *The Handbook of Emotion and Memory: Research and Theory.* Edited by Sven-Åke Christianson, pp. 3–31. Hillsdale, N.J.: Erlbaum.

Brenneis, Donald. 1990a. "Dramatic Gestures: The Fiji Indian *Pancayat* as Therapeutic Event." In *Disentangling: Conflict Discourse in Pacific Societies.* Edited by Karen Ann Watson-Gegeo and Geoffrey M. White, pp. 214–238. Stanford, Calif.: Stanford University Press.

Brenneis, Donald. 1995. " 'Caught in the Web of Words': Performing Theory in a Fiji Indian Community." In *Everyday Conceptions of Emotion.* Edited by J. A.

Russell, J. M. Fernándey-Dols, A. S. R. Manstead, and J. C. Wellenkamp, pp. 241–250. Dordrecht: Kluwer Academic Publishers.

Briggs, Jean L. 1970. *Never in Anger: Portrait of an Eskimo Family*. Cambridge, Mass.: Harvard University Press.

Brissenden, R. F. 1974. *Virtue in Distress: Studies in the Novel of Sentiment from Richardson to de Sade*. New York: Harper and Row.

Brooks, John I. III. 1998. *The Eclectic Legacy: Academic Philosophy and the Human Sciences in Nineteenth-Century France*. Newark, Del.: University of Delaware Press.

Brooks, Rodney A., and Lynn Andrea Stein. 1994. "Building Brains for Bodies." *Autonomous Robots*, 1:7–25.

Brownstein, Rachel. 1993. *The Tragic Muse: Rachel of the Comédie Française*. New York: Knopf.

Burack, Cynthia. 1994. *The Problem of the Passions: Feminism, Psychoanalysis, and Social Theory*. New York: New York University Press.

Butler, Judith. 1990. *Gender Trouble: Feminism and the Subversion of Identity*. New York: Routledge.

Butler, Judith. 1992. "Contingent Foundations: Feminism and the Question of 'Postmodernism.' " In *Feminists Theorize the Political*. Edited by Judith Butler and Joan W. Scott, pp. 3–21. New York: Routledge.

Butler, Judith. 1997. "Sovereign Performatives in the Contemporary Scene of Utterance." *Critical Inquiry* 23:350–377.

Butler, Judith, and Joan W. Scott, eds. 1992. *Feminists Theorize the Political*. New York: Routledge.

Cabanis, Pierre-Jean-George. [1802] 1815. *Rapports du physique et du moral de l'homme*. Paris: Caille et Ravier.

Carlisle, Robert B. 1987. *The Proffered Crown: Saint-Simonianism and the Doctrine of Hope*. Baltimore, Md.: Johns Hopkins University Press.

Caron, Jean-Claude. 1991. *Générations romantiques: Les étudiants de Paris et le Quartier latin (1814–1851)*. Paris: Armand Colin.

Caron, Jean-Claude. 1999. *A l'école de la violence: Châtiments et sévices corporels dans l'institution scolaire*. Paris: Aubier.

Carr, T. H., and D. Dagenbach. 1990. "Semantic Priming and Repetition Priming from Masked Words: Evidence for a Center-Surround Attentional Mechanism in Perceptual Recognition." *Journal of Experimental Psychology: Learning, Memory, and Cognition* 16:341–350.

Cassagne, Albert. 1906. *La théorie de l'art pour l'art en France*. Paris: Hachette.

Chartier, Roger. 1999. "Diderot, Richardson, et la lectrice impatiente." *MLN*, 114:647–666.

Chodorow, Nancy J. 1999. *The Power of Feelings: Personal Meaning in Psychoanalysis, Gender, and Culture*. New Haven, Ct.: Yale University Press.

Church, Timothy, Marcia S. Katigbak, and Stacia M. Jensen. 1998. "The Language and Organisation of Filipino Emotion Concepts: Comparing Emotion Concepts and Dimensions Across Cultures." *Cognition and Emotion* 12:63–92.

Clark, Margaret S. 1989. "Historical Emotionology: From a Social Psychologist's Perspective." In *Social History and Issues in Human Consciousness: Some*

Interdisciplinary Connections. Edited by Andrew E. Barnes and Peter N. Stearns, pp. 262–269. New York: New York University Press.

Clark, Ronald W. 1975. *The Life of Bertrand Russell.* New York: Knopf.

Clifford, James. 1988. *The Predicament of Culture: Twentieth-Century Ethnography, Literature, and Art.* Cambridge, Mass.: Harvard University Press.

Clifford, James, and George E. Marcus, eds. 1986. *Writing Culture: The Poetics and Politics of Ethnography.* Berkeley, Calif.: University of California Press.

Clore, Gerald L. 1994. "Why Emotions Vary in Intensity." In *The Nature of Emotion: Fundamental Questions.* Edited by Paul Ekman and Richard J. Davidson, pp. 386–393. Oxford: Oxford University Press.

Clore, Gerald L., and W. Gerrod Parrott. 1991. "Moods and Their Vicissitudes: Thoughts and Feelings as Information." In *Emotion and Social Judgments.* Edited by Joseph P. Forgas, pp. 107–123. Oxford: Pergamon Press.

Cobb, Richard. 1970. *The Police and the People: French Popular Protest, 1789–1820.* Oxford: Clarendon Press.

Cohen, J. D., and J. W. Schooler, eds. 1997. *Scientific Approaches to Consciousness.* Mahwah, N.J.: Erlbaum.

Collier, Jane Fishburne. 1997. *From Duty to Desire: Remaking Families in a Spanish Village.* Princeton, N.J.: Princeton University Press.

Conley, Thomas M. 1990. *Rhetoric in the European Tradition.* Chicago, Ill.: University of Chicago Press.

Cormenin, Louis. M. de L. 1842. *Livre des orateurs,* 12th ed. Paris: Pagnerre.

Cornut-Gentille, Pierre. 1996. *L'honneur perdu de Marie de Morell.* Paris: Perrin.

Cousin, Victor. 1828. *Cours de philosophie: Introduction à l'histoire de la philosophie.* Paris: Pichon et Didier.

Cousin, Victor. [1836] 1879. *Du vrai, du beau, et du bien.* 21st edition. Paris: Didier et Cie.

Crapanzano, Vincent. 1992. "Preliminary Notes on the Glossing of Emotions." In *Hermes' Dilemma and Hamlet's Desire,* pp. 229–238. Cambridge, Mass.: Harvard University Press.

Craveri, Benedetta. 1982. *Madame du Deffand et son monde.* Paris: Seuil.

D'Andrade, Roy G. 1992. "Schemas and Motivation." In *Human Motives and Cultural Models.* Edited by Roy D'Andrade and Claudia Strauss, pp. 23–44. Cambridge: Cambridge University Press.

D'Andrade, Roy, and M. Egan. 1974. "The Colors of Emotion." *American Ethnologist* 1:49–63.

D'Andrade, Roy, and Claudia Strauss, eds. 1992. *Human Motives and Cultural Models.* Cambridge: Cambridge University Press.

Darnton, Robert. 1985. *The Great Cat Massacre and Other Episodes in French Cultural History.* New York: Vintage.

Das, Veena. 1997. "Language and Body: Transactions in the Construction of Pain." In *Social Suffering.* Edited by Arthur Kleinman, Veena Das, and Margaret Lock, pp. 67–91. Berkeley: University of California Press.

Das, Veena. 1998. "Wittgenstein and Anthropology." *Annual Review of Anthropology* 27:171–195.

Daumas, Maurice. 1988. *L'affaire d'Esclans: Les conflits familiaux au XVIIIe siècle.* Paris: Seuil.

354   *References*

Daumas, Maurice. 1996. *La tendresse amoureuse, XVIe–XVIIIe siècles*. Paris: Perrin.

Davidson, Donald. 1984. *Inquiries into Truth and Interpretation*. Oxford: Oxford University Press.

Davis, Natalie Zemon. 1983. *The Return of Martin Guerre*. Cambridge, Mass.: Harvard University Press.

Dean, Carolyn J. 1994. "The Productive Hypothesis: Foucault, Gender, and the History of Sexuality." *History and Theory* 33:271–296.

DeJean, Joan. 1991. *Tender Geographies: Women and the Origins of the Novel in France*. New York: Columbia University Press.

DeJean, Joan. 1997. *Ancients Against Moderns: Culture Wars and the Making of a Fin de Siècle*. Chicago: University of Chicago Press.

Denby, David. 1994. *Sentimental Narrative and the Social Order in France, 1760–1820*. Cambridge: Cambridge University Press.

Dennett, D. C. 1991. *Consciousness Explained*. Boston: Little, Brown.

Derrida, Jacques. 1967a. *De la grammatologie*. Paris: Editions de minuit.

Derrida, Jacques. 1967b. *L'écriture et la différence*. Paris: Seuil.

Derrida, Jacques. 1973. "Differance." In *Speech and Phenomena and Other Essays on Husserl's Theory of Signs*. Translated by David P. Allison, pp. 129–160. Evanston, Ill.: Northwestern University Press.

De Sousa, Ronald. 1987. *The Rationality of Emotion*. Cambridge, Mass.: MIT Press.

Diesbach, Ghislain de. 1983. *Madame de Staël*. Paris: Perrin.

Dimock, Jr., Edward C., Edwin Gerow, C. M. Naim, A. K. Ramanujan, Gordon Roadarmel, J. A. B. van Buitenen. 1974. *The Literatures of India: An Introduction*. Chicago: University of Chicago Press.

Drevets, Wayne C., and Marcus E. Raichle. 1998. "Reciprocal Suppression of Regional Cerebral Blood Flow During Emotional Versus Higher Cognitive Processes: Implications for Interactions Between Emotion and Cognition." *Cognition and Emotion* 12:353–385.

Dreyfus, Hubert L., and Paul Rabinow. 1983. *Michel Foucault: Beyond Structuralism and Hermeneutics*. Chicago: University of Chicago Press.

Ehrard, Jean. 1970. *L'idée de nature à l'aube des lumières*. Paris: Flammarion.

Ekman, Paul. 1972. *Emotion in the Human Face: Guide-Lines for Research and an Integration of Findings*. Oxford: Pergamon Press.

Ekman, Paul. 1980. *The Face of Man: Expressions of Universal Emotions in a New Guinea Village*. New York: Garland STPM Press.

Elias, Norbert. 1978. *The Civilizing Process*, Vol. 1, *The History of Manners*. Translated by Edmund Jephcott. New York: Urizen.

Ellsworth, Phoebe C. 1994. "Levels of Thought and Levels of Emotion." In *The Nature of Emotion: Fundamental Questions*. Edited by Paul Ekman and Richard J. Davidson, pp. 192–196. Oxford: Oxford University Press.

Erdelyi, Matthew Hugh. 1990. "Repression, Reconstruction, and Defense: History and Integration of the Psychoanalytic and Experimental Frameworks." In *Repression and Dissociation: Implications for Personality Theory, Psychopathology, and Health*. Edited by Jerome L. Singer, pp. 1–31. Chicago, Ill.: University of Chicago Press.

Erdelyi, Matthew Hugh. 1992. "Psychodynamics and the Unconscious." *The American Psychologist*, 47:784–787.

Erdelyi, Matthew Hugh. 1994. "Hypnotic Hypermnesia: The Empty Set of Hypermnesia." *International Journal of Clinical and Experimental Psychology* 42:379–390.

Ewing, Katherine Pratt. 1990. "The Illusion of Wholeness." *Ethos* 18:251–278.

Ewing, Katherine Pratt. 1997. *Arguing Sainthood: Modernity, Psychoanalysis, and Islam.* Durham, N.C.: Duke University Press.

Fajans, Jane. 1997. *They Make Themselves: Work and Play Among the Baining of Papua New Guinea.* Chicago, Ill.: University of Chicago Press.

Farge, Arlette. 1986. *La vie fragile: Violence, pouvoirs et solidarités à Paris au XVIIIe siècle.* Paris: Hachette.

Farge, Arlette, and Michel Foucault. 1982. *Le désordre des familles: Lettres de cachet des Archives de la Bastille au XVIIIe siècle.* Paris: Gallimard.

Febvre, Lucien. 1944. *Amour sacré, amour profane.* Paris: Gallimard.

Feld, Steven. 1982. *Sound and Sentiment: Birds, Weeping, Poetics, and Song in Kaluli Expression.* Philadelphia: University of Pennsylvania Press.

Feld, Steven. 1995. "Wept Thoughts: The Voicing of Kaluli Memories." In *South Pacific Oral Traditions.* Edited by Ruth Finnegan and Margaret Orbell, pp. 85–108. Bloomington, Ind.: Indiana University Press.

Feldman Barrett, Lisa. 1998. "Discrete Emotions or Dimensions? The Role of Valence Focus and Arousal Focus." *Emotion and Cognition* 12:579–599.

Fermon, Nicole. 1997. *Domesticating Passions: Rousseau, Woman, and Nation.* Hanover, N.H.: University Press of New England.

Ferry, Luc, and Alain Renault. 1985. *La pensée '68: Essai sur l'anti-humanisme contemporain.* Paris: Gallimard.

Fischer, Kurt W., and June Price Tangney. 1995. "Introduction: Self-Conscious Emotions and the Affect Revolution: Framework and Overview." In *Self-Conscious Emotions: The Psychology of Shame, Guilt, Embarrassment, and Pride.* Edited by June Price Tangney and Kurt W. Fischer, pp. 3–24. New York: The Guilford Press.

Ford, Carolyn. 1994. "Private Lives and Public Order in Restoration France: The Seduction of Emily Loveday." *American Historical Review* 99:21–43.

Foucault, Michel. 1966. *Les mots et les choses.* Paris: Gallimard.

Foucault, Michel. 1969. *L'archéologie du savoir.* Paris: Gallimard.

Foucault, Michel. 1980. "Two Lectures." *In Power/Knowledge: Selected Interviews and Other Writings 1972–1977.* Edited by Colin Gordon. New York: Pantheon Books.

Foucault, Michel. 1985. *The Use of Pleasure: Volume 2 of the History of Sexuality.* Translated by Robert Hurley. New York: Pantheon.

Fraenkel, Béatrice. 1992. *La Signature: Genèse d'un signe.* Paris: Gallimard.

Frank, Robert H. 1988. *Passions Within Reason: The Strategic Role of the Emotions.* New York: W. W. Norton & Co.

Fraser, Nancy. 1992. "The Uses and Abuses of French Discourse Theories for Feminist Politics." *Theory, Culture, and Society* 9:51–71.

Fridlund, Alan J. 1992. "The Behavioral Ecology and Sociality of Faces." In *Review of Personality and Social Psychology,* 13 *Emotion.* Edited by Margaret S. Clark, pp. 90–121. Newbury Park, Calif.: Sage.

Fried, Michael. 1980. *Absorption and Theatricality: Painting and Beholder in the Age of Diderot.* Chicago, Ill.: University of Chicago Press.

Frijda, Nico H. 1994. "Emotions Require Cognitions, Even If Simple Ones." In *The Nature of Emotion: Fundamental Questions.* Edited by Paul Ekman and Richard J. Davidson, pp. 197–202. Oxford: Oxford University Press.

Frijda, Nico H., Andrew Ortony, Joep Sonnemans, Gerald L. Clore. 1992. "The Complexity of Intensity: Issues Concerning the Structure of Emotional Intensity." In *Review of Personality and Social Psychology* 13 *Emotion.* Edited by Margaret S. Clark, pp. 60–89. Newbury Park, Calif.: Sage.

Funke, Gerhard. 1947. *Maine de Biran: Philosophisches und politisches Denken zwischen Ancien Régime und Bürgerkönigtum in Frankreich.* Bonn: H. Bouvier u. Co.

Furet, François. 1981. *Interpreting the French Revolution.* Translated by Elborg Forster. Cambridge: Cambridge University Press.

Gasnault, François. 1986. *Guinguettes et lorettes: Bals publics à Paris au XIXe siècle.* Paris: Aubier.

Gauchet, Marcel. 1995. *La révolution des pouvoirs: La souveraineté, le peuple et la représentation, 1789–1799.* Paris: Gallimard.

Gauthier, Marie-Véronique. 1992. *Chanson, sociabilité, et grivoiserie au XIXe siècle.* Paris: Aubier.

Geertz, Clifford. 1973. *The Interpretation of Culture.* New York: Basic Books.

Gergen, Kenneth J. 1995. "Metaphor and Monophony in the 20th-Century Psychology of Emotions." *History of the Human Sciences* 8:1–22.

Goblot, Jean-Jacques. 1995. *La jeune France libérale: Le Globe et son groupe littéraire, 1824–1830.* Paris: Plon.

Goldstein, Jan. 1987. *Console and Classify: The French Psychiatric Profession in the Nineteenth Century.* Cambridge: Cambridge University Press.

Good, Mary-Jo DelVecchio, and Byron Good. 1988. "Ritual, the State, and the Transformation of Emotional Discourse in Iranian Society." *Culture, Medicine, and Psychiatry* 12:43–63.

Goodman, Dena. 1994. *The Republic of Letters: A Cultural History of the French Enlightenment.* Ithaca, N.Y.: Cornell University Press.

Gordon, Daniel. 1994. *Citizens Without Sovereignty: Equality and Sociability in French Thought, 1670–1789.* Princeton, N.J.: Princeton University Press.

Goswami, Roshmi. 1995. *Meaning in Music.* Shimla: Indian Institute of Advanced Study.

Gottman, John M., and Robert W. Levenson. 1988. "The Social Psychophysiology of Marriage." In *Perspectives on Marital Interaction.* Edited by Patricia Noller and Mary Anne Fitzpatrick, pp. 182–202. Clevedon, England: Multilingual Matters.

Greenblatt, Steven J. 1980. *Renaissance Self-Fashioning: From More to Shakespeare.* Chicago, Ill.: University of Chicago Press.

Greenspan, Patricia S. 1988. *Emotions and Reasons: An Inquiry into Emotional Justification.* New York: Routledge.

Greenwald, Anthony G., and Sean C. Draine. 1997. "Do Subliminal Stimuli Enter the Mind Unnoticed? Tests with a New Method." In *Scientific*

Approaches to Consciousness. Edited by Jonathan D. Cohen and Jonathan W. Schooler, pp. 83–109. Mahwah, N.J.: Erlbaum.

Greenwald, Anthony G., Mark R. Klinger, and Eric S. Schuh. 1995. "Activation by Marginally Perceptible ('Subliminal') Stimuli: Dissociation of Unconscious from Conscious Cognition." *Journal of Experimental Psychology: General* 124:22–42.

Griffiths, Paul E. 1997. *What Emotions Really Are: The Problem of Psychological Categories.* Chicago, Ill.: University of Chicago Press.

Grima, Benedicte. 1992. *The Performance of Emotion Among Paxtun Women.* Austin, Tex.: University of Texas Press.

Grimal, Pierre. 1988. *L'amour à Rome.* Paris: Les Belles Lettres.

Grogan, Susan. 1992. *French Socialism and Sexual Difference: Women and the New Society, 1803–1844.* New York: St. Martin's Press.

Gross, J. J., and R. W. Levenson. 1993. "Emotional Suppression: Physiology, Self Report, and Expressive Behavior." *Journal of Personality and Social Psychology* 64:970–986.

Gueniffey, Patrice. 2000. *La politique de la Terreur.* Paris: Fayard.

Gwynn, G. E. 1969. *Madame de Staël et la Révolution française.* Paris: A. G. Nizet.

Habermas, Jürgen. 1987. *The Philosophical Discourse of Modernity: Twelve Lectures.* Translated by Frederick G. Lawrence. Cambridge, Mass.: MIT Press.

Halévi, Ran. 1984. *Les loges maçonniques dans la France d'Ancien Régime: Aux origines de la sociabilité démocratique.* Paris: Armand Colin.

Hardin, C. L., and Luisa Maffi, eds. 1997. *Color Categories in Thought and Language.* Cambridge: Cambridge University Press.

Harré, Rom, ed. 1986. *The Social Construction of Emotions.* Oxford: Blackwell.

Hatfield, E., J. Cacioppo, and R. Rapson. 1994. *Emotional Contagion.* Cambridge: Cambridge University Press.

Hatfield, E., and R. Rapson. 1993. *Love, Sex, and Intimacy: Their Psychology, Biology, and History.* New York: HarperCollins.

Heider, Karl G. 1991. *Landscapes of Emotion: Mapping Three Cultures of Emotion in Indonesia.* Cambridge: Cambridge University Press.

Hemmings, F. W. J. 1987. *Culture and Society in France, 1789–1848.* Leicester: Leicester University Press.

Hess, Ursula, Pierre Philippot, and Sylvie Blairy. 1998. "Facial Reactions to Emotional Facial Expressions: Affect or Cognition?" *Cognition & Emotion* 12:509–531.

Hibbert, Christopher. 1981. *The Days of the French Revolution.* New York: Morrow Quill.

Higonnet, Patrice. 1998. *Goodness Beyond Virtue: Jacobins During the French Revolution.* Cambridge, Mass.: Harvard University Press.

Hirsch, Jean-Pierre. 1978. *La nuit du 4 août.* Paris: Editions Gallimard/Juillard.

Hirsch, Jean-Pierre. 1991. *Les deux rêves du commerce: Entreprise et institution dans la région lilloise (1780–1860).* Paris: Éditions de l'École des Hautes Études en Sciences Sociales.

Hochschild, Arlie R. 1983. *The Managed Heart: Commercialization of Human Feeling.* Berkeley: University of California Press.

Hollan, Douglas W. 1992. "Emotion Work and the Value of Emotional Equanimity Among the Toraja." *Ethnology* 31:45–56.

Hollan, Douglas W., and Jane C. Wellenkamp. 1994. *Contentment and Suffering: Culture and Experience in Toraja*. New York: Columbia University Press.

Holland, Dorothy C. 1992. "How Cultural Systems Become Desire: A Case Study of American Romance." In *Human Motives and Cultural Models*. Edited by Roy D'Andrade and Claudia Strauss, pp. 61–89. Cambridge: Cambridge University Press.

Houbre, Gabrielle. 1997. *La discipline de l'amour: L'éducation sentimentale des filles et des garçons à l'âge du romantisme*. Paris: Plon.

Howell, Signe. 1981. "Rules Not Words." In *Indigenous Psychologies: The Anthropology of the Self*. Edited by Paul Heelas and Andrew Lock, pp. 133–144. London: Academic Press.

Hughes, Cheryl F., Carmen Uhlmann, and James W. Pennebaker. 1994. "The Body's Response to Processing Emotional Trauma: Linking Verbal Text with Autonomic Activity." *Journal of Personality* 62:565–585.

Hunt, Lynn. 1984. *Politics, Culture, and Class in the French Revolution*. Berkeley: University of California Press.

Hunt, Lynn. 1992. *The Family Romance of the French Revolution*. Berkeley: University of California Press.

Irvine, Judith T. 1990. "Registering Affect: Heteroglossia in the Linguistic Expression of Emotion." In *Language and the Politics of Emotion*. Edited by Catherine A. Lutz and Lila Abu-Lughod, pp. 126–161. Cambridge: Cambridge University Press.

Irvine, Judith T. 1995. "A Sociolinguistic Approach to Emotion Concepts in a Senegalese Community." In *Everyday Conceptions of Emotion*. Edited by J. A. Russell, J. M. Fernández-Dols, A. S. R. Manstead, and J. C. Wellenkamp, pp. 251–65. Dordrecht: Kluwer Academic Publishers.

Isbell, John Claiborne. 1994. *The Birth of European Romanticism: Truth and Propaganda in Staël's De l'Allemagne, 1810–1813*. Cambridge: Cambridge University Press.

Isen, Alice M., and Gregory Andrade Diamond. 1989. "Affect and Automaticity." In *Unintended Thought: Limits of Awareness, Intention and Control*. Edited by J. S. Uleman and John A. Bargh, pp. 124–152. New York: Guilford Press.

Izard, Carroll E., Jerome Kagan, and Robert B. Zajonc. 1984. "Introduction." In *Emotions, Cognition, and Behavior*. Edited by Carroll E. Izard, Jerome Kagan, and Robert B. Zajonc, pp. 1–17. Cambridge: Cambridge University Press.

Jacob, Margaret C. 1991a. *Living the Enlightenment: Freemasonry and Politics in Eighteenth-Century Europe*. New York: Oxford University Press.

Jacob, Margaret C. 1991b. "The Enlightenment Redefined: The Formation of Modern Civil Society." *Social Research* 58:475–495.

Jacoby, Larry L., Andrew P. Yonelinas, and Janine M. Jennings. 1997. "The Relations Between Conscious and Unconscious (Automatic) Influences; A Declaration of Independence." In *Scientific Approaches to Consciousness*. Edited by Jonathan D. Cohen and Jonathan W. Schooler, pp. 13–48. Mahwah, N.J.: Erlbaum.

Jaggar, Alison M. 1989. "Love and Knowledge: Emotion in Feminist Epistemology." In *Women, Knowledge, and Reality: Explorations in Feminist Philoso-*

phy. Edited by Ann Garry and Marilyn Pearsal, pp. 129–156. Boston: Unwin Hyman.

Jameson, Kimberly A., and Roy D'Andrade. 1997. "It's Not Really Red, Green, Yellow, Blue: An Inquiry into Perceptual Color Space." In *Color Categories in Thought and Language*. Edited by C. L. Hardin and Luisa Maffi, pp. 295–319. Cambridge: Cambridge University Press.

Jenkins, Janis Hunter. 1991. "The State Construction of Affect: Political Ethos and Mental Health Among Salvadoran Refugees." *Culture, Medicine, and Psychiatry* 15:139–165.

Johnson, James H. 1995. *Listening in Paris: A Cultural History*. Berkeley: University of California Press.

Join-Lambert, A., ed. 1896. *Le mariage de Madame Roland: Trois années de correspondance amoureuse (1777–1780)*. Paris: E. Plon, Nourrit et Cie.

Joseph, Stephen, Tim Dalgleish, Sian Thrasher, William Yule, Ruth Williams, and Peter Hodgkinson. 1996. "Chronic Emotional Processing in Survivors of the *Herald of Free Enterprise* Disaster: The Relationship of Intrusion and Avoidance at 3 Years to Distress, at 5 Years." *Behaviour Research and Therapy* 34:357–361.

Jouffroy, Théodore. [1825] 1924. "Comment les dogmes finissent." In Théodore Jouffroy, *Le cahier vert; Comment les dogmes finissent*. Edited by Pierre Poux, pp. 59–80. Paris: Les presses françaises.

Kagan, J. 1984. "The Idea of Emotion in Human Development." In *Emotions, Cognition, and Behavior*. Edited by C. E. Izard, J. Kagan, and R. B. Zajonc, pp. 38–72. Cambridge: Cambridge University Press.

Kapferer, Bruce. 1979. "Emotion and Feeling in Sinhalese Healing Rites." *Social Analysis* 1:153–176.

Kay, Paul, and Chad McDaniel. 1978. "The Linguistic Significance of the Meanings of Basic Color Terms." *Language* 54:610–646.

Kitayama, Shinobu, Hazel Rose Markus, and Hisaya Matsumoto. 1995. "Culture, Self, and Emotion: A Cultural Perspective on 'Self-Conscious' Emotions." In *Self-Conscious Emotions: The Psychology of Shame, Guilt, Embarrassment, and Pride*. Edited by June Price Tangney and Kurt W. Fischer, pp. 439–464. New York: Guilford Press.

Kleinman, Arthur. 1995. "Pitch, Picture, Power: The Globalization of Local Suffering and the Transformation of Social Experience." *Ethnos* 60:181–191.

Kleinman, Arthur. 1996. "Bourdieu's Impact on the Anthropology of Suffering." *International Journal of Contemporary Sociology* 33:203–210.

Kleinman, Arthur, Veena Das, and Margaret Lock, eds. 1997. *Social Suffering*. Berkeley: University of California Press.

Kleinman, Arthur, and Joan Kleinman. 1991. "Suffering and Its Professional Transformation: Toward an Ethnography of Experience." *Culture, Medicine and Psychiatry* 15:275–302.

Kleinman, Arthur, and Joan Kleinman. 1997. "The Appeal of Experience; The Dismay of Images: Cultural Appropriations of Suffering in Our Times." In *Social Suffering*. Edited by Arthur Kleinman, Veena Das, and Margaret Lock, pp. 1–23. Berkeley: University of California Press.

Kosslyn, S. 1994. *Image and Brain: The Resolution of the Imagery Debate.* Cambridge, Mass.: MIT Press.

Laird, James D. 1987. "Mood Affects Memory Because Feelings Are Cognitions." *Journal of Social Behavior and Personality* 4:33–38.

Lakoff, George. 1987. *Women, Fire, and Dangerous Things: What Categories Reveal About the Mind.* Chicago: University of Chicago Press.

Lang, Peter J. 1995. "The Emotion Probe: Studies of Motivation and Attention." *American Psychologist* 50:372–385.

Langford, Paul. 1989. *A Polite and Commercial People: England, 1727–1783.* Oxford: Clarendon Press.

Lazarus, Richard S. 1982. "Thoughts on the Relations Between Emotion and Cognition." *American Psychologist* 37:1019–1024.

Lazarus, Richard S. 1994. "The Past and the Present in Emotion." In *The Nature of Emotion: Fundamental Questions.* Edited by Paul Ekman and Richard J. Davidson, pp. 273–279. Oxford: Oxford University Press.

Leavitt, John. 1996. "Meaning and Feeling in the Anthropology of Emotion." *American Ethnologist*: 514–535.

Lefebvre, Georges. 1932. *La Grande Peur de 1789.* Paris: A. Colin.

Levy, Robert I. 1973. *Tahitians: Mind and Experience in the Society Islands.* Chicago, Ill.: University of Chicago Press.

Levy, Robert I. 1984. "Emotion, Knowing and Culture." In *Culture Theory: Essays on Mind, Self and Emotion.* Edited by R. Shweder and R. LeVine, pp. 214–237. New York: Cambridge University Press.

Lofland, Lynn. 1985. "The Social Shaping of Emotion: The Case of Grief." *Symbolic Interaction* 8:171–190.

Logan, Gordon D., Stanley E. Taylor, Joseph L. Etherton. 1996. "Attention in the Acquisition and Expression of Automaticity." *Journal of Experimental Psychology: Learning, Memory, and Cognition* 22:620–638.

Lutz, Catherine A. 1986. "The Domain of Emotion Words on Ifaluk." In *The Social Construction of Emotions.* Edited by Rom Harré, pp. 267–288. Oxford: Blackwell.

Lutz, Catherine A. 1988. *Unnatural Emotion: Everyday Sentiments on a Micronesian Atoll and Their Challenge to Western Theory.* Chicago: University of Chicago Press.

Lutz, Catherine A., and Lila Abu-Lughod, eds. 1990a. *Language and the Politics of Emotion.* Cambridge: Cambridge University Press.

Lutz, Catherine A., and Lila Abu-Lughod. 1990b. "Introduction." In *Language and the Politics of Emotion*, pp. 1–23. Cambridge: Cambridge University Press.

Lutz, Catherine A., and Geoffrey M. White. 1986. "The Anthropology of Emotions." *Annual Review of Anthropology* 15:405–436.

Lynch, Owen, ed. 1990. *Divine Passions: The Social Construction of Emotions in India.* Berkeley: University of California Press.

Lyon, Margot L. 1995. "Missing Emotion: The Limitations of Cultural Constructionism in the Study of Emotion." *Cultural Anthropology* 10:244–263.

Lyons, Martyn. 1987. *Le triomphe du livre: Une histoire sociologique de la lecture dans la France du XIXe siècle.* Paris: Promodis.

Maine de Biran, Pierre. 1954–1957. *Journal.* 3 vols. Edited by Henri Gouhier. Neuchâtel: Editions de la Baconnière.

Mandler, G. 1984. *Mind and Body: The Psychology of Emotion and Stress.* New York: Norton.

Marcus, George E. 1992. "Introduction." In *Rereading Cultural Anthropology.* Edited by George E. Marcus, pp. vii–xiv. Durham, N.C.: Duke University Press.

Marglin, Frédérique Apffel. 1990. "Refining the Body: Transformative Emotion in Ritual Dance." In *Divine Passions: The Social Construction of Emotions in India.* Edited by Owen Lynch, pp. 212–236. Berkeley: University of California Press.

Martin, John. 1997. "Inventing Sincerity, Refashioning Prudence: The Discovery of the Individual in Renaissance Europe." *American Historical Review* 102:1309–1342.

Matthews, Gerald, and Trevor A. Harley. 1996. "Connectionist Models of Emotional Distress and Attentional Bias." *Cognition and Emotion* 10:561–600.

Matusik, Martin J. 1989. "Habermas on Communicative Reason and Performative Contradiction." *New German Critique* 47:143–172.

May, Gita. 1970. *Madame Roland and the Age of Revolution.* New York: Columbia University Press.

Maza, Sarah C. 1993. *Private Lives and Public Affairs: The Causes Célèbres of Prerevolutionary France.* Berkeley: University of California Press.

Maza, Sarah C. 1996. "Stories in History: Cultural Narratives in Recent Works in European History." *American Historical Review* 101:1493–1515.

Maza, Sarah C. 1997. "Luxury, Morality, and Social Change: Why There Was No Middle-Class Consciousness in Prerevolutionary France." *Journal of Modern History* 69:199–229.

McNally, Richard J. 1995. "Automaticity and the Anxiety Disorders." *Behaviour Research and Therapy* 33:747–754.

McNeill, David. 1992. *Hand and Mind: What Gestures Reveal About Thought.* Chicago Ill.: University of Chicago Press.

Ménétra, Jacques Louis. 1982. *Journal de ma vie.* Edited by Daniel Roche. Paris: Montalba.

Meyer, Michel. 1991. *Le philosophe et les passions: Esquisse d'une histoire de la nature humaine.* Paris: Le Livre de Poche.

Mogg, Karin, Brendan P. Bradely, and Rachel Williams. 1993. "Subliminal Processing of Emotional Information in Anxiety and Depression." *Journal of Abnormal Psychology* 102:304–311.

Montesquieu. [1721] 1963. *Lettres persanes.* Paris: Flammarion.

Moretti, Marlene M., and Brian F. Shaw. 1989. "Automatic and Dysfunctional Cognitive Processes in Depression." In *Unintended Thought: Limits of Awareness, Intention, and Control.* Edited by J. S. Uleman and John A. Bargh, pp. 383–421. New York: Guilford Press.

Morrill, Kirsten Elisa. 1998. "Politics, Prosperity, and Pleasure: Fashioning Identity in Second Empire Paris, 1852–1870." Ph.D. thesis, Duke University.

Muchembled, Robert. 1998. *La société policée: Politique et politesse en France, du XVIe au XXe siècles.* Paris: Seuil.

Musset, Alfred de. [1836] 1993. *La confession d'un enfant du siècle.* Paris: Flammarion.

Myers, Fred R. 1986. *Pintupi Country, Pintupi Self: Sentiment, Place, and Politics Among Western Desert Aborigines.* Berkeley: University of California Press.

Neuschel, Kristen. 1989. *Word of Honor: Interpreting Noble Culture in Sixteenth-Century France.* Ithaca, N.Y.: Cornell University Press.

Niedenthal, Paula M., and Caroline Showers. 1991. "The Perception and Processing of Affective Information and Its Influences on Social Judgment." In *Emotion and Social Judgments.* Edited by Joseph P. Forgas, pp. 125–143. Oxford: Pergamon Press.

Nye, Robert A. 1993. *Masculinity and Male Codes of Honor in Modern France.* Oxford: Oxford University Press.

Oatley, Keith. 1992. *Best Laid Schemes: The Psychology of Emotions.* Cambridge: Cambridge University Press.

Obeyesekere, Gananath. 1985. "Depression, Buddhism, and the Work of Culture in Sri Lanka." In *Culture and Depression: Studies in the Anthropology and Cross-Cultural Psychiatry of Affect and Disorder.* Edited by Arthur Kleinman and Byron Good, pp. 134–152. Berkeley: University of California Press.

Obeyesekere, Gananath. 1990. *The Work of Culture: Symbolic Transformation in Psychoanalysis and Anthropology.* Chicago: University of Chicago Press.

Oliver, A. Richard. 1964. *Charles Nodier, Pilot of Romanticism.* Syracuse: Syracuse University Press.

O'Rorke, Paul, and Andrew Ortony. 1994. "Explaining Emotions." *Cognitive Science* 18:283–323.

Ortner, Sherry. 1989. *High Religion: A Social History of Sherpa Buddhism.* Princeton, N.J.: Princeton University Press.

Ortony, A., G. L. Clore, and A. Collins. 1988. *The Cognitive Structure of Emotions.* Cambridge: Cambridge University Press.

Ortony, A., and Terence J. Turner. 1990. "What's Basic About Basic Emotions?" *Psychological Review* 97:315–331.

Pachet, Pierre. 1990. *Les baromètres de l'âme: Naissance du journal intime.* Paris: Hatier.

Palmer, R. R. [1941] 1989. *Twelve Who Ruled: The Year of the Terror in the French Revolution.* Princeton, N.J.: Princeton University Press.

Pandolfi, Mariella. 1991. *Itinerari delle emozioni: Corpo e identità femminile nel Sannio Campano.* Milan: FrancoAngeli.

Panksepp, Jaak. 1992. "A Critical Role for 'Affective Neuroscience' in Resolving What Is Basic about Basic Emotions." *Psychological Review* 99:554–560.

Parkinson, Brian, and A. S. R. Manstead. 1992. "Appraisal as a Cause of Emotion." In *Review of Personality and Social Psychology, 13 Emotion.* Edited by Margaret S. Clark, pp. 122–149. Newbury Park, Calif.: Sage.

Pennebaker, James W. 1989. "Stream of Consciousness and Stress: Levels of Thinking." In *Unintended Thought: Limits of Awareness, Intention, and Control.* Edited by J. S. Uleman and John A. Bargh, pp. 327–350. New York: Guilford Press.

Petrey, Sandy. 1988. *Realism and Revolution: Balzac, Stendhal, Zola, and the Performances of History.* Ithaca, N.Y.: Cornell University Press.

Pinch, Adela. 1995. "Emotion and History: A Review Article." *Comparative Studies in Society and History* 37:100–109.

Pinch, Adela. 1996. *Strange Fits of Passion: Epistemologies of Emotion, Hume to Austen*. Stanford, Calif.: Stanford University Press.

Plutchik, Robert. 1994. *The Psychology and Biology of Emotion*. New York: Harper Collins.

Pocock, J. G. A. 1975. *The Machiavellian Moment: Florentine Political Thought and the Atlantic Republican Tradition*. Princeton, N.J.: Princeton University Press.

Pontmartin, Armand de. 1885–1886. *Mes mémoires*. 2 vols. Paris: Calmann Lévy.

Prochasson, Christophe. 1997. *Les intellectuels et le socialisme*. Paris: Plon.

Quine, W. V. O. 1969. *Ontological Relativity and Other Essays*. New York: Columbia University Press.

Quinn, Naomi. 1992. "The Motivational Force of Self-Understanding: Evidence from Wives' Inner Conflicts." In *Human Motives and Cultural Models*. Edited by Roy D'Andrade and Claudia Strauss, pp. 90–126. Cambridge: Cambridge University Press.

Reddy, William M. 1984. *The Rise of Market Culture: The Textile Trade and French Society, 1750–1900*. Cambridge: Cambridge University Press.

Reddy, William M. 1987. *Money and Liberty in Modern Europe: A Critique of Historical Understanding*. Cambridge: Cambridge University Press.

Reddy, William M. 1992. "Postmodernism and the Public Sphere: Implications for an Historical Ethnography." *Cultural Anthropology* 7:135–168.

Reddy, William M. 1993. "Marriage, Honor, and the Public Sphere in Postrevolutionary France: *Séparations de Corps* 1815–1848." *Journal of Modern History*, 65:437–472.

Reddy, William M. 1997a. "Against Constructionism: The Historical Ethnography of Emotions." *Current Anthropology* 38:327–351.

Reddy, William M. 1997b. *The Invisible Code: Honor and Sentiment in Postrevolutionary France, 1815–1848*. Berkeley: University of California Press.

Reddy, William M. 1999. "Emotional Liberty: History and Politics in the Anthropology of Emotions." *Cultural Anthropology* 14:256–288.

Revel, Jacques. 1986. "Les usages de la civilité." In *Histoire de la vie privée*, vol. III, *De la Renaissance aux Lumières*. Edited by Roger Chartier, pp. 169–209. Paris: Seuil.

Roche, Daniel. 1981. *Peuple de Paris*. Paris: Aubier-Montaigne.

Roland, Jeanne-Marie. 1905. *Mémoires de Madame Roland*. 2 vols. Edited by C. Perroud. Paris: Plon.

Ronsin, Francis. 1992. *Les divorciaires: Affrontements politiques et conceptions du mariage dans la France du XIXe siècle*. Paris: Aubier.

Roper, Lyndal. 1994. *Oedipus and the Devil: Witchcraft, Sexuality, and Religion in Early Modern Europe*. London: Routledge.

Roqueplan, Nestor. 1853. *Regain: La vie parisienne*. Paris: Librairie nouvelle.

Rosaldo, Michelle Z. 1980. *Knowledge and Passion: Ilongot Notions of Self and Social Life*. Cambridge: Cambridge University Press.

Rosaldo, Michelle Z. 1984. "Toward an Anthropology of Self and Feeling." In *Culture Theory: Essays on Mind, Self, and Emotion*. Edited by Richard A. Shweder and Robert A. LeVine, pp. 137–157. Cambridge: Cambridge University Press.

Rosaldo, Renato. 1980. *Ilongot Headhunting: A Social History, 1883–1974*. Stanford: Stanford University Press.

Rosaldo, Renato. 1989. *Culture and Truth: The Remaking of Social Analysis*. Boston: Beacon Press.

Rosanvallon, Pierre. 1985. *Le moment Guizot*. Paris: Gallimard.

Rosenblatt, Helena. 1997. *Rousseau and Geneva: From the "First Discourse" to the "Social Contract," 1749–1762*. Cambridge: Cambridge University Press.

Rudman, Laurie A., and Eugene Borgida. 1995. "The Afterglow of Construct Accessibility: The Behavioral Consequences of Priming Men to View Women as Sexual Objects." *Journal of Experimental Social Psychology* 31:493–518.

Rumelhart, D. E., & J. L. McClelland, et al., eds. 1986. *Parallel Distributed Processing*, 2 vols. Cambridge, Mass.: MIT Press.

Russell, James A. 1983. "Pancultural Aspects of the Human Conceptual Organization of Emotions." *Journal of Personality and Social Psychology* 45:1281–1288.

Russell, James. A. 1994. "Is There Universal Recognition of Emotion from Facial Expression? A Review of the Cross-Cultural Studies." *Psychological Bulletin* 115:102–141.

Sahlins, Marshall. 1985. *Islands of History*. Chicago, Ill.: University of Chicago Press.

Saint-Just, Antoine-Louis. 1976. *Théorie politique*. Edited by Alain Liénhard. Paris: Seuil.

Saint-Simon, Louis de Rouvroy, duc de. 1947–1961. *Mémoires*, 7 vols. Paris: Gallimard.

Sand, George. [1832] 1984. *Indiana*. Paris: Gallimard.

Sarbin, Theodore R. 1986. "Emotion and Act: Roles and Rhetoric." In *The Social Construction of Emotions*, edited by Rom Harré, pp. 83–97. Oxford: Blackwell.

Schachter, S., and J. Singer. 1962. "Cognitive, Social, and Physiological Determinants of Emotional States." *Psychological Review* 69:379–399.

Schaub, Diana J. 1995. *Erotic Liberalism: Women and Revolution in Montesquieu's Persian Letters*. Lanham, Md.: Rowman and Littlefield.

Schein, Louisa. 1999. "Performing Modernity." *Cultural Anthropology* 14:295–322.

Schieffelin, Edward L. 1985. "Anger, Grief, and Shame: Toward a Kaluli Ethnopsychology." In *Person, Self, and Experience: Exploring Pacific Ethnopsychologies*. Edited by G. White and J. Kirkpatrick, pp. 168–182. Berkeley: University of California Press.

Schiesari, Juliana. 1992. *The Gendering of Melancholia: Feminism, Psychoanalysis, and the Symbolics of Loss in Renaissance Literature*. Ithaca, N.Y.: Cornell University Press.

Schneider, W., S. T. Dumais, and R. M. Shiffrin. 1984. "Automatic and Control Processing and Attention." In *Varieties of Attention*. Edited by R. Parasuraman and D. R. Davies, pp. 1–27. New York: Academic Press.

Schneider, Walter, and Mark Pimm-Smith. 1997. "Consciousness as a Message Aware Control Mechanism to Modulate Cognitive Processing." In *Scientific Approaches to Consciousness*. Edited by Johnathan D. Cohen and Jonathan W. Schooler, pp. 65–80. Mahwah, N.J.: Erlbaum.

Schooler, Jonathan W., and Stephen M. Fiore. 1997. "Consciousness and the Limits of Language: You Can't Always Say What You Think or Think What You Say." In *Scientific Approaches to Consciousness*. Edited by Johnathan D. Cohen and Jonathan W. Schooler, pp. 241–257. Mahwah, N.J.: Erlbaum.

Schwarz, Norbert, and Herbert Bless. 1991. "Happy and Mindless, but Sad and Smart? The Impact of Affective States on Analytic Reasoning." In *Emotion and Social Judgments*. Edited by Joseph P. Forgas, pp. 55–71. Oxford: Pergamon Press.

Schwarz, N., and G. L. Clore. 1983. "Mood, Misattribution, and Judgments of Well-being: Informative and Directive Functions of Affective States." *Journal of Personality and Social Psychology* 45:513–523.

Scott, Walter. [1823] 1946. *Quentin Durward*. New York: Dodd, Mead and Co.

Scribe, Eugène. [1827] 1878–1899. "Le Mariage d'argent: Comédie en cinq actes, Théâtre français, 3 décembre 1827." In *Oeuvres complètes*, 11 vols. I, 297–411. Paris: E. Dentu.

Searle, John R. 1989. "How Performatives Work." *Linguistics and Philosophy* 12:535–558.

Seigel, Jerrold E. 1986. *Bohemian Paris: Culture, Politics, and the Boundaries of Bourgeois Life, 1830–1930*. New York: Viking.

Sewell, William H., Jr. 1980. *Work and Revolution: The Language of Labor from the Old Regime to 1848*. Cambridge: Cambridge University Press.

Shaftesbury, Anthony Ashley Cooper, Third Earl of. [1711] 1999. *Characteristics of Men, Manners, Opinions, Times*. Edited by Lawrence E. Klein. Cambridge: Cambridge University Press.

Shaver, Phillip R., Hillary J. Morgan, and Shelley Wu. 1996. "Is Love a 'Basic' Emotion?" *Personal Relationships* 3:81–96.

Shaver, Phillip R., J. Schwartz, D. Kirson, and C. O'Connor. 1987. "Emotion Knowledge: Further Exploration of a Prototype Approach." *Journal of Personality and Social Psychology* 52:1061–1086.

Shiffrin, R. M., and S. T. Dumais. 1981. *The Development of Automatism*. In *Cognitive Skills and Their Acquisition*. Edited by J. R. Anderson, pp. 111–140. Hillsdale, N.J.: Erlbaum.

Simond, Charles, ed. n.d. *Marat: Biographie, bibliographie, choix de textes*. Paris: Louis Michaud.

Sinclair, Robert C., Curt Hoffman, and Melvin M. Mark. 1994. "Construct Accessibility and the Misattribution of Arousal: Schachter and Singer Revisited." *Psychological Science: A Journal of the American Psychological Society* 5:15–19.

Smallman, H. S., and R. M. Boynton. 1990. "Segregation of Basic Colors in an Information Display." *Journal of the Optical Society of America* 7:1985–1994.

Smith, Jay. 1996. *The Culture of Merit: Nobility, Royal Service and the Making of Absolute Monarchy in France, 1600–1789*. Ann Arbor: University of Michigan Press.

Solomon, Robert C. 1984. "Getting Angry: The Jamesian Theory of Emotion in Anthropology." In *Culture Theory: Essays on Mind, Self, and Emotion*. Edited by R. Shweder and R. LeVine, pp. 238–254. New York: Cambridge University Press.

Solomon, Robert C. 1992. "Existentialism, Emotions, and the Cultural Limits of Rationality." *Philosophy East and West* 42:597–621.

Sonenscher, Michael. 1989. *Work and Wages: Natural Law, Politics, and Eighteenth-Century French Trades.* Cambridge: Cambridge University Press.

Spiro, Melford E. 1992. "Cultural Relativism and the Future of Anthropology." In *Rereading Cultural Anthropology.* Edited by George E. Marcus, pp. 124–151. Durham, N.C.: Duke University Press.

Spitzer, Alan B. 1987. *The French Generation of 1820.* Princeton, N.J.: Princeton University Press.

Spurlock, John C., and Cynthia A. Magistro. 1994. "'Dreams Never to Be Realized': Emotional Culture and the Phenomenology of Emotion." *Journal of Social History* 28:295–310.

Staël, Germaine de. [1800] 1991. *De la littérature considerée dans ses rapports avec les institutions sociales.* Paris: Flammarion.

Staël, Germaine de. [1807] 1853. *Corinne, ou l'Italie.* New York: Leavitt et Allen.

Staël, Germaine de. [1813] 1894. *De l'Allemagne.* Paris: Garnier Frères.

Staël, Germaine de. [1818] 1983. *Considérations sur la Révolution française.* Paris: Editions Tallandier.

Stearns, Peter. 1994. *American Cool: Constructing a Twentieth-Century Emotional Style.* New York: New York University Press.

Stearns, Peter N., and Jan Lewis, eds. 1998. *An Emotional History of the United States.* New York: New York University Press.

Ste-Marie, Diane M., and Larry L. Jacoby. 1993. "Spontaneous Versus Directed Recognition: The Relativity of Automaticity." *Journal of Experimental Psychology: Learning, Memory, and Cognition* 19:777–788.

Strauss, Anne S. 1977. "Northern Cheyenne Ethnopsychology." *Ethos* 5:326–357.

Strauss, Claudia, and Naomi Quinn. 1997. *A Cognitive Theory of Cultural Meaning.* Cambridge: Cambridge University Press.

Strayer, David L., and Arthur F. Kramer. 1994. "Strategies and Automaticity: I. Basic Findings and Conceptual Framework." *Journal of Experimental Psychology: Learning, Memory, and Cognition* 20:318–341.

Stroop, J. R. 1935. "Studies of Interference in Serial Verbal Reactions." *Journal of Experimental Psychology* 18:643–662.

Tackett, Timothy. 2000. "Conspiracy Obsession in a Time of Revolution: French Elites and the Origins of the Terror, 1789–1792." *American Historical Review* 105:691–713.

Tait, Rosemary, and Roxane Cohen Silver. 1989. "Coming to Terms with Major Negative Life Events." In *Unintended Thought: Limits of Awareness, Intention, and Control.* Edited by J. S. Uleman and John A. Bargh, pp. 351–382. New York: Guilford Press.

Teichgraeber, Richard F., III. 1986. *"Free Trade" and Moral Philosophy: Rethinking the Sources of Adam Smith's Wealth of Nations.* Durham, N.C.: Duke University Press.

Toomey, Paul M. 1990. "Krishna's Consuming Passions: Food as Metaphor and Metonym for Emotion at Mount Govardhan." In *Divine Passions: The Social Construction of Emotions in India.* Edited by Owen Lynch, pp. 157–181. Berkeley: University of California Press.

Trawick, Margaret. 1990. "The Ideology of Love in a Tamil Family." In *Divine Passions: The Social Construction of Emotion in India*. Edited by Owen M. Lynch, pp. 37–63. Berkeley: University of California Press.

Uleman, James S. 1989. "A Framework for Thinking Intentionally About Unintended Thought." In *Unintended Thought: Limits of Awareness, Intention and Control*, edited by J. S. Uleman and John A. Bargh, pp. 425–449. New York: Guilford Press.

Uleman, J. S., and J. A. Bargh, eds. 1989. *Unintended Thought: Limits of Awareness, Intention, and Control*. New York: Guilford Press.

Urban, G. 1988. "Ritual Wailing in Amerindian Brazil." *American Anthropologist* 90:385–400.

Vincent-Buffault, Anne. 1986. *Histoire des larmes: XVIIIe–XIXe siècles*. Paris: Rivages.

Vincent-Buffault, Anne. 1995. *L'exercice de l'amitié: Pour une histoire des pratiques amicales aux XVIIIe et XIXe siècles*. Paris: Seuil.

Watson-Gegeo, Karen Ann, and David W. Gegeo. 1990. "Shaping the Mind and Straightening Out Conflicts: The Discourse of Kwara'ae Family Counseling." In *Disentangling: Conflict Discourse in Pacific Societies*. Edited by Karen Ann Watson-Gegeo and Geoffrey M. White, pp. 161–213. Stanford, Calif.: Stanford University Press.

Watson-Gegeo, Karen Ann, and Geoffrey M. White, eds. 1990. *Disentangling: Conflict Discourse in Pacific Societies*. Stanford, Calif.: Stanford University Press.

Wegner, Daniel M. 1994. "Ironic Processes of Mental Control." *Psychological Review* 101:34–52.

Wegner, Daniel M. 1997. "Why the Mind Wanders." In *Scientific Approaches to Consciousness*, edited by Johnathan D. Cohen and Jonathan W. Schooler, pp. 295–315. Mahwah, N.J.: Erlbaum.

Wegner, Daniel M., and R. Erber. 1992. "The Hyperaccessibility of Suppressed Thoughts." *Journal of Personality and Social Psychology* 63:903–912.

Wegner, Daniel M., and Daniel B. Gold. 1995. "Fanning Old Flames: Emotional and Cognitive Effects of Suppressing Thoughts of a Past Relationship." *Journal of Personality and Social Psychology* 68:782–792.

Wegner, Daniel M., and Laura Smart. 1997. "Deep Cognitive Activation: A New Approach to the Unconscious." *Journal of Consulting and Clinical Psychology* 65:984–995.

Wells, Rulon S. 1947. "De Saussure's System of Linguistics." *Word* 3:1–31.

Wenzlaff, Richard M., and Danielle E. Bates. 1998. "Unmasking a Cognitive Vulnerability to Depression: How Lapses in Mental Control Reveal Depressive Thinking." *Journal of Personality and Social Psychology* 75:1559–1571.

Whisner, William. 1989. "Self-Deception, Human Emotion, and Moral Responsibility: Toward a Pluralistic Conceptual Scheme." *Journal for the Theory of Social Behavior* 19:389–410.

White, Geoffrey M. 1990a. "Emotion Talk and Social Inference: Disentangling in Santa Isabel, Solomon Islands." In *Disentangling: Conflict Discourse in Pacific Societies*. Edited by Karen Ann Watson-Gegeo and Geoffrey M. White, pp. 53–121. Stanford, Calif.: Stanford University Press.

White, Geoffrey M. 1990b. "Moral Discourse and the Rhetoric of Emotions." In *Language and the Politics of Emotion*. Edited by Catherine A. Lutz and Lila Abu-Lughod, pp. 46–68. Cambridge: Cambridge University Press.

White, Geoffrey M. 1991. *Identity Through History: Living Stories in a Solomon Islands Society*. Cambridge: Cambridge University Press.

White, Hayden. 1978. "Foucault Decoded: Notes from Underground." In *Tropics of Discourse*, pp. 230–260. Baltimore, Md.: Johns Hopkins University Press.

Widdess, Richard. 1995. *The Ragas of Early Indian Music: Modes, Melodies, and Musical Notations from the Gupta Period to c. 1250*. Oxford: The Clarendon Press.

Wierzbicka, Anna. 1994. "Cognitive Domains and the Structure of the Lexicon: The Case of Emotions." In *Mapping the Mind: Domain Specificity in Cognition and Culture*. Edited by Lawrence A. Hirschfeld and Susan A. Gelman, pp. 431–452. Cambridge: Cambridge University Press.

Wikan, Unni. 1989. "Managing the Heart to Brighten Face and Soul: Emotions in Balinese Morality and Health Care." *American Ethnologist* 16:294–312.

Wikan, Unni. 1990. *Managing Turbulent Hearts: A Balinese Formula for Living*. Chicago, Ill.: University of Chicago Press.

Wikan, Unni. 1992. "Beyond the Words: The Power of Resonance." *American Ethnologist* 19:460–482.

Zajonc, Robert B. 1980. "Feeling and Thinking: Preferences Need No Inferences." *American Psychologist* 35:151–175.

Zajonc, Robert B. 1994. "Evidence for Nonconscious Emotions." In *The Nature of Emotion: Fundamental Questions*. Edited by Paul Ekman and Richard Davidson, pp. 293–297. Oxford: Oxford University Press.

Index

Abu-Lughod, Lila, 38–44, 47, 49–50, 60, 63, 74, 118, 130, 134–136, 318
Académie Française, 160, 246
activation
  and attention, 17, 84
  chronic, 29
  and culture, 52
  and emotion, 89, 93, 102–103, 110, 116, 287
  and emotional regimes, 126
  and goals, 120–122
  and mental control, 28–32
  and translation, 88–89, 94
  types of, 29–30
adrenaline, 13
agency
  and poststructuralism, 74
  and thought material, 94
  and translation, 87
Agulhon, Maurice, 151–153, 312
Alcoff, Linda, 71, 74–75, 78, 81, 110
Alton-Shée, Edmond de Lignères, comte d', 230–231
Ampère, Jean-Jacques, 227, 255
anger
  and activation, 91
  and arousal, 31
  on Bali, 60
  as basic emotion, 12
  on Ifaluk, 41, 57
  among Ilongots, 36–37, 56
anthropology
  and constructionism, 51
  debates in, 34–35
  and emotions, 34, 37–38, 56, 323
  and gender, 40
  and history, 45, 113
  and politics, 112
  and poststructuralism, 73
  psychocultural, 48–50

and suffering, 53
anxiety, and cognition, 19–20
Appadurai, Arjun, 58–59
Argyle, Michael, 14, 106
arousal
  and emotions, 6–7, 12, 19, 35–36
  and intensity, 22
  sexual, 31
  and subjective experience, 65
art
  in Victor Cousin, 223–224
  and emotional regimes, 125
  liberal view of, 235–236
  in nineteenth century, 207, 253, 259
  and *rasa*, 57
  and Romanticism, 240–242
  and sentimentalism, 145, 146, 149, 164–166
Asad, Talal, 52
attention, 16, 21, 25–26, 29, 31, 54
  and automatic processes, 17–18
  and goals, 120
  limits of, 15
  and translation, 80, 88–89, 94–95, 320–321
attorneys, *see* lawyers
Aulard, Alphonse, 186–188, 190–193, 195–196, 201
Austin, J. L., 64, 97, 322
automatic processes, 15, 83–84
  and attention, 17
  and cross-modality transfers, 80
  and culture, 52
  and emotions, 16
Averill, James R., 91, 100
Awlad ʿAli, 38–40, 43, 56–57, 130, 134–136

Baars, Bernard J., 119
Baasner, Frank, 155, 159, 161, 163, 165–166, 184, 189, 235

369

and happiness, 6
and self, 121, 332
and social interaction, 55
and translation, 80, 110, 320–322
Cohen, Jonathan D., 17, 63
Collier, Jane Fishburne, 45
Collot d'Herbois, Jean-Marie, 198
colors, 3–5, 12
Committee of Public Safety, 178, 191–194, 206
communities, and emotions, 55
Condillac, Etienne Bonnot de, 202, 220
Condorcet, Marie-Jean-Antoine-Nicolas Caritat, marquis de, 151, 186–187
Condorcet, Sophie de Grouchy, marquise de, 151, 160
Constant, Benjamin, 170
constructionism, and emotions, 35–45, 47, 49–50, 323
and Hindu tradition, 57
and honor codes, 132
and oppression, 114
and psychological research, 55
and Western subject, 66, 74
Convention, 173–176, 190–191, 195, 201
Corinne, ou l'Italie, 243–244, 253
Cormenin, Louis M. de L., 273
Cornut-Gentille, Pierre, 133, 286
courage
in Chateaubriand, 205
in Victor Cousin, 223
and French Revolution, 194, 206, 209
and sentimentalism, 174–175
Cousin, Victor, 208, 217, 234–235, 237, 241, 248
philosophy of, 219–228, 238, 249, 256, 259, 284, 332
Couthon, Georges, 194, 200, 206, 209
Crapanzano, Vincent, 319
Craveri, Benedetta, 150–151
Crousse, 278, 281–284
crying, icons of, 51
culture
and anthropology, 73
and constructionism, 38–44
and emotions, 34, 37, 40–41, 43, 47
theorizing, 130

Dagenbach, D., 17, 30
d'Alembert, Jean Baptiste Le Ronde, known as, 150–151, 160, 163, 187
Damiron, Jean-Philibert, 217
D'Andrade, Roy, 5, 24, 52, 90, 119
Danton, Georges, 181, 196, 200
Darnton, Robert, 154, 161
Das, Veena, 52–53
Daumas, Maurice, 91, 148, 153, 163, 275

David, Jacques-Louis, 165, 175
Davidson, Donald, 81, 110
Davis, Natalie Z., 260–261
De Sousa, Ronald, 15, 100, 104, 112
Dean, Carolyn, 74
Deffand, Marie de Vichy-Chamrond, marquise de, 150
DeJean, Joan, 91, 112, 143, 149, 159
Denby, David, 154–155, 161–162, 195, 204
Dennett, D. C., 86, 95
depression
and chronic activation, 89
and cognition, 19–21
and mental control, 27–28
Derrida, Jacques, 69–70, 76–77, 318
Descoutures, Frédéric, 257–258, 264–274, 276–277, 288–289, 313
Desmoulins, Camille, 198, 200
Destutt de Tracy, Antoine-Louis-Claude, 202, 218
Devadasi dancers, 58
d'Haussez, Charles, 229–230
Diamond, Gregory, 16, 20, 32, 55
Diderot, Denis, 163, 165, 175, 179, 218–219, 224
Diesbach, Ghislain de, 142, 163, 169–171, 204
Dimock, Edward C., Jr., 57
Directory, 201–202
discourse
and categories, 68–70
and emotions, 42–44
and freedom, 74
in poststructuralism, 75–78, 87
and subject, 73
see also codes; language
disgust, as basic emotion, 12
divorce, among Awlad 'Ali, 39
Drain, Sean C., 18
Drevets, Wayne C., 31, 80
Duchâtel, Tanneguy, 238
duels, in France, 133, 203, 231
see also honor

effort, emotional, 55–57, 62, 121, 129
on Bali, 60–61
and French Revolution, 196, 210
and goal conflict, 124
in Hindu tradition, 59
in Maine de Biran, 214, 252
in public sphere, 287
and translation, 84, 95
see also management, emotional; navigation, emotional
Ehrard, Jean, 159
Ekman, Paul, 12–13, 101
Elias, Norbert, 148, 324